BASIC
SOCIOLOGY:
AN
INTRODUCTION
TO THEORY
AND
METHOD

SOCIOLOGY SERIES

John F. Cuber, Editor
Alfred C. Clarke, Associate Editor

Alvin L. Bertrand
Louisiana State University

BASIC SOCIOLOGY: AN INTRODUCTION TO THEORY AND METHOD

New York

APPLETON-CENTURY-CROFTS
Division of Meredith Publishing Company

GRATEFULLY
DEDICATED TO
The instructors, colleagues, students, secretarial assistants, friends, and my family—who inspired, demanded, encouraged, or otherwise lent a helping hand.

PREFACE

The writer's decision to undertake the preparation of this text was prompted by two beliefs derived from many years of teaching sociology. The first is that beginning students are generally not introduced early enough to the basic terms and methods used in sociology and are seldom provided with sociological models that schematically portray social organization. This is why the second and third chapters in this work include a review of important concepts and techniques in sociology. The purpose of this arrangement of materials is to provide a sufficient theoretical and methodological background for the student so that he immediately begins "thinking like a sociologist."

The second belief is that systematic theory is often not distinguished clearly enough from content for the beginning student. The tendency has been to present descriptive accounts of research studies and to emphasize the findings rather than the conceptual frame of reference used. Although it is realized that there is danger in pushing the introductory student too fast and that it is often difficult to keep an analytical approach in mind when presenting the pragmatic aspects of research, it is nonetheless of paramount importance that theory be understood, appreciated, and consistently used. Complete chapters are devoted to the structure of groups and complex systems, to social power, to social disorganization, and to social control in an attempt to maintain a higher than usual level of theoretical orientation. In addition, several new concepts are introduced, and old themes revised.

Certain other features give this text some degree of uniqueness. First, while theory is stressed, the application and utility of sociology are also featured. Too long has the question gone at least partially unanswered for the neophyte sociologist, "What use is sociology?" The writer is a pragmatist and believes that sociology will grow and prosper to the extent that sociologists prove their worth to business, industry, and government, as well as to the academic marketplace.

The inclusion of relatively recent research materials which clarify certain processes is a second unique feature. A chapter on "The Human Being in Disaster" and a section on the acceptance of innovations are examples of such materials.

Third, a claim to distinctiveness is made on the basis of organization. A strenuous effort was made to arrange each part, chapter, and topic so that sociology would unfold logically and systematically before the student. For this reason several conventional discussions appear in unusual contexts and others receive less than the usual stress.

Finally, a deliberate attempt was made to cast all definitions relating to social structure and organization in such a way as to obviate or at least lessen the necessity of depending on psychological concepts, such as group identification, feelings of belongingness, and group acceptance. The idea was to deal with questions of system boundaries in purely structural fashion and thus maintain a more clear-cut sociological approach to analyses.

It is with a deep sense of gratitude that the writer acknowledges the debt owed the many persons who have contributed in one way or another to this volume. He is especially grateful to his departmental colleagues—Vera Andreasen, Perry Howard, Charles Glasgow, Eugene Griessman, and Jerome Salamone—who graciously consented to use working draft copies of the manuscript in their classes. The final version of the text owes much to their thoughtful suggestions. Dr. Walfrid J. Jokinen, the writer's department chairman, graciously lent the kind of support and encouragement which is vital to this type of project, and this assistance is sincerely acknowledged. Finally, full and deserving credit must be given John F. Cuber and Alfred C. Clarke for their exceedingly helpful critical evaluation and suggestions, which improved the quality of the volume immensely. No one deserves better editors.

A.L.B.

CONTENTS

Part IV

SOCIAL DISORGANIZATION, SOCIAL DEVIATION, AND SOCIAL CONTROL

Part V

MAJOR INSTITUTIONALIZED SOCIAL STRUCTURES

Part VI

THE DEMOGRAPHIC AND ECOLOGICAL ASPECTS OF SOCIAL DIFFERENTIATION

PART

I

THE
CONCEPTUAL
FRAME
OF
REFERENCE
AND
METHODS
OF
SOCIOLOGY

PART
I
INTRODUCTION

The three chapters in Part I are designed to give the beginning student a perspective regarding the theoretical and methodological approach of sociology. It is also intended that some appreciation of the field be gained, both as an intellectual endeavor and as an applied and useful science. Chapter 1 is largely standard for introductory texts. Its purpose is to give the student a working definition of sociology and to acquaint him with its nature as a social science. The latter part of the chapter anticipates the first question which disturbs many introductory students, "What use is sociology?", and tries to illustrate what Merton has called the "visibly practical accomplishments" of the discipline.* At the same time, some notes of caution are included to help the student avoid typical, but incorrect, assumptions which tend to lead to dangerous misconceptions.

The student should develop a working vocabulary of concepts at the very beginning of his introductory course in sociology. Likewise, he should become acquainted with the conceptual approach of the discipline. This is the aim of Chapter 2. Chapter 3 is devoted to the methods of research and study generally used by sociologists. The purpose underlying the inclusion of this chapter in the introductory part of the text is twofold—to acquaint the student with the rigor of the methods used in the discipline and to provide an answer to questions regarding the validity of the findings of research studies reported here and elsewhere.

* Robert K. Merton and Robert A. Nisbet, Eds., *Contemporary Social Problems* (New York, Harcourt, Brace & World, 1961), p. 697.

1
THE
NATURE OF
SOCIOLOGY
AS A
SPECIALIZED
DISCIPLINE

Sociology is the newest of the social sciences to achieve the status of a major discipline. Its beginnings can be traced back to the French philosopher, Auguste Comte, who put forth a challenge for the scientific study of society in a series of works published between 1830 and 1842. The Rue de Auguste Comte in Paris commemorates this great scholar, but he is far better remembered as the father of sociology. Although a few works besides Comte's, now considered classics, were produced before the turn of the century, sociology can be more accurately described as a twentieth century discipline.[1] The great body of concepts, theories, methods, and data trace no further back than 1900 and many are products of the last quarter century. The American Sociological Society (now Association) was not founded until 1905.

It is significant that sociology appeared as a special discipline when it became clear that the traditional social sciences and philosophy did not tell the complete story of human behavior. Psychologists interested themselves in the study and measurement of individual human differences; cultural anthropologists concerned themselves primarily with investigations of primitive or

[1] The youth of sociology is clearly brought out in the article by Talcott Parsons, "The Profession: Reports and Opinion," *American Sociological Review,* Vol. 24 (August, 1959), pp. 547-559.

preliterate group culture; political scientists were absorbed in the study of power structures; and economists delved into social behavior mostly as it related to the production, distribution, and consumption of wealth. Each of these disciplines, as well as the other social science areas, dealt more or less exclusively with some selected aspect of social life. The need for a discipline that would treat human relationships in their entirety gave rise to sociology. Interestingly enough, this need was felt by persons trained in widely separated disciplines more or less coincidently. Early sociologists were recruited from such diverse fields as biology, history, philosophy, economics, and natural science.

DEFINITION OF SOCIOLOGY[2]

The preceding introductory statement provides a clue to the definition of sociology. In simplest terms, sociology is the *study of human relationships*. A more elaborate definition might state that sociology is the *generalizing science and theory of social action systems,* but would not be more correct. The student will discover many differently worded definitions as he progresses from one reference to another. This should not be cause for concern since the *content* of definitions by reputable professional sociologists is essentially the same. The beginning student should be aware that works prepared for advanced students and for fellow professionals usually include definitions at a higher level of abstraction than are found in introductory texts. In reviewing definitions it should be understood that sociology focuses its primary attention on human relationships *per se,* and to this extent it is different from other studies. Said another way, sociologists interest themselves in human relationships merely because they are social in nature and not because they are related to a particular type of activity. This is not to imply that the discipline ignores the other social sciences, whose foci are on economic, religious, or other types of human interaction, when studying a given problem. On the contrary, all social sciences, including sociology, have an aspect of unity, although they maintain their distinct points of view. The relation of sociology to other disciplines will be apparent throughout this book.

RAISON D'ETRE FOR SOCIOLOGY

Two basic assumptions lie at the foundation of sociology.[3] The first is that *human behavior follows a pattern or order* similar to the patterning of natural

[2] For a succinct statement on the subject matter and definition of sociology see Alex Inkeles, *What Is Sociology?* (Englewood Cliffs, New Jersey, Prentice-Hall, 1964), Chapter 1.

[3] See Roland J. Pellegrin, "The Nature and Characteristics of Sociology," selection in Robert W. O'Brien, Clarence C. Schrag, and Walter T. Martin, *Readings in General Sociology,* 3rd ed. (Boston, Houghton Mifflin, 1964), pp. 7-11.

phenomena. One has but to observe the everyday activities of his fellows to determine that certain acts are performed in a more or less standardized way. It may be a surprising discovery to see how closely one can predict the group behavior of his acquaintances during the course of a day. Activities such as those relating to dress, eating habits, dating, family life, and driving automobiles are all predictable to a large extent. The processes whereby this patterning comes about make up an integral part of the subject matter of sociology.

The second factual basis of sociology is that *man is a social creature.* Numerous scholars, tracing back to Aristotle, have observed and recorded what has been called a natural tendency for men to associate themselves in groups. Occasionally, there are accounts of feral men who have lived with animals or of isolates who have remained away from human association for periods of time, but in such instances the individuals can scarcely be termed human.[4] If anything, these accounts reinforce the position that it is necessary to look for descriptions and/or explanations of human behavior within the realm of learning and experience, or in other words, in the group setting.

THE METHODS OF SOCIOLOGICAL INQUIRY

Sociologists and others have long debated whether or not the methods of sociology (and of the other social sciences) were those of a science, in the strictest sense of this term. This issue is an involved one and should not be of grave concern to the beginning student. It involves the basic questions of what science is and what the legitimate methods of science are. There is, however, no question that much sociological information is derived through use of the formal methods of science, and that the discipline includes "a body of systematically organized knowledge and theory." It is thus possible to refer to sociology as scientific without arbitrarily ruling on what are or are not the methods of science.

There are two methodological approaches which are foremost in sociological (and social science) researches—the formal scientific method and the informal *Verstehen* method.[5] Each has its champions, the extremists among whom hold that their way is the only valid one. The brief summaries which follow are designed to acquaint the student with the respective approaches. Chapter 3 elaborates on the techniques used in the application of these methods.

---

[4] See J. A. L. Singh and Robert M. Zingg, *Wolf Children and Feral Man* (New York, Harper & Row, 1942), and Kingsley Davis, "Final Notes on a Case of Extreme Isolation," *American Journal of Sociology* (March, 1947), pp. 432-437.

[5] One of the best summary statements on these approaches is found in John F. Cuber, *Sociology*, 5th ed. (New York, Appleton-Century-Crofts, 1963), pp. 33-42.

THE FORMAL SCIENTIFIC METHOD

In essence, science can be defined as a method of knowing that something is true or correct.[6] This definition lays aside the issue of whether there is more than one way of determining truth or fact. Our concern here is the formal scientific method which is based upon a number of postulates and practices and follows certain standardized procedures. The basic postulates are that there is order and uniformity in the universe which can be observed, verified, and classified into systems or patterns of knowledge. The procedure followed in determining and classifying the regularity in nature involves at least three major steps: (1) The formulation of an hypothesis or a statement which expresses the belief that one condition or thing is related in a specific way to another condition or thing. (2) The empirical testing of the relationships hypothesized. Findings backed by conclusive evidence are termed laws of science (such as the law of falling bodies in physics). Discoveries that lack final verification but for which considerable evidence exists, are often termed theories. (3) The systematic classification and description of what has been tested and observed into systems or patterns of knowledge.

THE INFORMAL VERSTEHEN METHOD

The informal method used by sociologists, sometimes also called the philosophical method, is in sharp contrast to the formal method just described. It seems to be best explained by the German word *Verstehen*. In a general sense *Verstehen* refers to insight, but it connotes a particular type of insightful understanding. This unique understanding has been compared to the artist's comprehension of a painting or a sculpture. Cooley explains how this type of understanding is developed. He states that *Verstehen*, ". . . is developed from contact with the minds of other men, through communication, which sets going a process of thought and sentiment similar to theirs and enables us to understand them by sharing their states of mind."[7]

The proponents of this method of inquiry hold that it is both a valid and necessary way of arriving at certain classes of knowledge.[8] They point out that factual information must be integrated into unified and meaningful wholes, a type of endeavor which does not lend itself to statistical manipulations.

[6] Some scholars hold that all facts are determined through use of the scientific method. See G. A. Lundberg, *The Foundations of Sociology* (New York, Macmillan, 1939).

[7] C. H. Cooley, *Sociological Theory and Social Research* (New York, Holt, Rinehart & Winston, 1939), p. 290.

[8] See Robert Bierstedt, "Sociology and Humane Learning," *American Sociological Review*, Vol. 25, No. 1 (February, 1960), pp. 5-9.

THE INTERDEPENDENCE OF
METHODS OF INQUIRY

If one is to judge by recent expressions, there is a growing consensus among sociologists that a judicious use of the formal and informal methods of inquiry provides the greatest enlightenment.[9] Whereas the details of interactional patterns and relationships can best be determined through use of empirical methods, the meaning of these relationships are best worked out through *Verstehen* operations. Both steps are essential to the development of new knowledge and to scientific progress.

THE GENERALIZING NATURE
OF SOCIOLOGY

Although sociology follows the scientific method, it concerns itself with general and recurrent human relationships rather than with unique ones. This point is introduced early because some students may have difficulty in understanding why sociology does not pursue interesting and obviously important studies of the specific or the particular. Actually, such investigations are left to the individualizing disciplines, such as history. Historians have as their proper task the study of the unique features of past and current events. The historian has made a contribution to his discipline when he discovers a particular way in which one war, or one religion, or one general, or one political movement differs from other wars, religions, generals, or political movements. By contrast, the sociologist, working within the framework of a generalizing science, makes his contribution when he demonstrates phenomena that *recur* in time and space. Thus, he seeks to find types of interaction common to certain types of wars, to given classes of religions, to certain types of military leaders, and to particular kinds of social movements. Behavior patterns that are determined to be recurrent and predictable can be considered as principles of human behavior.

---

[9] Almost all recent books of readings in sociology include sections which stress this point. See Milton L. Barron, Ed., *Contemporary Sociology* (New York, Dodd, Mead, 1964), Part I; John F. Cuber and Peggy B. Harroff, *Readings in Sociology* (New York, Appleton-Century-Crofts, 1962), Part I; and Alex Inkeles, Ed., *Readings on Modern Sociology* (Englewood Cliffs, New Jersey, Prentice-Hall, 1966).

THE PROBLEM OF OBJECTIVITY IN SOCIOLOGY

In contrast to the physical and natural scientists, sociologists and other social scientists are generally involved in the phenomena they investigate—religion, family customs and systems, and political institutions. These are "ways of life" toward which a sociologist, like anyone else, has a *personal* orientation. It is for this reason that great stress is placed in the training of sociology students on objectivity, on overcoming their preconceived ideas, emotional biases, and their tendency to make ethical judgments.

The problem of prejudice goes beyond the ability and willingness to study the facts in a given situation dispassionately and without prejudice. Because of the nature of his studies, it is not unusual for the sociologist to be confronted with an "audience" that feels qualified to speak authoritatively on his findings. Almost every nonscientist considers himself to be well informed on what is right and wrong in human relationships. Since the lay person seldom feels hindered by limited cultural experience, the social investigator may feel a more or less subtle pressure to come up with the "right" answer in terms of group ideas of morality. This type of pressure is much more likely to come into play on matters charged with strong feelings such as race relations, religion, and politics.

Some students may feel that in achieving objectivity they must give up their moral or religious convictions. This is a misinterpretation. Sociology as a science is concerned only with facts such as the moral significance that a particular group attaches to a given idea or object, or the different ways in which people worship their god or gods, or the number of wives included in a family system. Because they are descriptive and interpretive scientists, sociologists can never say what is good or bad, moral or immoral, ethical or unethical in and of itself. They can only do this in terms of the beliefs of a given society. Matters of this type can be studied objectively, but they cannot be judged good or evil by scientific means. It is thus that the scientist as well as the lay person finds it possible to reconcile his religious and other beliefs with his scientific investigations.

PREDICTION IN SOCIOLOGY

Social scientists are often criticized for the lack of preciseness of their predictions. The implication is that prediction is more exact and precise in the physical and natural sciences. While the relative exactness of one or another science may be argued *ad infinitum,* it is unquestionably true that sociology has not achieved the predictive level of certain other disciplines. There are, however, several good reasons for this. The first is the relative youth of sociology. Most of the physical or natural sciences trace their origins back hundreds of years. By contrast, man did not seriously begin studying his relations with others until this century.

A second reason for the higher predictive capacity of the physical sciences is that sociological prediction requires knowledge additional to that required in the sciences dealing with natural phenomena. The four general concepts or ideas of the so-called exact sciences—regularity, structure, function, and change—do not suffice for sociology or the other social sciences. There is the necessity of adding a fifth general concept, namely *meaning.*[10] Meaning acknowledges the fact that individuals act, not according to instincts or other rigid, unchanging patterns, but according to their *interpretation* of the situation and in part, at least, according to their intentions. This is demonstrated by the fact that the same situation may have entirely different meaning to persons having grown up in different cultures. For example, an Orthodox Jew and a Christian place a different meaning on a platter of ham and, therefore, they behave differently toward it.

The necessity of considering meaning separates sociology and the other social sciences from the physical sciences. Arnold W. Green illustrates this point well in pointing out that a chair, whether a very expensive Eames or a plain wooden electric chair, represents a whirl of electrons to the physicist. The sociologist, in sharp contrast, sees symbols which in the one instance represent high status and a given mode of life and in the second instance represent punishment for crime.[11]

Prediction in sociology, as in any other science, can only be done in light of relatively complete knowledge of the many variables in a given situation. However, forecasting may be done on the basis of educated guesses about the variables. It becomes necessary in real life, and sometimes in professional endeavors, to forecast the future. In these instances, one must expect to be wrong part of the time.

A major portion of this volume will be devoted to the theoretical frame of reference, the methods, and the tools which sociologists use in arriving at predictions and forecasts. The remainder of the chapter will contain illustrations of concrete ways in which sociological information has been or can be useful in planning for the future and in solving problems of human relations.

[10] John W. Bennett and Melvin M. Tumin, *Social Life* (New York, Knopf, 1948), p. 82.

[11] Arnold W. Green, *Sociology,* 4th ed. (New York, McGraw-Hill, 1964), p. 4.

THE APPLICATION AND USE
OF SOCIOLOGY

In earlier years sociologists, like other scientists, tended to argue for a pure science, devoid of immediate practical applications. This commitment to knowledge for knowledge's sake appears to have been partly an attempt to resist the so-called corruption which it was felt would take place when one was employed to find solutions to practical problems, and partly a defense mechanism for protection against being pressed to come up with solutions to difficult problems. The latter reason was quite rational because sociology is only now achieving a sufficient degree of theoretical and methodological refinement to be useful. Donald Young has listed some of the factors that handicapped the cooperation of the sociologist and the practitioner in the past: (1) sociology was a young discipline and thus had only a small store of useful knowledge; (2) the standard practices in the profession did not encourage or facilitate close collaboration with operating agencies; (3) sociologists were poorly prepared because of the way sociology was taught; (4) practitioners had an unrealistic expectation in terms of current sociological knowledge and techniques. Young goes on to make the important point that sociologists and practitioners often did not understand one another because the former were concerned with understanding and the latter with doing.[12]

At the present time, thousands of sociologists are employed in attempts to apply their knowledge of human behavior for some purpose considered important by political parties, industrial organizations, and government agencies. A recent book by Donald M. Valdes and Dwight G. Dean devotes over 500 pages to examples of sociology in use.[13]

The fact that sociology has an application does not imply that basic research should be or is neglected. Such research is often the foundation of good practice. Someone has said, "If there is anything worse than theory without practice, it is practice without theory." This is the view one generally encounters among sociologists. Some of the activities of sociologists and the purposes served by their work and study are as follows.

[12] Donald Young, "Sociology and the Practicing-Professions," *American Sociological Review,* Vol. 20 (December, 1955), pp. 641-648.
[13] Donald M. Valdes and Dwight G. Dean, *Sociology in Use* (New York, Macmillan, 1965).

PREPARING INFORMATION FOR LEGISLATIVE PROGRAMS

Local, state, and national governments are continually being faced with important social issues. Many times these issues are subject to legislation, and it falls to the lot of legislators to vote for or against certain propositions. It is impossible for a given legislator to be knowledgeable on all subjects, and indeed basic information is frequently lacking. Sociologists can be of use in a practical way in determining what facts apply in these situations. They can, on the basis of their research, provide legislators and others interested in a given issue or program with evidence helpful in decision making. A few examples will illustrate this application of sociological know-how:

(1) Major government programs relating to relief, rehabilitation, health, urban development, and poverty can be traced directly to the work of sociologists. Two examples demonstrate this fact. (a) Sociological research provided the factual base required to bring about the 1954 amendment to the United States Social Security Law. Studies made in Kentucky, Connecticut, Wisconsin, and Texas exploded the myth (rather well entrenched in the Congress) that farmers were so devoted to free enterprise and to individualism that they would not want to be included in the Social Security program. The findings turned up by sociologists were that farmers felt they needed some kind of assured retirement income and were, as a group, most interested in participating in social security programs.[14] (b) Sociological research done during the depression years (1930's) in the United States provided the basic information and support for a wide range of legislative programs relating to health insurance, chronic disease control, hospital construction, and medical care for the needy. This research was accomplished under the first National Health Survey organized by the U. S. Public Health Service and provided work relief by training unemployed workers under the Work Progress Administration Program.[15] A new National Health Survey was begun by the Public Health Service of the U. S. Department of Health, Education, and Welfare in 1957. The findings from this continuing research have already been widely utilized.

(2) The Arkansas School District Reorganization Act of 1948 reduced the state's school districts by over 1000. The basic data for this act was supplied by Lawrence Charlton, a sociologist at the University of Arkansas.[16]

(3) The federal programs relating to area redevelopment, community development, and poverty in the United States in recent years can also be

[14] See *Hearings before the Committee on Ways and Means*, House of Representatives (83rd Congress, 2nd Session) HR 7199 (Social Security Act Amendment of 1954), pp. 195-233.

[15] Valdes and Dean, *op. cit.*, p. 11.

[16] J. L. Charlton, *School Services in Rural Communities*, Agricultural Experiment Station Bulletin No. 398 (Fayetteville, Arkansas, 1940).

directly linked to sociological studies. Much of the basic work for determining areas of need was done under the direction of Margaret J. Hagood and Louis J. Ducoff.[17]

(4) Perhaps one of the most far-reaching and significant examples of how sociologists have been instrumental in implementing government programs is the case of the G. I. Bill of Rights. Stuart Dodd tells how the Morale Branch of the U. S. Armed Forces, a human relations surveying agency, was called upon to determine the best procedures for demobilizing and rehabilitating service men after World War II. Their findings and recommendations were used as the basis of the G. I. Bill of Rights, which proved highly successful.[18]

IMPLEMENTATION OF PROGRAMS

Not only are sociologists of use in providing information helpful for formulating legislation, they also perform a highly demanded service in providing the persons charged with implementing programs of government and nongovernment agencies with facts and understandings basic to planning. In addition, they serve to orient persons employed in these programs to the intricacies of human behavior and interaction. Without going into detailed citations, which are numerous, it can be noted that in so far as government planning is involved, sociologists have (1) provided much of the information used in program planning for health care, law enforcement, military personnel problems, disaster situations, communications and transportation problems, agricultural extension work, and education; (2) performed as consultants or speakers at many conferences, short courses, and workshops designed to implement programs; (3) served as members of work teams charged with important community or village development projects throughout the world; and (4) provided research know-how and conducted the research for almost every government agency charged with decision making and planning.[19]

Outside the government, sociologists render service to mass-media agencies, manufacturers, labor unions, voluntary health agencies, various welfare agencies, and industrial and retail organizations. In most of these organizations more and more positions have been formed for professionally trained sociologists. This is true because no other field of study gives the student such a broad and scientific acquaintance with human behavior. In this regard, many employers express preference for sociology majors in jobs requiring skills in another area. They base their preference on the fact that the given skill may be acquired on the job, but the knowledge of human behavior cannot.

[17] See *Development of Agriculture's Human Resources* (U. S. Department of Agriculture, Washington, D. C., April, 1955).

[18] Valdes and Dean, *op. cit.*, pp. 4-5.

[19] See Howard W. Beers, "Application of Sociology in Development Programs," The Council on Economic and Cultural Affairs, Inc., *CECA Paper* (January, 1963).

The account given by Ithiel de Sola Pool, Robert P. Abelson, and Samuel L. Popkin of the famous Simulmatics Project demonstrates the use of a new type of sociological service.[20] The Simulmatics Project was launched during the 1960 Presidential campaign in the United States. The research done by the social scientists working on the project utilized a new technique for processing public opinion poll data which involved computed simulation of how certain groups in the population would react to certain issues—and thus provide a more intelligent understanding of voter behavior. The Democratic Party employed the services of the project and the election of President Kennedy is attributed in part to the success of the research done and to the body of psychological and sociological theory upon which it was based. The idea has been dramatized in a highly interesting novel by Eugene Burdick.[21]

TEACHING, RESEARCH, AND ADMINISTRATION

Professional sociologists are in great demand and currently in short supply, as college teachers, and as researchers and administrators for government and private agencies. Two factors have combined to open wider the door of opportunity for sociologists as teachers. First, everywhere there is a growing conviction that education is not only the right of the individual, but a necessity for societal progress. This view, when coupled with rapidly increasing populations, explains the ever-increasing demand for teachers—sociology included. Second, sociology has become established in most colleges. Almost all medium-sized universities in the United States have departments of sociology which include 12 to 20 faculty members plus teaching assistants.

The use of sociologists as researchers has boomed in the last two or three decades. Olaf Larson notes that growth in budgets for research in government agencies is the most important base for the current growth and strength of sociology.[22] Harry Albert describes the government's growing recognition of social science and especially sociology with the vernacular phrase, "they never had it so good."[23] Many private organizations, such as opinion-polling and market-research groups, industrial and manufacturing organizations, and professional associations also maintain or support sociological research. For this type of employer, sociologists do studies of production efficiency, of morale, and of the attitudes, beliefs, and values of people which relate to their potential behavior. Large and small foundations of all sorts and types also give

[20] Ithiel de Sola Pool, Robert P. Abelson, and Samuel L. Popkin, *Candidates, Issues, and Strategies: A Computer Simulation of the 1960 Presidential Election* (Cambridge, M. I. T., 1964).

[21] Eugene Burdick, *The 480: A Novel of Politics* (New York, McGraw-Hill, 1964).

[22] Olaf F. Larson, "Uses of Sociology in Action Programs," paper read at August 31, 1962 annual meeting of the American Sociological Association in Washington, D. C.

[23] Harry Albert, "The Government's Growing Recognition of Social Science," in Valdes and Dean, *op. cit.,* p. 477.

much support to basic sociological research. The future looks even more promising.

Sociologists are being provided with an increasing number of opportunities to become administrators because of their understanding of human behavior and their consequent ability to analyze problems of human relations objectively. Many government bureaus and private agencies now use sociologists as administrators and subadministrators. Sociologists are considered qualified personnel for positions as personnel directors, labor relations specialists, members of clinical teams and other types of evaluative teams, and for many other positions where a knowledge of what is now being called "people problems" is important.

NONOCCUPATIONAL PURPOSES

Sociology has use for the nonspecialist as well as for the person making a career in this field. The complexities and problems of modern life are such that everyone must constantly face new issues and changed situations. Sociological training provides a perspective for participating effectively in the modern world because one so trained can understand and act more intelligently with regard to problems that frustrate the average citizen.

THE IMPORTANCE OF THINKING
AS A SOCIOLOGIST

Sociology, like other disciplines, involves a way of thinking. This way includes (1) a familiarity with sociological nomenclature—professional concepts are often initially confusing because the same *words* have a different popular meaning; (2) some understanding of the theoretical frame of reference of sociology, which conceives human behavior as patterned and predictable; (3) an ability to consider social phenomena dispassionately, that is, without letting personal biases obscure facts; (4) an ability to think in terms of trends, gradations, and continuums as contrasted to precise measurements and to popular dichotomies; and (5) an ability to keep from falling prey to the so-called common sense fallacy. The victim of this fallacy holds that sociology is nothing but good horse sense because research findings often agree with what is already known. The fact is many so-called well-known things also turn out to be quite false after careful research.[24] Perhaps the first clue to whether or not one is thinking sociologically comes when he begins to analyze the ordinary behavior of his friends and of himself in terms of ordered or socially structured action.

[24] See Paul F. Lazarsfeld, "Sociology and Common Sense," reprinted in Milton L. Barron, Ed., *Contemporary Sociology* (New York, Dodd, Mead, 1964), pp. 27-29.

WHAT SOCIOLOGY CANNOT DO

There is a tendency for some persons outside the field of sociology to expect more from sociology than it can now deliver. Those who expect the sociologists to provide complete answers to all social problems and explain perfectly all human behavior are bound for disappointment. Sociology is categorically no better—or worse—in the provision of answers than other sciences. One needs but to remember that the important breakthroughs in physics, medicine, and other disciplines have generally come only after years of concentrated research and have often involved the expenditure of vast funds. The sociologist should be accorded comparable patience. Actually, by some yardsticks, faster progress has been made on a great variety of problems than could have been expected in the light of the normal pace of science.

SOCIOLOGISTS MAINTAIN A HEALTHY DISAGREEMENT

It is most disturbing to some students to discover that the members of a profession are unable to agree completely on professional matters. The natural tendency is to conclude that the content of the discipline is therefore vague, lacking in authenticity, and, at best, unscientific. This note is to forewarn the student that sociologists are of many schools and few textbooks completely agree on all definitions and understandings. At the same time, there is a substantial core of conceptual agreement. The fact is that sociology or any other science could not expect to move forward without some disagreement among its practitioners. This is the way new ideas are tested and new bodies of theory developed. The youth of sociology may account for its great diversity of viewpoints, but this may at the same time be a measure of strength. With so many persons engaged in theory building, one must expect breakthroughs in theory and methods to be made continuously.

THE STUDY OF SOCIOLOGY IS NOT THE STUDY OF A GIVEN SOCIETY

One final admonition is in order. Many books used as introductory sociology texts are devoted primarily to the study of American society. This emphasis is worthwhile when the purpose in mind is to illustrate national patterns of behavior and national problems. However, it is likely to give the impression to the beginning student that sociology is really a study of the peoples in some one society. Also, the descriptions which are given (usually quite interesting to the student) are likely to detract from the basic theory which is the core matter. For this reason, the emphasis in this text is upon concepts and theoretical models. Certain illustrations taken from the United States and other societies are included; but a deliberate attempt is made to avoid too many interesting descriptive accounts of specific groups.

SUMMARY

Sociology is defined simply as the study of human relationships *per se*. The inspiration for this discipline is found in the facts that human behavior follows a pattern and man lives in groups.

Sociologists are divided on the proper role of formal scientific methods and informal *Verstehen* methods of inquiry in their search for knowledge. However, there is a growing consensus that these two methods can be used in a complementary fashion.

Sociologists concern themselves with objective studies of general and recurrent human relationships, rather than with unique ones. Although prediction in sociology still lacks the preciseness of certain other disciplines, there is a fast increasing use and application of sociological information. Such information is the basis for the formulation and implementation of many government programs as well as for much planning by private interests in business, industry, and politics. In addition, sociological training provides the individual with a perspective for more effective participation in the everyday affairs of life.

It is important that the beginning student of sociology develop a familiarity with concepts and keep from falling prey to his prejudices or to common sense fallacies. Also, he needs to be aware that sociology does not have complete answers for all social problems and that there is disagreement among sociologists. The disagreements which persist are seen as a healthy sign of active theory building—with the promise of future breakthroughs. Finally, to assure a proper perspective for his study of sociology, the student should be clear on the point that sociology is *not* the study of a given society, but of theory and method which is as applicable in one societal setting as in another.

Supplementary Readings

Each of the items in the suggested list of supplementary readings which appears at the end of the respective chapters has been selected with the introductory student in mind. The lists are relatively short since the purpose was to supplement text materials with readily available sources rather than compile a comprehensive bibliography. To this end, many of the references were selected because they are reprinted in one or another of the various books of readings prepared especially for the first courses in sociology. All of the books of this type consulted are listed below and identified in abbreviated form. This shortened form is used as an identifying code and placed at the end of the bibliographical information to show that the selection is available in more than one place. Articles that can be found in the Bobbs-Merrill reprint collection are identified by the small capital letters BM. The latter are available at a nominal cost.

Abbreviated Form	Books of Readings
BARRON	Barron, Milton L., Ed., *Contemporary Sociology* (New York, Dodd, Mead, 1964).
CUBER & HARROFF	Cuber, John F. and Peggy B. Harroff, *Readings in Sociology* (New York, Appleton-Century-Crofts, 1962).
INKELES	Inkeles, Alex, Ed., *Readings on Modern Sociology* (Englewood Cliffs, New Jersey, Prentice-Hall, 1966).
LASSWELL ET AL.	Lasswell, Thomas E., John H. Burma and Sidney H. Aronson, *Introductory Readings in Sociology* (Chicago, Scott, Foresman, 1965).
LEE	Lee, Alfred M., Ed., *Readings in Sociology* (New York, Barnes & Noble, 1951).
MIZRUCHI	Mizruchi, Ephraim H., *The Substance of Sociology: Codes, Conduct, and Consequences* (New York, Appleton-Century-Crofts, 1967).
O'BRIEN ET AL.	O'Brien, Robert W., Clarence C. Schrag and Walter T. Martin, *Readings in General Sociology* (Boston, Houghton Mifflin, 1964).
ROSS	Ross, H. Laurence, *Perspectives on the Social Order: Readings in Sociology* (New York, McGraw-Hill, 1963).
SCHULER ET AL.	Schuler, Edgar A., Thomas F. Hoult, Duane L. Gibson, Maude L. Fiero and Wilbur B. Brookover, *Readings in Sociology,* 2nd ed. (New York, Crowell, 1960).
YOUNG & MACK	Young, Kimball and Raymond W. Mack, *Principles of Sociology: A Reader in Theory and Research,* 3rd ed. (New York, American Book, 1965).
BM	*Reprint Series in the Social Sciences* (Indianapolis, Indiana, Bobbs-Merrill).

Readings for this chapter:

Bierstedt, Robert, "Sociology and Humane Learning," *American Sociological Review,* Vol. 25 (February, 1960), pp. 3-9; and also in BARRON; CUBER & HARROFF; and BM.

Hinkle, Roscoe C. and J. Gisela, *The Development of Modern Sociology* (New York, Random House, 1954).

Hopper, Janice Harris, "To Be a Sociologist," selection in ROSS.

Inkeles, Alex, *What Is Sociology?* (Englewood Cliffs, New Jersey, Prentice-Hall, 1964).

Lazarsfeld, Paul F., "Sociology vs. Common Sense," Excerpt in BARRON—from "Review of the American Soldier, Vols. I and II," in *The Public Opinion Quarterly*, Vol. 13 (Fall, 1949), pp. 378-380.

Schellenberg, James A., "Divisions of General Sociology," *American Sociological Review*, Vol. 22 (December, 1957), pp. 660-663; and also in BARRON.

Toby, Jackson, "Undermining the Student's Faith in the Validity of Personal Experience," *American Sociological Review*, Vol. 20 (December, 1955), pp. 717-718; and also in BARRON and YOUNG & MACK.

Valdes, Donald M. and Dwight G. Dean, *Sociology in Use* (New York, Macmillan, 1965).

Zetterberg, Hans L., *On Theory and Verification in Sociology*, 3rd ed. (New York, The Bedminster Press, 1965).

2

SOCIAL ORGANIZATION: BASIC CONCEPTS AND A SOCIAL SYSTEM MODEL

It was stressed in Chapter 1 that sociology is based on the observation that human behavior is characterized by regular and recurrent patterns. This fact sets the stage for a theory of sociology which allows for the *conceptualization of human interrelationships* in a systematic fashion. Physicists use the conceptual model of the atom to understand and explain the structure and functioning of physical aspects of the universe. This model allows physicists to better comprehend the *organization* of the physical world. Sociologists likewise, approach their phenomena in terms of models. The social organization models used facilitate the understanding of human behavior. The purpose of this chapter is to acquaint the student, first with certain basic terms and concepts which must be mastered before *social* organization can be understood; then with a conceptual model which will provide a perspective for working out explanations of human behavior.

Sociology will be meaningful and the sociological approach will make sense to the person who carefully studies the material presented in this chapter. To the person who does not grasp the broad frame of reference (theory) of sociology as presented here, the remainder of this text, and much other sociological writing will appear to be little more than an interesting (perhaps occasionally boring) agglomeration of facts and descriptions.

NATURE OF SOCIOLOGICAL CONCEPTS

The concepts of sociology, like those of other disciplines, are terms of general reference. They are used in each instance to refer to types or classes of events, persons, or relationships. Sociological concepts are not concerned with the nonrecurrent or unique, as brought out in Chapter 1. When defined and understood precisely, sociological terms are devoid of moral connotations. They do not imply that one event, group, or type of relationship is good and another bad; they simply communicate types of relationships such as a "polygamous" family, or a "caste" system.

Many of the concepts of sociology are used popularly in a different sense because they deal with features of everyday life. This is why such words as *society, status, culture,* and *race* must be defined with extreme care for professional usage. In this regard, sociological concepts generally have a higher level of abstraction than identical words do in ordinary discourse. It is easier to comprehend the above statement if one considers that most ordinary conversations deal with concrete situations and people—the hurricane Audrey or President Johnson—whereas the sociologist would think more abstractly of the former as a disaster situation and the latter as a status position. The distinction between popular and technical usage of words is one reason why popular writers often do not adequately present the findings of research scholars. It accounts for the fact that a discipline, such as sociology, can have a public image which is not in keeping with its true position. The sociologist has a responsibility to interpret his findings to the public, but it is not his responsibility to make every intelligent person a sociologist. Indeed, if he could do this in a short time, there would be no need for the long period of training which professional sociologists undergo.

The body of sociological concepts is growing at a fast pace. Increased knowledge often comes about through the formulation of more precise or more appropriate concepts for observed patterns of regularity. Rapid growth also sets the stage for a certain amount of terminological confusion, as old concepts are redefined or replaced by more appropriate terms. In this volume, an attempt is made to use generally accepted definitions. However, new understandings are given when they appear as a decided improvement on old concepts.

SOCIAL ORGANIZATION AS A CONCEPT

When a sociologist uses the term **social organization** in a generic sense he has reference to the vast, complex network of patterned human behavior which exists within each society. When he uses this term in a specific sense he has in mind the behavior of actors in subunits of society such as families, businesses, and schools. Robin Williams points out that, "Social organization refers to human action insofar as the actor takes into account the actions of others." He goes on to explain that, as persons interact, they develop mutual expectations and concerns and if interaction continues over a period of time, more or less definite patterns of behavior emerge.[1] It can readily be seen that if no patterns existed, the most ordinary situations would be baffling. The person who has visited in a country where he does not understand the language or customs finds himself in something of an unorganized state. If two drivers do not have a preconditioned expectancy, such as on which side of the street to drive, there is no social organization; if they have just enough understanding to know certain signals or signs, then there is at least minimal social organization.

Social organization is a dynamic process; the patterns of human relationships are constantly changing, despite the fact that they are also regular and predictable. It is thus that the sociologist studies social organization, both as a condition and as a process. On the one hand, he looks into the structure of social action and on the other hand, concerns himself with the processes of change in social action.[2] Both approaches will be elaborated in later discussions.

The important understanding for the beginning student is that in every society the behavior of persons and groups is somehow integrated into a more or less cohesive whole through patterns of interaction. In this regard, as Robin Williams points out, "There is organization precisely to *the degree that* the actions of individuals toward other individuals are recurrent and coordinated by the orientation of the acts of each to those of others."[3]

SOCIETY AS A CONCEPT

Social organization is generally studied within the limits of a society. When the word *society* is heard in casual conversation, it is likely the speaker will be

---

[1] Robin M. Williams, Jr., *American Society*, 2nd ed. (New York, Knopf, 1960), p. 472.

[2] This point of view is elaborated in J. O. Hertzler, *Social Institutions* (Lincoln, Nebraska, University of Nebraska Press, 1946), p. 13.

[3] Williams, *op. cit.*, p. 37.

referring to an upper-class person or group, or to a formal association of persons banded together to support a common cause, such as the Society for the Prevention of Cruelty to Animals. None of these understandings suffice for sociology. In the technical sense in which sociologists use the term, a *society* is, ". . . that group within which men share a total common life."[4] Said another way, a **society** is a collection of people with a common identification, who are sufficiently organized to carry out the conditions necessary to living harmoniously together. How this condition is met, is brought out in Chapter 8.

Three characteristics can be utilized in differentiating societies from less inclusive groups. First, there must be an aggregate of individuals of fairly large size. Second, these individuals must have relationships which assure their cooperation, at least at one level of interaction. Finally, the association of these individuals must be more or less permanent in nature. Following the above criteria, a football crowd, or a United Nations assembly, or any relatively small aggregate of persons whose association is temporary, could not be said to be a society. But one can legitimately speak of the French or the African Pygmies as belonging to a national and tribal society, respectively. (Although the term society is roughly synonymous with the term nation, it is also correct to speak of tribal societies, residing within national boundaries.)

SOCIAL INTERACTION AS A CONCEPT

We have noted that social organization conveys the meaning of an organized network of *social interaction*. The latter term is a basic, if not the most basic, concept in sociology. It refers specifically to the interstimulation and response (reciprocal contact) between individuals and groups. Alvin and Helen Gouldner describe **social interaction** as, ". . . action and reaction among people."[5] Thus, whether or not exchanges between men are friendly or antagonistic, whether they are formal or informal, whether they are face to face or through symbols like written language sent thousands of miles; they constitute social interactions as long as they elicit a response of some type.

Charles P. Loomis lists four important characteristics of interaction as follows[6]:

(1) A plurality of actors (two or more).
(2) Communication between the actors by means of symbols.
(3) A "duration" or time dimension possessing a past, present, and future, which in part determines the character of the ongoing action.
(4) An "objective" whether or not its specification from the standpoint of the actors coincides with that of an objective observer.

[4] Ely Chinoy, *Sociological Perspective* (New York, Random House, 1954), p. 21.
[5] Alvin W. Gouldner and Helen P. Gouldner, *Modern Sociology* (New York, Harcourt, Brace & World, 1963), p. 63.
[6] From Charles P. Loomis, *Social Systems: Essays on Their Persistence and Changes*, copyright 1960, D. Van Nostrand Company, Inc., Princeton, N.J., p. 2.

SOCIAL ORGANIZATION AND CULTURE

In presenting the basic concepts related to social organization, it is appropriate to explain why *culture* is not included among the terms treated at some length. The fact is that culture is such an important concept that an entire chapter is devoted to it later. However, it is not basic to the foundation of a sociological theory of organization, as some earlier writers implied.

Perhaps the easiest way to distinguish culture from social organization is to think of culture as a body of transmittable patterns for living—such as when to eat, how to dress, and how to greet people. By contrast, social organization is concerned with aggregations of people who are "bonded" together through communication and webs of interaction as social groups. Robin Williams clarifies the distinction between these two terms in this way. "The distinction arises from the fact that culture is not concrete behavior itself but contains the normative standards for behavior. The embodiment of cultural norms in concrete social relations marks the area of social organization."[7] A theory of social organization makes possible the explanation of such processes as conflict and, in addition, explains why culture changes. Culture, by contrast, only provides an orientation for action to actors who are members of concrete systems of action.[8] The reader is referred to Chapter 6 for a detailed review of the full implication and meaning of culture as a concept.

THE SOCIAL SYSTEM AS AN ANALYTICAL MODEL FOR THE STUDY OF SOCIAL ORGANIZATION

A conceptual model is the scientist's beforehand image of the way in which the phenomena he wishes to study is organized. Such models are worked out to guide the researcher as he searches for order in nature.

SOCIAL SYSTEM DEFINED

Perhaps the most generally accepted conceptual model of social organization used by sociologists is the *social system*. This model is designed to help one

---

[7] Williams, *op. cit.*, p. 37.

[8] See Scott A. Greer, *Social Organization* (Garden City, New York, Doubleday, 1955), pp. 11-12; and Talcott Parsons and Edward A. Shils, Eds., *Toward a General Theory of Action* (New York, Harper & Row, 1962, Harper Torchbook), pp. 6-8.

visualize that certain human collectives (groups) are systems whose parts are interdependent and which, as unities, are in turn interlinked with one another through mutual dependencies. The prerequisites for a social system are two or more people in interaction directed toward attaining a goal and guided by patterns of structured and shared symbols and expectations. The relationship among system members will normally persist over time, although it may be a short period on occasion.

Once the student accepts and understands the social system model, he will have taken a giant step in comprehending the sociological approach. It may be helpful to think of the social system as the basic unit of society in something of the same way that a cell is thought of as a basic unit in the make-up of an organism and an atom is thought of as the basic unit of matter.

The model of the social system presented here is in a tradition called the Structural–Functional School in sociology. It is selected for two reasons: because of its widespread use and because of the ease with which it can be used as an explanatory device.

THE ELEMENTS AND ELEMENTAL PROCESSES OF SOCIAL SYSTEMS

The term *element* is normally used to designate some basic part of a larger whole. Chemical elements for example, represent varieties of matter which singly or in combination make up all material things. Likewise, the **elements** of social systems are units of social interaction. The elements make up the structure of the social system—they are the parts of the system which hold it together.

Ten social system elements are described in some detail in this chapter including: (1) belief (knowledge); (2) sentiment; (3) end, goal, or objective; (4) norm; (5) status-role (position); (6) rank; (7) power; (8) sanction; (9) facility; (10) stress–strain.[9] In studying these elements, which are shown in graphic form in Figure 2-1, the student should keep in mind that they represent the analytical aspects of interaction most consistently used by sociologists, whether or not they are approached in the context of a social system model. The utility of certain of these concepts will become clearer in the discussions on social structure which appear in Chapter 8.

[9] Professor Charles P. Loomis must be given full credit for his masterful job of synthesizing, organizing, and describing of the first nine of these elements and the elemental processes that articulate them. The tenth element, stress–strain, has been added by the writer. The writer wishes to fully acknowledge the debt which he owes to Loomis for the material used in the greater part of the remainder of this chapter. See *Op. cit.*, Essay No. I; and Alvin L. Bertrand, "The Stress–Strain Element of Social Systems: A Micro Theory of Conflict and Change," *Social Forces*, Vol. 42 (October, 1963), pp. 1-9.

FIGURE 2-1. *Loomis' P.A.S. (processually articulated structural model of social systems) Model with Stress–Strain Element and Social Change Process Added.*

PROCESSES (ELEMENTAL)	STRUCTURAL FUNCTIONAL CATEGORIES	ELEMENTS
1. COGNITIVE MAPPING AND VALIDATION	1. KNOWING	1. BELIEF (KNOWLEDGE)
2. TENSION MANAGEMENT AND COMMUNICATION OF SENTIMENT	2. FEELING	2. SENTIMENT
3. GOAL ATTAINING ACTIVITY AND CONCOMITANT LATENT ACTIVITY AS PROCESS	3. ACHIEVING	3. END, GOAL, OR OBJECTIVE
4. EVALUATION	4. NORMING, STANDARDIZING, PATTERNING	4. NORM
5. STATUS-ROLE PERFORMANCE	5. DIVIDING THE FUNCTIONS	5. STATUS-ROLE POSITION
6. EVALUATION OF ACTORS AND ALLOCATION OF STATUS-ROLES	6. RANKING	6. RANK
7. DECISION MAKING AND INITIATION OF ACTION	7. CONTROLLING	7. POWER
8. APPLICATION OF SANCTIONS	8. SANCTIONING	8. SANCTION
9. UTILIZATION OF FACILITIES	9. FACILITATING	9. FACILITY
10. DISORGANIZATION DISINTEGRATION	10. DEVIATING CONFLICTING	10. STRESS-STRAIN

COMPREHENSIVE OR MASTER PROCESSES

1. COMMUNICATION	3. SYSTEMIC LINKAGE	5. SOCIALIZATION
2. BOUNDARY MAINTENANCE	4. INSTITUTIONALIZATION	6. SOCIAL CONTROL
	7. SOCIAL CHANGE	

CONDITION OF SOCIAL ACTION

1. TERRITORIALITY	2. SIZE	3. TIME

☐ indicates elements and processes added

Source: Charles P. Loomis, *Social Systems: Essays on Their Persistence and Change* (New York, Van Nostrand, 1960), p. 8 and Alvin L. Bertrand, "The Stress-Strain Element of Social Systems: A Micro Theory of Conflict and Change," *Social Forces*, Vol. 42, No. 1 (October, 1963), pp. 1-9.

BELIEF (KNOWLEDGE). Every social system includes certain *beliefs,* which its members embrace. Other less general beliefs may be variously associated with the system, but are not essential. It is not necessary that these beliefs be true in fact, but simply that they be accepted by the members of the system as true or right. The members of a religious sect, for example, may believe that fire or certain stones have divine power. Beliefs are an important element of social systems because people behave in terms of what they know, and they know that certain explanations and evaluations propounded in their systems are true, right, and good.

Beliefs must be acquired in one manner or another and the process by which knowledge is obtained is **validation** and **cognitive mapping.** The latter terms simply refer to some method of testing *which is considered adequate by members of a social system* to sustain a belief. In a science system, this may mean strict empirical methods such as is necessary before acceptance of a belief that a drug is harmless. In a preliterate society, it may be a simple matter of the pronouncement of a medicine man considered to be divinely inspired.

The number of beliefs (or amount of knowledge) and the intensity with which they are held vary from social system to social system. Likewise, the members of each system have their own peculiar devices for accumulating knowledge. Despite this diversity, belief is an important analytical tool. To illustrate, the investigator who determines that a given religious group does not believe in birth control can offer at least one explanation for a high birth rate.

SENTIMENT. The second element of social systems, *sentiment,* is related to the first, yet easily separated in an analytical sense. **Beliefs,** as brought out, represent what members of a system know about their worlds. **Sentiment** refers to what the members of the system feel about things, events, and places, regardless of how this feeling might have been obtained. Sentiments or feelings help explain patterns of behavior which cannot be explained otherwise. It explains why a father may risk his life to save his son, but may as a bombardier, have no special reluctance to drop bombs on a city inhabited by many children. He has sentiment in both instances, love for members of his family, hate for the enemies of his nation.

The elemental process which directly articulates sentiment is **communication of sentiment.** Sentiments, when communicated, are likely to arouse feelings which must be controlled at least to some extent. It is thus that **tension management** is brought into being. The boy and girl in love must manage or control their sentiment to a point, or they will elicit a different type of sentiment in their family social systems. Tension management is so important that most systems have special mechanisms to assist the individual in managing his tensions, such as sexual taboos for close kin, the affective neutrality which rules out sentiment for the social scientist in his investigations or for the police officer in his arrests.

END, GOAL, OR OBJECTIVE. Normally, when persons interact it is to achieve some purpose. The *goals* of most social systems are most clearly seen as functions of the system, i.e., there is little difficulty in recognizing reproduction of the species as a function or goal of the family or of seeing education as a function of the school. However, in some systems, interaction between members of a group is an end in itself, such as in play. Goals and objectives are less readily identified in such instances.

Goal attaining is, of course, the obvious process in the achievement of objectives. The football team runs plays to achieve a touchdown; the devout believer performs his rituals reverently and carefully to achieve a better life after death; and the student plods his way through course after course to achieve a bachelor's degree. Sometimes functions (or ends) are achieved which are not perceived, at least at first, by the actors in a system: The members of a football team achieve a strong *esprit de corps* off the football field, through playing together. Although this may not be the manifest purpose of the team, the activities of actors in the system still bring it about.

NORM. Social **norms** may be defined as required or acceptable behavior in given situations. Many sociologists consider the norm as the most critical element in the understanding and prediction of action in social systems. Norms represent the rules of the game; in other words they provide standards for judging behavior and for behaving. Some examples of norms are honesty, rules of a game, and laws. Norms become internalized in individuals through a long socialization process, which will be explained later.

At this point, it is possible to consider the question why human behavior is orderly. The answer is found in the nature of norms. Orderliness comes from adherence to norms which represent certain universal elements found in all cultures including: (1) **folkways** or commonly accepted rules of conduct, which do not have a compulsive or "must" status; (2) **mores** or "must" behaviors, which are strictly enforced; (3) **laws** that codify and reinforce the mores and control behavior outside the scope of the mores.

Recourse to norms is the basis for **evaluating** the behavior of individuals and groups. The sociologist, in his analysis of behavior, strives to determine what is the normative pattern. Once he has established what is normal behavior in a group, he can then predict behavior of members of the group in given situations, because he knows how they will evaluate the situation. In the United States, for example, one may predict that the driver of an auto will normally not enter a street which has an arrow shaped sign marked with the words "one way" and pointing in the opposite direction. In Europe, a circular sign with a white bar on a red background conveys the same meaning, although it may baffle the uninitiated American because it is not normal for him.

STATUS (POSITION) AND ROLE. A **status** may be defined as a position in a social system independent of given actors, whereas a *role* can be described as a part of a status position consisting of a more or less integrated subset of social norms.[10] All social systems, by virtue of the fact that they involve two or more actors, are characterized by different status positions such as husband, wife, son, or daughter. A person's status position determines the nature and degree of his responsibilities and obligations as well as his superior–inferior relations to other members of his society.

Status position must not be thought of as synonymous with the individual who, at the moment, occupies the given place in a group structure to which it is attached. It is simply the established collection of responsibilities, obligations, and rights associated with a certain position that is recognized and understood in a given society. This can be illustrated by referring to the well-known fact that in each society the status position of wife or husband is associated with certain rights and duties, and these rights and duties are independent of any particular man or woman. Literally millions of men and women occupy the same status position and enjoy essentially the same rights and responsibilities.

An individual comes to occupy status positions in two separate ways. **Ascribed statuses** are acquired at birth or later without effort on the part of the individual. Through ascription one automatically gets such status positions as social class, race, sex, and age placement. **Achieved statuses** come to the individual only after effort or at least choice on his part. Such places in society are subject to competition and include status positions such as doctor, lawyer, governor, farmer, or pole vault champion. It is a general rule that the more complex the society, the more opportunity each individual has to achieve or choose from a variety of status positions.

Each status position carries with it certain rules that guide the social relations of the occupier of the position. Patterns of behavior expected of those who occupy particular status positions as pointed out, are defined as **roles.** In every society, social roles are prescribed for every status position and social interaction is predictable to the extent that individuals behave in accordance with the acceptable patterns for their roles. *Status-role performance* is thus the process which articulates status positions and roles as structural elements of social systems.

It is a general rule that social roles fit together in such a way as to be *reciprocal* in terms of duties, rights, and obligations. For example, the roles of husband and wife, employer and employee, or doctor and patient immediately suggest certain obligations for the persons playing each role.

POWER. Social **power** as a concept has not been easy for sociologists to define. At present, there is rather widespread consensus that the term should be

[10] Frederick L. Bates, "Position, Role, and Status: A Reformulation of Concepts," *Social Forces*, Vol. 34 (May, 1956), pp. 313-321.

used to refer to "the capacity to control others." The power of one individual or group to control another individual or group is seen as residing in the control exercised over the things the other group values, regardless of what these might be.[11] Power is often classified into two basic types of control, authoritative and nonauthoritative. Established or authoritative power always rests in a status position while nonauthoritative power such as coercion and the capacity to influence others, is not implicit in status positions.

The element of power is made apparent through **decision-making.** Action in a social system comes about when decisions are reached and initiated into action by those in power positions because they wield authority or are able to influence others. In the first instance the ranking officer makes the decisions and gives the orders in the armed services, the quarterback (or the coach) calls the plays for the football team, and the judges decide which aspirant will be the new Miss America. In the second instance, one officer might influence a second officer to go along with his order, the quarterback might convince the coach that his play is better, and one judge would let the other sway his vote. In each instance, the incumbent actor can make a decision because he occupies a status or has influence which gives him power. This concept is elaborated in Chapter 10.

RANK. **Rank** as an element of social systems can be understood as "social standing." Rank depends on status-positions and role relationships. It is possible to have persons with a *similar* rank in a system but there is no system where all have the *same* rank, at all times. The latter situation would rule out all status symbols, a condition which has never been reported.

Each actor in a social system is constantly evaluating the other actors in the system to determine their rank relative to his own. Thus, **evaluation of actors** is the elemental process that triggers action involving the structural element of rank. After evaluation by his fellow actors, a given individual is allocated a status or statuses (and ranked) according to the appraisal of his worth by his fellows to the system. Appraisal of actors may be done in terms of skills, experience, schooling, or any other criterion important or trivial. However, performance is usually the key to movement up or down in the system. The substitute may be moved to first string; or the winless coach may be "promoted" to another position.

SANCTION. The term **sanction** is used by sociologists to mean the system of rewards and punishment worked out and employed by members of a society to encourage behavior in keeping with the norms. **Positive sanctions** (or rewards) may include as little as a word of praise or as much as a large monetary prize; whereas **negative sanctions** may be something as the loss of rank, or ultimately, banishment or death.

[11] Richard M. Emerson, "Power-Dependence Relations," *American Sociological Review,* Vol. 27 (January, 1962), pp. 31-32.

The **application of sanctions** is done in order to bring about the changes in behavior and can thus be recognized as the elemental process which articulates sanctions. Whether or not a deviation from the norms is subject to sanction is dependent on many factors, the crucial one being public awareness. However, everyone is involved in one or another way with sanctions in every system to which he belongs. The student, to take an easy example, is rewarded by his family for good grades with money and privileges or deprived of allowance and privileges for poor marks. In each instance, the application of sanction is an indication of departure from average behavior—in the former instance, a positive sanction was applied to recognize and encourage superior performance with respect to established norms. In the latter instance, negative sanctions were used to indicate performance below levels of expectation.

FACILITY. **Facility** is defined broadly as any means which may be used to attain ends within the system. A facility may be a building, any item of technology, or it might be a block of time over which control is maintained, such as when appointments can be set. The use of the facility, rather than its nature, determines its significance to social systems. A piece of ground may be a field for cultivation to a farmer; another may be a graveyard for a church congregation; and still a third might be the football field.

The sociologist concerns himself with the **utilization of facilities,** which he recognizes as a process closely related to value systems. To illustrate, some early settlers refused to use the iron plow because they were afraid it would poison the soil; in other words their beliefs and sentiments prevented them from readily adopting this facility. In today's world, there are people who will not eat pork or beef and still others who pass up horse meat. Yet swine, cattle, and horses represent a facility as food for many others whose values differ. General theorists have developed models which relate systems of social organization to number of and degree of utilization of facilities. In these schemes, the more primitive, the more rural, or the less developed, are generally shown to have fewer and simpler facilities. All in all, facilities are an important element of all social systems.

STRESS–STRAIN. It is inescapable that every social system have an element of stress–strain. This is because no two members of a given system will ever have exactly the same interpretations about roles and status positions. To the extent that there are differences in interpretation which are translated into action patterns, the system undergoes **stress**. Perhaps it will be possible to see this element more clearly if one thinks of the way in which one brick or other building unit places a stress on another brick or unit in a building. One actor, in a similar conceptual manner, places a stress on the second actor in a social system. **Strain** is a behavioral manifestation which cannot be separated from its source of stress. It relates to the degree of control which the given individual or group exercise over their tendency to deviate from norms because of role conflict, such as the teen-age son who accepts the decision of his parents on hair and dress styles, although he feels such a decision should be left to him. Some writers have phrased this as the ability to manage tensions, although it is not to be confused with tension management related to sentiment on another level of analysis.

A social system is subject to stresses and strains from the moment of its inception. Specific stresses may come and go but stress–strain forces are continuous because of uneven socialization. (See Chapter 10.).

Conflict, deviation, and nonconformity stem from stress–strain and result in **disorganization.** However, stress–strain is articulated by the process of disorganization which can be looked upon as part of the dynamics of social change. In other words, no social system is completely organized or in complete equilibrium. There is always some degree of disorganization because stress–strain is continuous. A system is more or less organized as measured by goal-oriented activity depending on the magnitude of the stress–strain element. A monastery conceivably would be relatively free of stress–strain and exhibit little disorganization, whereas a prison might be a setting for much conflict and resultant disorganization.

THE COMPREHENSIVE OR MASTER SOCIAL SYSTEM PROCESSES

It was mentioned previously that the comprehensive or master social system processes articulate or involve more than one of the elements of a social system at a time. Seven such processes are identified here.[12] Each one provides the sociologist with an analytical tool for studying human behavior.

COMMUNICATION. There is no process that is more basic to social systems than communication. Without means of communicating the actors in a system would have no way of transmitting information or of indicating their feelings, attitudes, or needs. It is not an exaggeration to say that without communication there would be no social organization.

BOUNDARY MAINTENANCE. All systems have certain ways of protecting their identity, of keeping the outside world out, so to speak. This may be done by building walls, by restriction of use of facilities to "members only," by secret ritual, or by insistence upon subscription to a religious or other creed. The closer knit the system, the more solidarity will be exhibited in excluding

[12] The first six master processes are listed and described by Loomis, including communication, boundary maintenance, systemic linkage, institutionaliztion, socialization, and social control. See Loomis, op. cit., pp. 30-37. The seventh process, social change, has been added by the writer in an attempt to provide a more systematic frame of reference for studying this process. See Bertrand, op. cit., p. 8.

outsiders. Periods of crisis, such as wars, often bring stricter enforcement of boundary maintenance, because of the obvious malicious intent of members of enemy groups.

SYSTEMIC LINKAGE. The process whereby one social system establishes a bond or tie with another system is known as systemic linkage. The best test of such a linkage is if there is close cooperation between the individuals and groups of the two systems in the attainment of a goal. Loomis puts it this way: "**Systemic linkage** may be defined as the process whereby one or more elements of at least two social systems is articulated in such a manner that the two systems in some ways and on some occasions may be viewed as a single unit."[13] An example would be when the officials of a local school are delegated as representatives of a county school organization at a state or national convention.

Subsystems form larger systems through systemic linkage. The many local school systems, for example, are linked in such a way as to form regional, state, national, and master societal systems of education. Family systems have links with other families and with economic, political, religious, and educational systems as well. In short, the web of human relationship which symbolizes social organization is fabricated to a great extent through systemic linkage.

SOCIALIZATION. Socialization is a fundamental process, insofar as sociological understanding is concerned, and a later chapter will be devoted to a detailed explanation of it. Briefly, it may be defined as the process through which the individual acquires the social and cultural heritage of his society. Through socialization, one becomes a functioning member of his group. In essence, he is transformed from an organism into a person, since personality is derived from the interaction involved in the process of socialization. Socialization as a master process articulates all the elements of a system to a greater or lesser extent.

SOCIAL CONTROL. The term social control implies a process of restriction of behavior. In social systems, this is the process whereby deviancy or nonconformity (regardless of the reason) is corrected or maintained within tolerable limits. The elements most closely related to social control are norms, power, and sanctions. Various mechanisms are used to assure proper behavior. They range from informal means such as ostracism, ridicule, and gossip to formal means related to law and order.

INSTITUTIONALIZATION. Institutionalization is the process whereby certain patterns of behavior become legitimized, that is, accepted as right and

[13] From Charles P. Loomis, *Social Systems: Essays on Their Persistence and Changes,* copyright 1960, D. Van Nostrand Company, Inc., Princeton, N.J., p. 33.

proper. In a given society, this may take place gradually through an evolution-ary process or it might be accomplished rapidly by a decree backed by popular will. "The family" and "education" are social institutions because they are characterized by a body of formalized relationships from which deviancy be-yond a point is not tolerated. At another level of abstraction, it is an institu-tionalized practice to drive on the right side of the road in the United States.

SOCIAL CHANGE. Social change is conceived as some alteration in patterns of interaction. Use of such a definition makes it possible to consider the change process without the encumbrance of such value-laden terms as progress and retrogression. As a master systemic process, change always articulates the stress–strain element in conjunction with other elements, such as power and sanction. The elemental process of disorganization, insofar as it connotes con-stant reorganization, establishes the comprehensive nature of change as a proc-ess. In this regard, a state of organization or equilibrium can only be visualized in the abstract since social systems are dynamic in nature and characterized by continual change.

SOCIAL SYSTEMS VERSUS SOCIAL GROUPS

Since the term *social group* is often used interchangeably with the term *social system* in sociological analysis and prediction, it is necessary, before terminat-ing this chapter, to make clear the distinction between these two terms. The distinction is at the abstract level, because in concrete situations the terms may be used interchangeably. Bredemeier and Stephenson discuss the differ-ence between groups and systems and point out that the members of a group cannot be changed without changing the character of the group, while the system remains the same whether the group of people acting in it change or not.[14] In other words a **social group** is a concrete reality with actors acting in terms of status positions which are units of a social system. In the same sense that a status position (such as an airplane pilot) may be thought of as inde-pendent of an actor, a social system may be seen as independent of groups of ac-tors. However, groups are studied as concrete realities acting collectively in terms of the structure of the social system; for example, John Eagle may be pilot and employee of the XXX Air Line. To illustrate further, the family may be seen as a social system in the abstract, but the John Doe family is a con-crete social group as well as a social system. The family as a system will per-sist long after the John Doe family is dead and gone, although for the moment this family group can be identified as a social system.

[14] Harry C. Bredemeier and Richard M. Stephenson, *The Analysis of Social Systems* (New York, Holt, Rinehart & Winston, 1962), pp. 34-35.

SUMMARY

The concepts of sociology are used to refer to types or classes of events, persons or relationships, while theoretical models are designed to show in a beforehand way how sociological phenomena are organized. Basic concepts and models must be mastered if the sociological approach is to be meaningful.

Social organization, when used in a general sense, refers to the vast, complex network of patterned human behavior (interaction) which is characteristic of all societies. Societies represent a relatively large collection of people, who are sufficiently organized to carry out the conditions necessary to live harmoniously together. Social interaction refers to the reciprocal contact between individuals and groups.

The basic conceptual model of social organization is that of a social system or group (the concrete manifestation of a system). Such models are designed to show that human groups are made up of interdependent parts and are interlinked one with another to form the broad fabric of social structure. The elements of social systems include: (1) belief (knowledge); (2) sentiment; (3) end, goal, or objective; (4) norm; (5) status-role (position); (6) rank; (7) power; (8) sanction; (9) facility; and (10) stress–strain. Each of these elements is articulated or involved in the system by an elemental process. In order, these processes are (1) cognitive mapping and validation; (2) tension management and communication of sentiment; (3) goal-attaining activity; (4) evaluation; (5) status-role performance; (6) evaluation of actors; (7) decision making; (8) application of sanctions; (9) utilization of facilities; and (10) disorganization. Every social system includes in its make-up seven comprehensive or master processes, which involve more than one of the elements of the system at a time. They are communication, boundary maintenance, systemic linkage, socialization, social control, institutionalization, and social change.

Supplementary Readings

Bates, Frederick L., "A Conceptual Analysis of Group Structure," *Social Forces,* Vol. 36 (December, 1957), pp. 103-111.

Bertrand, Alvin L., "The Stress-Strain Element of Social System: A Micro Theory of Conflict and Change," *Social Forces,* Vol. 42 (October, 1963), pp. 1-8.

Bredemeier, Harry C. and Richard M. Stephenson, *The Analysis of Social Systems* (New York, Holt, Rinehart and Winston, 1962), Chapter 2.

Greer, Scott A., *Social Organization* (Garden City, New York, Doubleday Co., 1955), chapters 1-3.

Homans, George C., "A Conceptual Scheme for the Study of Social Organization," *American Sociological Review,* Vol. 12 (February, 1947), pp. 13-26; and also in BARRON.

Johnson, Harry M., *Sociology: A Systematic Introduction* (New York, Harcourt, Brace & World, 1960), Part I.

Loomis, Charles P., *Social Systems: Essays on Their Persistence and Change* (Princeton, New Jersey, Van Nostrand, 1960), Essay I.

Parsons, Talcott and Edward A. Shils, Eds., *Toward A General Theory of Action* (New York, Harper & Row, 1962, Harper Torchbook), Chapter 4.

Williams, Robin M., Jr., *American Society,* 2nd ed. (New York, Knopf, 1960), Chapter 12.

3

THE METHODS
AND
TECHNIQUES
OF
SOCIOLOGICAL
RESEARCH

The conceptual approach of sociology was introduced in the preceding chapters. However, nothing was said about *how* data are obtained and manipulated or about the necessary first steps before analysis. The methods of sociological research are essentially the ones used in all scientific inquiry. As brought out in Chapter 1, the scientific method includes several steps from the formulation of an hypothesis to the collection, validation, and classification of data. These methods should not be confused with the techniques of the various sciences, which are the technical tools used for gathering and analyzing data. Each science is characterized by the use of techniques which are uniquely adaptable to its investigations, such as the use of radiographic techniques in many biological and physical sciences. Our purpose in this chapter is to describe the more important techniques used by sociologists in the application of the scientific method.[1]

[1] For a recent work devoted to this theme see Phillip E. Hammond, Ed., *Sociologists at Work* (New York, Basic Books, 1964).

STEPS IN SCIENTIFIC RESEARCH

Every research undertaken by a sociologist or other scientist follows certain steps in order to satisfy the acceptable standards of scientific method. It is not necessary that these steps be taken in a particular sequence, but it is usual to follow a logical order. The researcher does not necessarily have to formalize his procedures by putting them into written form, but he has to think them through and work out each procedure so that he has it clearly in his mind. The steps listed here are those generally considered as basic to sociological investigation.[2]

(1) *Selection of a Problem Worthy of Study:* Many questions that come to mind or are brought to our attention represent interesting hypotheses. Yet, only a fraction of these problems are worthy of scientific investigation. Some are beyond the realm of testing, at least at the present state of knowledge; others are not sufficiently profound or important to warrant the necessary expenditure of time and resources; and still others represent so many hindrances to the objective approach that findings from them are always suspect, such as situations where a political line must be adhered to. In the selection of a research problem, one must strive for an area of inquiry which will yield more or less important information (to someone) and which can be studied scientifically, that is, in accordance with the rules of scientific method.

(2) *Comprehensive Review of Pertinent Theory and Knowledge:* It is a constant source of amazement to discover how many problems selected for study have already been investigated. This fact, plus the necessity of developing a background of information, makes it mandatory for the serious scholar to carefully review the literature pertinent to the problem he wishes to study. Generally speaking, this step can be carried out in the library.

(3) *Plan the Research Design:* The design of a study corresponds to the blueprints drawn by an architect. It is the researcher's plan, including specific rules and procedures, for gathering and organizing the facts he seeks. Each particular problem presents the researcher with numerous alternative choices for assembling and systematizing his data. Matilda White Riley has prepared a checklist of some of the common choices confronting researchers.[3] This list is reproduced on page 39 as Table 3-1. The student can use this list, if he wishes to indulge in a brief exercise, in classifying research designs encountered in this book or elsewhere.

[2] For a comprehensive statement on the steps in scientific research see Roy G. Francis, "The Nature of Scientific Research," chapter in John T. Doby, *et al.*, Eds. *An Introduction to Social Research* (Harrisburg, Pennsylvania, The Stackpole Company, 1954), pp. 12-16.
[3] Matilda White Riley, *Sociological Research I: A Case Approach* (New York, Harcourt, Brace & World, 1963), pp. 17-25.

TABLE 3-1. *Some Alternatives of Sociological Research Design.*

I. Nature of research case:
   Individual in role (in a collectivity)
   Dyad or pair of interrelated group members
   Subgroup
   Group, society
   Some combination of these

II. Number of cases:
   Single case
   Few selected cases
   Many selected cases

III. Sociotemporal context:
   Cases from a single society at a single period
   Cases from many societies and/or many periods

IV. Primary basis for selecting cases (sampling):
   Representational
   Analytical
   Both

V. The time factor:
   Static studies (covering a single point in time)
   Dynamic studies (covering process or change over time)

VI. Extent of researcher's control over the system under study:
   No control
   Unsystematic control
   Systematic control

VII. Basic sources of data:
   New data, collected by the researcher for the express purpose at hand
   Available data (as they may be relevant to the researcher's problem)

VIII. Method of gathering data:
   Observation
   Questioning
   Combined observation and questioning
   Other

IX. Number of properties used in research:
   One
   A few
   Many

X. Method of handling single properties:
   Unsystematic description
   Measurement (of variables)

XI. Method of handling relationships among properties:
   Unsystematic description
   Systematic analysis

XII. Treatment of system properties as:
   Unitary Collective

Source: Matilda White Riley, *Sociological Research I: A Case Approach* (New York, Harcourt, Brace & World, 1963), p. 18.

Riley poses three questions that may be used to check the usefulness of a research design.[4] (a) Has the design been worked out to fit the conceptual model decided upon? (b) Will the design be appropriate in terms of the theory to be tested? (c) Is the design practical, that is, have suitable techniques been developed to carry it out and will it lead to the relevant facts? In essence, the worth of a design depends upon achieving a balance between the requirements of the conceptual model being followed, the nature of the facts to be studied, and the facilities and resources available.

(4) *Collection of Data:* The data for a study are collected in accordance with the research design worked out. Sometimes this is a simple procedure, such as referring to a census volume; at other times it is an involved procedure. In field studies, for example, before data can be obtained the necessary instruments such as questionnaires or interview guides must be created and tested; sampling procedures must be worked out; and finally, the data must be gathered as efficiently as possible. With regard to the latter, it is frequently necessary to spend considerable time recruiting and training a team of interviewers. The various methods used by sociologists to collect data are explained in detail in this chapter.

(5) *Analysis of Data:* Once the data have been collected, the next step is a determination of findings and the drawing of conclusions. This involves various steps of tabulation, classification, measurement, and comparison, all of which depend on the complexity of the data. Larger studies are normally machine processed, whereas smaller undertakings may be done by hand with the aid of desk calculators. Any techniques of analysis (such as scales, indexes, or ratios) planned in the research design are applied at this stage. Unanticipated results must be faced on occasion and adapted to the research design insofar as possible through reformulation of hypotheses. In the end, certain conclusions are reached in the light of the evidence at hand.

(6) *Report the Findings:* The final, but not the least important step in research is a report of findings. This is the way the body of scientific knowledge is increased. The research report, if done well, will become a part of the intellectual heritage of the particular discipline. It will have theoretical implications, either in the application of concepts or in the development of new concepts. It will suggest new areas for investigation and at the same time provide a basis for making decisions, some of which may literally change national policy. The reports of investigations which are truly outstanding become classics and serve as the important bench marks for future researchers. The many term papers and the theses and dissertations which graduate students write, serve as basic training for the writing of research reports.

[4] *Ibid.,* pp. 24-25.

THE TECHNIQUES UTILIZED IN SOCIOLOGICAL RESEARCH

A research design, in any field of science, includes plans for the utilization of certain techniques to test hypotheses. Techniques vary somewhat from one discipline to another, a fact which has confused even learned persons on occasions. It is not unusual for sociologists to be questioned about the validity of procedures which appear strange and without precision, simply because the questioner has no experience in a social science discipline. The fact is, all methods that can pass valid tests of causal relationships are worthy as scientific techniques.

The techniques of sociological research are the ones generally used in the other social sciences: (1) statistical techniques; (2) field-survey techniques; (3) experimental techniques; (4) case-study techniques; (5) participant-observation techniques; and (6) constructive-typologies techniques. These approaches to the collection and manipulation of data are described in some detail in the remainder of this chapter. It is important to note that very few studies utilize only one technique. Normally, several techniques will be used in a given investigation.

All studies have time either built into or implicit in their design. When a study is related to a single point in time, a snapshot of social action, it is known as a **cross-sectional study.** A study which extends over a period of time, that is, involves an element of history, is known as a **longitudinal study.** A study comparing similar units across time or in different places is called a **comparative study.**

STATISTICAL TECHNIQUES[5]

Statistical techniques represent an important method used in sociology as in other sciences. Not only can statistical methods show relationships, but they provide some assurance that certain types of bias are minimized.

Perhaps the simplest of statistical methods used is **enumeration.** Everyone is familiar with the decennial census of the United States. From the mere tabulations of the responses to the various questions included in the census, one can learn about the quantitative and qualitative character of the population of the nation. Vast stores of enumerative data are available at the state and federal levels of government which, with some statistical processing, provide many important facts about human behavior.

[5] Refined statistical methods such as analysis of variance and scaling and indexing techniques are not discussed because they were deemed out of place in an introductory volume.

Some studies call for a higher level of statistical methodology than the mere tabulation of data into usable categories. One of the first such refinements is the *use of graphic forms* to make data more easily interpreted. Graphs and charts often allow the researcher to see relationships which would be hard to detect in a long array of detailed data. Note in Figure 3-1 how the growth pattern of the population of the United States from 1935 can be seen at a glance. Imagine how long it would take to digest each independent statistic in a study of growth rate using tabular data only. Graphic presentation is important enough to sociologists that books have been prepared on the subject for advanced students in the discipline.[6]

It is seldom possible to obtain information from every individual in a given group one wishes to study. Limitations of money and time force the researcher to use a statistical technique called **sampling.** Through use of statistical formulas of probability, one can select a **representative sample** of a given population which will give results within a tolerable margin of error from total enumerations. Sampling techniques are reliable to an extent which justifies large outlays of money for national sample surveys of one kind or other. For example, the National Health Survey conducted to determine the health characteristics of the people in the United States sampled 115,000 persons out of a national population of approximately 190 million. Yet the data obtained are sufficiently reliable to plan needed health programs and to provide a basis for future health legislation.[7]

EXPERIMENTAL TECHNIQUES

Experimental design is most appealing. No doubt all of us have been conditioned to respect it because of familiarity with experiment in the physical sciences. Although sociologists do not use this method as exclusively as physical scientists, it is a valid technique in the field.

The late Samuel A. Stouffer makes a case for more use of experimental designs in sociology and illustrates a simple model of a controlled experiment with the four-cell diagram shown as Figure 3-2.[8] In this diagram one can quickly and clearly see that the function of the control group is to test change in a manipulated or experimental group. When a significant difference appears between *d* (the difference that occurred over time in the experimental group) and *d'* (the difference that occurred over the same time in the control group), one can assume that the manipulation of the experimental group produced the difference. Of course, caution must be observed to prevent extraneous factors from interfering with the experiment.

[6] For an example see Calvin F. Schmid, *Handbook of Graphic Presentation* (New York, Ronald, 1954).

[7] Implemented under the National Health Survey Act, Public Law 652, 84th Congress.

[8] Samuel A. Stouffer, "Some Observations on Study Design," *The American Journal of Sociology*, Vol. 55 (January, 1950), pp. 355-361.

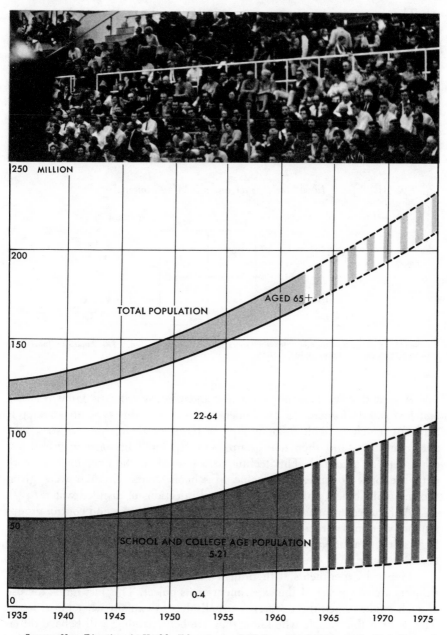

FIGURE 3-1. *Population Trends in the United States, 1935–1975.*

Source: *New Directions in Health, Education, and Welfare* (Washington, D.C., U. S. Dept. of Health, Education, and Welfare, Office of the Secretary, 1963), p. 3. Photograph courtesy of United Nations Organization.

There are several common ways of setting up an experimental design. One way which was pioneered by F. Stuart Chapin, is known as the *"ex post facto* experiment."[9] An *ex post facto* design is one that seeks to relate a current situation with earlier events or conditions. The term itself, connotes that the experiment has already taken place, that is, the control was somehow established before the research was begun. An example would be a comparison of the marital and divorce rates of the graduates of a state university and of a privately endowed university. The fact of graduation provides the necessary control, whereas marriage and divorce are the variables.

FIGURE 3-2.   *Ideal Model of a Controlled Experiment.*

	BEFORE	AFTER	
EXPERIMENTAL GROUP	x_1	x_2	$d = x_2 - x_1$
CONTROL GROUP	x_1'	x_2'	$d' = x_2' - x_1'$

Source: Samuel A. Stouffer, "Some Observations on Study Design," *The American Journal of Sociology,* Vol. 55 (January, 1950), p. 356.

A second way of setting up a test and control group is known as the *matched-pair technique.* In experimental designs of this type an attempt is made to match individuals or groups in terms of their characteristics—age, size, education—and then one group is manipulated in some way and the other kept as a control. This technique was used in the experimental work with the Salk poliomyelitis vaccine in schools. Some children were given vaccine while others unknowingly received injections of distilled water.

A third experimental approach is to select test groups and control groups randomly from a larger population. The idea is to have groups sufficiently large so that variations are minimized and the averages of the two groups are about the same.

Planned experiments with human subjects are most reliable when the subjects are not aware of the experiment or its object. This fact limits the use of such studies since the researcher usually has to explain what he is doing. The point is that people who know they are being studied will behave differently than normally, a phenomenon known as the Hawthorne effect. This term derives from studies made in the Hawthorne Plant of the Western Electric Company, which showed that employees responded to both brighter lights

[9] F. Stuart Chapin, *Experimental Designs in Sociological Design* (New York, Harper & Row, 1947).

and dimmer lights with temporary increases in productivity, simply because they were the object of attention and not necessarily because of a better work situation.[10]

FIELD-SURVEY TECHNIQUES

Perhaps more sociologists engage in what are known as *field-survey studies* than in any other type of study. Field surveys are planned when the facts sought are not recorded or otherwise available and it is necessary to go to people for answers. Field studies are accomplished in three major ways: by mailed questionnaires, by personal interviews, and more rarely by direct observation. These techniques are much more complicated than may appear at first glance.

The first two steps in the implementation of a questionnaire or interview study are essentially the same. Initially, the characteristics of the population to be studied must be determined as far as possible. This type of information provides a basis for working out a representative sampling procedure and gives clues as to how questions should be worded and approaches made. The second step is the development of an efficient "instrument"—questionnaire or an interview guide. Here, many factors must be considered. How should the questions be phrased to avoid bias? How long can the instrument be and still continue to hold the informant's attention? How can touchy subjects, like income and delinquent behavior, best be approached? How should one approach problems of measuring? What adaptations should be used in the interests of computer processing? These and other questions must be faced and worked out before a study can get under way.

Mailed questionnaire studies also face problems that are somewhat different in nature from interview studies. The unique problem of the mailed questionnaire approach is to obtain a sufficiently large return of completed instruments to make the study valid. Certain groups in our society are notably difficult to get to complete a mailed questionnaire, either because of busy schedules or because of a reluctance to commit themselves in writing. Various gimmicks are used to increase returns, such as enclosing self-addressed envelopes, having important persons write cover letters, or the use of follow-up letters.

The special problem of the interview approach is the conduct of the interview. It is difficult for untrained persons to keep from interjecting their personal biases into the interview, either while recording the answers received or by influencing the responses of interviewees verbally or by subtle gestures made while asking questions. This is why such a large segment of time is spent in training graduate sociology students to conduct interviews. Several books and many sections of books have been devoted exclusively to this prob-

[10] F. J. Roethlisberger, *Management and Morale* (Cambridge, Massachusetts, Harvard University Press, 1949).

lem.[11] It is customary for the researcher to conduct training sessions before sending a group of interviewers into the field. Also, the completed interviews are carefully graded to determine if consistent error or bias occur.

When conducted properly, questionnaire and interview studies are quite reliable. They are used in planning advertising campaigns, as a basis for policy and program planning, in detecting voter interest and concern (by politicians), and in many other ways. Two illustrations—one from a rural area in Australia and one involving a national sample survey in the United States —illustrate how such studies proceed.

In the early 1960's a team of researchers (including E. A. Wilkening, Joan Tully, and Hartley Presser) was dispatched to a study area located in the Goulburn Valley of northern Victoria, Australia—a prosperous dairy area. Their charge was to determine the way in which information about farm matters and new practices was transmitted, how decisions were made, and how social and psychological characteristics of farmers affect the adoption of different types of farm practices. The research was sponsored by a Fulbright research grant, the Commonwealth Scientific and Industrial Research Organization of Australia, the University of Melbourne, and the University of Wisconsin. The researchers describe their sampling and interview procedures in this manner:[12]

The area from which the sample was drawn was outlined to include the supervisory districts of three dairy supervisors in the two shires of Rochester and Deakin. This appeared to give an area uniform in land and water characteristics, farming type, and milk markets. This area included 1,073 dairy farmers. In order to eliminate the influence of variables extraneous to the study, the following restrictions were placed upon the population to be sampled:
   (1) The farmer must milk 25 or more cows.
   (2) The main part of his income must come from dairying.
   (3) His farm must not be a stud farm for selling pedigreed stock.
   (4) The farmer must have operated the farm for at least one year.
   (5) He must use irrigation water from the State Rivers and Water Supply Commission.
   (6) The owner must reside in the study area.
After the elimination of those who did not qualify, a population of 535 remained. From this population 100 cases were chosen at random for personal interviews. These interviews lasted from one and a half hours to most of the day. When feasible, the interviewer walked over enough of the farm to gain first-hand knowledge of the problems and practices followed.

11 For three examples see P. R. Sheatsley, "The Art of Interviewing and a Guide to Interview Selection and Training," selection in M. Jahoda, *et al., Research Methods in Social Relations* (New York, The Dryden Press, 1951); Anne F. Fenlason, *Essentials in Interviewing* (New York, Harper & Row, 1952); and R. N. Adams and J. J. Preiss, *Human Organization Research* (Homewood, Illinois, The Dorsey Press, 1960).

12 E. A. Wilkening, Joan Tully, and Hartley Presser, "Communication and Acceptance of Recommended Farm Practices Among Dairy Farmers of Northern Victoria," *Rural Sociology*, Vol. 27 (June, 1962), pp. 122-123.

In early 1954, Stouffer undertook a national opinion survey with two major aims in mind: (1) to determine the attitudes of the people of the United States toward the danger of the Communist conspiracy outside and inside the country and (2) to determine the reaction of citizens toward the danger of sacrificing certain traditional individual liberties in the effort to thwart the Communist conspiracy.[13] The study was carefully planned and administered. After pretesting, the interview schedule was administered to 6,466 men and women throughout the nation. The sampling procedure included the following steps: (1) drawing a random sample of *primary sampling units* from all the counties and metropolitan areas in the United States; (2) drawing a random sample of urban blocks and rural segments within each primary sampling unit; (3) drawing a random sample of dwelling units within each selected block or segment; (4) selecting one adult within each dwelling unit for interview according to a predetermined randomly worked out procedure. This procedure did not allow the interviewer to make substitutions. Repeated calls had to be made until the interview was accomplished and every effort was made to track down absentees. All interviews were conducted by specially trained interviewers of two national research agencies.

Although it may seem that six or seven thousand interviews are too few to be representative of the total United States population, the care with which the study was planned assured successful achievement of its objectives within a small margin of error. The probability method of selecting respondents eliminated any possible bias which might have occurred had the interviewers been allowed to use their judgment in dropping difficult cases from the sample group.

THE PARTICIPANT-OBSERVER TECHNIQUE

There is considerable logic to the argument that a researcher cannot come to know the true character of a group without personal experience as a member of the group. It is understandable, therefore, that the *participant observer* conducts his investigation while taking part as an active and accepted member of the particular community, union, or gang, which he is studying. Often, his identity as a scholar cannot be revealed because of the jeopardy to his study. West describes the problems of becoming accepted as follows[14]:

Final widespread acceptance of my role as investigator resident of Plainville came slowly, however, and only after I had gained the cooperation of one particular man. He was a "politician," forty-three years old, divorced from his wife, and "batching it," a disabled veteran and small "pensioner" of the first World War, a voracious reader but able to write only slowly, personally very ambitious but pas-

[13] This survey is reported in Samuel A. Stouffer, *Communism, Conformity, and Civil Liberties* (Garden City, New York, Doubleday, 1955).

[14] James West, *Plainville, U. S. A.* (New York, Columbia University Press, 1945), pp. x-xi.

sionately interested in community reform. He had great ability in manipulating rumor and opinion, and his local knowledge and social insights were astounding. For example, once after inquiring into the techniques by which I worked, he elaborated a plan for studying a community which corresponded very closely with the well-known "genealogical method." This man became convinced of the value of my work in October, 1939. Thenceforth, without pay ("You ain't got enough money to hire me!") he vouched for my "safety" as a repository of confidences and arranged numerous interviewing situations for me. Through the same techniques, he employed in any "political" manipulation, he set rumor to working for me, rather than against me, and I finally came to be considered a full fledged community member, welcome in men's loafing centers, in church, and in many homes, able to talk confidentially with numerous people in situations of my own devising, and free to record any private conversations I wanted to record, in the presence of informants, without arousing any apparent embarrassment. People often said, "People wouldn't talk to you when you come here, but now they've adopted you everybody will talk to you." Of great aid toward this "adoption" were the facts that I drove a two-year-old car, "knew how to loaf and joke" on the street, wore "old clothes" and otherwise imitated the average level of everyday life, and already knew how to speak accurately whatever dialect level of the language was being spoken at any moment.

Information obtained through participant observation must generally be presented in a descriptive rather than statistical fashion, since it is not obtained in a standard way. The same questions and situations cannot be maintained as the researcher moves from one social situation to another. This approach also has the other disadvantage inherent in the case-study approach in that generalization must be made with extreme caution. The great hurdle that the participant observer must overcome is the tendency to become emotionally involved in the affairs of the group he is studying. When he reaches the point of wanting to defend or of being biased in favor of the group, he loses his perspective as a scholar. The technique involves behaving as if emotionally involved while maintaining a dispassionate or objective attitude.

Participant observations cannot be carried out without some type of interviewing. Usually this will be accomplished skillfully in the course of an ordinary conversation, and the informant will not be aware that he has been questioned. However, on occasions, and especially when one's role as an investigator is known, direct and pointed questions can be used. The researcher can use this approach with the assurance of receiving honest answers. The type of insight (in this instance about social class) which may be obtained through this technique is illustrated by the following account reported by W. M. Williams in his study of an English village.[15]

. . . Discussing the baptism of a child of lower class parents, a housewife commented, "I wonder how many more they'll have. Yance (before) ower people used to have big families, but now it's only them sort have kids every year."

15 W. M. Williams, Gosforth: The Sociology of an English Village (Glencoe, Illinois, The Free Press, 1956), p. 102.

THE CASE-STUDY TECHNIQUE

Sometimes circumstances are such that study must be limited to one phenomenon, from which it is hoped generalization can be made for similar classes of phenomena. This would be true for disasters such as Hurricane Audrey in which over 400 people lost their lives. The case nature of a hurricane is obvious in this description[16]:

> During the predawn hours of June 25, 1957, a disaster agent subsequently known as Hurricane Audrey, struck the marshy coast of Cameron Parish in southwest Louisiana with an estimated wind velocity of 140 miles per hour, bringing an unprecedented high tide of approximately 11 feet which swept inland for about 15 miles with waves of 12 to 14 feet.

Social movements, such as a religious movement or a farmer's movement or a union movement might be studied as particular cases. A particular family, community, business, or any organization could also be selected as a case for thorough detailed study.

CONSTRUCTION-OF-TYPOLOGIES TECHNIQUE

The last methodological technique to be discussed is known as the *constructed types technique.* Since it does not involve a statistical or experimental procedure *per se,* and since no field research for data is made or mathematical formulas applied, it may be difficult for the student to envision what this technique involves and what utility it has. The following paragraphs are designed to clarify these points.[17]

First, the student should be aware that all concepts are constructs, that is, they are devices for defining what is to be observed. For example, economists speak of capitalistic systems or socialistic systems and historians identify epochs or eras as being characterized by feudal systems or manorial systems. Constructed typologies are one step removed from ordinary concepts in that they state or infer the ideal limits of a case. This character makes it possible for such types to be used in comparing concrete occurrences, even to the point of measurement. McKinney emphasizes this point by stating that the scientific function of the constructed type is ". . . to order concrete data so that they

---

[16] Charles W. Fogleman and Vernon J. Parenton, "Disaster and Aftermath: Selected Aspects of Individual and Group Behavior in Critical Situations," *Social Forces,* Vol. 38 (December, 1959), p. 129.

[17] For two of the most comprehensive discussions on "constructed" of "ideal" types see Llewellyn Gross, Ed., *Symposium on Sociological Theory* (Evanston, Illinois, Harper & Row, 1959), Part II; and John C. McKinney, *Constructive Typology and Social Theory* (New York, Appleton-Century-Crofts, 1966).

may be described in terms which make them comparable. . . ." He sees constructed types as a particular type of concept especially created for purposes of prediction. He further states, "The constructed type is a heuristic device. It is an abstraction taken for the purpose of eliminating the research minutiae and achieving a structured order of observations that more readily lend themselves to statement and verification."[18]

FIGURE 3-3. *Sacred versus Secular Authority and Interaction Patterns.*

A— AMISH FAMILY   f— STUDENTS' FAMILIES
D— DITCH ASSOCIATION   m— STUDENTS' MILITARY UNITS
                          G— GOVERNMENT BUREAU

AT POSITION 5 THE PARTICIPANT WHO HAS THE MOST AUTHORITY IS CONSIDERED BY THE PARTICIPANTS AS BEING DIVINE IN SOME RESPECTS. INTERACTION OF SUBJECTS AND THE EMPEROR IN PREWAR JAPAN APPROACHED THE REQUIREMENTS OF POSITION #5.

FAMILISTIC GEMEINSCHAFT

AT POSITION 5 PARTICIPANTS ARE SHOWN NO PARTICULAR RESPECT; ANY DEFERENCE IS ONLY A MEANS TO SPECIFIC ENDS AS IN THE CASE OF HAGGLING IN THE MARKET OR STRUGGLING FOR POWER.

CONTRACTUAL GESELLSCHAFT

Source: Charles P. Loomis, "The Nature of Rural Social Systems—A Typological Analysis," *Rural Sociology,* Vol. 15 (June, 1950), p. 168.

In other words, constructed types are simply some sort of polar types which state the ideal limits of the case under scrutiny. Their great utility as a technique is in reducing highly complex relationships to a general level, which can be described by one concept and used to understand real situations. In the sense that the relations between characteristics are held constant, the constructed type is a theoretical model and functions as an analytical device in a more comprehensive theoretical frame of reference. In sociology, the typology constructed by Ferdinand Tönnies—*Gemeinschaft* and *Gesellschaft*—illustrates this point.[19] *Gemeinschaft* was used by Tönnies to typify group relationships which developed unconsciously or subconsciously and which were familistic in nature, whereas *Gesellschaft* was used by him to indicate group relationships entered into deliberately to achieve recognized ends.

Loomis used Tönnies' typology to scale five concrete social systems.[20] On his scale, position 5 on the left represented an extremely nonrational or *Gemein-*

18 John C. McKinney, "Constructive Typology and Social Research," selection in John T. Doby *et al., op. cit.,* pp. 144-145.

19 Ferdinand Tönnies, *Community and Society: Gemeinschaft and Gesellschaft,* translated and edited by Charles P. Loomis (New York, Harper & Row, 1957).

20 Charles P. Loomis, "The Nature of Rural Social Systems—A Typological Analysis," *Rural Sociology,* Vol. 15 (June, 1950), pp. 156-174.

schaft position. Each social system, the Amish Family, the Spanish American Ditch Association, the Government Bureau, the Students' Military Units, and Students' Families, was rated by competent judges according to a series of continua to establish a social system profile. In the illustration shown (Figure 3-3), the ranks of each of the social systems on Sacred versus Secular authority is plotted. This illustrates graphically the analytical use of typologies.

SUMMARY

The methods of sociological research are essentially the ones used in all scientific inquiry. The investigator, carrying a project through to completion, follows six steps including (1) the formulation of a problem worthy of study; (2) the review of pertinent theory and knowledge; (3) the planning of a research design; (4) the collection of data; (5) the analyses of the data collected; and (6) the preparation of a report so others can learn about his findings.

Several basic techniques are utilized to test hypotheses and validate theories. Statistical methods are used to show relationships and to minimize bias; experimental techniques are used to test the effects of change; field surveys are conducted to obtain data not otherwise available; participant-observation is done to obtain knowledge in depth of group ways; case studies are made of particular happenings; and typologies are constructed to better define and explain what is observed. All the above techniques are valid tests of causal relationships. Normally, several of them will be used in one investigation to assure reliability.

Supplementary Readings

Adams, R. N. and J. J. Preiss, *Human Organization Research* (Homewood, Illinois, The Dorsey Press, Inc., 1960). (For an anthropological approach.)

Doby, John T., *et al.*, Eds., *An Introduction to Social Research* (Harrisburg, Pennsylvania, The Stackpole Company, 1954).

Hammond, Phillip E., Ed., *Sociologists at Work* (New York, Basic Books, 1964).

McKinney, John C., *Constructive Typology and Social Theory* (New York, Appleton-Century-Crofts, 1966).

Riley, Matilda White, *Sociological Research I: A Case Approach* (New York, Harcourt, Brace & World, 1963).

Stephan, Frederick F., "Sampling," *The American Journal of Sociology,* Vol. 55 (1950), pp. 371-375; and also in YOUNG & MACK.

Stouffer, Samuel A., "Some Observations on Study Design," *The American Journal of Sociology,* Vol. 55 (1950), pp. 335-361; and also in LASSWELL ET AL.; ROSS; and BM.

Thomlinson, Ralph, *Sociological Concepts and Research* (New York, Random House, 1965).

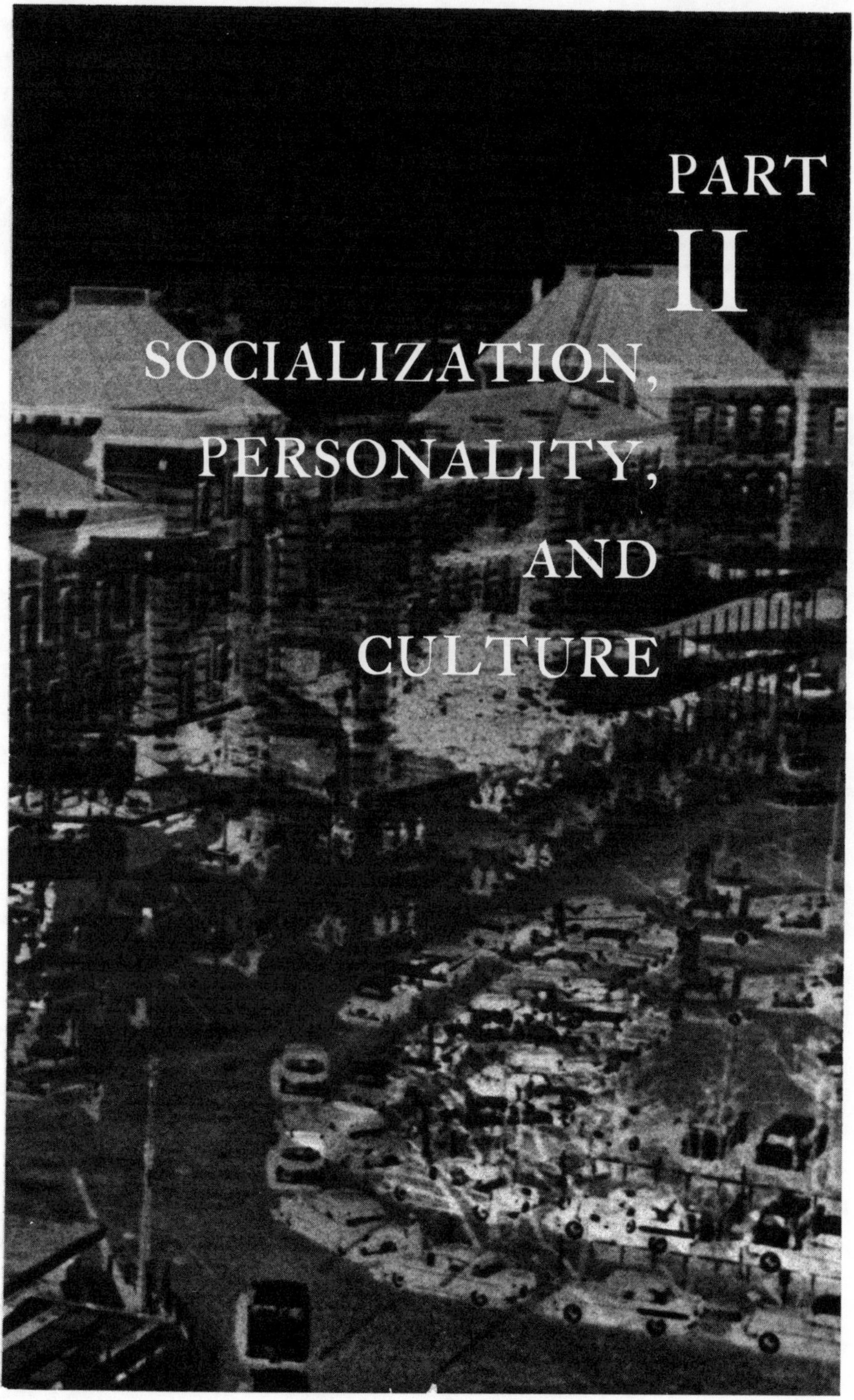

PART II

SOCIALIZATION, PERSONALITY, AND CULTURE

PART
II
INTRODUCTION

Part II, in a way, can be called the core of the sociological argument. Each of the four chapters included elaborates a different facet of the theme that human behavior is predictable because man is a social animal. Chapter 4 sets the stage by reviewing the work of scholars which explains the social origin of the self. This chapter also demonstrates how personality is a product of socialization. In logical order, Chapter 5 is devoted to an explanation of values in personality and societal organization. Here an attempt is made to show how value systems become internalized in individuals and groups through the process of socialization. Both chapters 4 and 5 serve to elaborate the personality-factor aspect of social organization. Chapters 6 and 7 move to an explanation of the broader cultural base which provides a framework for patterned behavior. The purpose of these chapters is both to clarify the concept of culture for the student and to show how the socialization process indoctrinates the individual with the culture of his society. Sociocultural factors are of primary importance as a component element of social structure and organization. The final chapter in Part II, Chapter 8, is included to acquaint the student with the dynamics of social life. Here social change is explained and the processes which articulate change are described. Knowledge of this type has a very practical application. Groups and individuals interested in bringing about change, for example, in getting new ideas, new products, or new ways accepted, have to understand the principles and procedures which have been derived from studies of this type.

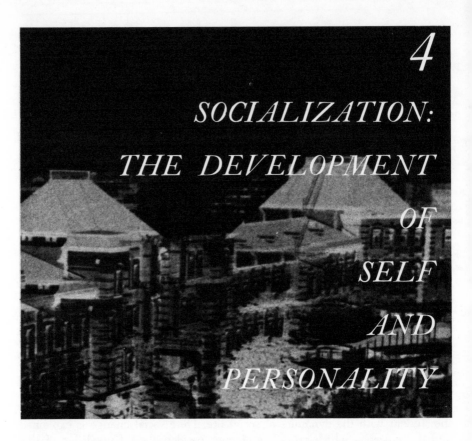

4

SOCIALIZATION: THE DEVELOPMENT OF SELF AND PERSONALITY

Socialization was defined earlier as the process by which the human organism is made into a person, that is, converted from his original unsocialized state to his ultimate state as a civilized human being. This process may be viewed as one of conditioning wherein the individual gradually learns the requirements for getting along in his culture. Once he has internalized these requirements as habits of behaving and thinking, then his behavior is not only predictable to a large extent, but he has acquired a self and a personality. Personality is vital to sociological understanding because it is one of the components or causative factors in the structure of behavior. The purpose of this chapter is to show how the self and personality emerge from the process of socialization and to describe the environmental influences which account for differences in individual personalities.

PERSONALITY AS A CAUSATIVE FACTOR IN BEHAVIOR

The question sometimes arises as to why sociologists concern themselves with the study of self and personality. Queries of this type are in order since such investigations seem more appropriate for psychologists. They need to be clarified before the material in this and the following chapter is presented.

Preceding discussions have emphasized the fact that sociologists are primarily concerned with patterns of social behavior. The model of the social system was introduced to show these patterns in a general sense. In order to understand them in a specific sense, attention must be given to the factors which *cause* behavior to be structured. Three basic sets of factors are identified and included in most theoretical models of behavior causation: (1) **the sociocultural structure,** that is, the expected (ideal) patterns of behavior; (2) **situational factors,** that is, all the physical and social conditions in which a social system exists and to which it must adjust; and (3) **personality factors,** that is, all the psychological and biological factors which affect the behavior of individual actors.[1]

Personality factors thus can be seen as an integral part of social organization. Without such factors, the deviation which occurs in social systems from the ideal behavior prescribed by the cultural structure could not be fully explained, nor could the socialization process be totally understood. Said another way, the maladjustments which occur between the sociocultural structure, situational factors and personality factors provide a conceptual scheme for analyzing and explaining the structural stress which occurs in all systems. Each group of variables is vital to explanations of social disorganization and social change as well as social organization. These facts make it mandatory for sociologists to treat personality as well as culture and situation as part of the basic theory of sociology.

SELFHOOD: AS A PRODUCT
OF SOCIALIZATION

It has been said that the clearest distinction between humans and lower forms of life is the inclusion of *selfhood* in the former. Thus the question arises as to what self is and how it is achieved. These queries have presented a challenge to social scientists and philosophers through the years. There is now a general consensus of opinion as to the nature of self, although some schools of thought differ in their approaches to the study of self.

The **self** may be defined, in a subjective way, as the *awareness* that one has of other personalities and of how one differs from others. Essentially it is the consciousness which is expressed by the pronouns "I" and "me." The subjective self is not easily studied even by the subject himself, since no one is

[1] Nix and Bates have worked out a model of behavioral causation which shows the relationship of these three sets of factors. See Harold L. Nix and Frederick L. Bates, "Occupational Role Stresses: A Structural Approach," *Rural Sociology*, Vol. 27 (March, 1962), p. 9.

completely objective in introspection. The student might convince himself of the fact by trying to answer questions such as, "What am I?", "Where do I exist?", and "Do I change?" without reference to the physical aspects of his body. In an objective way, it is possible to refer to the self and to study its origin and characteristics.

Robert Bierstedt points out that three of the most notable students of the self—Charles Horton Cooley, George Herbert Mead, and Sigmund Freud —agree on certain points: (1) the self is social, (2) the self requires society for its full explanation, and (3) individual consciousness of self arises from interaction with others.[2] These points are the focus of our attention.

SOCIAL ORIGIN OF SELF

For the purposes of this discussion, the newborn infant can be considered as a pliable but not completely plastic organism which can be molded into one or another type of person within limits. Only certain reflexes (such as sucking) and drives (such as hunger) are possessed and even these are subject to social conditioning. Humans have no instincts, or biologically rooted behavior patterns, such as the migration and nest-building instinct of certain birds. The search of a baby for the nipple has been likened to the peristalsis in the walls of the stomach, which is a biological stimulus. Instinctivist theories were exploded by L. L. Bernard in 1924, when he proved that the so-called human instincts were culturally acquired attributes.[3]

The molding of the not wholly passive infant into a human being begins almost with birth. Interaction with others is immediate because of the helplessness of a baby, and since the human organism has a capacity to learn, it is not long before the newborn child comes to associate the presence of others with some kind of experience for itself. The mother comes to be recognized as one who feeds, changes, and fondles, and also a bit later, as one who may frustrate from time to time by forcing on shoes or by interfering with pleasures in some other way. Other persons in the infant's world likewise have something to do with his needs and wants, each having a particular type of interaction with the child. Gradually, an older sister may almost become a substitute mother, a younger brother may pinch and pummel as the occasion presents itself, and become an object of fear, and so on.

The infant's awareness of others develops from constant interaction with others, and it is coincident with the discovery that others expect certain behavior from him in given situations. At the time when he begins to view himself objectively, that is, behave as he thinks others want him to, social self is in evidence. When a little boy anticipates the consequences of his acts—mommy

---

[2] Robert Bierstedt, The Social Order, 2nd ed. (New York, McGraw-Hill, 1963). p. 215.
[3] L. L. Bernard, Instinct: A Study in Social Psychology (New York, Holt, Rinehart and Winston, 1924).

will spank if I cross the street, or daddy will take me for a ride, if I am a good boy—his social self is emerging and he has begun the long journey to taking his place as an acceptable member of his society.

Broom and Selznick identify three important ways in which socialization creates a self.[4] First, socialization creates a self-image in the sense that the individual takes on a view of himself from observing how others treat and regard him. A harmful self-image can come from judgments that constantly project an image of the unwanted, unworthy, or untrustworthy. On the other hand a beneficial self-image may come from judgments that one is lovable, good, and trustworthy.

Secondly, socialization creates the ideal self in the sense that the individual discovers what he should do in order to secure approval and affection. The ideal self serves to promote adherence to societal norms as most persons have strong desires for approval. Two of W. I. Thomas' famous four wishes—the wish for response (expressed in man's longing for friendship and love) and the wish for recognition (expressed in man's desire to be appreciated by his fellows)—indicate the need of humans to belong and be accepted by their groups.[5] The other two wishes are the wish for new experience (expressed in man's search for variety and adventure in his life) and the wish for security (expressed in man's need for a safe place to retreat from his troubles and problems).

The third way in which socialization creates the self is by developing an ego. The *ego* may be generally defined as the "integrative, controlling function of the self." In a popular definition it may be likened to the conscience. As a person matures he is expected to develop controls so that he behaves as if he is being observed, even though he is not under surveillance by any one who matters to him. The girl who remains chaste and the boy who refuses to drink when in a college atmosphere, away from the watchful eyes of parents and friends, are demonstrating a self capable of directing and controlling its own behavior in keeping with certain reference group norms. This is an ego function.[6]

IDENTIFICATION: A MECHANISM IN THE DEVELOPMENT OF SELF

Perhaps the most important mechanism that is evident in the creation of the self is *identification*. When identification is carried to the extreme it may be

[4] Leonard Broom and Philip Selznick, *Sociology*, 3rd ed. (New York, Harper & Row, 1963), pp. 101-102.

[5] For the best brief statement of this theory see W. I. Thomas, *The Unadjusted Girl* (Boston, Little, Brown, 1923).

[6] For a list of ego functions see Fritz Redl and David Wineman, *Children Who Hate: The Disorganization and Breakdown of Behavior Controls* (Glencoe, Illinois, Free Press, 1951), Ch. 3.

termed *imitation*. In either instance, behavior is such as to indicate that one has taken over the values (ideas, attitudes, or habits) of another.

Identification is dependent to a large extent on imagination, that is, the ability to perceive not only how another looks and behaves but to develop an idealized image of the other worth imitating. This is why children are such great imitators. They have not developed the mental blocks to precise imitation so often found in adults. The little boy playing soldier or cowboy, or the little girl playing nurse or mother are identifying with their *significant others*. **Significant others** are defined as persons considered worth emulating because of personal experience which indicates they are to be held in high esteem.

One cannot identify with another without at least attempting to play the role associated with the status being emulated. When a child identifies with a soldier he must be brave, willing to undergo hardship, and otherwise take on the hopes, fears, attitudes, and even the reputation of the soldier. He advertises to the world that he is now a soldier by wearing a replica of a soldier's uniform, by carrying toy weapons off to mock wars with enemies, and by using the proper vocabulary. He actually undergoes the emotions he imagines the soldier has, is happy at conquering an imaginary outpost and insists on being addressed in terms of the role he is assuming.

Identification is part of the normal process of growing up and represents one way in which culture is transmitted from one generation to the next. There are, of course, degrees of identification, from teen-ager crushes on ideal figures, such as teachers or movie actors or actresses, to adult identification with job, political party, or profession.

THE DIMENSIONS OF SELF

Many great minds have grappled with the question of whether man can ever be completely socialized, that is, have a self that is in harmony with society. The theories of Cooley, Freud, and Mead have long enjoyed popularity with regard to this question. The recent writings of Goffman have also received considerable attention. The theories of all four scholars are briefly reviewed here.

CHARLES H. COOLEY. Cooley's views were that self and society represented a harmonious unity. He argued that a person's values as seen in ideas, attitudes and loyalties, represented one dimension of self, the subjective self, but that these values were derived from others and thus a second dimension of self, the objective self, could be seen. Because the objective self was derived from others, Cooley maintained the self was not in conflict with the social order. He developed his famous looking-glass self model to illustrate his view. This model includes three steps which the individual goes through to derive a self-conception from others. Each step is followed in sequence, consciously or subconsciously, whenever intimate social interaction occurs and includes: (1) imagination of how others see us, that is, how our dress or manners appear to them; (2) imagination of how others judge what they see in us, that is, our dress is in fashion or out of fashion, we have been courteous or rude; (3) some sort of feeling such as pride, mortification, elation, or disappointment, which occurs as a result of our imagination of what others think of us.[7]

Cooley's ideas have proved very useful in understanding the self. Thorough testing of his theories has served to validate them in a general sense. Criticism has been based on two limitations of his model, the first being that it is more useful in explaining the behavior of some groups in highly differentiated societies than of others. Teenagers, for example, are much more susceptible to the views of others than are the aged, who tend to ignore or stay away from those with whom they are not compatible. Secondly, the model is criticized as being somewhat oversimplified, in that it does not account for a mature personality appraising the behavior of others as well as his own. Green terms this a sort of discrimination and feels the looking glass should be seen as developing a double image at some indeterminate point in life history.[8]

SIGMUND FREUD. Freud's view of self included three dimensions or parts. The **id** he identified in essence as the biological core of the self, that is, one's desires or drives. The **ego** he saw as a sort of mediator trying to work out a compromise between one's desires or drives and the demands of society. Ego, in the Freudian sense, can be roughly summarized as reason. The third dimension of self postulated by Freud was the **superego,** or "social conscience." The superego served as a sort of policeman built into the self, but apart from the essential self. It served to overrule motivations stemming from sexual, agressive, and other drives.[9]

Freud's ideas, as Cooley's, have been tested rather thoroughly. His central idea, that society or the social environment is in constant conflict with the self and eternally blocks pleasure goals has been corroborated in studies of child behavior. Children are dominated by personal pleasure seeking more than adults, and raw hostility is quickly manifested over frustrations stemming from the claims or authority of others. Anyone having experience with three- to five-year olds, will have observed this type behavior which is evidenced in defiance of adult wishes, in refusal to take turns with others on the playground, or in attempts to take things away from smaller children by force. Freud used this type of reasoning to develop a whole approach to psychoanalysis, which assumed that neurosis, as a product of guilt and anxiety, could be measured according to the extent the superego dominated the id and ego.

[7] Charles H. Cooley, *Human Nature and the Social Order,* rev. ed. (New York, Scribner, 1922).

[8] Arnold Green, *Sociology,* 4th ed. (New York, McGraw-Hill, 1963), p. 134.

[9] See Sigmund Freud, *Civilization and Its Discontents,* Joan Riviere, Translator (New York, Cape and Smith, 1930); and Sigmund Freud, *An Outline of Psychoanalysis* (New York, Norton, 1949).

In this way he emphasized the repressive and frustrating aspects of group life and painted a very dreary picture of an evolving complex civilization with so many opportunities for guilt feelings. In such a society, hostility would remain near the explosive level and happiness would be continually forfeited.

The major criticism of Freud's views stem from his failure to adequately stress man's ability and willingness to repress his aggressive tendencies and physical drives. Through the development of cultural definitions of morality, man defines certain acts as wrong and these definitions become even more integral as a part of his personality than do aggression, cruelty, or sexuality. It must be concluded, however, that there is a dimension or part of the self which is never completely socialized and a debt is owed to Freud for this understanding.

GEORGE MEAD. Mead, called a pragmatist philosopher and social psychologist, divided the self into two dimensions. The first dimension he identified as the "me" and defined it as the part of self which takes into account the attitudes and opinions of others. This has been characterized as the passive and conventional part of the self. The second dimension of the self, called the "I" by Mead, was seen as the active part, that is, the part which was actively and creatively engaged in influencing rather than being influenced by society.

The unified or conventional self emerges, according to Mead, at the time the child begins to act toward himself from the viewpoint of the total group or community which he knows and not from the standpoint of any one individual, such as his mother. This stage is seen when the child begins to act out roles of others, such as storekeeper, nurse, mother, or mailman. In these roles he gains a new perspective of himself, in effect getting outside himself and making an object of himself. As his experience broadens he becomes completely identified with the organized community of which he is a part. Mead viewed the organization of roles taken over from the community as a "generalized other." The notion of the generalized other makes it possible to explain the continuity and consistency of self as one engages in numerous interactions with others, since all others are simply lumped or consolidated into a generalized other which is identical with the social group or community. The latter may be thought of as the "people" in the question which we so often pose or hear, "What will people think?"[10]

Mead's point that the self has a creative spontaneous aspect is a notable contribution, although it presents a difficult problem of measurement. It may be elaborated in this manner. When he acts, the individual takes into account the attitudes and values of others, which he has internalized; but the demands of the social situation pose a problem which must be solved with some originality. The football player knows what his coaches and fellow players expect of him in given play situations, but he may and does exercise a certain amount of initiative and creativity in the way he carries out his assignment. This

[10] George H. Mead, *Mind, Self, and Society* (Chicago, The University of Chicago Press, 1934).

part of his behavior is the acting self or "I." It is controlled by the "me," and this is why members of a close knit group, such as a primitive society, are characterized by extremely conventional behavior. In modern societies, where a premium is placed on innovation, the "I" potential is exploited through greater freedom of expression. In this regard, it is important to note that Mead felt that the "I" always took account of the "me" but did not necessarily have to be dominated by it.

ERVING GOFFMAN. Recent personality theorists have departed radically from the views of earlier writers on the subject. The new approach assumes a mass society and focuses on the relations of the individual to social groups. The characteristics of a mass society will be given in a later chapter. Its features are urbanism, industrialization, mass production, marketing, mass communication, and bureaucratization. The concept of the social role is utilized and considered most appropriate for the presentation of the self in such a society. The description of self in these terms has been done most cleverly by Goffman.[11]

The major premise on which Goffman builds his theory is that when an individual interacts with others he has certain motives for attempting to control the social situation. In other words, the pattern of action which is followed is in keeping with a routine designed to elicit a particular type of response from others. Martindale contrasts this approach with earlier ones in this manner[12]:

> The contrasts with the theories of James, Cooley, and Mead are striking. In place of the small town, Goffman presupposes the mass society as the back drop to the self. In place of the conception of the self as an autonomous moral agent or as the humanistic man of taste, there appears only the opportunist observing at best, purely discretionary rules.

Goffman identifies three crucial roles which are found in every interactional situation—those who perform, those performed to, and outsiders. In public performances he identifies other or "discrepant" roles which include (1) informer—a person who pretends to be a member of the team or in-group but who sells out to the audience (public); (2) shill—one who acts as though he is a member of the audience, but who is in reality a member of the team; (3) spotter—presumably a member of the audience, but serving to protect the public from fraud by the team; (4) shopper—the foreigner or observer, not a true member of team or audience; (5) go-between or mediator—one who knows the secrets of both sides and gives the impression to each side that he will keep their secrets. Another type of discrepant role is represented by the "nonperson"—some one present when the roles are played, but who remains completely aloof, such as a servant, a secretary, or photographer.

[11] Erving Goffman, *The Presentation of Self in Everyday Life* (Edinburgh, University of Edinburgh Social Science Research Center, 1956).
[12] From Don Martindale, *American Society*, copyright 1960, D. Van Nostrand Company, Inc., Princeton, N.J., p. 72.

As Goffman interprets the presentation of self, the individual always accentuates some matters and hides others. This represents a deliberate attempt to manipulate, to create awe, to maintain social distance, or to achieve an advantage. In this regard, the current popularity of self-improvement literature is evidence of the kind of world Goffman describes. Martindale points out that practical students of personal relations readily adopt the language and categories of merchandising. He cites the success of Dale Carnegie's *How to Win Friends and Influence People* to prove his point. (This volume has sold over five million copies since 1936 and continues to sell over 250,000 copies annually.) He puts Carnegie's two principles for handling people—praise but don't flatter and never criticize—into the terms of Goffman as follows[13]:

A most crucial set of roles in everyday life are those intended to get the other person to do one's bidding. For all such roles there are three basic techniques of self-presentation that will go far toward achieving one's objective. (1) Never attack other persons, at least not directly; it only puts them on guard—in fact sometimes they counter-attack when they are wounded. (2) Soften them up with a little praise; that is, "honest, sincere appreciation." (3) Always disguise the form of influence you wish to exercise as something the other man wants.

In essence, then, Goffman shifts the analysis of personality to social appearances which take place in terms of role playing in given social settings, presupposed to exist as part of the complex social life of the mass society. To him, man is an opportunist out to get what he wants out of life by acting in a discretionary manner designed to create the desired impressions. This view is in contrast to earlier theories of man as a moral agent—either from the religious or humanistic point of view.

Goffman's theories have received a great deal of attention in recent writings. However, there remains some reluctance to fully accept such a radical notion of the structure of the self.

No doubt the student can detect certain similarities in the theories of Cooley, Freud, Mead, and Goffman. These theories of self all have one thing in common—they require society. For this reason they are explicitly sociological. As Bierstedt puts it, "The individual has a self only because he first acquires a society."[14]

PERSONALITY: A PRODUCT OF SOCIALIZATION

Occasionally the term *personality* is used in ways which would indicate it is synonymous with selfhood. This usage, though erroneous, is accounted for

[13] From Don Martindale, *American Society*, copyright 1960, D. Van Nostrand Company, Inc., Princeton, N.J., p. 73.
[14] Bierstedt, *op. cit.*, p. 204.

by the fact that both personality and selfhood are products of the socialization process. Personality, in contrast to self (the awareness of others), refers to what is distinctive about a person in terms of traits and values. Cuber gives a good general definition of **personality** as, ". . . the sum total of the observed and observable characteristics of a person."[15] When used in this inclusive way, personality not only refers to physical traits, such as curly hair, blue eyes, or handsome physique; but also includes habits, such as laziness or promptness; attitudes, such as liberalness on political issues or prejudices against Catholics or Protestants, as the case may be; and other observable traits. A personality trait is one aspect or facet of a total personality.

The term *personality* connotes something quite different from the popular understanding of people who are outgoing and well-liked, such as the life-of-the-party type; or of important figures, such as movie actresses, who have the designation of "personalities." Everyone has a personality, though the personality of one person may differ radically from that of another. No one personality can be judged good or bad, except through use of some arbitrary moral standard. The latter is not the prerogative of the sociologist, although he may describe personalities in terms of a given cultural standard.

The personality is formed, maintained, and changed as the socialization process moves along. There are at least four important determinants of personality: (1) biological inheritance, (2) geographic environment, (3) social environment, and (4) cultural environment. The peculiar nature of these influencing factors account for differential socialization and differences in personality. Hence, the final part of this chapter is devoted to a discussion of each in turn.

BIOLOGICAL INHERITANCE AND PERSONALITY FORMATION

Man is born with an anatomy, physiology, and neural structure which set certain limits to his social behavior and to this extent biological inheritance is important in socialization. The great significance that the raw materials of biological inheritance have for personality formation is that they are relatively fixed and unchangeable. In other words, they set limits beyond which individuals cannot go and these limits are influential in a social way. Some of these limits are mere matters of physical endowment, whereas others link physical attributes with cultural interpretations, as will be seen in the discussion which follows.

BIOLOGICAL VARIABILITY IN HUMANS. Differences between men and women, between men, and between women play an important part in social life everywhere. Variability among humans is of two types, discrete and

---

[15] John F. Cuber, *Sociology: A Synopsis of Principles,* 5th ed. (New York, Appleton-Century-Crofts, 1963), p. 213.

continuous. Discrete variation is such as that found between the sexes, and continuous variation is represented by differences in height, weight, and head size, or other traits that everyone has.

The relationship of biological variability to personality formation can be seen at two operational levels. First, the mere fact that one individual is not endowed by nature as generously as another, in one or another way, places this individual in a poor competitive position. Homely girls are automatically eliminated from most beauty queen contests and 125-pound boys will seldom make the college football squad. Second, because of cultural definitions which evolve through time, some biological traits become more socially desirable than others and these traits serve as a basis for social class distinction, as well as for a competitive advantage. A classic example is the peculiar status position of racial hybrids who will rarely mix socially with their lower status ancestral groups, but who are not socially acceptable by their higher status ancestral groups.[16]

The importance which such factors as intelligence, sex, age, size, physical beauty, and physical prowess have for one's personality are so obvious as to preclude elaboration. Race differences have enough significance for social relations to warrant specific treatment at a later place. The student should understand that the culture of every known people includes many requirements and taboos with respect to the human body. What parts of the body can be exposed, how parts of the body should be groomed, what body characteristics are desirable or undesirable, as well as how body processes should be carried out are all examples of how culture (and consequently human behavior) and biology are related.

MATURATION AND SOCIALIZATION. When used in a biological sense, the term maturation refers to the changes in the human body (or other organism) which take place with increasing age. There exists a definite relationship between maturation and socialization, which has important implications for personality formation. The more obvious aspects of this relationship are those which relate to growing up and growing old. The infant is a completely helpless creature, which has to be fed, clothed, and washed. Adolescence, with puberty, represents another stage of maturation fraught with psychological and sociological implications. Adulthood, middle age, and old age follow in inevitable sequence and each in turn is characterized by physiological changes which have personality consequences. The frustrations of aging are in large part associated with the deterioration of the physical self. In modern societies, the adjustment problems of the adolescent and the aged represent major societal concerns.

---

[16] There are many such communities throughout the United States, most involving peoples with white and Negro ancestors. See Vernon J. Parenton and Roland J. Pellegrin, "The Sabines: A study of Racial Hybrids in a Louisiana Coastal Parish," *Social Forces*, Vol. 29 (December, 1950), pp. 148-154.

Maturation, as a biological process, relates to socialization and personality is a more subtle way than the association between physical development and deterioration. This second relationship is seen in the unevenness with which maturation takes place from one individual to another. Everyone is familiar with the fact that girls mature physically (reach puberty) at an earlier age than boys. This fact has certain consequences (sometimes dire) for social relations between teen-age boys and girls. Maturation also occurs differently in different individuals, because of glandular and other biological abnormalities. Some persons never quite develop adult traits, others have strong or weak drives, still others tend toward characteristics of the opposite sex. To the extent to which such deviations elicit special societal attention, or affect cultural competition, they have an effect on socialization and personality.

THE GEOGRAPHIC ENVIRONMENT AND PERSONALITY FORMATION

The geographic environment in which we live has four major aspects: location, climate, topography, and natural resources. All four represent important influences on human activity. These influences are so profound at their extremes, such as the ice and snow of the arctic and the humidity and heat of the tropics, that even relatively recent writers have tended to assign them as *the* determining factor in human behavior.[17] However, the studies of many reputable scholars verify that geography does not cause men to behave in one way or another, it merely influences behavior by setting limits to activity. Geographic limits are constantly changing in the face of an increasing technology and this is evidence of the validity of the previous statement. The discussion that follows is designed to show the several ways in which the geographic environment may influence human activity and hence socialization as a process.[18]

THE PHYSICAL SETTING OF SOCIAL LIFE. All of us grow up with more experience in one or another geographic setting. This setting might include greater or lesser abundance of sunshine, food, water, shelter, good soil, useful minerals, and attractive topography. Some among us, for example, may have lived in fertile regions characterized by gentle, rolling plains and a temperate climate. Others may come from desert regions with their fierce, hot daytime climate and shifting sands while still others call a cold, mountainous region home. Each person will have had to face nature as he found it in

[17] This thesis is put forth in Ellsworth Huntington, *Mainsprings of Civilization* (New York, Wiley, 1945).
[18] The discussions which follow on the influences of the geographic, social, and cultural environments on social life are adapted from a previous work by the writer. A. L. Bertrand, Ed., *Rural Sociology* (New York, McGraw-Hill, 1958), pp. 25-33.

his home environ and in so doing he cannot help but develop customs, practices, and personality traits compatible to his existence.

INTENSITY OF EXPERIENCE WITH THE NATURAL ENVIRONMENT. We have just seen how variable experiences with geographic factors account for personality differences. Geographic experience is important in another way in socialization—the intensity with which one encounters nature. Two persons may come from the same general locale, but one may be a farmer while the second is a city dweller. The farmer, by virtue of his occupation, does his work in close association with sun, the open air, the soil, and living, growing things. He may come to commune with plants and animals as if they were almost human. The city man, in contrast, may work, eat, and play indoors most of the time, and abhor contact with plants or animals. The farmer, thus, would characteristically feel ill at ease in a situation where he would have to remain cooped up, whereas the urbanite would flee the hot sun and hand work of farm life for the air conditioning and pencil pushing of his city existence.

Intensity of experience with geographic factors is also a function of the degree to which one is pitted against raw nature. Certain persons, by virtue of residence, occupation, war, or disaster, have to struggle against and endure the caprices and extremes of nature, while others never experience great discomfort from such sources. The farmer, on occasion, sees his year's work wiped out by a hailstorm, an early frost, or a drought; the fisherman knows days and seasons when storms and other contrary conditions thwart his efforts; or the miner fights floods, gas, and the vagaries of geologic strata. These individuals may be more religious, more superstitious, and more fatalistic in their approach to life than other persons because of their experience in dealing with the inscrutable powers of the natural environment.

THE CULTURAL ENVIRONMENT AND PERSONALITY FORMATION

The cultural environment awaits the newborn infant in perhaps a more positive way than even the geographic environment. It is through culturally established limits to behavior that each society indirectly selects the type of personality which will be most successful in it. In this regard, in spite of the uniform influence of culture, no two individuals can ever be socialized in exactly the same way, and as a result cannot have identical personalities. This phenomenon is explained by differences in cultural participation. Despite certain universal or general cultural influences, which each person in a society experiences, each person also has certain areas of experience which serve as specific influences on his personality. Specific influences are always present since no culture is ever transmitted in its entirety, and there are also ranges of tolerable behavior in all cultures. With this in mind, we may examine some of the cultural influences on personality.

RELATIVE SIMPLICITY OF CULTURAL MILIEU. It is easy to contrast the differences which one finds as he travels from a relatively undeveloped part of the world to a highly developed country. Three types of cultural differences usually stand out: (1) the relative simplicity of cultural expressions, such as music, clothes, dwellings, and tools; (2) differences in variety of knowledge and skills possessed which may run the gamut from those things required for existence in a hunting- and fishing-type of economy to those necessary for existence in a highly industrialized society; (3) differences in systems of social control, which may vary from highly familistic, informal systems where the injured, the total society, or some authoritative figure metes out more or less arbitrary punishment to offenders; to formal systems where the mechanisms of a highly formalized police and court system are utilized for social control. The opportunity for personality differences varies almost directly with the complexity of the given society.

VARIATIONS IN LEVELS AND STANDARDS OF LIVING. Another general way in which the cultural environment may account for personality differences is in terms of degree of participation in the culture. Cultural participation, to a point, is a matter of choice. One may decide whether or not he wants a television set in his house, providing television is a part of his culture milieu. The presence of certain consumer items in a home, such as television, telephone, piano, inside bathroom, and central heating, provide a measure of level of living. They indicate rather precisely what part of the available material culture is utilized by the individual or group and also provide some clues to his participation in the nonmaterial culture (for example, presumably he is exposed to political issues and social problems through massmedia paraphernalia). Obviously some people have cultural standards, that is, things they know about and would like to have, which they cannot achieve because of lack of resources. Just as obviously others know about things which they can readily afford but for which they have no desire; at least they do not value the object or thing enough to purchase it. Still others are ignorant of things which are available, which they can afford and would like very much. In each case we see differential cultural participation related to levels of living rather than to cultural milieu as such. Our point is that personality development has a subcultural component as well as a total-cultural aspect.

THE SOCIAL ENVIRONMENT AND PERSONALITY FORMATION

The fourth major influence in socialization comes from the social environment. In a way, social influences are a function of cultural influences; the distinction lies in that only individuals are culture bearers. This distinction makes it possible to distinguish between those socialization factors which exist purely in the nature of group experience and those which occur because of differences in the cultural orientation of members of the group. One may, for example, grow up in a close-knit small family or in a large orphanage, both with essentially the same cultural milieu and level-of-living items, but have an entirely different group experience. The number and kind of social groups in which a person has experience influences his personality to no small extent. It is in group settings that he learns loyalty, devotion, sympathy, respect, and cooperation among other personality traits. In fact, it is possible to tell what kind of person an individual is if one knows the groups to which he belongs.

PREDOMINANCE OF PARTICULAR GROUP CONTACTS. We will see later that groups vary along a continuum from those characterized by intimate, face-to-face association to those held together by one or a few special-interest type of bonds. It is easy to see how the person whose associations are overwhelmingly in groups where relations are close and personal would be socialized differently from a person whose typical experience was in groups where relations were more or less contractual and formal in nature. In the first instance the person would likely experience less loneliness and frustration, while in the second instance the individual might be less narrow and localized in his outlook on life. Many studies show that mental disease, delinquency, and personal pathologies such as alcoholism, are closely related to the group experience of individuals.

The number of different groups within which one has regular interaction is also a factor in personality development. One of the major differences between urban and rural communities as socializing agents stems from this fact. The urban attitude of superiority, which is almost universal, can be accounted for in part by differences in number and variety of experience in group participation.

At this point two terms which the student will encounter frequently have significance. The first is *peer group* and the second is *reference group*. A **peer group** is one whose members are about the same age. It is not unusual for such groups to include only persons of the same sex. Peer groups become very important and studies have shown that teen-agers, especially, may agree with and abide by the norms of peers in contradiction to those of their parents.[19]

A **reference group** (usually a group, but may be individuals as well) is one used by an individual as a standard for comparison, that is, one from which the individual gets his values. Reference groups values may not be in keeping with those of the larger society, for example, when religious organizations oppose war at time of national conflict. However, many conscientious objectors

[19] Bernard C. Rosen, "Conflicting Group Membership: A Study of Parent-Peer Group Cross-Pressures," *American Sociological Review*, Vol. 20 (April, 1955), pp. 155-161.

used such organizations as reference groups and refused to take up arms. Reference groups, like peer groups, offer an important key to one's personality.[20]

DEGREE OF SOCIAL MOBILITY. The circulation of people within a given strata of society or from one social strata to another is referred to as **social mobility.** This concept will be developed later. Our point here is that the person who, because of necessity, good or bad fortune, or other circumstances has experience in several social classes, or in several settings within the same class, is bound to have his personality affected. Many studies have documented this finding. Perhaps the most dramatic are those of persons who have crossed the color line, to live in a white world after having lived as a Negro for some time.[21]

Societies with many or few class strata, or those characterized by much or little freedom to move from one strata to another, provide an opportunity for social mobility to this degree. This accounts for some of the differences in the personalities of ruralites and urbanites. It also explains some of the personality differences which are typical of persons from different castes in a closed class society. The personality contrasts between persons with only local experience (a localite) and persons who are widely traveled and experienced (a cosmopolite) are related to mobility as well.

NOTE ON HOW THE DETERMINANTS OF PERSONALITY COMBINE

There is, at present, no way to measure just how heredity, geography, culture, and social experience combine to form a given personality. The best that can be said is that there is some measure of each blended into everyone. This leads us to the statement that the determinants of personality are combined in an individual according to what Green calls his "particular experiences."[22] Particular experiences are of two types—those which originate from continuous association and those which happen suddenly by chance and are nonrecurrent.

Continuous types of association are experienced in family groups, neighborhood and community settings, schools, play groups, and in all other groups in which individuals have a rather prolonged tenure. Nonrecurrent events which can have personality implications run the range from extremely traumatic experiences, such as witnessing a bloody accident or undergoing attack by a vicious criminal, to extremely pleasurable experiences like a wonderful

[20] T. M. Newcomb, Ralph H. Turner, and Philip E. Converse, *Social Psychology* (New York, Holt, Rinehart & Winston, 1965), p. 109.
[21] See St. Clair Drake and Horace R. Cayton, *Black Metropolis* (New York, Harcourt, Brace & World, 1945), pp. 159-173.
[22] Green, *op. cit.,* pp. 124-125.

day in the country as a child or being chosen football queen as an unsuspecting high school coed. Scholars tend to discount the notion (idea) that unique experiences have lasting effects on personality, but there is no doubt that these experiences make some impact on one's future behavior.

In concluding our discussion on personality, we must readily admit that outside determinants do not explain one's behavior altogether. There is always the meaning or interpretation which the individual attaches to situations that he encounters, and this meaning expresses a unique, individual perception.

SUMMARY

Human behavior in a specific sense is explained in terms of three sets of interdependent factors, which account for patterns of regularity and variability in interactional relationships. These three types of factors are related to (1) cultural structure, (2) situation, and (3) personality. Culture and personality become a part of the make-up of the individual actor through the master process of socialization, which is the focus of attention of Part II of this text. How personality is developed and conditioned is explained first.

The human infant is born with a capacity to learn, but with no instinctive patterns for behaving in given situations. However, it is not long before an awareness of others is developed—and it is at this moment that the self is created and personality formation begun. Identification with others is one of the most important mechanisms in the continued development of the personality.

Many persons have contributed to an understanding of the self. Cooley demonstrated that the objective self was derived from others in large part; Freud called attention to the fact that the self is in rather constant conflict with the social environment; Mead made it clear that the self has a creative, spontaneous aspect; and Goffman, representing a contemporary approach, shifted the analysis of personality (and self) to discretionary role playing in the complex social setting of mass society. All theories relating to the self which require society as a backdrop, as the above, are sociological in nature.

Personality, refers to what is distinctive about a person and a personality trait is one aspect or facet of a total personality. "The" personality is formed, maintained and changed as the process of socialization takes place. The four important determinants of personality include (1) biological inheritance (which accounts for factors of individual variation in mentality, and in physical appearance and in maturation); (2) geographic environment (which accounts for different experiences in adjusting to the physical world); (3) cultural environment (which accounts for differential participation in the total culture); (4) social environment (which accounts for differential participation in group life). All of these determinants of personality combine in some measure, which is determined by an individual's particular experience, to form his personality.

Supplementary Readings

Blau, Zena S., "Changes in Status and Age Identification," *American Sociological Review,* Vol. 21 (April, 1956), pp. 198-203; and also in BARRON.

Bronfenbrenner, Urie, "The Changing American Child—A Speculative Analysis," *Merrill-Palmer Quarterly of Behavior and Development,* Vol. 7 (April, 1961), pp. 73-84; and also in LASSWELL ET AL.

Cooley, Charles H., *Human Nature and the Social Order,* rev. ed. (New York, Scribner, 1922); also some parts included in MIZRUCHI.

Freud, Sigmund, *Civilization and Its Discontents,* Joan Riviere, translator (New York, Coxe and Smith, 1930).

Martindale, Don, *American Society* (Princeton, New Jersey, Van Nostrand, 1960), pp. 61-75; and also in CUBER & HARROFF.

Mead, George Herbert, *Mind, Self & Society: From the Standpoint of a Social Behaviorist,* edited by Charles W. Morris (Chicago, University of Chicago Press, 1934), pp. xx-xxvi; and also in SCHULER ET AL. and MIZRUCHI.

Merrill, Francis E., "The Self and the Other: An Emerging Field of Social Problems," *Social Problems,* Vol. 4 (January, 1957), pp. 200-207; and also in BARRON.

Rose, Arnold M., "Reference Groups of Rural High School Youth," *Child Development,* Vol. 27 (September, 1956), pp. 351-363; and also in CUBER & HARROFF.

Wrong, Dennis H., "The Over-Socialized Conception of Man," *American Sociological Review,* Vol. 26 (April, 1961), pp. 185-193; and also in BARRON; CUBER & HARROFF; INKELES; and MIZRUCHI.

5
SOCIALIZATION: VALUES IN PERSONALITY AND SOCIETAL ORGANIZATION

In the preceding chapter it was shown how the individual developed a self and personality through the process of socialization. However, very little was said about what might be termed the structure of personality. In this chapter we focus on values which largely make up the structural component of personality. More specifically, the discussions are designed to demonstrate (1) how values come to be a part of personality in the socialization process, and (2) the significance of values for behavior.

DEFINITION OF VALUES

The term *value* has many popular and technical connotations in the English language. For this reason, one has to be careful to stipulate what definition he is following when using the term and to state what discipline his definition has relevance for. Sociologists think in terms of **social values**, which can be defined as ". . . a relatively enduring awareness plus emotion regarding an object, idea, or person."[1]

[1] Arnold W. Green, *Sociology: An Analysis of Life in Modern Society*, 4th. ed. (New York, McGraw-Hill, 1964), p. 143.

Robin Williams lists four qualities of values as follows[2]:

(1) They have a conceptual element which is more profound than mere sensations, emotions, or needs. In this sense, values can be thought of as abstractions drawn from one's experiences.

(2) They are affectively charged, or involve some understanding which has an emotional aspect. Emotion may not be actually expressed but is always a potential.

(3) They are not concrete goals of action, but do relate to goals in that they serve as criteria for their selection. One strives for those things he places value on.

(4) They are important matters and not in the least trivial to the individual. This can be seen in the fact that values relate to choices, which in turn precede action.

Williams goes on to point out that social values are shared by many individuals and thus, by an effective consensus of the group, considered as matters of collective welfare. Viewed in this sense, social values held by an individual or group may or may not be identical with ethical or moral values, that is, ideas of what is good or right set by the larger society. For example, the conscientious objector holds an ethical or moral value against killing, which is in conflict with a war being fought as a matter of collective welfare by members of his national society.[3]

Beliefs are sometimes confused with values because of their close relationship. The two must be distinguished if values are to be understood properly. Beliefs, in contrast to values, are convictions that some explanation or description is real or factually true. It was brought out in Chapter 2 that it is not necessary for beliefs to be empirically verifiable. A superstitious person believes (that is, holds a belief) that a black cat crossing his path will bring him bad luck. Although there is no scientific evidence to support this belief, it is as much a belief for him as a belief that the world is round, or that there is a God in heaven. Values are usually derived from beliefs. For example, an expressed preference not to continue on a path which a black cat has crossed is indication of a value orientation.

The chief distinction between values and beliefs can be stated this way. Beliefs are ideas about those things considered facts, that is about which knowledgeable persons will entertain no dispute. Values are feelings about what is desirable or undesirable, or about what should or should not exist. Gouldner and Gouldner have prepared a list of beliefs and related values held by many Americans which is helpful in understanding the distinction between the two terms[4]:

[2] Robin M. Williams, Jr., *American Society: A Sociological Interpretation*, 2nd. ed. (New York, Knopf, 1960), p. 400.

[3] *Ibid.*

[4] Alvin W. Gouldner and Helen P. Gouldner, *Modern Sociology* (New York, Harcourt, Brace & World, 1963), p. 109.

BELIEFS	VALUES
Red-haired people lose their tempers quickly.	People should control their tempers.
A college education is necessary to get a good job.	A college education is a good thing.
Excessive driving speeds lead to accidents.	People should not exceed the lawful speed limits.
Objects are held in place by the laws of gravity.	It is desirable to explore outer space.
Students sometimes cheat on examinations.	Cheating is wrong.
The United States is a democracy.	Democracy is a desirable form of government.

Beliefs, except as they are translated into values, will not be discussed further. They have already been identified in Chapter 2 as a structural element of social systems. Values, in the sense that they represent preferences, are revealed when social systems are used as a conceptual tool in the analysis of social action. They are a characteristic of the system as a whole, rather than a component part. We turn now to a description of the various features of values.

LEVELS OF SOCIAL VALUES

Arnold Green has developed a very insightful classification for understanding the organization of values within personality.[5] He distinguishes three levels of values—abstract sentiments, moral norms, and the self as a social value—which are found in every one's personality. Each level may be described briefly as follows.

ABSTRACT SENTIMENTS

All of us, indeed members of every society, have ideas which are independent of action directed toward recognizable goals. These ideals may be identified as *abstract sentiments*. They are illustrated by such expressions as "all men are born free and equal," "it is better to give than to receive," "justice prevails in the end," and "good sportsmanship."

The importance of abstract sentiments comes from the fact that they are widely used as a basis for individual decision and as standards for group behavior. They are also handy ways for an individual or group to justify or rationalize something they want to do (behavior). The catch is that many abstract sentiments are contradictory, that is, they support a type of behavior

[5] Green, *op. cit.*, pp. 143-150.

which is in direct opposition to behavior by a second sentiment. An individual may strongly defend a statement such as, "there is a brotherhood of all mankind" and equally strongly disfavor sharing national wealth or military secrets with other nations because of sentiments related to national defense and interests.

Most of us turn quickly to the sentiments which support our interests of the moment whether or not these sentiments are in conflict with stands we have taken before. Normally conflicts in abstract sentiment lose their inconsistency for us, which might lead to personality breakdown because we are able to compartmentalize our thinking and behavior. The latter is possible for two reasons: (1) Our behavior of the moment is in keeping with the norms of groups in which we are acting. (2) Our societies function in such a way as to make contradictory sentiments legitimate or logical as ways of life in given contexts. To illustrate, most nations are characterized by sentiments against murder in peacetime, but other sentiments which may actually glorify killing are adopted in time of war. The change of social context provides an escape for the individual personality.

MORAL NORMS

Moral norms were defined earlier as standards of behavior which serve as a frame of reference for social interaction. It was pointed out that the folkways, mores, and customary and enacted law exemplify the norms. As a part of one's personality organization, norms can be seen in another, though not altogether separate, way. This is as one's reaction to the demands of the group that he act in the group's collective interest.

The individual is more aware of moral norms as part of his self-conception than he is of abstract sentiments. This is because the norms represent specific and pressing demands from the group to act in a certain way. For most people the norms take precedent over abstract sentiments which may be in opposition to expected behavior. A father and mother may preach "a penny saved is a penny earned" to their children, but go heavily in debt trying to "keep up with the Joneses," that is, live according to expected or normative standards for their social class. Interestingly, although moral norms generally take precedence over abstract sentiments, in almost every instance the norms are justified by reference to some abstract sentiment. The extravagance of the family in the above illustration would usually be justified by reference to abstract sentiments as "one must keep up a good front in our profession" or "we do not want to deprive our children of the advantages we missed."

In some situations the norms of one group can be recognized as in conflict with the norms of the greater society. For example, the criminal gang has strong norms which members adhere to in many instances even though societal norms are to the contrary. This is seen clearly in the withholding of evidence (a criminal code) from the police. Examples of this type indicate that subgroup social control mechanisms are more effective than societal mechanisms and therefore take precedence in the individual personality. However, the usual case is for subgroup and societal norms to be similar and to be integrated to a greater or lesser extent in personality organization.

Moral norms can be contradictory within the same group as well as between groups. A good example is seen in the case of a woman who has embarked on a professional career, but has not been able to shed her socialization as a member of a traditional family. On the one hand, she has adopted liberal norms with regard to the place of the woman in the family and may argue for husband–wife equality and career wives. On the other hand, she agrees that women should play the traditional role of wife and mother, that is, stay at home and care for the children, and leave the prerogative of major decision making to her husband.[6]

All types of inconsistencies in moral norms, as in the cases of abstract sentiments, are resolved by the individual personality in such a way as to minimize guilt feelings. In most instances contradictions are neatly ignored in the self, by a sort of compartmentalization of personality. In other words two separate value systems exist, but conflict is evaded by never calling on the two for rational explanations at the same time. Men who serve in the armed services tend to adopt values (moral norms) which are in sharp contrast to the values they express as members of a civilian world. The transition from the military world to the civilian world is accomplished smoothly because the disciplinary, responsibility, recreational, and other behavior norms of the military establishment are sealed off in one compartment of the personality and seldom, if ever, compared with the behavior expected in the nonmilitary world.

It should be noted that the intellectual is more likely to be disturbed by conflicting norms. This fact helps explain why some intellectuals are active in attempts at reform, and at the same time provides a basis for understanding why such persons suffer certain types of maladjustment. Whereas, the average person ignores or forgets about conflicts and inconsistencies in his own and in his group's behavior, the intellectual may develop feelings of shame or guilt. The important point here is that the moral norms occupy a central place in terms of the make-up of the personality.

THE SELF AS A SOCIAL VALUE

The third and perhaps the most important level of values in personality is the self. It has already been pointed out that the self arises out of social experience, yet remains distinctive from and, to some degree, resistant to group expectations. Stated another way, the self-conception is never completely derived

---

[6] Georgene H. Seward, "Cultural Conflict and the Feminine Role," *Journal of Social Psychology*, Vol. 22 (November, 1945), pp. 177–194.

from others' evaluations. There is, however, a constant striving to make a favorable impression and thus inflate self-importance. In this respect, the self-conception remains the first concern of every person throughout his lifetime. Because of this fact, individual behavior is inextricably related to the self as a social value.

The above point may be made somewhat clearer if one thinks of moral and ethical conduct as a function of the fact that one thinks such conduct is flattering to the self. Said another way, when individuals behave according to group expectations, they are accepted, praised, and otherwise rewarded, all of which boost the ego. By way of illustration, we can note that martyrs, such as the Buddhist monks who burned themselves as a protest against the policies of the Vietnamese government, performed the act after considerable publicity and in view of a large audience. This act called for a highly developed sense of morality and a self-conception of an act that would aggrandize the self. The reader should not confuse this acknowledgment of the self as a value in behavior to mean one can have no genuine social idealism. The fact is, the cause or reason for such an act must be sought in the values of the group. Without a group interpretation of morality, the individual could not realize a favorable self-conception for an act of martyrdom. In other words, the cause of the group is advanced by the sacrifice of the individual, which would never have taken place had he had no conception of himself as one who would be glorified as the supreme upholder of group morality.

CHARACTERISTICS OF VALUES

There are several ways in which values might be characterized beyond their nature as folkways, mores, and laws. The more useful designations relate to their character as more or less internalized and as more or less dominant. A description of the nature of these types of variations is given here.

By way of introduction to the discussions in this section, it may be noted that values vary along a continuum. Values should not be conceived as dichotomous in nature, that is, as having discrete or clearly separated classes. Rather, they should be seen as differing in degree of intensity, and along a range from extremely positive to extremely negative. This phenomenon will be clearer as the reader comes to know what is meant by *internalized* and *dominant values*.

INTERNALIZED VALUES

Despite the fact that values are learned, many of them may become a part of the subconscious personality. At this level they provide a basis for virtually automatic reaction to behavior situations. Values held in this manner can scarcely be said to have an existence apart from the individual and are thus termed *internalized* values.[7] Such values form the basis for conscience, and violation of them can result in deep feelings of guilt or shame which are difficult to fathom. A rather standard approach in psychiatry is to probe for conflicts in internalized values which might produce personality disturbances.

From the above it can be seen that the individual may have so completely internalized a value that he cannot conceive of alternative modes of behavior as being acceptable. A deeply religious person suffers tremendous mental discomfort at the violation of one of his religious norms. Likewise, a soldier in combat faces great risk to help a wounded comrade, and a father flirts with death in an attempt to save his drowning child, because of internalized values. Values which are not so deeply held normally would not trigger such spontaneous unreasoning action.

Internalized values often serve to unmask deliberate or inadvertent attempts to cover up one's feelings. It is part of the process of accommodation to attempt to avoid conflict by seeming to agree with certain abstract sentiments and norms when in reality one holds different values. A parent, for example, may tell his child to behave passively and refrain from fighting, in order not to conflict with group norms, yet be extremely disappointed if the youngster did not defend himself in the face of an insult or blow from the local bully. He cannot help showing his disappointment because it represents a value below the conscious level. It is also probable that all parents take the same subconscious pride in the fact that their children do not always behave precisely as they are told in school or in play groups, that is, their behavior is not in keeping with idealized group norms. In each instance the observed behavior of the parent is the clue to his or her internalized values. Their verbal admonitions to their children to abide by group values thus have an element of sham.

DOMINANT VALUES AND NORMS

The socialization process is a complicated one, as we have seen, and helps explain why individuals vary in the degree to which they assimilate values. This fact sets the stage for understanding values in terms of a hierarchy of dominance. Those values which take precedence over others are said to be **dominant,** whereas those values which are judged of lesser significance are identified as **subordinate** in nature.

Dominant values are evident in choices made relative to alternate courses of action in everyday activities. The more basic dominant values are considered good in and of themselves. They thus fall within the realm of the mores.

[7] Olen E. Leonard, "Rural Social Values and Norms," Chapter in Alvin L. Bertrand, *Rural Sociology* (New York, McGraw-Hill, 1958), p. 36.

These values make up the value system of a given society. The major value orientations in the United States will be discussed in the final part of this chapter to illustrate value systems. In essence, dominant values serve as a background or frame of reference for everyday behavior.

Williams has worked out some concrete tests of value dominance which are most helpful in studying this phenomenon.[8] He states that within a given group or social system as a whole, dominance of values can be roughly ordered or ranked according to the four criteria below.

(1) Extensiveness of the value in the total activity of the system. (Measured in terms of the proportion of the population and of its activities which manifest the value.)
(2) Duration of the value. (Measured in terms of the persistence of the value over a period of time.)
(3) Intensity with which the value is sought or maintained. (Measured in terms of effort, crucial choices, verbal affirmation, and reactions to threats to the value.)
(4) Prestige of value carriers, that is, of persons, objects, or organizations considered to be bearers of the value. (Measured in terms of heroes, high status, reputation, etc.)

THE NATURE OF VALUE SYSTEMS

Previous discussions have made it quite clear that values not only vary from individual to individual but from group to group and in another sense from one locality to another. At the same time, these variations were described as all bearing a certain relationship to a normative theme. These facts provide the foundation for the value-system approach to the study of societal values.[9] Most national and other societies obviously cannot be studied as a whole in terms of specific values because of the great range of interests, beliefs, and knowledge, which characterize its individual members.

When the sociologist speaks of the *value system* of a given society, he has reference to what has been called the *core values* found in that society. A given core value is not necessarily held by every person or every group in the society, but a sufficient number of its members subscribe to the value to make it one of the important determinants of behavior. Williams makes the further point that when one speaks of value systems he implies that values are not simply distributed at random but are patterned and represent a set of relationships that could *not* happen by chance.[10] The researcher who sets out to describe the

[8] Williams, *op. cit.*, pp. 409-410.
[9] *Ibid.*, pp. 412-413.
[10] *Ibid.*, p. 415.

value system of a given society looks for overriding relationships and interconnections which help explain order in the society. Normally he would focus his attention on the distinctive elements of these systems rather than on the universal elements which would be found in all societies. Williams' study of the United States is one of the best examples of a study of national value systems. His findings are presented as an illustration of the study of value at the societal level.

VALUE SYSTEMS IN THE UNITED STATES

Despite the difficulties inherent in the study of values in a nation as large and complex as the United States, Williams, as mentioned, has developed a comprehensive list of value orientations found in American society.[11] The student should keep in mind that such a list, although representing a tremendous effort, could be worked up for any society. Lists of this type provide a simplified, if generalized, picture of behavior potential in the given national or tribal society, or a portrait of the value system. They also serve as conceptual models from which comparisons can be worked out, for example, regional and individual variations can be compared. Since societal value systems are abstractions, one can never hope to find an individual or group which will have completely internalized the exact same list of dominant values worked up for a given society. In fact, in a nation as diverse as the United States, certain core values will conflict to an extent with other core values.

(1) *Achievement and Success.* This value is seen in the stress placed on personal achievement, especially occupational success. The self-made man theme so popular in the United States, evidences this value. Throughout the nation, achievement is measured to a great extent by economic criteria. Professional eminence, as a measure of success, normally is equated with an ability to attain wealth. However, the method of acquiring wealth is important as a dimension of the value of achievement and success. The gangster or others known to have acquired their wealth in ways not morally sanctioned are not usually considered successful.

(2) *Activity and Work.* Almost all observers note the stress which United States citizens place on activity. Laski, to illustrate, states that not many Americans are happy unless they are doing something.[12] Work, in early United

---

[11] *Ibid.*, pp. 415-468. For two other lists of core values in U.S. society see John F. Cuber, William F. Kenkel, and Robert A. Harper, *Problems of American Society: Values in Conflict,* 4th ed. (New York, Holt, Rinehart & Winston, 1964), p. 396, and Lee Coleman, "What Is American? A study of Alleged American Traits," *Social Forces,* Vol. 19 (May, 1941), pp. 492-499.

[12] Harold J. Laski, *The American Democracy* (New York, Viking, 1948), p. 6.

States, was often said to be next to godliness. The emphasis on work as an end in itself has diminished in recent years, but one can still find a strong value orientation in this direction.

(3) *Moral Orientation.* The people of the United States tend to see the world in moral terms, that is, as good or bad, right or wrong, moral or immoral. This value theme derives largely from Judeo-Christian ethics and has a strong puritan base. It explains why the conduct of individuals and groups tends to be tested against ethical principles, and also the obvious aspiration of most citizens to a higher plane of life.

(4) *Humanitarian Mores.* Despite many actions which might not be described as humanitarian, the people of the United States are known for responses to those in need. Newspaper stories of deserving cases usually bring immediate donations of cash as well as other forms of help which bespeak values related to kindness, the giving of aid and comfort, and charity. At another level, humanitarianism is evident in the success of the appeals of the voluntary health and welfare agencies such as those of the American Heart Association and the Red Cross. The annual receipts of such agencies go into the millions of dollars.

(5) *Efficiency and Practicality.* The high regard which is found for efficiency in the United States has long impressed outside observers. It has been related to the high degree of standardization and the mass production techniques typical of industrial production in the nation. The practicality theme is closely related to efficiency and simply asserts that things must be done for a more or less useful purpose.

(6) *Progress.* Progress as a value orientation is not as easily visualized as certain other themes. However, from the beginning of their history the people of the United States have been imbued with an optimism toward the future. Thus, in almost all their activity, the future is emphasized rather than the past or present. This value orientation is apparently part of a generally accepted feeling that man progresses toward an ever-increasing enlightenment.

(7) *Material Comfort.* The United States has long been characterized as a materialist-oriented nation, where people placed a high value on material comfort. There is a challenging intellectual question as to whether or not opportunity and ability to secure items of "creature" comfort are causally related to hedonistic values, that is, pleasure-giving activities. Nevertheless, the fact remains that people in the United States make full use of the accessibility of material things, and can be said to have a value orientation to material comfort to this extent.

(8) *Equality.* There has never been a time when a majority of the people of the United States would not espouse a theme of equality. The question of what is meant by equality, however, is one with a wide range of answers. Yet, the behavior of people in everyday situations clearly indicates a strong belief in a basic equality with those with whom they interact, at least at one or another level of interaction.

(9) *Freedom.* No word is used with more gusto in the United States than the word freedom. How much individual freedom exists in the nation is a constant source of debate. Nevertheless, the reality of a strong value orientation to freedom cannot be doubted. Evidence for this fact is found in the frequent references to the word "freedom" by political speakers and by people supporting causes.

(10) *External Conformity.* Standardization, mass production, public education, strong moral convictions, and a universal desire for approval all have worked to bring about what Williams calls external conformity.[13] This trend is further stressed by a high rate of internal migration which necessitates quick adjustment in new localities and new positions. External conformity may be more a matter of adjustment to the demands of a complex society than anything else. It has been pointed out that most families and individuals in the United States also place a high value on individuality, which might be seen as an internal level of nonconformity.

(11) *Science and Secular Rationality.* Science is clearly viewed as the way to progress and a better life in the United States. In addition, science has been easy to reconcile to a rationalistic, individualistic tradition because of its practicality and honesty aspects. Science also provides for rational mastery of nature, which leads to a strong belief that gradually the secrets of the universe will be unfolded.

(12) *Nationalism-Patriotism.* The intensity of nationalism-patriotism in the United States is quickly evidenced by the vehemence with which words like un-American are used. It is also seen in the ethnocentrism or culture centeredness of the populace. Patriotic organizations are well supported as are national defense programs.

(13) *Democracy.* The meaning of democracy quite decidedly varies from individual to individual in the United States, but a belief in democracy is universal. In the popular mind, democracy is related in some ways to form of government, in some ways to equality of opportunity, and in other ways to freedom and to individual liberty, all of which represent dominant values in the United States.

(14) *Individual Personality.* When the United States citizen is asked to outline the best techniques for child rearing, he will likely stress educational processes which emphasize individual integrity, independence of action, individual responsibility, and self-respect. It is also likely that he will say one must be worthy of concern and respect in one's own right and one must above all live his own life. The fact that not all persons live this sort of life does not detract from this very basic value orientation.

(15) *Racism and Related Group-superiority Themes.* It is a validation of the inherent inconsistency of individually and group-held values that the United States could be characterized by group-superiority themes. Yet, throughout the history of the nation ascribed status related to race, ethnic

[13] Williams, *op. cit.,* pp. 450-454.

background, or religious belief has served to set groups apart. The only way such behavior can be reconciled to the value orientation stressing the value and dignity of the individual is through compartmentalization of values in the personality. Themes of group-superiority are under great challenge at the moment, but still command enough following in the nation to be designated as a value orientation.

THE BROAD FUNCTION OF VALUES

In concluding this chapter on values, it is appropriate to show how the study of values has more than theoretical utility. Despite the difficulties which researchers face, the knowledge attained from studies of values has served a broad but vital function for sociology. This function may be generally expressed as the provision of substantial clues for the prediction of behavior, which in turn gives sociology an important practical justification. The findings from studies of values have been applied to problems at three levels, that of the individual, that of the community, and that of the national society. Each is illustrated in turn.

In recent years many studies have been made of individual values. These studies have demonstrated that a specific set of values may be the key factor in the acceptance or rejection of a new or more efficient practice. In one example, Harold Pederson demonstrated that Danish farmers in a Wisconsin county adopted recommended dairy practices more quickly than neighboring Polish farmers because of differences in attitudes and values. The values of the Danish group facilitated the introduction of new ideas, whereas the values of the Polish group tended to perpetuate the status quo.[14] In another example, it was demonstrated that individual levels of values are found in highly sophisticated settings. A study at Harvard done in 1958 revealed that many graduate students would not enroll in elementary language courses, although this was considered the best way of fulfilling the language requirement for their degrees. When asked why they did not attend these courses, they replied that it seemed degrading for them to be in a lower level course.[15]

Values at the community level have also been the subject of study and have been helpful to community development planners. One study of two communities in the Southwest revealed why divergent reactions to community development were experienced. The first community, a Mormon community deeply endowed with values of cooperation at the community level, was able to achieve enviable goals in building a gymnasium, paving streets, and expanding its road system. The second community of equal size and resources,

[14] Harold A. Pederson, "Cultural Differences in the Acceptance of Recommended Practices," *Rural Sociology*, Vol. 16 (March, 1951), pp. 37-49.
[15] Study by J. P. Elder, reported in George M. Foster, *Traditional Cultures: And the Impact of Technological Change* (New York, Harper & Row, 1962), p. 71.

but characterized by perhaps more typical United States values of individual rather than community initiative, was unable to achieve the necessary cooperation to attain similar goals.[16]

Finally, knowledge of value systems of a given national society or group can be very useful in predicting the behavior of the group in response to a specific stimuli. Leonard points out how centralization of action is a value orientation in Latin American countries.[17] He suggests it would be an extremely difficult task to convince the people of a Latin American community that they should take the responsibility for initiating and implementing plans to build a new school or other public building. This would be true because they believe that such planning should be undertaken by the central government. By contrast, the people of a United States community would typically object if it were suggested that the Federal Government should intervene in the construction of schools.

SUMMARY

The socialization process accounts for the structural components of personality, which are largely manifested in social values. Values are defined as feelings about what is good or bad, desirable or undesirable, or about what should or should not exist. They are in contrast to beliefs, which are defined as ideas *about* things.

Three levels of social values are recognized: (1) abstract sentiments, or the ideals held by individuals; (2) moral norms, or the standards used to judge the real behavior of individuals; and (3) the self, or the creative part of one's personality, which is not derived from others' evaluation.

Values are characterized in several ways beyond their nature as folkways, mores, and laws. They are said to be internalized when they become a part of the subconscious personality, and evoke action without thought, so to speak. Those values which take precedence over others in given situations are said to be dominant, those of less importance are termed subordinate. Dominant values are reflected in the choices which are made when there are alternative courses of action.

The core values are relatively widespread among the members of the society. Fifteen core values were recognized as making up the value system of the United States: (1) Achievement and success, (2) moral orientation, (3) humanitarian mores, (4) efficiency and practicality, (5) activity and work, (6) progress, (7) material comfort, (8) equality, (9) freedom, (10) external conformity, (11) science and secular rationality, (12) nationalism-patriotism,

---

[16] Evon Z. Vogt and Thomas F. O'Dea, "Comparative Study of the Role of Values in Social Action," *American Sociological Review*, Vol. 18 (December, 1953), p. 648.

[17] Leonard, *op. cit.*, pp. 39-40.

(13) democracy, (14) individual personality, (15) racism and related group-superiority themes.

The study of values serves a basic function in connection with many types of planning for the future. When it is determined that an individual, a community, or a society, is characterized by a certain value orientation, steps may be taken to allow for or change this orientation.

Supplementary Readings

Cuber, John F., William F. Kenkel and Robert A. Harper, *Problems of American Society: Values in Conflict,* 4th ed. (New York, Holt, Rinehart & Winston, 1964), Part III.

Du Bois, Cora, "The Dominant Value Profile of American Culture," *American Anthropologist,* Vol. 57 (December, 1955), pp. 1232-1239; and also in O'BRIEN ET AL.; and SCHULER ET AL.

Kluckhohn, Clyde and Others, "Values and Value-Orientations in the Theory of Action," selection in Talcott Parsons and Edward A. Shils, Eds., *Toward a General Theory of Action* (Cambridge, Massachusetts, Harvard University Press, 1959), pp. 388-433.

Lipset, Seymour Martin, "The Value Patterns of Democracy: A Case Study in Comparative Analysis," *American Sociological Review,* Vol. 28 (August, 1963), pp. 515-531.

Useem, Ruth Hill and John Useem, "Images of the United States and Britain Held by Foreign-Educated Indians," *The Annals,* Vol. 295 (September, 1954), pp. 73-82; and also in SCHULER ET AL.

Vogt, Evon Z. and John M. Roberts, "A Study of Values," *Scientific American,* Vol. 195 (July, 1956), pp. 25-30; and also in SCHULER ET AL.

Vogt, Evon Z. and Thomas F. O'Dea, "A Comparative Study of the Role of Values in Social Action," *American Sociological Review,* Vol. 18 (December, 1953), pp. 645-654; and also in YOUNG & MACK.

Williams, Robin M., Jr., *American Society,* 2nd ed. (New York, Knopf, 1960), Chapter 11.

6

CULTURE:

THE

GOAL

OF

SOCIALIZATION

The general meaning of culture was brought out in Chapter 2. In Chapter 4 it was pointed out that culture is a vital component of social structure. In this chapter the concept is elaborated in much greater detail. The focus of the material presented is on culture as the major part of what is transmitted to the individual in the process of socialization. In this sense, culture is seen as the goal of socialization.

CULTURE VERSUS SOCIETY

Although the terms culture and society have been defined, they have not been distinguished one from the other. It is appropriate that this be done because the two are commonly confused.

Specifically, culture may be thought of as all the learned and expected ways of life which are shared by the members of a society. Culture includes all buildings, tools, and other physical things as well as techniques, social institutions, attitudes, beliefs, motivations and systems of value known to the group.[1] From this definition one can see that culture not only consists of commonly accepted ways of thinking and acting, but includes the more tangible achievements of group life as well.

[1] This definition is essentially the same as the popular definition of E. B. Tyler. See *Primitive Culture,* 7th ed. (New York, Brentano's, 1924), p. 1.

It will be recalled from earlier discussions that a society is a group of people who are sufficiently organized to carry out the conditions necessary for living harmoniously together. A society is able to function because its members agree on certain basic rules of conduct. These rules, in a general sense, constitute the *culture* (and account for the fundamental order) of the societal group, but do not account for the people themselves. This is the basic distinction between society and culture.

It is difficult to speak of culture or society without relating the terms, because they are interdependent. In other words, a culture cannot exist without a society, and vice versa. But, the evolution of a culture can be studied and the development of a society can be traced independently because the behavior patterns which constitute the specific culture are learned and *passed on* by the members of a society.

In this regard, it is helpful to think of culture as consisting essentially of a *collection of behavior patterns* or, in a technical sense, norms, and to think of society as being made up of a *group of people,* whose behavior and organization is determined by the culture, and who create culture. A distinction of this type makes it clear that culture relates to such things as ideas and beliefs, whereas society relates to people. The two terms are closely related because people *enact* a culture.

THE FORMS OF CULTURE

There are a number of ways whereby the content or make-up of culture might be classified. However, the various classifications worked out by social scientists vary in specificity rather than in content. Sociologists are in general agreement that content of culture can be divided into two distinct component elements, *material* and *nonmaterial.*[2]

MATERIAL CULTURE

The **material** part of a culture includes those things which men have created and use which have a tangible form. Such components may range from the clay vessels crudely constructed by a primitive people to the space capsules assembled and launched by top scientists in an advanced society. Both items are characterized by a physical form and this is what places them in the realm of material culture. In other words, concrete existence as a man-made product, regardless of size, intricacy, purpose, or form, distinguishes material culture. Our houses, clothing, automobiles, ships, buildings, and television sets, all provide good examples of this part of our culture.

[2] William F. Ogburn, *Social Change* (New York, The Viking Press, 1927; new ed., 1950).

Despite the fact that material culture is easily identified, it has a relationship to the nonmaterial aspects of culture which is not so easy to comprehend. This is evidenced in the fact that the same object may have different uses or meanings in different cultures. The bow and arrow may represent a weapon for defense and means for securing game to the primitive tribesman, while in an advanced society bows and arrows are manufactured as toys or as sporting equipment. In this regard, the important question of values (norms) as well as the question of degree of technology, has relevance. However, a discussion of the former is more appropriate to the topic of nonmaterial culture which follows.

NONMATERIAL CULTURE

The **nonmaterial** aspect of culture encompasses all those creations of man which he uses to explain and to guide his actions, but which are not found except in his mind. Two categories of nonmaterial culture are recognized. The first category includes what may broadly be defined as individual norms, the second encompasses groups of norms which form social institutions.

NORMS: Norms have been defined as the standards of behavior which are found in all societies, such as how to dress on given occasions or how to greet different classes of individuals. As a part of the nonmaterial culture they represent idealized conceptions of behavior—blueprints for action. It is true, of course, that behavior is closely related to what one thinks is right; nevertheless, the actual behavior is considered an aspect of social organization, as brought out previously, rather than culture. The norms are formalized in the folkways, mores, and laws of a given society.[3]

The term norm is interpreted to include knowledge, beliefs and values. These concepts have already been defined and discussed as elements of social systems in some detail, so there is no purpose in elaboration here. However, it serves a purpose of review to state that all the understandings men hold about themselves, their worlds, and their relations to their fellows make up their body of ideas (norms). In a cultural sense, ideas embrace folklore, theological doctrines, scientific theories and principles, philosophies of education and government, rules for sports, abstract sentiments, and systems of morality and ethics, as well as all other explanations of the world in which one lives.

Norms differ to a greater or lesser extent from one individual or group to another for the reasons brought out in previous discussions. The systems of values and beliefs which develop in given societies set them apart culturally from other societies where other values and beliefs have evolved. This is one

[3] Bierstedt feels that ideologies and technologies (techniques of doing things) are not clearly identifiable as ideas or norms separate from the material world. Robert Bierstedt, *The Social Order*, 2nd ed. (New York, McGraw-Hill, 1963), pp. 170-174.

of the facts which provides the sociologist with an explanation of differences in behavior.

INSTITUTIONS: **Social institutions** are in effect bodies of norms (social structures) which have been worked out to serve a function for society. They differ from norms as discussed above only in the sense that they include a cluster rather than an individual norm. Institutions develop through time, and may or may not call for behavior contrary to that expected outside an institutional setting. One thinks of "the family" as a social group but he must not confuse this concept with THE FAMILY—a social institution. As a social institution, the family is not a group but a set of behavior patterns related to the functions of procreation and the provision of society with members having a social identity. The family as a social group performs multiple institutional functions associated with social institutions other than THE FAMILY, such as religion or politics.[4]

Norms and institutions can be related in this way. Beliefs in monogamy or in a single deity are ideas which are classifiable as single norms. The institutions of THE FAMILY and religion are made up of a composite of norms which includes the norm of marrying only one wife in the first instance and the norm of worshipping only one god in the second instance. Social institutions and institutionalized social structures are treated in detail in Part V.

THE STRUCTURAL COMPONENTS OF CULTURE

The investigator interested in a careful and detailed analysis of a given culture generally makes reference to what may be called the *structural components* of culture. This is a way to look at the content or makeup of culture, which has certain analytical advantages. Primarily it tends to make possible the cataloging of concrete behavior which may be characteristic of a given individual or group. Classification is possible because culture is not simply an accumulation of ideas (norms), but an organized system of behavior. The structural components of culture as concepts help one to visualize this organization.

CULTURE TRAITS

The smallest unit of culture which can be identified is termed the **culture trait.** At this point the student should be careful not to confuse raw materials

[4] See Frederick L. Bates, "Institutions, Organizations, and Communities: A General Theory of Complex Structures," *The Pacific Sociological Review,* Vol. 3 (Fall, 1960), pp. 67-68.

with culture. For example, a pencil may be identified as a culture trait because it represents a material product of learned behavior. To quibble over whether the wood, the lead in the pencil, the paint on it, and its eraser are also culture traits is to miss the point. Unless the unit under question represents a combination of material, acts, and ideas related to a particular need or situation, it is not legitimately called a trait. In other words, traits must relate to a greater cultural totality, as will be seen in the discussion of culture complexes which follows.

A trait of the material culture is perhaps more readily identifiable than a trait of the nonmaterial culture. Examples of the former would be such things as a football, a wrench, a pencil, a tie, a lipstick, or an arrowhead. Nonmaterial culture traits would include such actions and practices as the rule that a touchdown is scored when the goal line is crossed, a regulation that girls living in dormitories must be in their rooms by 11:00 P.M. on Wednesday nights, addressing one's superior officer with the proper "sir," the requirement of a C average for graduation, and the law that one must be 21 years of age before being eligible to vote. One needs little imagination to see that each culture contains literally thousands of traits, which may be thought of as the foundation units of the culture.

CULTURE COMPLEX

It was brought out in the preceding discussion that culture traits seldom, if ever, exist in isolation from other traits in a given culture. The term used to describe a combination of related traits which make up the cultural requirements for given situations or activities is **culture complex.** The game of football represents a culture complex, which includes the football and a given rule as traits, among many others, of course.

There is sometimes confusion about the difference between the words *trait* and *complex.* Actually, the same item of culture may be referred to as a trait in one instance and a complex in another. This apparent contradiction is reconciled in terms of the context of the conversation. To illustrate, an automobile would be identified as a culture trait when one had reference to a transportation complex. However, a tire would be a culture trait when the discussion was centered on the automobile as a culture complex. A good rule to observe is that traits represent the smallest units or parts which have direct significance for the understanding of the given culture complex.

CULTURE PATTERN

Culture complexes also combine to form larger units of culture. The latter are termed **culture patterns** or **configurations.** To follow through with our example of football, a national culture pattern of sports emerges when the football, baseball, basketball, and track, culture complexes are brought together to form a sports pattern. Likewise, automobiles and other mechanical cultural complexes are the earmarks of a technological culture pattern within a given society.

TYPES OF CULTURAL PARTICIPATION

Social scientists are indebted to the anthropologist Linton for his lucid clarification of types of cultural participation.[5] He distinguished three levels of participation as follows: (1) **Universals** are the culture traits which are required for all members of a society. Cultural universals are necessary for existence within a given national society, and include laws and customs which relate to family life, to schooling, to business activities, and to certain government activity. Specific examples might be the proper way to greet a friend, the necessity for a wedding license, or compulsory schooling to a certain age. It can be seen that without certain cultural universals it would be impossible to carry on an organized national existence.

(2) **Alternatives** are the situations where the individual has a choice of several courses of action which are equally, or nearly so, acceptable by the greater society. We may illustrate by following through with the specific examples of culture universals used above. In a given cultural setting, one may greet acquaintances in several ways which would be considered proper—by shaking hands, by kissing (in the proper situation), or by a verbal response, all of which represent alternative choices. However, these choices might not go so far as to include rubbing noses, or shaking one's own hand, which would be greetings acceptable in other cultures. In the second instance, one has a choice of being married in a church, in a magistrate's office or on a ship at sea —so long as the marriage license is a proper one. In most states of the United States one must attend school until the age of 16; however, there is no requirement that one attend a particular school in a given section of the country. Whenever such choices exist, they represent cultural alternatives. It is important to note that a given cultural trait may represent a universal in one culture and an alternative in another.

(3) **Specialties** are unique aspects of culture which are not shared by the general populace. All large societies include groups which may be identified as specialists in a professional, occupational, or religious sense. By virtue of their special training and experience members of these groups know things and are allowed to do things which others are not. Many examples can be brought to mind, such as the work of doctors, secret service men, teachers, etc. In effect,

[5] Ralph Linton, *The Study of Man* (New York, Appleton-Century-Crofts 1936), pp. 272-274.

specialists are a function of division of labor, and vary according to sex, age, education, class and other status positions.

THE CONCEPT OF SUBCULTURES

All large, complex societies are characterized by the presence of groups of persons who have their own peculiar ways of behaving. The behavior of such groups is tolerated by the greater society as long as societal values are not jeopardized, although there is a general awareness of the difference which exists. Actually, there is a range of toleration which moves from a position of little anxiety on the part of the greater society (such as when the peculiar culture traits of the nonconformists are within the realm of the folkways), to a position of great anxiety when the mores are threatened or violated. For example, the members of a religious sect may insist on wearing homespun clothes and ride in buggies, but otherwise be ideal citizens. By contrast another nonconforming group, such as a teen-age gang in a large city, may take to stealing cars for joy rides, or experiment with narcotics; both acts fall within the realm of mores.

The term that is used to describe groups within a society with a clearly recognized pattern of behavior is **subculture.** Such groups share the total culture of the society, but their special culture traits are too numerous and too unique to their members to be termed specialties, in the sense this term was previously described. Subcultures may develop for a number of reasons, such as differences in national background, occupational differences, race differences, religious differences, and other peculiar experiences. Ethnic groups often resist assimilation into the larger culture to a greater or lesser degree and thus take on the character of a subculture. In the United States, one can find German–American, Spanish–American, Italian–American, Greek–American and many other types of communities. The most important subcultures are those characteristic of the major regions of a nation. (See Chapter 22.)

One of the most persistent subcultures in the United States has been that of the French in South Louisiana. After more than 200 years, one still finds the language being spoken, a particular way of cooking, and a way of life quite distinct from the surrounding national culture.[6] Other examples of subculture are found in the world of adolescents, the life of men and women in the Armed Services, and the various social classes set aside by economic and other criteria, such as poverty groups. Likewise, the members of an occupational group, such as electricans, musicans, teachers, or even astronauts have

[6] Alvin L. Bertrand, *The Many Louisianas: Rural Social Areas and Cultural Islands* (Baton Rouge, Louisiana, Louisiana Agricultural Experimental Station Bulletin No. 496, 1955), and Alvin L. Bertrand and Calvin L. Beale, *The French and Non-French in Rural Louisiana: A Study of the Relevance of Ethnic Fctors to Rural Development* (Baton Rouge, Louisiana, Louisiana Agricultural Experimental Station Bulletin No. 606, 1965).

a world, to some degree, of their own and to this extent participate in a sub-culture.

A person may participate in several subcultures in the course of a lifetime and may or may not disassociate himself with previous groups as he progresses from one to the other. It is not unusual that cultural conflict, both at the individual and group level, may develop as contact with other subcultures or with the greater culture increases. To illustrate, the children of first generation immigrants are often caught between two culture worlds. They want to be accepted outside their homes, which means adopting the ways of the local community, and in their homes, which means the way their parents brought from their native countries. In the same way, families moving from remote rural places to urban centers often experience conflict between younger and older members. All in all the concept of subculture makes it possible to account for many types of behavior peculiarities or differences within a national setting.

THE CONCEPT OF CULTURAL LAG

The term *culture lag* was introduced by Ogburn to explain the situation when one part or phase of a culture lags or falls behind another part and results in some sort of unevenness.[7] Ogburn was convinced that the technological aspects of culture (materials and things, especially) tended to develop faster than the ways of using technological items or the adaptation to them. The lapse between the time an innovation was introduced and the time it was generally accepted and adjustment to it accomplished, he termed **culture lag.**

Examples of culture lag are easy to find. In an advanced culture, such inventions as the automobile and airplane are accepted and used without proper thought being given to laws involving road systems, driver education, and so on. Similarly, advances in communication, such as movies, television, and other types of visual aids, are made long before full use of such devices is made in schools, by governments, and in businesses.

It is usual that new inventions require new regulations and understandings which go counter to old laws and ways of doing things. Some societies are attuned in such a way that change is expected and accepted without tremendous culture lag. Others are more traditional in nature and the period of culture lag is usually much longer, if indeed change ever comes about. Two examples will illustrate this point. In a study of a community of Spanish–American farmers in New Mexico, it was discovered that the efforts of the local county extension agents to introduce hybrid corn had eventually failed, though apparently successful at first. After investigation it was found that the farmers' wives complained about the taste, texture, and color of the corn dough which was used by them to make tortillas. In the value system of this com-

---

[7] Ogburn, *op. cit.* (new ed.), pp. 200-213.

munity it was more important to revert to a low-yield corn variety than to give up these traditional food characteristics.[8] In contrast, in England a battery system in which hens are placed in cages just large enough to hold one bird and in which a light burns 18 hours a day was adopted to increase egg production, despite protests by some persons who construed this practice as cruelty to the hens.[9] The period of culture lag in the latter instance was much less because of the greater susceptibility of the general culture to change, although a similar economic factor was present in both instances. The reasons for cultural lag will be discussed in Chapter 8.

The term *cultural survival* is related to cultural lag in that it represents a traditional way that has not changed with the times. However, it is a distinct concept in the sense that it is used to designate a practice which has lost its functional significance completely and which survives solely on the basis of custom. Many examples of cultural survival can be found in even the most advanced cultures. One may note the ornaments which remain on the hood (bonnets) of automobiles long after the radiator has disappeared underneath the hood. Men continue to wear ties although the practice is a vestigial survival of the shoulder shawls worn by seventeenth century Croats, and men walk on the street side when escorting women on a sidewalk despite an extremely remote possibility of danger from runaway horses and splashed water and mud.

CULTURAL RELATIVISM: ITS MANIFESTATIONS AND SIGNIFICANCE

Standards of behavior are relative to the culture in which they appear, a phenomenon termed **cultural relativity.** Cultural relativism explains why a given act like wearing a topless dress is considered proper attire in one culture and an absolutely immoral act in another culture. The same explanation would hold true for views with regard to government or religion which would be considered right and good in one setting, but evil and forbidden in another culture. What is good or bad, desirable or undesirable is, then, relative to one's definition of the situation, which is done in terms of cultural preconditioning. This is why social scientists are careful to analyze behavior in the context of the given culture.

The relative nature of culture provides an explanation for behavior. Three of the more important behavioral manifestations and consequences of

[8] Anacleto Apodaca, "Corn and Custom: The Introduction of Hybrid Corn to Spanish American Farmers in New Mexico," selection in E. H. Spicer, Ed., *Human Problems in Technological Change* (New York, Russell Sage Foundation, 1952), pp. 35-39.
[9] George M. Foster, *Traditional Cultures and the Impact of Technological Change* (New York, Harper & Row, 1962), p. 77.

cultural conditioning are reviewed here: (1) *ethnocentrism,* (2) *culture shock,* and (3) *culture conflict.*

ETHNOCENTRISM

The astute observer, as he travels from one country to another, will note that almost all the individuals he encounters will consider his culture superior to others in one or another way. The Frenchman will boast of his beautiful language, the Italian of his music, the American of his material possessions, and the oriental of his ancient wisdom. It not infrequently comes as a shock to find that others are less than prone to agree with one's notions of superiority. The tendency is to question the knowledgeability of the person who does not see that one's way of doing things is natural and the best way. **Ethnocentrism** is the term used to connote the tendency to evaluate other cultures in terms of one's own. Most individuals, even those with high levels of sophistication and education, fall victims of ethnocentrism at one time or another. Foster relates this account, told by a highly trained woman anthropologist (Virginia Gutierrez de Pineda) doing field work amongst the cattle-raising Guafiro Indians of the Guafira Peninsula of Colombia.

I remember when once I spoke with an Indian woman of high social class about marriage, and the Indian custom of giving money and cattle to buy the wife. I had not yet come fully to understand the Indian culture, and while the woman spoke of her price I felt terribly sad that a Colombian woman could be sold like a cow. Suddenly she asked, "And you? How much did you cost your husband?" I smugly replied, "Nothing. We aren't sold." Then the picture changed completely. "Oh, what a horrible thing," she said. "Your husband didn't even give a single cow for you? You must not be worth anything." And she lost all respect for me, and would have nothing further to do with me, because no one had given anything for me.[10]

It is the responsibility of sociologists to be aware of and to avoid ethnocentrism as much as possible in their work. A thorough understanding of cultural relativism is helpful in the discharge of this responsibility. It is also helpful, in a careful analysis, to distinguish between the **ideal culture** of a society (that is the culture its members think they possess and verbally express in terms of abstract sentiments) and the **real culture** of the society [the behavior (organization) actually manifested in everyday activity]. It is likely one will lose a degree of ethnocentrism after such an exercise with his culture as the subject. What we do is frequently quite the opposite of what we say ought to be done or that which we believe to be right.

Ethnocentrism has certain advantages to cultural stability and integration. Personality traits such as patriotism, loyalty to one's nation, and provincialism are closely related to ethnocentrism and sometimes termed functions of ethno-

[10] *Ibid.,* p. 69.

centrism. However, besides its hindrance to scientific objectivity, ethnocentrism also hinders relations between cultures and slows down the assimilation of divergent groups into a larger society.

CULTURE SHOCK

The expression cultural shock was first popularized by Kalervo Oberg.[11] He used this term to describe what he called an occupational disease of people who have been suddenly transplanted in a different culture than their own. Oberg described culture shock as a form of mental illness—one of which the victim was not aware. He states that this malady is precipitated by the anxiety which results from losing all one's familiar signs and symbols of social intercourse. When the thousand and one familiar cues for orienting oneself in social situations are missing—such as when to shake hand, how to say no gracefully, how to make purchases, how to give orders to servants, what facial expressions to use, and on and on and on—both peace of mind and efficiency are lost.

Oberg outlines four stages which represent the full cycle of culture shock for career persons (others could be expected to follow a similar pattern). The first or *incubation* stage (sometimes called the honeymoon stage) is one of an exciting new experience. During this stage there is a great probability that one is living in a better than accustomed way, probably in a hotel, and there is adventure in finding a new home, in arranging for servants (which one could not afford at home) and in being wined and dined by local important persons. This period may last from a few days to a few weeks depending on situational factors.

The second stage strikes with a vengeance and is appropriately called the *crisis* stage. It is characterized by everything going wrong—language trouble precipitates maid trouble, school trouble, and all sorts of other trouble. It is during this stage that the victim becomes aggressive and bands together with his fellow countrymen to criticize in a derogatory way the host country, its ways, and its people; and the cocktail circuit fairly boils with stereotyping which offers an easy rationalization for one's troubles. The complaining includes remarks as, "These people are stupid," "They are a bunch of thieves," and "You can't get anything done here." The extreme symptoms of culture shock in this stage are characterized by Oberg as excessive washing of the hands and great concern over drinking water, food, bedding, fear of physical contact with native domestics, an absent minded, far-away stare (known as the tropical stare), a feeling of dependence, fits of anger over unavoidable minor frustrations, a morbid fear of being cheated or robbed, great concern over minor infections and pain, and a terrible yearning to be back home.

The patients who successfully weather the second stage of culture shock more than likely survive. This is why the third stage is termed the *recovery*

---

[11] *Ibid.*, pp. 187-194; and Kalervo Oberg, "Do You Suffer From Cultural Shock?" published in 10 installments in *Abadan Today* (June 13-July 4, 1956).

stage. At this time the individual begins to understand the cues which orient him in the new culture, he knows enough of the language so as not to be completely isolated and the solutions to the ordinary problems of living are worked out without undue frustration. The best test of recovery is a returning sense of humor. When one can joke about his plight and at the same time speak with authority and pride about the new country, recovery is nearing the complete stage.

When complete or full recovery is achieved, the fourth and final stage known as the *adjustment* stage is evident. This does not mean that the individual waxes eloquent about everything in the new country, but simply that he does not rebel against its people or customs; in other words he has lost his anxiety. In a matter of time most people develop a real sense of exhilaration about their overseas experience and some actually begin finding considerable shortcomings with their native lands. When they cut vacations and leaves short to get back to their foreign home, there is actually some suspicion that culture shock is working in reverse.

A knowledge of culture shock and its symptoms is very important to all persons planning to work or reside in a foreign country for a considerable length of time. There is no guarantee of immunization in this knowledge, but it usually suffices to reduce the severity of the shock.

CULTURE CONFLICT

Mention has already been made of the conflict which may develop between members of one culture with those of another. This is such an important aspect of culture that culture conflict needs emphasizing as a special concept. The pages of history are filled with accounts of war and of suffering which can be traced directly to conflicts in culture. Every student is familiar with the religious wars which have interlaced the history of known civilizations. Different beliefs with regard to government, economic practices, family life, and education have all served to trigger culture conflict. In the United States, there are currently many persons who evince culture conflict in their views toward such things as birth control, the reading of the Bible in schools, and race relations. The conflict between parents and their teen-age children, can in some part be termed culture conflict and the problems of recent immigrants mentioned before are of this nature.

Conflict is considered a normative element of social organization, as brought out in Chapter 2. This accounts for the fact that sociologists are seriously engaged in developing subspecialties, such as military sociology. The latter is concerned with "organized activities for carrying on aggression against other societies," among other things.[12]

[12] Charles H. Coates and Roland J. Pellegrin, *Military Sociology: A Study of American Military Institutions and Military Life* (University Park, Maryland, The Social Science Press, 1965), p. 10 (Distributed by the Maryland Book Exchange, Inc., College Park, Maryland).

SUMMARY

The socialization process is never complete, but progress toward socialization can be measured in terms of the individual's knowledge and understanding of his culture. In this sense, the goal of socialization can be said to be culture or the individual's acquaintance with culture. This is why it is important to understand the problems related to this concept.

The first distinction which should be clear is that between culture and society. These terms are often confused because of their interdependency. They can be readily distinguished if one thinks of a society as made up of people who generally act according to certain basic rules of conduct which they have worked out and which represent their culture. The form or content of culture is classified as material in nature if it has a concrete existence, that is, if it can be seen and felt. It is classified as nonmaterial in nature if it is used by man to explain and guide his actions, but represents nothing more tangible than creations of his mind. The norms, which are the ideas and values that relate to standards of behavior, are in the realm of the nonmaterial culture, as are the social institutions, which are made up of clusters of norms.

The structural components of culture provide a frame of reference for cataloguing and analyzing concrete behavior. Culture traits are seen as the smallest unit of culture which can be identified. A combination of related traits which make up the necessary requirements for given activities are visualized as a culture complex. Culture complexes in turn combine to form larger units of culture called culture patterns. The latter represent cultural configurations such as sports, whereas a culture complex would be simply *the* sport of football, and a culture trait would be a football or a rule of football.

Three levels of cultural participation can be distinguished. Cultural universals include the traits which represent required behavior by all members of a society, such as the necessity of a wedding license to legalize marriage. In situations where the individual has a choice of how to act, such as the many "proper" ways in which a friend may be greeted, cultural alternatives are provided. When, by virtue of special training or qualities, a person is permitted to behave in a way that is denied others, a cultural specialty is in evidence. The work of doctors, teachers, and lawyers include many specialties.

All large, complex societies are characterized by the presence of groups of persons who have their own somewhat different cultural orientations. The term which is used to describe such groups is subculture. Cultural lag refers to the situation which exists when one aspect of culture falls behind another, such as when technological developments outdate laws. When a practice has completely lost its functional significance, but survives on the basis of custom, it is known as a cultural survival.

Standards of behavior are relative to the culture in which they appear, a phenomenon termed cultural relativity. Ethnocentrism, the practice of evaluating other cultures in terms of one's own, is a problem which stems from the relativeness of culture. Culture shock, the mental state which some people develop when transferred to new cultural settings, is also related to cultural differences. Culture conflict, manifested in wars and in other ways, stems directly from the fact that what one thinks and believes is relative to culture.

From the above it can be seen that most of the behavior of men can be understood in terms of his cultural conditioning or socialization.

Supplementary Readings

Duncan, Otis Dudley, *William F. Ogburn on Culture and Social Change* (Chicago, The University of Chicago Press, 1964), Chapters 4-7; excerpts also in INKELES; LASSWELL ET AL.; LEE; and BM.

Foster, George M., *Traditional Cultures: and the Impact of Technological Change* (New York, Harper & Row, 1962), pp. 187-194.

Minor, Horace, "Body Ritual Among the Nacirema," *American Anthropologist*, Vol. 58 (June, 1956), pp. 503-507; and also in MIZRUCHI; O'BRIEN ET AL.; ROSS; and YOUNG & MACK.

Polsky, Ned, "The Village Beat Scene: Summer, 1960," *Dissent*, Vol. 8 (1961), pp. 339-359; and also in ROSS.

Redfield, Robert, "A Critique of Cultural Relativism," Selection in SCHULER ET AL. taken from *The Primitive World and Its Transformations* (Ithaca, New York, Cornell University Press, 1953), pp. 130-164.

Redfield, Robert, "The Folk Society," *American Journal of Sociology*, Vol. 52 (January, 1947), pp. 293-308; and also in BARRON; LASSWELL ET AL.; and BM.

Sumner, William Graham, *Folkways* (Boston, Ginn, 1904 and 1940 Centennial Edition). Excerpts also in CUBER & HARROFF; LASSWELL ET AL.; LEE; MIZRUCHI; and SCHULER ET AL.

Yinger, J. Milton, "Contraculture and Subculture," *American Sociological Review*, Vol. 25 (October, 1960), pp. 625-635; and also in BARRON.

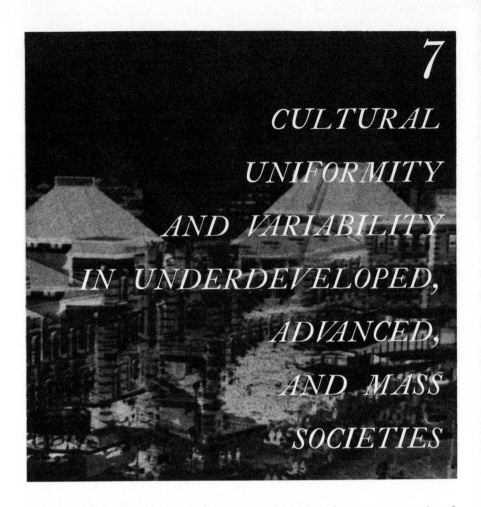

7
CULTURAL UNIFORMITY AND VARIABILITY IN UNDERDEVELOPED, ADVANCED, AND MASS SOCIETIES

Preceding discussions have made it quite clear that there is great cultural variability between individuals and among societies. The reasons for this variability were also accounted for by reference to differential socialization. It is the purpose of this chapter to (1) distinguish more clearly between the elements and forms of culture which represent near universal uniformities and the content of culture which varies infinitely in its concrete details; (2) compare and contrast cultural variation within and between advanced and underdeveloped societies; (3) and describe the evolving mass society and outline its implications for cultural uniformity and variability.

UNIVERSAL CULTURE PATTERNS

The major uniformities among cultures center around the capabilities and basic needs of humans. In every society there are special types of behavior related to communication, legitimate procreation, government, economic activity, recreation, and religion. These are the elements and forms of cultures —the institutional structures—which constitute and may be recognized as the universal culture patterns.

Since the universal patterns of culture are seen and appear at what might be termed a generic level of analysis, it is not incongruent to note that there is wide variability in the way that these patterns are manifested. In fact, the main body of this chapter is devoted to illustrations of this sort of variability. The conceptual picture which the student should develop is one which portrays universal patterns as behavior related to certain basic functions, biologically or culturally derived, which are found everywhere. These types of functions are illustrated by the list of universal behavior patterns which is reproduced below. There is no need to elaborate on these patterns because of their universal nature—they are so much a part of all cultures that to do more than provide a list is to introduce redundancy. However, each pattern varies infinitely in its specific manifestations; language, for example, is universal; but languages other than our own are always termed "foreign." The study of this type of variation is both enlightening and interesting. Cultural variation is so widespread as to justify a rather extended descriptive treatment.

BEHAVIOR PATTERNS FOUND IN EVERY KNOWN HUMAN SOCIETY[1]

(1) Language—not necessarily written language.

(2) A sex-marriage-family system—widely variable as to details of content, but always present.

(3) Age and sex differentiation, that is, a somewhat different and often strikingly different set of behaviors required of males and females and of persons of different ages.

(4) Government functions—a generally recognized set of ideas and practices designed to handle disputes between persons, between groups, and to make for cooperation to preserve the society from aggression.

(5) Religion—a set of ideas and practices relating to the society's conception of the sacred.

(6) Knowledge—a system of propositions regarded as true or correct, sometimes built up as mythology, and sometimes by more or less scientific derivation.

(7) Economic system—a set of beliefs and practices pertaining to making a living, property rights, and the relative importance of economic matters in the whole scheme of life.

(8) Recreational or play activities—participation in certain activities for amusement.

[1] John F. Cuber, *Sociology*, 5th ed. (New York, Appleton-Century-Crofts, 1963), p. 111.

(9) Art—some kind of attempt to portray situations and create objects in nonutilitarian form.

VARIABILITY AMONG CULTURES

There are many ways by which the great variation is the specific content of culture might be illustrated. However, the purposes of this volume are served by giving rather brief illustrations which show some of the major differences between and within distinct types of societies set apart on the basis of complexity and social organization. In this regard, the so-called primitive tribes are not treated specifically, although they might be classified as peoples from underdeveloped areas.

VARIATION IN ADVANCED CULTURES

The advent of modern systems of communication and the ease with which travel can be accomplished might lead one to the conclusion that modern advanced cultures would differ less than cultures with simpler forms of social organization. A recent study by Howard E. Bracey of subdivision life in the United States and England provides evidence to the contrary by showing the infinite variety of subtle and not so subtle ways in which neighbors and neighborly activities differ in these two countries.[2] The findings of this study with regard to educational, religious, and recreational aspects of life suffice to illustrate how two major advanced cultures with highly complex forms of social organization can vary even though they share language and other gross features of culture.

Bracey discovered that American householders placed a good school system at the top of the list of their reasons for choosing a neighborhood in which to live. English householders, in contrast, did not mention schools at all among their reasons for selecting a given home site. The explanation for this difference in outlook is found in the fact that the English educational system is a national one and standards do not vary greatly from locality to locality. Since American schools are generally controlled and operated by local government bodies, there is considerable variation in curricula, standards, and facilities. Americans are thus justified in showing real concern over schools. Schools are also closely related to many government, economic, and social aspects of life and in this way account for a great number of national cultural peculiarities.[3]

[2] Howard E. Bracey, *Neighbors: Subdivision Life in England and the United States* (Baton Rouge, Louisiana, Louisiana State University Press, 1964).
[3] *Ibid.*, pp. 39-41.

The churches and the pattern of church going in the United States and England also exhibit a number of striking contrasts, according to Bracey. In the first place, he found that many more Americans than British in his sample population attended church with a degree of regularity—an estimated 75%–80% compared to 10%–12%. Another impressive difference was seen in the effort which American churches made to get newcomers to attend church services and in general to make them welcome in the neighborhood. By contrast, in no English home studied was there evidence that any church had made an effort to get the newcomer and his family to attend church services. After outlining the various social activities planned by rather typical American churches for their teen-agers, including game rooms, places to dance, and canteens where refreshments are served, Bracey states, "One shudders to think of the reaction of the average English minister who discovered such goings-on in the Church Hall on Sunday evening."[4] Other differences are pointed out, but the above suffice to illustrate cultural variability in this important social institution.

A final illustration of cultural variation is found in one type of neighborhood party described by Bracey—the coffee party. He comments that the importance of the coffee party in the life of American women is difficult to describe to an Englishwoman, because her life has no counterpart. The suggestion that as many as a dozen neighbors might get together in one of their homes during the morning or afternoon for a coffee party would be unthinkable to the Englishwoman, both because of her notions of propriety and because of economic and transportation reasons. Bracey explains that afternoon tea has never been the social occasion for English working and professional classes which Americans have been led to believe. He goes on to observe that "The American homemaker has been brought up on coffee and 'cokes' since she was a teen-ager," and states that he found coffee drinking and parties fascinating because, ". . . it was so different from anything we had met in England and perhaps because we envied the speed with which neighbors were able to 'get acquainted' through the everyday action of drinking a simply prepared non-alcoholic beverage."[5]

VARIABILITY WITHIN MODERN ADVANCED CULTURES

There is, as brought out before, much cultural variation within modern societies as well as between modern societies. In the United States, regional differences in speech patterns, in typical dress, and in food habits are mere minor manifestations of these differences. More important and involved cultural variations are found in values associated with such important issues as

[4] *Ibid.*, pp. 146-162.
[5] *Ibid.*, p. 98.

race relations, states rights, and socialized medicine. Green accounts for variability within American culture (all advanced cultures parallel one another to
a notable degree) in terms of three characteristics as follows: (1) A relative
lack of institutional integration—that is, the major social institutions such as
the family, the church, government, and education are isolated in function
and activity. (2) Separative organization—that is, the myriads of local, state,
and national organizations, some of which are opposed in purposes. (3) Specialization—that is, such a high degree of division of labor that culture is
transmitted in a very complex manner.[6]

The following account serves to demonstrate how culturally derived
differences are manifested within a modern societal setting. It is taken from
a study of how important planning decisions were reached in Chicago, one of
the three largest cities in the United States, concerning a public housing
project.[7] The specific problem was to decide where the sites for low-rent public housing projects were to be located. The project was originally inspired by
federal housing assistance acts and public opinion in support of slum clearance
projects. The preliminary proposal for the project, which called for building
40,000 units of low-rent housing over a six-year period, was worked out by
the Chicago Housing Authority and put before the mayor and City Council
in July, 1949. Because of many problems, it was not until 1952 that the site
questions were largely decided upon. Those who were most active in the
politics of this particular decision-making were divided into five major opinion-interest groups by Meyerson and Banfield, the authors of the study. These
groups reflect the cultural variability which occurs within a modern society,
and at the same time suggest why this cultural variability arises and the types
of problems which it creates.[8]

The first opinion-interest group was composed mainly of department store
executives, who had business interests in the Loop area. Their concern
stemmed from the steady exodus of people to the suburbs. They wanted the
slum areas near them redeveloped into "high class" neighborhoods. The members of this group, by virtue of their wealth and close relationships with real
estate and management interests, had considerable influence. However, because they did not live locally, but in the fashionable suburbs around Chicago
and because of other reasons—one being they were accustomed to buying
what they wanted—they usually did not appear openly on the political scene.

The second opinion-interest group was made up of North Side residents
—an area which included most of the city's high-income neighborhoods. These
individuals were in large measure Republican, middle class, and civic minded.
They were characterized by the authors as likely to take the editorial and
news columns seriously and to vote a split ticket. The spokesmen for numerous

[6] Arnold W. Green, Sociology: An Analysis of Life in Modern Society, 4th ed.
(New York, McGraw-Hill, 1964), pp. 103-110.
[7] Martin Meyerson and Edward C. Banfield, Politics, Planning, and the Public
Interest (New York, Free Press, 1964).
[8] Ibid., Chapter 4.

church and civic organizations lived on the North Side and they had a personal humanitarian interest in the public housing issue. All residents tended to take a "community-regarding" rather than a self- or "neighborhood-regarding" view toward this issue and generally supported the public housing project.

The slum dwellers themselves made up a third opinion-interest group, but were far from being united in support of the housing project. Their diversity of opinion stemmed from the fact that only about one-third of the families were eligible to live in it. Obviously, the Authority could not provide places of business for persons such as prostitutes, gamblers, dope peddlers, and other "undesirable" types. At the same time many "respectable" people in the slum area earned just enough to make them ineligible for new housing and still others had incomes—from rentals, pushcarts, and various other operations—which would be affected by the clearance activities. Some persons held positions, such as politicians, clergymen, storekeepers, which had been gained on the basis of personal relationships with their clients or church members. These persons were not too enthusiastic about starting over again. The group to be affected most, was therefore quite split on the housing issue, and understandably so.

The Negroes, who constituted the largest group among slum dwellers, represented another group with a division of opinion and interest. Those with the lowest income, the underlying broad base of the Negro population, had much to gain by the destruction of the slum, and clearly were in favor of the housing project. However, the middle- and upper-class Negroes were actively opposed to project sites which would move Negroes to outlying areas of the city because they feared the continuation of segregation. The slogan "Slum clearance is Negro clearance," which was prominently displayed, reflected this fear. Others were against the change, but not for such humanitarian reasons. They were the local political and business leaders, who stood to lose their positions of power.

The last opinion-interest group, and by far the most influential one, was made up of the owners and residents of the "conservation" areas, those not to be cleared. Most of the inhabitants of these neighborhoods were white and a large percentage lived in single-family dwellings which they owned. Most belonged to the Catholic church and generally Irish-Catholics were predominant. It was against these neighborhoods that the Negro slums were exerting a steady and irresistible pressure to expand. The residents of the conservation area were dismayed at the prospect of their "nice" neighborhoods becoming engulfed by the slum. The strong resistance which these neighborhoods put up against the public housing projects was based on the following factors, according to Meyerson and Banfield.[9] First, a fear of criminals; second, a dislike of people who were dirty, unkempt, and disorderly; third, a dislike of people with whom they were not compatible, that is, could not communicate with as neighbors; fourth, a dislike of people of lower social status; fifth, a

[9] *Ibid.*, p. 103.

dislike of people who maintained different manners of speech, dress, etc.; sixth, a dislike of people with different physical characteristics (other than skin color); seventh, a dislike of people with a different skin color. The reader will readily see that many of the factors were associated with racial and ethnic prejudice. At the same time a purely racial explanation of the feelings exhibited would be unrealistic because of the importance of economic and social class factors definitely involved.

The above brief account of how the people in one city were divided on an important and generally recommended project to better the living conditions in a city, dramatically demonstrates cultural variability. Whatever personality or situational factors were involved in the behavior patterns manifested, they were far outweighed by the cultural factors. In other words, the various opinion-interest groups were members of subcultures and, as such, socialized in such a way that they considered their behavior relating to the public housing issue the right or normative way.

VARIATION BETWEEN UNDERDEVELOPED AND ADVANCED CULTURES

The world is divided roughly into societies which are termed developed, that is, have a relatively high degree of cultural advancement, and those which are underdeveloped. There are various definitions of "underdeveloped," but the consensus of most writers has been captured by Eugene Staley. He defines an underdeveloped country as, "A country characterized by mass poverty which is chronic and not the result of some temporary misfortune, and by obsolete methods of production and social organization, which means that the poverty is not entirely due to poor natural resources and hence could presumably be lessened by methods already proved in other countries."[10] The underdeveloped countries have commanded such international attention within the recent past that they cannot be overlooked in terms of cultural characteristics.[11] They encompass all examples of preliterate cultures as well as most of the world's people who have not advanced beyond rudimentary plow culture.

The contrast between advanced and underdeveloped cultures is marked by two important differences. First, underdeveloped cultures tend to be more homogeneous and integrated culturally speaking. All the major social institutions are quite closely integrated, because living and making a living is an integral part of religion, government, and family life, as well as that of economic life. Specialization is also much less extensive, as much of the work is still done by hand. Poverty, ignorance, superstition, and traditionalism are

[10] Eugene Staley, *The Future of Underdeveloped Countries* (New York, Harper & Row, 1954), p. 13.
[11] See Lyle W. Shannon, *Underdeveloped Areas* (New York, Harper & Row, 1957).

usual characteristics of underdeveloped cultures. To illustrate, as late as 1958, Agaton P. Pal found that approximately 78 percent of the beliefs of rural household heads in Negros Oriental Province of the Phillipines about health had no basis in science. Over two-thirds of these household heads attributed sickness to "bad air," which was said to be ordinary air that was used by the evil spirits as a medium of their power in doing harm to man.[12]

The range of cultural variation between underdeveloped and advanced cultures is such that it is almost beyond the scope of comprehension. Suffice to say that individuals socialized in one or the other are separated by wide cultural differences. Perhaps, the way that food is produced provides the most dramatic emphasis for this fact, since the more effort and time men take to fill their stomachs, the less time they have to develop other aspects of their culture. The descriptions below highlight differences in the "culture" of food production in underdeveloped and advanced cultures. Figure 7-1 graphically portrays other gaps between these broad classes of countries.

The way of life of the Ibans, who live in Borneo, is characteristic of vast numbers of people in Asia, Africa, and Latin America.[13] Farming, for them, is not only an occupation but a total pattern of living interwoven with religion and all other aspects of culture. The Iban farmer typically cares for three acres of land located on a steep, rugged mountainside rising from the bank of the Regang River. The rainfall of the Sarawak area of Borneo averages 160 inches a year and forces nearly all the farmers to practice shifting from one field to another—moving back to a field about every twelfth year. At this time they burn the heavy growth of brush and timber which has grown, an operation which leaves a residue of ashes to nourish the rice plants. The burning operation is critical, since the rainless days are few. The vegetation must be cut and allowed to dry at just the right time, or crop failure will result. The Iban farmer prays for a "good burn" which will make his paddies of rice "happy, fertile, and thrifty."

All farming operations carried on by the Ibans are steeped in custom. Once the men have chopped down and burned the overgrowth on the fields, they have very little else to do until threshing time but set traps for wild animals. The women plant the rice by making a small hole with a stick for the seed. Several varieties of paddies are differentiated, including the sacred *paddy pun*. The latter is planted last and special rituals are conducted for it during the growing and harvesting season, because a "happy" crop of *paddy pun* helps to assure a good yield of the main crop. At the proper time, the women do the harvesting, collecting the heads of rice one at a time. Threshing is a joint work effort between men and women and something of a social

[12] Agaton P. Pal, *The Resources, Levels of Living, and Aspirations of Rural Households in Negros Oriental* (Diliman, Quezon City, University of the Phillipines, Community Development Research Council, 1963), pp. 190-191.

[13] This account of farming in underdeveloped countries is taken from I. W. Moomaw, *To Hunger No More* (New York, Friendship Press, Inc., 1963), pp. 73-76.

FIGURE 7-1. *The Gap between the Underdeveloped and the Developed Countries in Health and Education (top graphs), and in Economy (bottom graphs).*

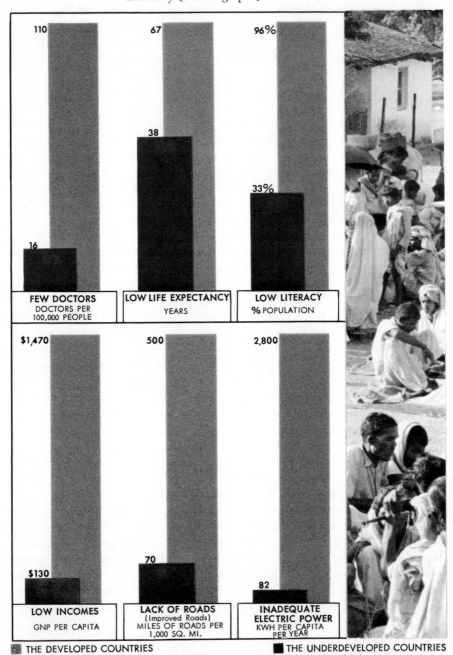

110   67   96%

38

33%

16

FEW DOCTORS
DOCTORS PER
100,000 PEOPLE

LOW LIFE EXPECTANCY
YEARS

LOW LITERACY
% POPULATION

$1,470   500   2,800

70

82

$130

LOW INCOMES
GNP PER CAPITA

LACK OF ROADS
(Improved Roads)
MILES OF ROADS PER
1,000 SQ. MI.

**INADEQUATE
ELECTRIC POWER**
KWH PER CAPITA
PER YEAR

THE DEVELOPED COUNTRIES   THE UNDERDEVELOPED COUNTRIES

Source: *A New Program for a Decade of Development for Underdeveloped Areas of the World* (Washington, D.C., Bureau of Public Affairs, 1961), p. 7. Photograph courtesy of United Nations Organization.

occasion. The men tread out the rice grains with their bare feet, rather than resort to use of a flail of some type. To the Ibans, rice is too precious to be disrespected by beating. Once the rice is cleaned it is stored in freshly cleaned vessels and according to correct ritual to assure it will last longer.

The customs of the Iban, as mentioned, are quite typical of the type of cultural practice followed in underdeveloped countries. Some variations occur, but they are a matter of slight degree. For example, on Mindanao in the Phillipines, a farmer might plow his small field with a carabao rather than prepare it by hand. In West Pakistan, the middle-class farmer might have the usual hand tools supplemented by a yoke of oxen and simple plows and cultivators. In some areas of Mexico, the burro is used as the primary beast of burden; in the Andes of Ecuador, the slopes are still dug by hand with hoes and spades. In all these areas, the natural elements are faced with primitive tools and knowledge at best.

In contrast to the ways of farmers in underdeveloped countries, a typical farmer in an advanced nation is a highly trained business and technical expert. A review of James Svedman's story and of his operation dramatizes the nature of farming in societies, such as the United States.[14]

Jim Svedman was born in Windsor, Colorado in 1926 on a farm homesteaded by his grandfather in 1885. He started raising cattle in 4-H Club work in 1939. Income from his 4-H projects and a merit scholarship financed his five years of college—he earned a bachelor's degree in animal husbandry and did a year of graduate work in business law and economics at Colorado State University. His wife, Shirley, earned a degree in dietetics and nutrition and helps him manage a farm of over 1400 acres near Fort Collins, Colorado. About one-third of his land is irrigated and 1250 acres more or less are in crop land, the remainder is in pasture. He grows corn, alfalfa, barley, winter wheat, and sugar beets on a commercial scale. He feeds about 1000 head of cattle in partnership with his father each year and produces most of the feed for them. He has a registered herd of about 100 Angus cattle besides his commercial herd. Jim pays close attention to fertilizing, rotating crops, stripcropping, contour farming, stubble mulching, controlled irrigation, and land leveling. His careful management has brought substantial reductions in death losses and improvements in his fattening ration and feeding system. He adds new equipment, such as tractors, hay harvesting equipment, and automatic feeding systems when he is convinced they will pay off in savings of crops and reduction in productions costs. He employs only two or three men the year round.

The Svedmans are active in a number of civic, church, and community groups, and in cattlemen's organizations and the Farm Bureau. Jim seeks technical assistance from such agencies as the Extension Service, the Soil Conservation Service, and the Agricultural Stabilization and Conservation Com-

[14] Taken from *After A Hundred Years* (Washington, D. C., The Yearbook of Agriculture 1962, U. S. Dept. of Agriculture), pp. 64-65.

mittee. Mrs. Svedman helps her husband keep the detailed records that are essential to modern farming operations. Their house is full of labor-saving devices, including a two-way radio to her husband's pick-up truck.

It is belaboring the obvious to note the cultural contrasts in the way an Iban-type farmer and a Jim Svedman-type farmer go about their business. These two types of operations are repeated in the cultural arenas which are respectively termed underdeveloped and developed societies.

MASS SOCIETY: ITS IMPLICATIONS FOR CULTURAL UNIFORMITY AND VARIABILITY

The growing preoccupation with what has been termed *mass society* is manifested in almost all current literature devoted to evolving social trends. Many themes and various approaches are highlighted, but all writers suggest that drastic cultural changes are involved. This fact makes it fitting to conclude the present chapter with a review of the characteristics attributed to this phenomenon. It should be noted that the concern expressed by many over the meaning of mass society is closely related to man's continuous attempt to understand changes in his social environment. It also relates directly to the matter of cultural uniformity and variability.

DEFINITION OF "MASS SOCIETY"

It is misrepresentative to imply that there is a clear consensus of opinion about what a mass society is, that is, about the nature of its cultural structure and its social organization. There is, however, an agreement on the general features of such a society. The latter provides a basis for a definition: A **mass society** *is a society within which the overall activities of the total population are integrated to such an extent that all daily behavior is given direction by a central core of institutionalized structures.*[15]

In the interest of clarifying the above definition, it may be pointed out that the integration necessary for mass society is dependent on (1) a technological and industrial order which is advanced to the degree that facile communication is possible throughout the society and (2) an occupational structure which is highly diversified and specialized. The latter includes a highly developed bureaucratic type of organization, with the key position being in the hands of a "power elite." (See Chapter 11.)

A mass society is also dependent on an urbanized setting. Such a setting

[15] For an elaboration of this definition see Philip Olson, Ed., *America as a Mass Society* (New York, The Free Press, 1963), pp. 3-4.

provides an arena for its distinctive operations. The popular or mass culture which is used as a guide to behavior flows everywhere from large urban centers. The flow is made possible by communication networks, which could not exist without the facilities of large cities. The large metropolises also provide homes and/or work sites for the power elite, and make possible the centralization upon which bureaucratic activity is dependent.

THE EMERGENT NATURE OF MASS SOCIETY

There is a very real temptation to speak of mass society as something which is here and now. This impression must be corrected because as yet there is no example of a completed mass society. In fact there is a very real question if such a type of social structure can ever be fully realized. Any large-scale society will always manifest regional cultural variation and these "natural" differences may be too great to be removed. Leaving this possibility aside, it is still true that mass society is seen only in an emerging state at the present time. This fact does not invalidate the concept nor does it preclude an analysis of the basic features of such a society.

THE BASIC FEATURES OF MASS SOCIETY

The important features or characteristics of mass society were identified in the definition presented at the beginning of this discussion. These features are elaborated here.

(1) *Large size:* The mass society must, by virtue of its nature, be a large-scale society. This means it must include populations which number in millions and encompass rather large territorial masses. Both criteria rule out small-scale societies whether they be clan or tribal groups or national entities. However, a mere aggregation of people on a large block of land is not enough to make a mass society; these requirements only set a minimum condition.

(2) *Urban character:* As noted before, an urban setting is a prerequisite for a mass society. When people live in scattered places or in small communities, it is impossible to develop the kind of relationships which provide the foundation for a mass culture. Again, urbanization is only a condition for mass society. It is not synonymous with it.

(3) *Mass production:* This feature of mass society is characterized by mass production of standardized products. Such production, as Martindale points out, is a special type of factory production in which the principles of power, accuracy, economy, system, continuity, speed, and repetition are realized. Efficiency is achieved by the transfer of skill from the artisan to the machine, and increased by the standardization of machines themselves. It is

improved by the synchronization of men and machines. The ultimate in mass production is achieved in the operation of the continuous flow system where raw materials are transferred entirely by machines controlled by a few men manipulating an electronic control board.[16]

(4) *Mass marketing:* Leaving aside the academic question of whether market demand must precede production, it is possible to say that mass marketing is a vital component of mass society. Once mass production gets under way, it tends to be self-generating in the sense of mass markets. The former artisan is forced into taking a job in a factory or into service institutions and he thus becomes a more prolific consumer of goods. Martindale describes what he terms strategies which are designed to create sufficient demand for an ever increasing production. The first strategy is to change behavior in such a way that consumer credit and installment buying effectively replace old practices of savings and cash payments. The second strategy is to create markets by the transformation of tastes. Massive advertising campaigns are the vehicle for the latter and success is achieved by (a) motivating the consumer to select one brand rather than another of essentially the same product and (b) creating psychological obsolescence, that is, stimulating a desire for change even though the item possessed is still serviceable.[17]

(5) *"Welfare" government controls:* In a mass society the activity of all citizens is controlled closely to protect the innocent or weak and to provide for certain needs of the total populace. To this end, everyone is subjected to an increasing number of taxes, rules, regulations, and other types of controls. On the one hand, licenses, insurance (of all types—such as liability, health, old-age security), standardization (of drugs and commodities, for example), and conformity (such as immunization programs, auto safety devices, and building codes) are required. On the other hand, the indigent are fed, clothed, and given medical attention, the unfortunate are provided with elaborate systems of care and rehabilitation, education is provided for the capable but needy, and so on. There is continuing pressure to pass more laws and, in effect, to make more and more people behave alike. In this way the mass society character of institutionalized behavior is developed and fostered.

(6) *Mass communication:* The question arises as to how conformity can be quickly achieved in such areas as production and consumption, and how government controls can be efficiently disseminated and enforced. The answer lies in mass communication. A mass society must have ways of spreading mass culture—such as through telephone, radio, television, newspapers, and by transportation means. Harvey Cox, who has helped portray the character of mass society in his *The Secular City,* uses two images to dramatize mass communication. The first is the *switchboard,* which he sees as linking human beings everywhere to one another through modern electronics magic. The

---

[16] Don Martindale, *American Society* (Princeton, New Jersey, Van Nostrand, 1960), pp. 3-23.

[17] *Ibid.,* pp. 24-50.

second is the *cloverleaf* (on super highways) which symbolizes simultaneous mobility in many directions.[18]

The above listed features help portray the nature of mass society. We turn now to the implications for social life, which are inherent in this type of cultural configuration.

THE IMPLICATIONS OF MASS SOCIETY FOR PERSONALITY AND COMMUNITY

There are two schools of thought regarding what happens to personality in mass society, and in turn to the quality of interpersonal relations which make up social structures through the level of community. The proponents of the first view are clearly pessimistic, and foresee the day when man will be motivated by nothing more idealistic than crass opportunism and communities will be held together by nothing stronger than superficial relationships. The second more optimistic view admits the inevitability of the disappearance of certain traditional social structures, like small rural neighborhoods and communities, but maintains that the individual will derive a larger degree of personal freedom through being released from the time-consuming obligations which structures of this type demand.

The writers who represent the pessimistic approach are well known in current social science literature. Such names as Riesman, Whyte, Mills, Fromm, and Martindale come readily to mind.[19] In *The Lonely Crowd*, Riesman speaks of "other-direction," as a condition that occurs when individuals look to others for their standards of correct and incorrect behavior. Whyte writes of an "organization man" who belongs first and foremost to a corporation and secondarily to wife and home. Mills notes a "higher immorality" which is illustrated by the disregard of members of the power elite for moral precepts. Fromm describes the development of a "marketing orientation" as an evolving type of insecure social relation. Goffman talks of a new personality type characterized by the working out and employment of a "routine" to create the impression necessary to manipulate others. It can be deduced that if mass society follows the general outline described by these writers very little will remain of traditionally conceived moral orders. In extreme form, it can be conceived that a state completely devoid of individuality and community, with personal freedoms and initiative gone and people responding to central agencies run by an elite, will evolve.

[18] Harvey Cox, *The Secular City* (New York, Macmillan, 1965), p. 38.
[19] See David Riesman, Ruel Denny, and Nathan Glazer, *The Lonely Crowd* (New Haven, Yale University Press, 1950); William Whyte, Jr., *The Organization Man* (New York, Simon and Schuster, 1956); C. Wright Mills, *The Power Elite* (New York, Oxford University Press, 1956); Erich Fromm, *Escape From Freedom* (New York, Farrar & Rinehart, 1941); and Martindale, *op. cit.*

The champions of the optimistic view are much fewer in number. They are typified by Shils and Bell, who see the mass society as freeing man from old restricting bonds.[20] Adherents of this school generally agree that central unifying social institutions will grow, but they do not see this trend as contributing to the loss of individual and collective freedoms. Rather they feel that all persons will experience a new opportunity for creativity because of the release from previous systems of self-control and self-denial. The rise of an urban-industrial order is seen as providing a much broader opportunity for self-expression and achievement than possible under old primordial, traditional, and hierarchal social orders.

In conclusion, it is impossible at present to evaluate the full implications of mass society. There is no question that the consequences of a mass type of social structure are of vital import and of the fact that much of the world, including major parts of Europe and North America, seems to be moving in this direction. In this context, it may be noted that the varying points of view and interpretations regarding mass society has led Shils to term this concept "a specter haunting sociologists."[21] Although it may take time, perhaps more than many of us have, the trend toward mass society will eventually be assessed and its nature more fully recognized.[22] Whatever the final development may be, the principles of cultural uniformity and diversity can safely be predicted to prevail.

SUMMARY

All cultures include certain patterns, such as language, religion and family systems, which are termed uniformities. However, each cultural group exhibits infinite variation in the specific ways in which these patterns are expressed. These variations were highlighted in this chapter through the use of concrete illustrations.

Findings from a study of subdivision life in the United States and England were utilized to show how two advanced cultures can and do differ one from the other. These findings indicated that American householders were concerned with the local school system in seeking a new home while English householders were not, because English schools were more uniform in program. It was also found that Americans attended church with a greater degree of regularity and that the morning or afternoon type of coffee party, so common in the United States, had no counterpart in England.

The cultural variation within a modern culture was illustrated with an

[20] Daniel Bell, *The End of Ideology* (New York, Free Press, 1960); Edward Shils, "The Theory of Mass Society", selection in Olson, *op. cit.*, pp. 30-47.

[21] *Ibid.*, p. 30.

[22] For a pioneering example of an attempt to empirically test hypotheses about mass society see Richard E. Du Wors, Robert Batsemand, Margaret Daffron, "The 'Mass Society' and 'Community' Analyses of the Social Present," *Papers*, C. P. S. A. Conference on Statistics (1960).

account of the differences of opinion and interest of Chicago residents. Five groups were distinguished in terms of their opinions regarding the selection of sites for a slum-clearance housing project. The department store executives of the Loop Area wanted to redevelop a "high class" neighborhood to upgrade business; the North Side residents, not specifically affected one way or another, adopted a community wide view that the project was worthwhile; the slum dwellers to be directly affected were for or against the project, depending on their income and the legality of their activities, and their vested interests. The Negroes were also split in opinion; some upper-class Negroes feared further segregation and were against the project; lower-class Negroes were for it in the hope of improved housing. The people living near by the slums were definitely opposed to public housing projects on the basis of social class and race prejudices and other related factors.

Variation between underdeveloped and advanced cultures was demonstrated by describing farming operations in Borneo and the United States. Farming in the Iban section of Borneo was described as a hand operation on a small plot carried on within the context of deeply held customs and practices and a near subsistence level existence. The farm in the United States described was a highly commercial operation, carried on in a rational manner and utilizing the latest technology.

The discussion of mass society which concluded the chapter was designed to show the emerging pattern in advanced cultures. A mass society was described as one in which all activities were directed from centralized agencies. It was further characterized as having a large number of people, a large territorial base, a high degree of urbanization, mass production, mass marketing, mass communication, and welfare-type government controls. Some feel mass society will mean the loss of both individual freedom and the spirit of community, whereas others think the individual will enjoy an escape from the restrictions of traditional groups and have more opportunity for expression. The future must decide which view is the correct one.

Supplementary Readings

Bracey, Howard E., *Neighbors: Subdivision Life in England and the United States* (Baton Rouge, Louisiana, Louisiana State University Press, 1964).

Martindale, Don, *American Society* (Princeton, New Jersey, Van Nostrand, 1960), Chapter 1-4.

Meyerson, Martin, and Edward C. Banfield, *Politics, Planning and the Public Interest* (New York, Free Press, 1964).

Olson, Philip, Ed., *America as a Mass Society* (New York, Free Press, 1963).

Shannon, Lyle W., *Underdeveloped Areas* (New York, Harper & Row, 1957).

Staley, Eugene, *The Future of Underdeveloped Countries* (New York, Harper & Row, 1954).

Wilensky, Harold L., "Mass Society and Mass Culture," *American Sociological Review*, Vol. 29 (April, 1964), pp. 173-196; and also in MIZRUCHI.

8

SOCIAL CHANGE AND CULTURE GROWTH

Once it is understood what is meant by culture and cultural differences, it is logical to raise questions related to the growth of culture within a given society and to the processes by which changes in culture are brought about. This chapter is designed to answer queries of the above nature. The first section of the chapter sets the stage by defining and characterizing social change. The second section describes the process of communication, without which there would be no transmission of culture and hence no culture change. Subsequent discussions explain how new elements of culture are obtained and elaborate on the processes involved in the acceptance of innovations.

SOCIAL CHANGE IN PERSPECTIVE

Social change can be defined in a general way as *a continuous process which is manifested in alterations in social relationships.* Although this understanding is in keeping with popular usage, there are certain characteristics of social change which are not generally appreciated. First, social change is a normative aspect of social life. All societies (and cultures) are, in fact, constantly changing although some much more rapidly than others. Wilbert Moore underscores this point by entitling the first chapter in his monograph on

Social Change, "The Normality of Change."[1] The universality of change is explained in terms of the stress–strain element of social system, as brought out in Chapter 2.[2]

The second point regarding social change which should be noted concerns an interpretation. There are some sociologists who distinguish between social and cultural change, maintaining that the former involves changes in the structural aspects of society and the latter changes in the culture, *per se.* This distinction is a highly technical one because in concrete situations it is virtually impossible to decide which type of change is apparent. Therefore, the common approach is to use the two terms interchangeably. This is the understanding followed throughout this chapter and text.

Another understanding about social change which must be made clear, is that this process cannot be explained in terms of single causal factors. Robin Williams makes it clear that monofactorial determinisms have gone out of fashion, and that modern sociology will not revert to one-sided interpretations which attribute change to a single set of factors.[3] The numerous and diverse changes which are of interest to sociologists are too complex to be explained by a simple formula.

Finally, it must be noted that there exists no systematic theory of change which answers all the questions relating to this phenomenon. An adequate theory of change, according to Olaf Larson and Everett Rogers, should encompass these basic questions[4]: (1) What is it that has changed? (2) How much has it changed (extent)? (3) How quickly has it changed (rate)? (4) What were the conditions before and after change? (5) What occurred during the transition? (6) What were the stimuli that induced the change? (7) Through what mechanism(s) did change occur? (8) What brought stabilization at a particular point in change? (9) Can directionality be observed in change?

The discussions which follow indicate how many of the answers to the above questions have been derived. There is also a considerable body of social change theory presented. Yet, it would be misleading to indicate that any one theory answered all the questions, or that it has been determined that there should actually be a separate social change theory.[5]

[1] Wilbert E. Moore, *Social Change* (Englewood Cliffs, New Jersey, Prentice-Hall, 1963).

[2] Alvin L. Bertrand, "The Stress–Strain Element of Social Systems: A Micro Theory of Conflict and Change," *Social Forces,* Vol. 42 (October, 1963), pp. 1-9.

[3] Robin M. Williams, Jr., "American Society in Transition," selection in James H. Copp, Ed., *Our Changing Rural Society: Perspectives and Trends* (Ames, Iowa, Iowa State University Press, 1964), p. 30.

[4] Olaf M. Larson and Everett M. Rogers, "Rural Society in Transition: The American Setting," in James H. Copp (ed.), *Our Changing Rural Society: Perspectives and Trends* (Ames, Iowa: Iowa State University Press, 1964), p. 40.

[5] The argument has been well stated that a theory of change should be part of a general theory of action, rather than a unique phenomenon. See Robert C. Bealer and Frederick C. Fliegel, "A Reconsideration of Social Change in Rural Sociology," selection in Copp, *op. cit.,* pp. 288-306.

THE NATURE AND FUNCTION
OF COMMUNICATION

HUMAN COMMUNICATION DEFINED

It is quite obvious that communication is at the heart of culture. This is true because in its broadest sense **communication** can be defined as a process by which information (culture traits) is transferred from one place (individual) to another. Smith, Bealer, and Sim emphasize this understanding in their treatment of communication. They state that communication is the process by which a message which includes a set of meanings is conveyed to a person or persons so clearly that the meanings received are equivalent to those which the initiator(s) of the message intended.[6] The above definition is focused on human communication since this is a text in sociology. The fact that there is a type of communication among lower forms of life and between man and various animals is amply demonstrated, and indeed, a case for communication between machines can be made. However, these matters are properly discussed as part of total communications theory which is much broader than human communication.

Human communication is unique in one major respect. It is accomplished through *learned, arbitrary* signs or symbols manifested primarily in that part of culture which is referred to as language. Said another way, the words and other symbols used to communicate are not instinctive or inborn nor is there a necessary similarity between the sign or symbol and the thing it refers to. For example, the young English or French child would never, as an act of voluntary creativity, produce noises that sound precisely like "dog" or "chien." Much less would he associate such a sound with a certain type of animal until he was properly conditioned, that is, learned to associate the above sounds with the meaning intended.

Language permits man to communicate beyond the level of simple feelings and intentions. Highly complicated sentiments, involved abstract ideas, elaborate mechanisms of one kind or another, as well as detailed instructions are all successfully communicated through language, written or spoken. In fact, it is doubtful if one could think very coherently, much less communicate, without language.

LANGUAGE AS AN INTEGRAL
PART OF CULTURE

The integral place which language holds in culture is manifested in several ways. First, it is a cardinal principle of sociology and anthropology that one

[6] Joel Smith, Robert C. Bealer, and Francis M. Sim, "Communication and the 'Consequences' of Communication," *Sociological Inquiry* (Winter, 1962), p. 112.

must know a group's language intimately before he can fully understand the culture of the group. The subtleties of humor, of pathos, and of finer meanings are generally lost without an intimate knowledge of language. The writer is reminded of the embarassment of a friend, a serious student of the Cantonese dialect of China, who used the wrong intonation at a formal Chinese gathering, changing the meaning of the words *"Ngoh-tei chung-yi tong-yan"* from "I like Chinese people" to "I like to kill people."

A second way in which culture and language are closely linked is seen in the necessity to invent new words or combine old words in a new way to identify new items of culture. The space age has literally inserted dozens of words in the vocabularies of all modern languages. In English, words such as "sputnik," "blast-off," and "count-down" were little known before the successful orbiting of space crafts in the mid 1950's.

Language is also important to the spread of culture and this is the third way in which language as an important part of culture can be envisioned. The student, for example, who is proficient in one or more foreign languages has a great advantage in studying topics which are widely treated in foreign journals and texts. Free communication fosters many exchanges which language barriers can block or slow down, as any person who has traveled in foreign lands well knows.

FUNCTIONS OF HUMAN COMMUNICATION

The purposes for communicating are varied but have been grouped into two general classes—to inform and to motivate—by Alfred Kuhn.[7] Kuhn construes the information purpose or function as designed to alter a receiver's concepts (what he knows) and the motivation function as designed to change the receiver's preferences or feelings. All human communication is subject to rather involved, though interesting problems which stem from the above functions. This is especially true since most actual communication has an interactional dimension as well as an informative or motivational aspect. A parent does not just instruct his child about "the facts of life"; he seeks to influence the child's attitude about morality, as well as to add to his information. Likewise, a teacher might not only attempt to motivate a bright student toward advanced education, but to influence his views and feelings about the worth of science and the responsibility of the gifted person.

PROBLEMS OF HUMAN COMMUNICATION

The problems of human communication are essentially problems of *signs*. A whole discipline, *semiotics,* is devoted to the study (or science) of signs. A

---

[7] Alfred Kuhn, *The Study of Society: A Unified Approach* (Homewood, Illinois, Richard D. Irwin, Inc., and The Dorsey Press, 1963), p. 181.

sign may be defined as, ". . . a collection of signals which constitute a sufficient cue for purposes of communication."[8] A cue is sufficient when it contains enough information to enable the identification of a *referent,* that is, a concept or other sign.

Semiotics is divided into three main branches including: *Semantics, Syntactics,* and *Pragmatics.* Each of the latter deals with a particular type of problem in communication.

Semantics is concerned with the relation of signs to their referents. Problems in semantics arise in the interpretation of words and other language signs. Such problems are so common as to make illustrations redundant. Suffice it to point out that many a debate (or domestic scene) could be avoided if the words (or intonations and expressions) used by the first party conveyed the meaning intended to the second party. It is, of course, impossible to obtain precisely the same meaning, because no two persons ever have quite the same conceptualization.

Syntactics problems are inherent in misinterpretations of the relations of signs to other signs. Verbal syntax, as the student is aware, is referred to as grammar and grammatical problems are legion. The relationship of nouns to verbs, the place of punctuations, and word orders all represent problems of this nature. In a humorous vein, the instruction of the old South Louisiana Frenchman to the new "Anglo" hired hand to "throw the cow over the fence, some hay" is an illustration of a syntactic problem in communication. A rearrangement of words ("throw some hay over the fence to the cow") would have reduced the problem, if not solved it completely.

Pragmatics deals with the relations between signs and their users and problems stem from the ability of signs to convey the desired information. In a way, such problems are the practical ones of whether the purpose or function of communication intended is accomplished. The teacher of an introductory course in sociology will quickly introduce such a problem to his students if he insists on using the language and level of abstraction which are found in the professional journals of the discipline. The practical problem of communication, introducing the student to sociology in this instance, can only be accomplished if the sender (professor) and receivers (students) share common concepts.

CONDITIONS FOR SUCCESSFUL COMMUNICATION

In concluding this brief discussion of human communication as a part of culture which is directly related to culture growth and change, it is appropriate to review the conditions under which communication can be successful. The conditions listed here are set forth by Kuhn and relate to the specific types of

[8] *Ibid.,* p. 155.

problems outlined above.[9] First, the communicator must use signs (words) in the repertoire of the receiver of the communication—there must be common cues for conceptualization. Second, each sign used must have the same referent (meaning) for the communicator and the receiver of the communication, at least within certain rather narrow limits. Third, the communicator and the receiver of the communication must accept the same syntactic rules, for example, the same technical interpretations of grammar, which apply to one or several signs. When these conditions are met, the pragmatic goal of transferring information relatively accurately will be achieved, and culture will be transmitted to this extent. The test of communication is *feedback,* that is, the degree to which the performance or behavior response of the receiver of the communication corresponds to that called for by the communicator. Feedback may be discerned from quite informal signs, such as a smile or nod of approval, or from extremely formal tests, as a written examination on lecture materials.

THE GROWTH AND SPREAD OF CULTURE

The preceding discussion attempted to show how culture is transmitted from one individual to another via communication of some type. However, before culture can be passed on, it must be acquired in some way by the members of a society. There are two ways through which a given culture may secure new elements, that is, be modified in some way. The first is by the *invention* (including discovery) of new things and ideas; the second is through *diffusion,* which involves the borrowing of cultural items from other societies. These two sources of new traits and patterns of culture are considered in turn.

INVENTION AS A SOURCE OF NEW CULTURE

DEFINITION OF INVENTION. The term invention connotes the creation of something new. An inventor is thus someone who is able to combine known elements of culture into something not heretofore known. This something may be in the form of a new artifact, that is, in the realm of material culture; or it may be a new idea of some sort. The latter point is important because of the popular tendency to think of inventions solely in terms of such things as mechanical devices. A new plan for consolidating local units of government is just as much an invention as a tubeless automobile tire.

    Some scholars differentiate between invention and discovery on the basis

[9] *Ibid.,* p. 182.

that the latter simply involves the perception, often fortuituous, of something not previously recognized or if recognized, not understood to have a particular significance. Invention, by contrast, is seen as having a degree of manipulation over and beyond mere detection. However well taken this point may be, there is difficulty in clearly distinguishing between the two terms. Each invention has some element of discovery and most discoveries can be traced to some new understanding. For the latter reasons, **invention** is used here as a generic or inclusive term to mean the creation of new ideas or things, either through manipulation of previously known elements or by the perception of relationships not previously recognized.

RELATION OF INVENTION TO CULTURAL BASE. It was stated in the previous section that culture grows through invention. With this fact in mind, it becomes important to know what factors affect the rate of invention in a given culture. Ogburn addressed himself to this question, and after a great deal of study and research concluded that invention was the function of three variables: (1) mental ability, (2) demand, and (3) existing knowledge.[10] Ogburn's reference to mental ability was simply to the pool of brain power available. He saw large countries as being well endowed in this sense. By "demand," Ogburn had reference to felt needs which built up to such proportions that the whole society might divert a substantial part of its energies to satisfying the need. An illustration is the demand for many types of devices in order to more successfully prosecute a war. Training and education must be an inherent part of demand as a function of invention, else the demand is likely not to be effective. "Existing knowledge" is directly related to invention in that a new invention is in Ogburn's words, ". . . a combination of existing inventions and knowledge."[11] The broader the base of technology, for example, the greater variety and abundance of inventions one can expect. Ogburn, in fact, saw very little hindrance to continued technological progress in modern advanced societies.

The above listed variables clearly establish the relationship of invention to the culture of a given society. In traditional cultures, where there is no broad base of science, invention is likely to proceed from trial-and-error attempts to improve existing ways. However, it is not usual that invention is encouraged, nor is it assured that an invention will be accepted. Frequently there is strong resistance to change in keeping with the traditional nature of the culture—in fact, this may be what keeps it traditional. In a highly advanced culture, inventions are not only anticipated but planned for. Huge sums of money are dedicated to the development of new things, as a space ship or a polio vaccine, and top scientists are put to work in elaborate facilities to bring about the desired invention.

[10] William F. Ogburn, *The Social Effects of Aviation* (New York, Houghton Mifflin, 1946), pp. 58-59.
[11] *Ibid.*, p. 59.

Invention is related to the culture base in a second way, which is of importance. This may be seen in the way that the broad value orientation of a given people dictates the type of inventions they strive for. For example, in the United States, would-be inventors think largely in terms of monetary returns for their efforts. They thus strive for an invention which will capture mass fancy or fit into a widely utilized technological complex. In a society which did not reward the individual directly in proportion to the demand for his invention, the rate and focus of invention could be expected to be considerably different. The latter part of this chapter, which is devoted to the acceptance of innovations, will provide many illustrations of the relationship between values and the adoption and acceptance of new things.

DIFFUSION: THE SPREAD OF CULTURE

DEFINITION OF DIFFUSION. A given society may enrich its culture by borrowing culture traits or patterns from other societies as well as by invention. The process by which an item of culture spreads geographically from its source of invention is known as **diffusion.** Diffusion is differentiated from **social inheritance,** which is the transmission of culture from one generation to the next and is solely through time rather than space and time. Both diffusion and social inheritance may be involved in the socialization process, however.

Culture may be diffused between individuals, between regions, between nations or indeed, between the members of any spatially separated groups. Diffusion is direct when there is actual personal exchange, as when an invading army takes over a conquered nation or immigrants settle in a new country; it is indirect when culture is spread through means of communication such as magazines, newspapers, books, and movies.

FACTORS RELATED TO RATE OF CULTURAL DIFFUSION. The rate of culture diffusion is dependent on a number of factors. Some of the more important criteria which govern the speed with which items of culture will be diffused, are as follows: (1) The form of culture—normally material items are diffused much faster than ideas or ideologies. For example, the Japanese have been much quicker to adopt the dress and technology of western nations than their religious and government systems. (2) Degree of coercion—a conquered people must submit to the wishes of their masters, and to the extent one cultural group has power over another group it can force the group to accept its ways. (3) Intensity of cultural contact—when communication is facile and continuous, diffusion is usually faster than when contacts are difficult and accomplished only on occasion. Peoples living on national borders are usually more adept in the language of neighboring nations than persons living in the interior of their nations, for this reason. (4) Amount of cultural inertia—many individuals and groups resist culture change for a variety of reasons. It may be that they hold strong taboos against change of certain types, or it may be that apathy prevails to such an extent that only those new things requiring little or no effort are accepted. (5) The presence of a crisis situation —people who face disasters such as floods, hurricanes, and earthquakes, accept any new way which offers advantages in meeting their crisis situations rather quickly, both at the individual and group level.

THE STUDY AND ANALYSIS OF DIFFUSION. Rogers has identified four elements which are important in the analysis of culture diffusion, that is, in the study of this process.[12] The first is the *innovation,* defined as an idea perceived as new, whether or not it is a recent invention. In a particular diffusion study, the researcher would attempt to isolate the innovation or innovations and trace its or their movement in space. The second element of importance in the analysis of diffusion is *communication.* Here the essence of study is the interaction which takes place as one person communicates or passes on a new idea to another person, either directly or indirectly.

The third element of analysis is the *social system*(s) in which the individual(s) operates with relation to the given innovation. In some instances group decisions are imposed on all, such as in the case of the acceptance of fluoridation of drinking water. Social systems also encourage or discourage the adoption of innovations in all the ways which affect the rate of culture diffusion outlined previously.

The final element which must be analyzed in the study of diffusion is the *time element.* The adoption process, as will be shown in the following parts of this chapter, involves several steps. Those persons who adopt readily have characteristics which differ from those persons who wait or take more time to adopt. The researcher is interested in time, both as a measure of innovations and as a basis for classifying rate of diffusion.

ACCEPTANCE OF INNOVATIONS

Diffusion research by sociologists (especially rural sociologists) became extremely popular during the 1950's. Because of the relative recency of this type of research, there has not been too much time for systematic syntheses of the findings of the investigations made. However, the results disseminated to date have attracted a large audience and aroused much interest in professional and lay circles alike. It is remarkable that 80,000 copies of a report prepared by a committee of rural sociologists, in 1955, on the general conclusions from diffusion studies, were distributed by 1962, with translations available in sev-

[12] Everett M. Rogers, *Diffusion of Innovations* (New York, Free Press, 1962), pp. 12-20.

eral languages.[13] Also since 1955, a talk prepared by two Iowa State University sociologists has been delivered by them or by persons using material prepared by them before literally hundreds of groups of persons having roles as "change agents," such as agricultural extension workers, salesmen, dealers, advertising agency personnel, and managers.[14]

The discussion which follows is an attempt to pull together the more important findings of studies that were addressed to problems relating to the acceptance of innovations.[15]

PURPOSE OF STUDIES OF ACCEPTANCE OF INNOVATIONS

It is true that much of the world is now in a cultural milieu of rapid change. Even in the relatively underdeveloped countries, new items of technology and new ideologies are being introduced at an increasingly accelerated rate. In fact, these countries are now aptly being called the developing countries. Despite these facts, the time lag required for an innovation to reach wide acceptance remains extensive, even in nations where attitudes toward science and technology are generally favorable. A good illustration comes from the United States, where the average farmer currently supports himself and approximately 30 other persons; but if the farmer adopted already developed and proven innovations he could easily support an additional 20 persons. It has also been estimated that the average United States school lags 25 years behind the best known practices in teaching.[16]

The purpose of research on the acceptance of innovations is inherent in the above paragraph. In explicit terms it is to determine methods by which the adoption of new ideas might be hastened. Before this objective can be accomplished, diffusion problems must be studied (and solved) and the findings of such studies disseminated. The remainder of this chapter is devoted to the latter task. In this regard, the reader should not assume that the diffusion and adoption of innovations is always good, or indeed desirable. As will be seen later, change sometimes precipitates social disorganization, which can be quite disruptive to societal progress. Too, the diffusion of given innovations may be undesirable because of implications for moral norms. A new way of counterfeiting money may be diffused among the criminal element with disastrous effect on a given community.

[13] *How Farm People Accept New Ideas,* North Central Rural Sociology Subcommittee for the Study of Diffusion of Farm Practices. (Ames, Iowa Agricultural Extension Service Special Report 15.—RS.)

[14] Professors George M. Beal and Joe M. Bohlen.

[15] The works of George M. Beal, Joe M. Bohlen, Everett M. Rogers, and of Eugene Wilkening previously cited and of Herbert F. Lionberger served as a primary source for the material used. See Herbert F. Lionberger, *Adoption of New Ideas and Practices* (Ames, Iowa, Iowa State University Press, 1960).

[16] Rogers, *op. cit.,* p. 2.

THE ADOPTION PROCESS

Rogers defines the adoption of innovations process as, ". . . the mental process through which an individual passes from first hearing about an innovation to final adoption."[17] This process is similar to learning and other decision-making processes.

Studies made indicate that it is rare for an individual to adopt a new practice or idea as soon as he hears about it. This is especially true in some cultural settings where people are notably conservative. The research done indicates that the final decision to use a new idea is usually the result of a series of influences operating over a period of time.

The adoption process, for most people, includes a series of distinguishable stages. The first stage, is the *awareness stage*. It is simply the time at which first knowledge of the idea or practice is gained. Awareness, of course, is a function of communication, which has already been treated in general terms.

Once a person is aware of something new, he may, if he favors it to some degree, go to a second adoption process stage, *interest*. At this stage, the individual is led to seek detailed information regarding the innovation. In other words, his behavior becomes purposive in that he seeks more knowledge. When enough information to assess the usefulness of the innovation is obtained, the individual arrives at the third adoption stage, which is termed the *evaluation stage*. It is at this point, that he weighs the evidence at hand, and decides whether or not to go on to the next stage, the *trial stage*. During the trial stage, a limited application of the innovation is generally attempted. If tests prove successful, the final *adoption stage* follows in logical sequence.

The above five stages are not always followed in the adoption process, nor do they always represent a set pattern of progression. Such factors as social class, education, age, and sex characteristics affect the adoption process. Also, an innovation may be rejected, that is, a decision made not to adopt, at any stage in the adoption process. When rejection occurs after adoption, the behavior is termed a *discontinuance*. The latter has not been studied extensively, but research available suggests the extent of discontinuances varies with the nature of the idea and with the characteristics of the individuals adopting.

CHARACTERISTICS OF INNOVATIONS WHICH AFFECT RATE OF ADOPTION

When given cultures are studied, it is found that some innovations require years to become widely used, whereas others are adopted almost overnight. This phenomenon has prompted research designed to answer questions related

[17] *Ibid.*, p. 76.

to the characteristics of innovations which might affect the rate at which they would be diffused in given social systems. This research has shown that the adoption of a new practice or technical item is not always directly correlated with the usefulness or the advantage the innovation may have for the adopter. What is important, is the individual's perception of its usefulness; in other words, how he sees the advantages it may or may not have for him. Rogers cites the story of Analoze—"the pill that failed"—to illustrate this point. Analoze was developed as a combination pain killer and stomach sweetener, cherry flavored, which could be taken without water. Preliminary tests proved highly successful and an elaborate advertising campaign using the words "works without water" was unleashed in several major cities being used as test market areas. Although dealers were enthusiastic and early prospects appeared bright, the public did not come through with purchases and the product was finally withdrawn from the market cities. After much study and investigation it was decided that the fatal mistake had been the "works without water" feature. People just could not believe that a tablet dissolved in the mouth was as effective as one taken with water.[18]

Innovations which possess the following characteristics are more readily adopted than others. First, the innovation must have *relative advantage*. Sometimes the advantage is not readily recognized and must await a crisis situation where its superiority can be proved. For example, 15 years are normally required for an education innovation to be adopted by the first three percent of the public schools in the United States. However, 87 percent of the schools, in one study, adopted driver training education in the first 15 years. Why was driver education adopted so readily? Principally, because the need for driver education had been called to national attention by high accident rates and because local car dealers, local insurance companies, and the local branches of the American Automobile Association encouraged this change by showing its advantages.[19]

The second characteristic an innovation must have is *compatibility*. This term is used to indicate the degree to which the new idea is consistent with currently held values and patterns of behavior. In one study, only 24 percent of the upper class in a community had adopted television, whereas 72 percent of the lower class had accepted this innovation. Conversely, 72 percent of the upper class played canasta, but only 12 percent of the lower class indulged in this pastime. The conclusion reached was that these innovations were not compatible with social class values in each instance of low acceptance.[20]

The third characteristic of an innovation important to its adoption is its *complexity*. If it is too complicated and involves learning too many new and

---

[18] *Ibid.*, pp. 122-123.

[19] Donald H. Ross, "Rate of Diffusion of Driver Education," *Safety Education,* Vol. 32 (1952), pp. 16-32.

[20] Saxon Graham, "Class and Conservatism in the Adoption of Innovations," *Human Relations,* Vol. 9 (February, 1956), pp. 91-100.

unfamiliar procedures, it will likely be passed up. One reason chess is not more popular is its complexity—it has detailed and difficult features which have to be mastered and many persons do not feel the reward is worth the effort.

The fourth characteristic of an innovation which determines how quickly it will be accepted is *divisibility*. This refers to its nature. Can it be tried on a limited basis? Some things can not be divided into units, and individuals have to go "whole-hog." A farmer, for instance, might hesitate before buying an expensive harvester costing thousands of dollars, but might be willing to try one sack of a new fertilizer immediately.

The fifth and final characteristic which determines how quickly an innovation will be accepted is its *communicability*. Some things are easily observed and readily described. Others are not. Some can be shown in a short demonstration. Others must wait a number of years before results are apparent. Television swamped the nation in a few short years, because it was easily demonstrated and highly visible.

ADOPTER OF INNOVATIONS CATEGORIES (IDEAL TYPES)

From preceding discussions it is clear that all individuals do not adopt innovations at the same time. The fact that adoption in a given social system is along a continuum has made it possible to classify adopters into categories or classes on the basis of their innovativeness. In this instance, as is generally true where classifications are made somewhat arbitrarily, the classes listed are ideal types which have conceptual utility, but which may be somewhat more difficult to identify in a concrete setting. Studies have shown that adopter distributions follow a bell-shaped curve over time, which is to say the same relative percentage of each adopter class can be expected wherever a normal situation is found.

On the basis of innovativeness, that is, the degree to which an individual is relatively earlier in the adoption of a practice than the other members of his social system, five categories of adopters have been listed. The first class is tagged the *innovators*. Innovators are known as a venturesome group, and are characterized by a strong desire to try out new ideas. In other words, they do things that are considered rash by the majority of people. They are willing to take a risk, even though it means an occasional failure, to test out a new idea.

The second adopter category takes in the persons known as the *early adopter*. Persons in this class are usually respected in their local communities. They are the local leaders and are just a little ahead of the average individual. Their great contribution is to serve as guides for the mass of the more conservative persons.

Third on the adopter list are the persons classified as the *early majority*. This class includes those who are deliberate in their decision-making, but who are a bit ahead of the diehards or confirmed skeptics.

The fourth class of adopters is known as the *late majority*. This class refrains from accepting a new idea or practice until the weight of public opinion is overwhelmingly in favor of it. They are the "show-me" element in all groups.

The last adopter category is called, rather appropriately, the *laggards*. Individuals in this class are extremely conservative and traditional in behavior, and tend to live in rather isolated places. When laggards finally adopt an idea, there is a likelihood it has already been superceded by something newer.

CHARACTERISTICS OF EARLY ADOPTERS

It is important to know the characteristics of *early adopters* because of their important role in getting general acceptance of new and improved practices. The characteristics of this class have been subjected to considerable research, and it is possible to give a general description of this type of individual.

First, early adopters are younger in age than later adopters. Second, they have higher social status than later adopters. Third, they are characterized by a more favorable financial position than later adopters. Fourth, they make more use of impersonal sources of information, such as the radio, newspaper, magazines, and television, than later adopters. Fifth, they are more likely to use sources of information outside their local communities—that is, national and international sources—than later adopters. Sixth, they are also more likely to use sources of information which are in closer contact with the origin or originator of the new ideas. For example, they may work more closely with representatives of industrial firms, educators, or experiment stations. They also utilize a greater number of different information sources than do later adopters. Finally, early adopters are characterized by higher education and a different type of mental ability than later adopters. In this regard early adopters are less rigid and dogmatic in their thinking.

It can be seen from the above that early adopters are more cosmopolitan than later adopters and that their activities are not as closely tied to their local communities. They are usually the opinion leaders of their communities.

THE ROLE OF THE CHANGE AGENT

The present discussion on acceptance of innovations is logically closed with a brief look at the *change agent* whose purpose is to promote innovation. By definition, *a **change agent** is a person who is formally dedicated to influencing decisions to adopt innovations.* Change agents may have the interests of their clients foremost, such as county agricultural extension agents and Peace Corp workers, or they may have primarily selfish interests, as salesmen or other persons with "causes." Whatever their motivation, change agents function as a communication link between two social systems, a professional system (government or private) and a client system.

Studies have been made of the success of various types of change agents and some preliminary conclusions are worthy of consideration here. First, commercial change agents (salesmen or dealers, for example) are more important at the awareness and trial stages of the adoption process and have more hearing from early adopters than later adopters. Professional change agents (teachers or county agents, for example) are given more creditability than commercial persons and thus function more efficiently at the evaluation and adoption stages of the adoption process. This is explained by the fact that many clients feel the commercial change agent has a vested interest in promoting the overadoption of new ideas. Second, all change agents appear to have more communication with the higher status members. However, the agent must tailor his program of change to fit the cultural values and experience of his clients, whatever their status, if he is to be successful. Thirdly, change agents have more success in the long run if they concern themselves more with improving the competence of their clients in evaluating the new ideas they wish to have accepted and less with the promotion of a given item. For example, a chemical spray salesman will sell more spray to farmers after they are acquainted with the value of insecticides generally. Finally, change agents are more successful when they concentrate their efforts upon the opinion leaders in a social system during the early stages of the introduction of an innovation, which they hope to diffuse widely. If they succeed in selling the opinion leaders, their chances of getting widespread acceptance is much greater.

SOCIAL MOVEMENTS AND SOCIAL CHANGE

The discussions in this chapter until now have been concerned with culture change generated from the development, discovery, or borrowing of something new or different. In this last section of the chapter we consider briefly the relation of *social movements* to culture change.

Some writers consider social change on a societal scale to be a direct function of social movements. They define the latter as collective enterprises which arise to establish a new order of some type.[21] Such a definition is limited since some "collective enterprises" are for the purpose of maintaining the *status quo,* rather than for bringing about a change. For this reason a definition which is less restrictive is in order. In a general sense *a* **social movement** *may be defined as a conscious striving by a relatively large group of persons to bring about or resist societal change.*[22] It should be noted that those movements which have as

[21] For one example see Herbert Blumer, "Social Movements," article in Alfred McClung Lee, Ed., *College Outline Series: Principles of Sociology* (New York, Barnes & Noble, 1951), pp. 199-220.

[22] Ralph H. Turner and Lewis M. Killian, *Collective Behavior* (Englewood Cliffs, New Jersey, Prentice-Hall, 1957), p. 308.

their objective some type of change are likely to receive more attention than those designed to resist change. This fact has led Heberle to point out that one of the main criteria of most social movements is some sort of change in the basic institutions of property and labor relations.[23]

Social movements must be distinguished from social trends and what have been called *cultural drifts*. Trends, such as industrialization, urbanization, or centralization of government are not usually promoted by organized groups as are social movements—they simply occur over a period of time. **Cultural drifts** are identified as the process whereby minor alterations in culture which occur over a period of time eventually change the whole way of life of a society.[24] The development of a democratic society from a feudal society would be an example.

THE STAGES OF SOCIAL MOVEMENTS

Social movements originate at periods of time when a considerable number of persons become deeply dissatisfied with certain cultural developments. Usually dissatisfaction stems from feelings that inequalities exist or from feelings of insecurity and frustrations. Such feelings represent the first stage of social movements, known as the *social unrest* stage.[25] Not all unrest culminates in a genuine social movement, but it is the necessary first step.

The second stage of social movements is identified as the *excitement* or *popular* stage. It is at this time that attention becomes focused on an enemy and there is widespread feeling that the trouble should be eliminated by direct action. This is the time when the voice of a prophet or prophets with plans for deliverance begins to be heard above the clamor of the masses. Slogans and mottos are coined, appeals are made to abstract sentiments and idealized values —with the end result that a great deal of enthusiasm is generated.

If the movement continues, the third stage is one of *formalized organization*. At this point a definite organization takes shape, including a characteristic bureaucratic structure, with a hierarchy of officials, definite goals and a network of local leaders and workers. It is at this period that the "cause" is proclaimed far and wide, with every effort being made to attain the desired goal. If little or no success crowns these efforts, the movement fizzles out rather quickly.

The fourth stage, *institutionalization*, is the final aim of all movements. It is characterized by general societal acceptance of the goal sought. If some particular change has been the goal, such as women's suffrage, institutionalization

[23] Rudolf Heberle, *Social Movements* (New York, Appleton-Century-Crofts, 1951), pp. 6-10.

[24] Melville J. Herskovits, *Man and His Works* (New York, Knopf, 1949), p. 581.

[25] W. E. Gettys is given credit for first suggesting these stages of a social movement. See Carl Dawson and W. E. Gettys, *Introduction to Sociology* (New York, Ronald, 1934), pp. 708-709.

may come about at once, such as when laws are passed legalizing voting rights for women. When the movement is concerned with more general goals, such as civil rights, it may take some time for general acceptance to come about.

It is interesting to note that the members of the bureaucratic structure of a social movement literally work themselves out of business by accomplishing their goals. They may try to perpetuate themselves by adopting a new objective, but this is seldom a successful maneuver. Most movements disappear soon after achievement of their objectives.

TYPES OF SOCIAL MOVEMENTS

There are a number of ways to classify social movements because of their many characteristics. Some are secular in nature, others sacred; some are inclusive of whole national groups, others appeal only to smaller special-interest associations; some have one kind of leader and some another. However, several important ideal types can be recognized, and a listing of these is helpful in understanding the concept of social movements.

Reform movements are perhaps the most popular, if one uses numbers as a measure of popularity. Such movements are concerned with modifying some part of society. The history of all nations is spotted with examples of such movements—including themes such as civil rights, conservation, beautification, birth control, poverty and tax reforms among many others.

Movements which have as their goal a perfect society, are classed as *utopian* types. This kind of movement is not as popular today as in the eighteenth and nineteenth centuries, but still persists. Communism is sometimes classified as a utopian movement because it purports to promote a perfect, that is, classless, society.

Revolutionary movements seek to overthrow existing social systems and to replace them with something new and better. This aim serves to distinguish reform movements from revolutionary movements, since the former are only concerned with modifications of the existing system. Rex Hopper, a long-time student of revolution, states that, "The emergence of a numerically significant, economically powerful, and intellectually informed marginal group is one of the earliest indications of an impending revolution."[26] Almost any one can think of a dozen or more revolutionary movements, such as the American Revolution or the French Revolution or at another level the "Progressive Education" movement.

Resistance movements are in contrast to both reform and revolutionary movements. They arise because people feel that impending change or recent change is not desirable. In the United States, several such movements were be-

[26] Rex D. Hopper, "Cybernation, Marginality and Revolution," Selections in Louis Horowitz, Ed., *The New Sociology: Essays in Social Science and Social Theory in Honor of C. Wright Mills* (New York, Oxford University Press, 1965), pp. 313-330.

gun after the Civil Rights Legislation of the 1950's. Two notable examples are The White Citizens' Councils and The John Birch Society. In England, efforts in 1965–1966 to place speed limits on highways met with great resistance, as have many efforts to change to the decimal system of money and to change the patterns of driving on the left side of the road. Almost every change which affects large numbers of people is the target for a resistance movement.

Some writers include *expressive* movements and *migratory* movements as major types of social movements. However, such movements do not follow the same stages of development as reform, revolutionary, and resistance movements and there is some question as to whether or not they represent a different class of phenomenon. It is the writer's feeling that expressive movements—which are characterized by fads and fashions at one level and by rejection of conventional values (such as wearing beards and presenting an unkempt appearance) at another level—are more of a cultural drift than anything else. Migratory movements, such as the exodus of Negroes from the southern part of the United States, or of displaced Europeans, can be seen as social trends which are the by-product of reform or revolutionary movements.

SUMMARY

The culture of any given societal group grows at a greater or lesser rate, depending on a multitude of factors. These factors are implicit in the process of social change, which is defined as alterations in social relationships.

The study of social change begins with communication, which is the process by which information is transferred from one individual to another. Human communication has two primary functions—to inform and to motivate. It is unique in that it is accomplished through learned arbitrary symbols or signs manifested primarily in language. Human communication is subject to three classes of problems, which represent the three main branches of the science of signs—semiotics. Problems in semantics arise in the interpretation of the words or other signs used. Syntactics problems develop from misinterpretations of the relation of signs to other signs, such as the relation of nouns to verbs. Pragmatics problems stem from the inability of signs to convey the desired information. For communication to be successful the communicator must use signs (words) in the repertoire of the receiver, signs which have the same meaning for both and follow rules accepted by both.

Culture grows through the invention of new things and ideas and through the diffusion of cultural items from one society to another. The diffusion of culture is related to several criteria including the form of the cultural item, the degree of coercion involved, the intensity of cultural contact, the amount of cultural inertia, and the presence of a crisis situation.

The adoption of new and improved items of culture by individuals has been the subject of study for some time. These studies indicate the adoption process includes a series of stages, including awareness, interest, evaluation, trial, and adoption. When rejection occurs after adoption, the behavior is termed a discontinuance. Some innovations are adopted more readily than others. The characteristics which appear to enhance chances of adoption are: relative advantage, compatibility, complexity, divisibility, and communicability.

Individuals are classed according to their degree of innovativeness or willingness to accept new cultural items. Those who adopt first are termed innovators, they are followed in turn by early adopters, the early majority, the late majority, and the laggards. Persons who are in the early adopters groups are generally younger, have more money available to them, enjoy higher social status, and make more use of impersonal sources of information. Change agents play an important role in influencing decisions to accept innovations. Commercial change agents (such as salesmen) are more influential at the awareness and trial stages of the adoption process, but professional change agents (such as teachers) function more efficiently at the evaluation and adoption stages.

Social movements are related to social change at the societal level. They are characterized by collective action designed to promote or retard change of some kind. Most movements which persist go through four stages of development or growth. The first or social unrest stage occurs when widespread dissatisfaction with some cultural development comes about. This stage is followed by an excitement or popular stage when a leader is chosen, usually because he is vocal and has a plan for making right whatever is considered wrong. The third stage is one of formal organization into a bureaucratic structure and formalized efforts to achieve the specific goals in mind. Institutionalization, the final stage, occurs when the battle is won and the new order established or defeated, as the case might be. Social movements are typed as reform, utopian, revolutionary, or resistance movements, according to their nature.

Supplementary Readings

Barnett, H. G., *Innovation: The Basis of Cultural Change* (New York, McGraw-Hill, 1953).

Barringer, Herbert, George I. Blanksten, and Raymond W. Mack, *Social Change in Developing Areas* (Cambridge, Massachusetts, Schenkman, 1965).

Berlo, David K., *The Process of Communication* (New York, Holt, Rinehart and Winston, 1960).

Cottrell, W. F., "Death by Dieselization: A Case Study," *American Sociological Review*, Vol. 16 (June, 1951), pp. 358-365; and also in YOUNG & MACK and BM.

Cressey, Paul Frederick, "Chinese Traits in European Civilization: A Study in

Diffusion," *American Sociological Review,* Vol. 10 (October, 1945), pp. 595-604; and also in ROSS.

Foster, George M., *Traditional Cultures: and the Impact of Technological Change* (New York, Harper & Row, 1962), Chapters I and II.

Friedman, Georges, "Technological Change and Human Relations," *British Journal of Sociology,* 1952, pp. 95-116; and also in MIZRUCHI.

Kuhn, Alfred, *The Study of Society: A Unified Approach* (Homewood, Illinois, Richard D. Irwin, Inc. and The Dorsey Press, 1963), Chapter 10.

Moore, Wilbert E., *Social Change* (Englewood Cliffs, New Jersey, Prentice-Hall, 1963).

Rogers, Everett M., *Diffusion of Innovations* (New York, Free Press, 1962).

PART
III
SOCIAL
STRUCTURE
AND
INTERACTION

Preceding discussions have been designed to prepare the student logically for an understanding of social organization. Part III is devoted to this body of theory. Chapter 9 represents a theoretical frame of reference for the study of social groups. The role theory approach followed was developed by Bates and first appeared in the late 1950's. Chapter 10 devoted to social stratification and social mobility, is intended to take the student one step beyond groups in the theory of social structure and organization. It is followed by a discussion of social power in Chapter 11, the key to social organization and structure. The last chapter, Chapter 12, treats the processes and conditions of social adjustment. The traditional interactional social processes are defined and, in addition, two new processes are introduced.

THE STRUCTURE
OF GROUPS
AND
COMPLEX
SOCIAL
SYSTEMS

This chapter is concerned with the structure and functioning of social systems and with various types of social systems. Its majoi purpose is to show how the observed and perceived organization of societies and lesser groups are analyzed. The discussions in the first part of the chapter focus on the concepts which are used in analyses of social structure at all levels. Some of these concepts have already been introduced and defined, but their interrelationships are described here for the first time. In the latter part of the chapter attention is turned to descriptions of the behavior of real actors in concrete situations.

THE DIMENSIONS OF
SOCIAL STRUCTURE

In its commonly accepted definition, a structure denotes a fixed relationship between the elements or parts which make up a whole. We speak of the component parts of an automobile, the various units of an army, and the elements of a chemical compound. A social structure is likewise made up of elements or component units which are related to each other in a definite way, as was implied in Chapter 2, when the ten basic elements of a social system were outlined.

Robin Williams and others explain that social structure, as a concept, has two important dimensions. The first dimension is culture and the second is social organization.[1] Both these concepts have already been defined but they should be briefly reviewed in the present context.

The cultural part of social structure is conceived as a series of ideal patterns of behavior (norms) to which people are oriented: People expect others to behave in certain standard ways in given situations. In contrast, the social-organization aspect of the social structure is seen as the actual behavior of people. The cultural structure is related to social organization in the same way that the written rules of a game, such as football, are related to the actions of players during an actual game. The rules of the game are referred to as "football" and the actions of players during a game are likewise referred to as "football." If "social structure" is substituted for "football" in the above illustration, it may be seen how this term relates to both cultural structure and social organization. The former provides a standard for analyzing the latter. Said another way, by referring to the rulebook, one can determine how player's actions deviate from expected patterns of behavior.

THE ANALYSIS OF SOCIAL STRUCTURE

Group structure, because of its nature, can be analyzed efficiently in terms of role theory. In fact, this approach is the only one which makes it possible to describe the place of an actor in a social structure. Role theory also provides a way to explain how separate social systems are linked together to form social organization networks.[2] In addition, utilization of role theory is efficient analytically. The cultural, situational, and personality aspects of all social systems are automatically accounted for when the elements which are actor-centered are analyzed. Said another way, elements such as belief, sentiment, goals, power,

[1] Robin H. Williams, Jr., *American Society*, 2nd rev. ed. (New York, Knopf, 1960), pp. 22-38.

[2] The writer was faced at this point with the problem of selecting a systematic approach to the theory of social structure, which introductory students might follow readily. His selection of Bates' work in no way discounts the important approaches of Robert K. Merton, Talcott Parsons, Edward A. Shils and Robert P. Bales, Neal Gross, Ward Mason, and Alexander McEachern, among many others. The theory of group structure worked out by Bates and followed closely in this section is presented in three articles: Frederick L. Bates, "Position, Role and Status: A Reformulation of Concepts," *Social Forces*, Vol. 34, No. 4 (May, 1956), pp. 313-321; and Frederick L. Bates, "A Conceptual Analysis of Group Structure," *Social Forces*, Vol. 36, No. 2 (December, 1957), pp. 103-116; and Frederick L. Bates, "Institutions, Organizations, and Communities: A General Theory of Complex Structures," *Pacific Sociological Review*, Vol. 3, No. 2 (Fall, 1960), pp. 59-70.

sanctions, stress–strain, rank, and facilities are inherent in any consideration of norms, roles, status positions, and other actor-related units of social structure.

The structural concepts used in the analysis of social structures have already been introduced with two exceptions.[3] The smallest unit in this conceptual framework is a *norm*. As brought out before, a norm is a learned behavior expectation, held in common by the members of a social system.

The second conceptual unit is the *role*. In an operational or concrete study sense, a role is seen as a part of a status position which is made up of a subset of norms. This subset of norms is distinguishable from other sets of norm included in the status position. Figure 9-1 shows schematically how

FIGURE 9-1.   *Status Position.*

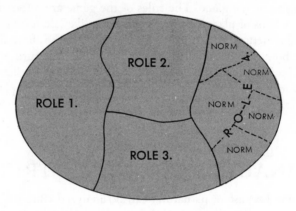

Source: Frederick L. Bates, "Institutions, Organizations, And Communities: A General Theory of Complex Structures," *The Pacific Sociological Review,* Vol. III (Fall, 1960), p. 59.

several norms (the number varies with the role) make up a role; and in turn how several roles make up a *status position*. The latter is the third primary conceptual unit in the analysis of social structure. To illustrate: a father's role of provider is made up of several norms related not only to what he should provide, but what quality he should provide—type of house, kind of food, educational opportunities, for example. But his role of provider is only one of the roles which makes up his status position as father. He must also play such roles as disciplinarian, teacher, and husband, each of which also includes many norms.

[3] Robert J. Dolan worked out the classification presented here which is a modification of Bates' classification. See *An Analysis of the Role Structure of a Complex Occupation with Special Emphasis on the Value and Role Orientations Associated with the County Agent Status* (Ph. D. Dissertation, Louisiana State University, June, 1963), Vol. I.

The fourth analytical concept, *situs,* is used to locate or place an actor in more complex social structures, those including more than one social group. Since this concept has not been introduced previously, some elaboration is in order. In Bates' words, ". . . there are constellations of positions which are *customarily* occupied by a *single actor* or type of actor."[4] The type of action engaged in by the actors may vary widely and include work routines, family life, religious activity, and political actions.

Bates terms the set of positions customarily occupied by the same actor in a multigroup structure as his **situs.** He gives many examples of situses including the following:

(1) *Occupational Situs* (Defined as all the positions a person who pursues a given occupation is expected to occupy). The situs of a college professor might be made up of the following positions:

Position (a): Member of a Department of Instruction.
Position (b): Member of University Courses and Curricula Committee.
Position (c): Member of the Graduate Faculty Council.
Position (d): Member of American Sociological Association.
Position (e): Instructor for social organization class and modern sociological theory seminar.

(2) *Kinship Situs* (Defined as all the positions a person holds in his family groups). Such a situs might include the following positions, among others:

Position (a): Father in a restricted conjugal or nuclear family.
Position (b): Husband in a nuclear family.
Position (c): Son in a family of origin.
Position (d): Brother or sister in a family of origin.
Position (e): Son-in-law, brother-in-law, and so forth, in wife's kin group.

Situses, as roles and status-positions, may vary widely in their characteristics. Some may be composed of only a few simple status-positions, such as the occupational situs of a janitor or other relatively uncomplicated work position. Some may be comprised of many complex status-positions, such as the occupational situs of the president or prime minister of a large nation. Since status-positions are related to prestige and power, it may be expected that the larger number of positions in a given occupational (or other) situs the more prestige and power the holder of the situs will have. A situs is illustrated graphically in Figure 9-2.

The final concept which has utility in primary analyses of social structure is termed *station.* Bates defines **station** as ". . . the location of an actor in the

[4] Frederick L. Bates, "An Outline of Structural Concepts" (Mimeographed, Baton Rouge, Department of Sociology, Louisiana State University, December, 1958).

FIGURE 9-2.   *Situs.*

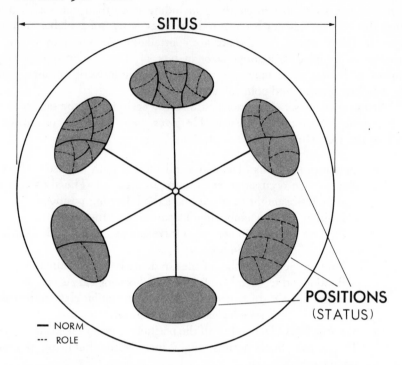

Source: Drawn by Robert J. Dolan from an illustration by Frederick L. Bates. See *An Analysis of the Role Structure of a Complex Occupation With Special Emphasis on the Value and Role Orientations Associated With the County Agent Situs,* Vol. 1 (unpublished dissertation, Louisiana State University, June, 1963), p. 111.

total structure of a community or society . . ." and points out that a person's station is made up of the total collection of his situses.[5] To determine the station of an individual, one has to determine his economic, political, religious, familial, educational, and other situses. See Figure 9-3.[6]

THE STRUCTURE OF A SOCIAL GROUP

It was pointed out in Chapter 2 that social groups are the concrete manifestations of social systems. At that time a group was defined as "two or more people in definable interaction directed toward attaining a common goal and ori-

[5] *Ibid.*

[6] Second-level analytical concepts are not included because they are considered beyond the scope of an introductory volume. Such terms as norm-set, role-set, position-set, and situs-set are at this level of analysis. See Dolan, *op. cit.,* and Robert K. Merton, *Social Theory and Social Structure* (New York, Free Press, 1957), pp. 368-386.

FIGURE 9-3. *Station.*

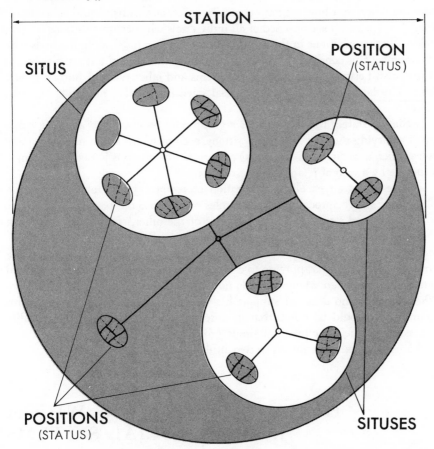

Source: Drawn by Robert J. Dolan from an illustration by Frederick L. Bates. See *An Analysis of the Role Structure of a Complex Occupation With Special Emphasis on the Value and Role Orientations Associated With the County Agent Situs,* Vol. 1 (unpublished dissertation, Louisiana State University, June, 1963), p. 114.

ented through a pattern of structured and shared symbols and expectations."
We are now ready to consider the structure and characteristics of social groups in more detail. A group is a social system which may be isolated from other systems for analytical purposes. A complex organization includes a multigroup system with various forms of linkage between its component social groups.

Bates outlines two conditions which provide a means for distinguishing a group and delineating one group from another. His first condition is the requirement that there be ". . . at least two individuals who interact with each other as the occupants of two positions, each of which contains at least one role reciprocal to a role in the other position." This condition makes it simple to determine when and how a group comes into existence. His second condition is that, ". . . a group is composed of *all* individuals who occupy positions reciprocal to *all other* positions in the group structure and includes no individuals who do not meet this condition."[7] The application of this second test enables one to distinguish between bona fide social systems and other types of human groupings. The latter are of interest to social scientists but are not units of social structure.

Simply stated, the structure of a group may be visualized as being made up of a varying number of status-positions, each of which contains one or more roles which are composed of a set(s) of norms. The group is joined into a single structure by a web of reciprocal role relations.

Bates gives an excellent illustration of reciprocal role relationships. Explaining that, "reciprocality between roles means that the performance of one role implies and requires the performance of the other," he points out that in the structure of a family, ". . . the performance of the father-husband's 'provider role' implies and requires the performance of the wife-mother's 'dependent role.' "[8] The norms applying to each role are culturally defined and societal sanctions are applied when actors do not play their roles in acceptable fashion. The husband who does not support his wife and children may be jailed, for example. It should be noted that in order to have the bilateral reciprocality necessary for the structure of a single group the occupants of the two status-positions involved must always be two different actors.[9]

HUMAN ASSOCIATIONS WHICH ARE NOT SOCIAL SYSTEMS

There are at least three types of sociologically significant human groupings which are not social systems.[10]

(1) *Statistical Aggregates:* Statistical aggregates are the product of sociologists and other social scientists, who form them for study purposes. Examples of such groups are persons in the United States (or the world) with a secondary school education, persons less than 25 years old, or persons earning

[7] Frederick L. Bates, "A Conceptual Analysis of Group Structure," *Social Forces* (published by the University of North Carolina Press), Vol. 36, No. 2 (December, 1957), pp. 104-105.

[8] Bates, "Institutions, Organizations, and Communities: A General Theory of Complex Structures," *op. cit.*, pp. 59-60.

[9] *Ibid.*, p. 62.

[10] Although Bierstedt uses the term association rather than social system or social group, he gives an excellent description of the types of human aggregates that are not groups. See Robert Bierstedt, *The Social Order*, 2nd ed. (McGraw-Hill, 1963), pp. 293-301.

less than $3,000.00 annually. Statistical groups may be sociologically significant, but they fulfill none of the conditions for a social system. They are *not* characterized by social interaction between their members, and there is no other aspect of social organization.

(2) *Societal Classes:* Societal classes are made up of individuals who are similar in some way. These similarities may be biological, such as age, sex, or race; they may come from national heritage, as Italians or Australians; they may be adherents of a particular school of thought, fashion, or creed; or they may be members of an occupational group, such as electricians or sociologists. As long as people who are similar do not band together in some type of formal organization, they represent a societal class. Again, the individuals making up such classes do *not* manifest the characteristics of social organization, although they do recognize one another by some kind of symbol or interest.

(3) *Congregations or assemblies.*[11] A third type of human grouping is called a congregation or assembly because its members congregate or assemble together at one time or another. Such groups have many forms. They include crowds, audiences, casual play groups, church congregations, spectators at a sporting event, passengers on a ship or airplane, and other similar groups. The interaction between members of congregate groups is generally casual, such as a vague mutual awareness of one another. However, there is no reciprocality of roles, such as is found in a bona fide social system.

The line between the various types of groups outlined above is very fine and may change almost instantly. To illustrate, two sociologists living in different towns may be studied as part of a statistical aggregate by a third sociologist. In the course of study, they may become aware of each other and thus assume a societal class relation. After the study is completed they may be called together, along with other sociologists interviewed, to hear the results of the investigation. At this gathering they are members of an audience, a congregate group. Finally, stimulated by the professional atmosphere of the research they contributed to, they both join some professional association. Now they are mutual members of an organized social system.

THE STRUCTURE OF MULTIGROUP SYSTEMS

Multigroup structures, as was previously indicated, are of several different types. The two types most commonly identified are (1) *organizations* (or "complex" organizations) and (2) *communities* and *societies*. **Organizations** typically consist of a number of subgroups or subsystems with specialized

[11] This term is used in lieu of Bierstedt's "social" groups, which is substituted for his associational groups. (*Ibid.*, p. 296) The attempt at semantic clarity in no way reflects on the conceptual utility of the types of groups differentiated by Bierstedt.

functions, linked together through bilateral and reflexive role reciprocality, but *which are devoted to a common goal.* (Roles are **bilaterally** reciprocal when two different actors occupy the status positions they link; they are **reflexive** when the same actor occupies the two positions.) Some examples would be (1) universities, with their various colleges, departments and schools; (2) industrial plants, with their various divisions and departments; and, (3) government agencies, with their various bureaus and sections. It should be noted that all systems have elements of stress–strain, such as subgroups which do not subscribe wholly to organization goals. However, such groups tend to be eliminated when they are completely out of accord with the greater goal of the system.

In contrast to organizations, which are linked together into a single structure by reciprocal relationships and dedication of roles to a common goal, communities and societies are seen as multigroup structures linked or held together by social relationships that are *not* necessarily directed toward common endeavors. Roles are played by actors toward various actors in other groups, but in each instance the other actor is pursuing a different end. For example, a husband and father must play roles to achieve the goal of supplying and caring for his family in his occupational pursuits; in his contacts with plumbers, carpenters, and others, from whom he needs service, with the internal revenue officers at tax time, and many others. None of the roles played by the persons with whom he interacts in these various situations is necessarily concerned with the welfare of his family. In fact, each may have a distinctly separate goal in mind. Yet, in each instance, the roles played must be played in conjunction with another role—hence the term *conjunctive role* as compared with reciprocal role. Again, Bates terms such roles as bilateral when the two statuses are occupied by different persons within the community structure and reflexive when the two statuses are occupied by the same person within the structure.[12]

In summary, the structure of organizations can be seen as made up of groups, and that of communities and societies as made up of groups and organizations. In terms of an actor-centered analysis, communities and societies include stations made up of situses, positions, roles, and norms.

THE BASIC TYPES OF SOCIAL GROUPS

The social structure of societal groups should now be clear to the student. However, the types of groups found in a complex society represent a great diversity in characteristics. Classifications of groups can be worked out on the basis of almost any criteria which one might select. For example, groups have

[12] For a discussion of "bilateral" and reflexive" reciprocal and conjunctive relationships see Bates, "Institutions, Organizations, and Communities: A General Theory of Complex Structures," *op. cit.,* pp. 62-63.

been classified according to size, according to stratification patterns, according to permanence, on the basis of whether or not membership is voluntary or involuntary, in terms of the number of social bonds (reciprocal roles) holding group members together, on the basis of exclusiveness, and at another level, in terms of ethnic, age, race, sex, or other like characteristics. All of these classifications have a certain sociological usefulness. However, the central core of group analysis is to be found in the nature of the role relations existing between group members. Many scholars have worked out classifications of groups based on the nature of social relations. We shall limit ourselves here to the three schemes which seem to predominate in current literature. The reader will quickly note that the differences among them are perhaps more in nomenclature than substance.

PRIMARY VERSUS SECONDARY GROUPS

The concept *primary group* was originated by Professor Charles H. Cooley. In a classic work, he stated, "By **primary** groups I mean those characterized by intimate face-to-face association and cooperation."[13] From this definition, one can easily gather that such groups are ones in which relationships are on a personal basis and that members are interested in each other over and beyond the mere selfish implementation of a goal. In fact social relationships are likely to be ends in and of themselves. Examples of primary groups would include a family, a local chapter of a fraternity or sorority, a neighborhood group, and so on. Primary groups can be recognized by the fact that individual personalities are so fused with one another, that the group manifests a common total life and purpose to a large extent.

Professor Cooley never used the term *secondary group*, but other scholars introduced the term to refer to group relationships which were in contrast to primary-group relationships. Thus, groups where personal association is more casual, less frequent, more special-interest directed, and more compartmentalized are typed as **secondary** groups. Secondary groups usually are much larger than primary groups and they are always more formal in nature. Some examples would be professional associations, trade unions, corporations, and all other groups not identifiable as primary groups.

The functions of primary and secondary groups are different in a major sense. In primary groups, where one is likely to find sympathy, affection, and a general sharing of problems as well as good fortune, there is an ideal climate for personality formation. One can also develop personality in secondary groups, but the traits developed tend to be formal in nature. Secondary groups provide an effective mechanism for achieving certain goals or expressing certain interests, but may well demand the suppression of deeper feelings and of frustrations. A student seldom will dare express himself openly to a professor on an opinion he may disagree with, but he will hesitate less to dis-

---

[13] Charles H. Cooley, *Social Organization* (New York, Scribner, 1915), p. 23.

pute his father. Of course, this situation may be reversed on occasion, depending on the authoritarian structure of the student's family and the classroom atmosphere provided by his instructor.

GEMEINSCHAFT VERSUS GESELLSCHAFT GROUP RELATIONS

The German scholar, Ferdinand Tönnies, developed two concepts—*Gemeinschaft* and *Gesellschaft*—to refer to special classes of social relations. These terms are in popular use today.[14] Although both terms were briefly defined in Chapter 3, they may be expanded somewhat here.

Tonnies termed a "social order" (social groups) which was based on a consensus of wills and harmony developed by the folkways, mores, and religion as **Gemeinschaft** in nature. Thus, a *Gemeinschaft* society was one in which relationships were personal or traditional or both. Loomis points out that, "In the work teams, families, communities, societies and other collectivities which are *Gemeinschaft*-like, human relations are ends in themselves; intimacy and sentiment are expected among the actors; norms are traditional. . . ."[15] The similarity of this notion with that of Cooley's primary group is obvious.

In contrast to the traditional ways of *Gemeinschaft* societies, a **Gesellschaft** society is one in which neither personal association nor customary rights and duties are important. The "contract" becomes all important and the relationships between men are determined by bargaining and defined in written agreements. Cold-blooded economic considerations take precedence over sentiment and relationships are specialized and formal rather than general and informal in nature. Said another way, the term *Gemeinschaft* is used to refer to those group relationships which develop unconsciously or subconsciously while *Gesellschaft* refers to group relationships which are entered into deliberately for the achievement of recognized ends.[16]

INFORMAL VERSUS FORMAL GROUPS

Another way of classifying groups which is gaining increasing importance in sociology is also in terms of what might be called the institutionalized struc-

---

[14] Ferdinand Tönnies, *Community and Society: Gemeinschaft and Gesellschaft*, Translated and Edited by Charles P. Loomis (New York, Harper & Row, 1963). (Originally published in German in 1887.)

[15] From Charles P. Loomis, *Social Systems: Essays on Their Persistence and Change*, copyright 1960, D. Van Nostrand Company, Inc., Princeton, N.J., p. 59.

[16] Rudolf Heberle, Tönnies' son-in-law, has done an excellent job of interpreting Tönnies' sociological system. See, for example, Rudolf Heberle, "The Sociological System of Ferdinand Tönnies: 'Community' and 'Society'," in E. E. Barnes, Ed., *An Introduction to the History of Sociology* (Chicago, University of Chicago Press, 1948), Chap. 10.

ture of the group. The classification informal versus formal has many of the connotations of primary versus secondary and *Gemeinschaft* versus *Gesell-schaft*. An **informal** group is recognized as one which evolves without explicit design and which is not specifically organized to attain a given end. In contrast, a **formal** group is one which usually has a definite purpose, explicit procedures and which is characterized by division of labor which is highly specialized. Agreements in formal groups normally would be written and decisions handed down from those in authority positions through a chain of command. In other words, the total structure of the group is formal, from the recruitment of members who have specialized abilities, to the rigid status-role structure.[17]

Informal groups are usually small in size, and can exist within the structure of formal groups. In fact, when a group increases in size it is likely to become formal in nature. Informal groups have been studied as *small groups* by a number of sociologists.[18] Examples of such groups are cliques, friendship groups, small work groups, and families. This type of group is rather easily set apart from formal groups such as government bureaucracies, large business and industrial enterprises, military establishments, and universities. The latter types of groups have received a considerable attention within recent years, although they have been identified as *complex* or *modern* organizations in some instances.[19]

It is also worth noting that the classifications reviewed here, as well as those of other scholars who have addressed themselves to classifications of groups based on their structural nature, have differentiated between those groups which are rationally conceived and whose structure is deliberately and consciously created, and those which have more or less just happened.

GROUP SOCIAL STRUCTURE: CONCRETE EXAMPLES

The theory of group structure was outlined in the preceding sections of this chapter. In this section, findings of actual studies are described to show how groups are held together in real-life situations. Four types of group structures are illustrated: a single informal group, a single formal group, a complex organization, and a community. The social relationships described are greatly oversimplified and abbreviated, but serve the purpose of illustration.

[17] See Peter M. Blau and W. Richard Scott, *Formal Organizations* (San Francisco, Chandler, 1962), pp. 5-8.
[18] Although the precise definition of small group may be more a function of size than the character of social relationships, the term informal very closely parallels what is described as small groups. See Michael S. Olmsted, *The Small Group* (New York, Random House, 1959).
[19] See Harry M. Johnson, *Sociology: A Systematic Introduction* (New York, Harcourt, Brace & World, 1960), Chapter 12; Amitai Etzioni, Ed., *Complex Organizations: A Sociological Reader* (New York, Holt, Rinehart & Winston, 1961); and Amitai Etzioni, *Modern Organizations* (Englewood Cliffs, New Jersey, Prentice-Hall, 1964).

THE PLAINVILLE FAMILY: SELECTED NORMS AND ROLES RELATED TO SEX AND PREGNANCY

The major unit of social structure in Plainville, the small community studied first by Carl Withers and 15 years later by Art Gallaher, Jr., was, as in most Western communities, the nuclear family.[20] Such a family includes the status-positions of husband-father, wife-mother, and children varying in sex and number. The norms which apply to the family roles of husband and wife are described at length by Gallaher. From his account, it is possible briefly to exerpt certain norms which apply to sex and pregnancy as a concrete illustration of the partial structure of an informal group.

Both are expected to exhibit mutual respect and familial support in all matters involving one or the other. Thus, a wife should be submissive (sexually), but a "good" husband refrains from making demands upon her "when she doesn't feel like it, at least two months before a child is born, and for a similar period after birth." In matters of sex both partners are expected to maintain fidelity throughout marriage, and neither should "look with favor" upon another man or woman. . . . The sharp tongues of neighbors immediately react to known, or assumed, violations of this norm.[21]

Gallaher goes on to report that the norms with regard to having children are changing, with young people not wanting to have children as soon or in as great a number as their parents. However, "Ideally, a wife should be happy whenever she suspects or learns that she is pregnant."[22] Her husband is told right away but no one else is informed before the couple is "sure." In keeping with changing folkways, young pregnant wives are not embarrassed to be seen in public because pregnancy is "natural." All but low-status "backward" women consult a physician during pregnancy and have a physician in attendance at childbirth.

In the above account, the norms associated with the roles which make up each status-position and which apply to a given situation can be seen. It is also possible to identify sanctions which the greater society applies to assure conformity to the norms. The roles are reciprocally related and clearly involve both rights and responsibilities, even though the group has no formal structures which outlines either. In our second example of a single group structure, the element of formality will be introduced.

[20] Art Gallaher, Jr., *Plainville: Fifteen Years Later* (New York, Columbia University Press, 1961), pp. 116-134.
[21] *Ibid.*, p. 116.
[22] *Ibid.*, p. 117.

THE NORWEGIAN MASKINRING: A NEW TYPE OF FARMERS' COOPERATIVE[23]

Many European farms are too small to allow their owners or operators to take full advantage of modern machine methods. Until recently, attempts made in various countries to solve the mechanization problem for small-size farms were without notable success. In 1959, seven farmers in the south central district of Nes, Hedmark, Norway succeeded in working out a very satisfactory answer to the high cost and other problems which faced farmers on small plots of land when they turned to mechanization. This scheme was so successful that, in 1963, some 70 such groups had already been organized in Norway.

The seven farmers mentioned organized themselves into a formal small group, which they called a *maskinring*. The *maskinring* was formally set up with by-laws and a hierarchy of officers to govern cooperation with regard to the purchase and use of machines and for the regulation of work by members. A brief review of the goals of this small formal group, and of its other structural elements provides an understanding of formal small group structure in a concrete situation.

The goals of the *maskinring* members are, ". . . to improve their income, make the daily routine as well as the seasonal work easier, get some leisure time, get things done at the proper time, relieve farm women of some of their heavy tasks, and achieve an output which they could not undertake or achieve without collaboration. . . ."[24] The by-laws which regulate the *maskinring* not only state the goals, but divide the functions (labor) among members, clearly defining rank and power (authority) of each status-position, and spell out the sanctions to be applied when roles are not properly played. Division of functions (labor) is worked out within particular seasons and over the entire year as well. Each task to be done is identified and a given member put in charge of the operation. In connection with seasonal activity, one man might be assigned the responsibility of transporting the machines from one farmer's field to another's field, a second man might see to the servicing of the machines, and a third would be in charge of spraying for insects. In each instance the remaining members would work under and respect the authority of the man in charge of the given specialization. A yearly assignment to one man might involve learning about and keeping posted on new machines and farming techniques, and to another the responsibility for working out all income and other taxes. The sanctions formally worked out to control members are applied by steps or degrees. The member who violates a rule of the *maskinring* first gets a warn-

[23] The information for this section is taken from a study made by John Hornslien of The Royal Agricultural Society of Norway. See John Hornslien, "New Type of Farmers' Cooperatives," *Sociologia Ruralis*, Vol. IV, No. 2 (1964), pp. 116-125.

[24] *Ibid.*, p. 118.

ing from the Board of Directors. If he continues his misbehavior, the next step is a fine and possibly a claim for damages. Finally, if the misdeeds continue, the offending member is thrown out and forfeits his claims to the jointly owned property of the *maskinring*. Since these rules are clearly outlined before a person joins, there is no question of the authority of the *maskinring*, and disloyalty to the cooperative is quickly discouraged.

The difference between the family as an informal small group and the *maskinring* as a formal small group is clear. Yet the same group structural elements—norms, roles, and status-positions—are readily identifiable. In complex organizations, which are always formal in nature, the additional structural element of the situs would be present, since more than one group is involved.

A LABOR UNION AS A COMPLEX SOCIAL ORGANIZATION: THE TORONTO DISTRICT OF AMALGAMATED CLOTHING WORKERS OF AMERICA

Labor unions are typical of complex organizations. It is possible to visualize the structural aspects of such organizations by very briefly outlining the social relationships which bind the members of the Toronto District of Amalgamated Clothing Workers of America together and to their international union.[25] At the time it was studied by Herbert Shepard, this union district was made up of nine local unions divided roughly on ethnic, linguistic, and craft distinctions. Each of the locals had an elected executive board whose function it was to handle routine business, take care of disputes among members, administer discipline, and prepare agendas for local meetings. Ties with the district and international organizations were maintained in several ways. First, resolutions and by-laws might be passed by the local and sent through channels for higher administrative consideration. Second, delegates from the local were selected and sent to district and international conventions. Third, each local elected three members to the Joint Board of the District Organization.

In addition to belonging to a local, a union member also belonged to a shop organization which consisted of the employees of the firm for which he worked. Members of different locals might work in the same shop and belong to the same shop organization. Each shop elected its own committee, including a chairman and several assistants, whose major function was to settle grievances of shop members and maintain a smooth flow of work. Complaints which could not be settled with the shop foreman were taken to the business agent from the District Joint Board for him to take up with higher management.

The District Joint Board included a Board of Directors which served as

[25] The account in this section is from the article Herbert A. Shepard, "Democratic Control in a Labor Union," *The American Journal of Sociology*, Vol. 54 (January, 1949), pp. 311-316.

its executive committee. One of the three members selected from each local served on the Board. The network of social relations moved from the district board to the general executive board of the international union. The latter had a structure which enabled the exertion of pressure on management, if and when it was deemed necessary.

The intricacies of the district organization of this union clearly identify it as a complex organization. For example, one man could hold a position in a shop group, a local, and serve on the district board, as well as be a delegate to the international conventions. Each level of his particpation would be in a different group and the constellation of his status-positions make up his situs in the organization. The complexity of the structure of social relations is further enhanced by the fact that the six paid representatives on the district board were elected by a different group, such as journeyman tailors, cutters, and trimmers (Italian-speaking and English-speaking locals) or the Jewish locals.

As in the case of simple groups, the norms, roles, and status-positions which make up the structure of the organization are apparent. In one illustration, the business agent is required to play a complex role which involves the more difficult bargaining with management. However, he must please his fellow-workers who elect him and who have a clear notion of what his behavior should be (norms) in this role. The moment he deviates from their role expectations, he is reprimanded and continued role deviation jeopardizes his position.

LIFE IN TURRIALBA: THE MANIFESTATIONS OF THE SOCIAL STRUCTURE OF A COMMUNITY

Turrialba, Costa Rica is a trade center community of some 19,000 inhabitants located near the "crossroads of the Americas." This community was studied in order that personnel assigned to technical cooperation programs might have some way of familiarizing themselves with societies in which they might be working.[26] The accounts given serve to show how individuals and groups interact in such a social system. The student should attempt to visualize the many roles which an individual community member plays as he moves from one situation to another, that is, from his primary group to his secondary group contacts. The norms of each role are implicit in each actor's behavior, as is the constellation of roles which make up his situses and the various situses of which his station in the community is composed. The conglomerate of stations are woven into the fabric of social structure which is the community.

[26] Charles P. Loomis, Julio O. Morales, Roy A. Clifford, and Olen E. Leonard, *Turrialba* (New York, Free Press, 1953).

The day in Turrialba begins early. Around five o'clock in the morning farm laborers are already on the streets. . . . Trucks from some of the farms come into town for the workers who stand packed against each other as the trucks move off.

People bound for early Mass are also astir. Older women, especially, can be seen with their black shawls over their shoulders, on their way to church. Soon farm youths and small farm operators arrive in town with produce which they spread on the sidewalks for sale near the Triangulo. Those people whose business will take them out of town for the day are already near the railway station to catch the 6:15 train going to San Jose or are waiting at the bus station to get good seats in the early buses which also cover this route. People in need of medical services are lining up around the doors of the Social Security section of the Canton hospital in order to get medical attention during the day.

Women, men, and children are out to get foodstuffs needed for the day's meals. They gather in the butcher shops to get their meat early while there is still opportunity to choose the tenderer pieces. After the milk is bought, the bread purchased from the bakeries, and the vegetables from the stands, they return to their homes with the purchases. . . .

Classes in the elementary school are scheduled to start at seven. As this hour approaches, boys and girls, mostly shiningly clean and barefoot, slowly gather around the school grounds. Meanwhile the noise of carreta wheels is heard as the brightly decorated ox-carts bring to town loads of plaintains, firewood and other products from outlying farms.

The afternoon between two and three o'clock is marked by the return of the farm laborers from the fields. . . . By three-thirty most of the school children are free from school and are playing in the streets or running errands for their families. The younger men and boys commonly gather around the sports ground and practice soccer. Dinner for most families is served around four or five o'clock. Soon after dinner one sees increasing numbers of younger women on the front porches. By this time the pool rooms are open and are frequented by men mostly from the middle classes.

Before seven o'clock groups of young men and girls appear on the Pavimentada and start to walk slowly back and forth along the street between the railway station and the Triangulo. . . .

The Club El Rancho is the only place in town where dances are regularly held. . . . Juke-box music and drinks are available. . . .

The two local theaters present movies every night. . . . During the evenings the movie-goers appear to be mostly of the middle and upper class levels, whereas Sunday matinees, being less expensive, attract proportionately more of the lower class people.

. . . Most of the stores are open all day Saturday and on Sunday morning, for these are their busiest days. The rural people who form a large part of these crowds are somewhat identified by the interest with which they observe everyday urban activities. Beggars, shoe-shine boys, peddlers of Saints' pictures, sellers of clay works, fruits, vegetables, and other items, turn the central streets and sidewalks around the Triangulo into a large open-air marketplace. The lottery vendors are an important part of the scene. . . .

The Sunday Masses in the Catholic church are well attended. In the opinion of the parish priest half of the people in Turrialba are Catholic in "every sense of the word" who attend Masses regularly, marry through the church, baptize their children and see that their children take their first Communion. . . .

Breaks in the routine pattern of life in Turrialba are introduced by the religious fiestas of the Roman Catholic calendar which are celebrated by the Church, the schools, and in the homes, and by many days dedicated to civic and patriotic observances. . . .

On the occasions of civic and religious fiestas there are erected in central parts of the town open-air stands which offer refreshments and games of chance. The chance games, especially, draw great numbers of participants.

Other important gatherings are at soccer games, weddings, baptisms, and birthdays. Attending funeral wakes, "ir a las velas," is also a custom. The friends of the deceased call on the latter's family and many stay in the watch during the whole night and may alternately pray, eat, drink, or gossip.

There are several Catholic organizations in the town. . . . The members of the organizations meet with the priests once a week for a meeting consisting mainly of religious lectures. . . . The Vincentinas occupy themselves with charity. . . . Similar charity activities are carried on by the Evangelical church.

There is a local chapter of the Lions International organization in Turrialba. To it belong most of the professional men and the more successful businessmen. The Lions Club has dinners once a month and sponsors some civic activities. The Masons also have an active lodge in the town, while the Sports Club (Club Deportivo), functions for the advancement of sports activities.[27]

The above brief account of life in Turrialba shows the type of relationships which hold the community together. A more complex community might have a larger number and more specialized roles, but a structure would be present and quite similar in its broad outline.

SUMMARY

The significance of a knowledge of social structure is found in the opportunity which this knowledge provides for systematically analyzing human behavior. The conceptual framework presented in this chapter makes it possible to relate various aspects of human interaction quickly and clearly to group, multigroup, and community or societal structures. Such structures have two important dimensions, cultural and social organization. The cultural dimension is conceived as a series of ideal patterns of behavior to which people are oriented and the social organization dimension is seen as the actual behavior of people in real-life situations.

Role theory provides an efficient approach to the analysis of social struc-

[27] Reprinted with permission of The Free Press from *Turrialba* by Charles P. Loomis, Julio O. Morales, Roy A. Clifford, and Olen E. Leonard. Copyright 1953 by Charles P. Loomis. (Pages 21-27 in Chapter 2, "The Setting of the Study," written by Paul C. Morrison, Charles P. Loomis, Sakari Sariola, Julio O. Morales, and Juvenal Valerio.)

ture, since all social system elements are accounted for by the actor-related structural units of such systems. The norms (learned behavior expectations) are seen as making up roles, which in turn make up status positions. Situses are made up of status positions and are used to locate or place an actor in complex or multigroup structure. The final role concept used in the analysis of group structure is station, which is defined as the location of an actor in the total structure of a community or society. A person's station is made up of the total collection of his situses.

The structure of a social group is differentiated from the structure of multigroup systems in two ways, although all roles in both types of structures are oriented toward the specific goal of the systems. In groups all individuals occupy positions reciprocal to all other positions in the structure. These criteria differentiate bona fide social groups or systems from other types of human associations such as statistical aggregates, societal classes and congregations or assemblies. In a multigroup system all roles are not bilaterally reciprocal as in single group structures, some roles are reflexively reciprocal, that is, played by the same actor but relating to positions in two separate groups. In larger structures, such as communities or societies, roles are conjunctive (that is, do not require the performance of a specific other role) as well as reciprocal and roles are not dedicated to the same goal.

Social groups may be classified according to a number of criteria. However, the role relations between group members appears to be the most basic approach to classification. Three such classifications were presented. The first, associated with C. H. Cooley, distinguished between primary groups characterized by intimate face-to-face association and secondary groups which are formal in nature and serve a special-interest function. The second classification, that of Tönnies, used the term *Gemeinschaft* to refer to social relations based on a consensus of wills and a condition of harmony in keeping with tradition, and the term *Gesellschaft* to refer to social relations which were strictly contractual in nature. Finally, a formal group was described as having a definite purpose, explicit procedures and a high degree of specialization of roles, and an informal group was characterized as one with intimate, personal relations and a lack of formal structure.

Supplementary Readings

Bates, Frederick L., "A Conceptual Analysis of Group Structure," *Social Forces,* Vol. 36 (December, 1957), pp. 103-116.

Bates, Frederick L., "Institutions, Organizations and Communities: A General Theory of Complex Structures," *Pacific Sociological Review,* Vol. 3 (Fall, 1960), pp. 59-70.

Blau, Peter M., "Formal Organizations: Dimensions of Analysis," *American Journal of Sociology,* Vol. 63 (July, 1957), pp. 58-69; and also in BARRON.

Etzioni, Amitai, *Modern Organizations* (Englewood Cliffs, New Jersey, Prentice-Hall, 1964).

Merton, Robert K., *Social Theory and Social Structure* (New York, Free Press, 1957), pp. 368-386.

Perrow, Charles, "The Analysis of Goals in Complex Organizations," *American Sociological Review*, Vol. 26 (December, 1961), pp. 854-866; and also in BARRON.

Tönnies, Ferdinand, *Community and Society*, Charles P. Loomis translation (New York, Harper & Row, 1957, Harper Torchbook), pp. 1-102; and also in LEE.

Warriner, Charles K., "Groups Are Real: A Reaffirmation," *American Sociological Review*, Vol. 21 (1965), pp. 549-554; and also in MIZRUCHI.

Williams, Robin H. Jr., *American Society*, 2nd rev. ed. (New York, Knopf, 1960), Chapter III.

10
SOCIAL
STRATIFICATION
AND
MOBILITY

By now, the student is aware of the many ways in which men differ from one another. Differences in heredity, cultural participation, and physical environment account for differences in conditioning and thus in ways of behavior, as was brought out in the various discussions of socialization. Differences in individual behavior are, in turn, necessary for the proper functioning of society, if many specialized tasks are to be done efficiently. These facts set the conceptual framework for defining and understanding social stratification as one aspect of social organization.

DEFINITION OF SOCIAL
STRATIFICATION

It will be recalled that roles are evaluated as inferior or superior and there is attached to each some varying amount of prestige, honor, power, and reward. Since every individual occupies numerous social positions and plays many roles, it is possible to classify persons into status-role categories, which are ranked in terms of the relative position of their roles taken as a whole. This is social stratification in essence. Robin Williams' definition, taken from Talcott Parsons' work, puts this idea in succinct form. He conceives social stratification as, ". . . the ranking of individuals on a scale of superiority-inferiority-equality, according to some commonly accepted basis of valuation."[1] John

[1] Robin M. Williams, Jr., *American Society*, 2nd ed. (New York, Knopf, 1960), p. 89.

Kelley elaborates the definition of stratification: "**Stratification** is defined as an explicitly or implicitly recognized functional system of differentiation and ranking of positions within groups, associations, communities, and the society, itself, which is standard for the society or a major segment of its structure (e.g., communities, tribal associations, clan associations), in terms of the unequal distribution of power, which system is relatively durable (stable) over a period of generations."[2]

From the above definitions it can be seen that there are several essential elements of stratification: (1) a system of ranking of positions, (2) applicable to a large segment of the societal structure, and (3) durable over an extended period of time.[3]

The above definition of social stratification makes it clear that it is a form of social differentiation. However, it is a distinct kind of social differentiation. Other forms of differentiation, such as family or kinship roles, sex roles, or age roles are determined initially by individual qualities. By contrast, one's first position in the social order is determined by the rank his family happens to occupy, regardless of what individual attribute he might possess.[4]

THE FUNCTION OF SOCIAL STRATIFICATION

Social stratification is universal. This generalization holds, despite some quibbling over whether extremely small, homogeneous societies, such as tribes and bands, are stratified. The latter are characterized by enough social differentiation on the one hand and represent such a small fragment of the known peoples of the world on the other hand, as not to invalidate the claim of universality. Social stratification is so widespread because, like other universal culture patterns, it serves a social function. This function is to provide for a division of labor which obviates the necessity of each individual handling all the duties deemed worthwhile by his society—an obviously impractical if not impossible task.[5]

The precise way in which social stratification functions in bringing about an effective division of labor is still within the exploratory realm. Kingsley Davis and Wilbert Moore have presented what has been called the "struc-

[2] John D. Kelley, "The Sociology of Stratification: A Theory of the Power Structure of Society," Ph.D. Dissertation (Louisiana State University, 1961), pp. 375-376.

[3] *Ibid.*, p. 376.

[4] Hodges contends that the family could not survive if its members were born into different levels of the stratification system. In a general sense, this may be true because children are associated with the status of their parents. However, a neat analytical problem is posed where parents do not hold equal social rank. Harold M. Hodges, Jr., *Social Stratification* (Cambridge, Massachusetts, Schenkman Publishing Co., 1964), p. 9.

[5] See Kingsley Davis and Wilbert E. Moore, "Some Principles of Stratification," *American Sociological Review*, Vol. 10 (April, 1945), pp. 242-249.

tural-functional argument," the thesis of which is as follows.[6] Because of greater social reward, some roles come to be prized more highly than others. These roles are generally those that demand more risks, education, or other types of dedication, such as test pilot, doctor, or atomic physicist. Were the rewards of money, prestige, and power lacking, a society would have great difficulty recruiting individuals for these or like positions.

The above thesis has been challenged by writers who raise questions regarding the inevitability of social stratification as a feature of social organization. In essence, they argue that social inequality does not necessarily have to be a core feature of all future societies and that stratification can be dysfunctional as well as functional. Others have taken issue with the view that role performance is the key to social stratification—maintaining that social inheritance (family lineage) and "demand and supply" explain social position more realistically than the theory that holds that the most important and most highly remunerative positions are held by the best qualified persons.[7]

Despite the fact that the structural-functionalists have not been able to explain some things about social stratification, their central argument that unequal rewards are prevalent in all societies and necessarily relate to the division of labor has not been invalidated.[8]

In the above connection, a word of elaboration is in order regarding the lags or incongruities which appear in most cultures, whereby some positions requiring little effort are highly rewarded, and others requiring relatively great effort are poorly rewarded. Such cases are found more frequently in rapidly changing societies. The former instance is seen in the example of the person who owns a plot of "worthless" land which suddenly becomes most valuable because a new technological development makes it the source of a valuable mineral (uranium is a case in point); the second case is typified by a prolonged building boom which raises the salaries of plumbers, brick masons, and carpenters above those of teachers and other professionals, despite the latter's greater expenditure of effort and time on education and training. In another example of this type, teachers and other professionals might be compared to "pop" singers or even racketeers. Both types of lag tend to be worked out in the course of time as the society stabilizes.

Social stratification may, then, be looked upon as a basic and important fact of social life. Although the average person may not be, indeed usually is not, completely aware of the details of the stratification system in which he lives, his actions during the course of an ordinary day more than likely involve

[6] Ibid.

[7] See Melvin Tumin, "Some Principles of Stratification: A Critical Analysis," American Sociological Review, Vol. 18 (August, 1953), pp. 387-394; Walter Buckley, "Social Stratification and Social Differentiation," American Sociological Review, Vol. 23 (August, 1958), pp. 369-375; and Richard Simpson, "A Modification of the Functional Theory of Stratification," Social Forces, Vol. 35 (December, 1956), pp. 132-137.

[8] Dennis H. Wrong emphasizes this point. "The Functional Theory of Stratification: Some Neglected Considerations," American Sociological Review, Vol. 24 (December, 1959), p. 773.

considerable behavior dictated primarily by social class relationships. This fact makes it worthwhile for the student of sociology to become acquainted with the various types of social stratification systems.

SYSTEMS OF SOCIAL STRATIFICATION: IDEAL TYPES

When the world picture is considered, it is possible to isolate at least three major systems of social stratification. None of these systems can be found in "pure" form, but as ideal constructs they serve a useful purpose. Systems of social stratification differ in degree of rigidity and can vary along a continuum from completely open to completely closed extremes. They also vary in the symbols used to portray class position and in the rewards (such as power and prestige) accorded members of the various social strata. There is also variation over time and between subsystems, such as a rural community and metropolitan area, within a given society. The major systems of social stratification are *caste, estate,* and *class systems.*

CASTE SYSTEMS

A **caste system** is characterized by a system of horizontal classes or castes (strata) which represent functional areas within a society. Each such area (religion, education, government, or business) is ranked according to the functional importance it has to the society. The determination of rank order is sometimes the result of a successful struggle for power by certain groups within the society and at other times is the result of conquest by outside groups. In either case, the system is stabilized through appeals which relate to society-wide values, values that are supported by all castes.

Figure 10-1, which shows a tentative model of the Hindu caste system in India, demonstrates the functional basis for such a system. Each caste or subcaste is restricted in terms of occupational specialization—for example, priestly castes are not allowed to perform economic or political activities. In this regard, caste systems are generally recognized as the most rigid of the so-called closed societies. Ideally, class position is inherited from one's family and is ascribed for life. Very few exceptions are made, even for outstanding personal attributes or accomplishments. Indeed, ambition to move from one's class is effectively blocked by strong sanctions, typically of a religious nature.

Caste systems flourish best in more or less self-sufficient societies, those characterized by a pre-industrial and a pre-market economy. They also must have some visible criteria for distinguishing between members of upper and lower castes. Traditionally, the Indian caste system has been given as the best

FIGURE 10-1. *Tentative Model of Caste System Power Structure in Hindu India.*

BRAHMAN CASTE

PRIESTS
INTELLECTUAL LEADERS
TEACHERS

MAIN CASTES
AND SUBCASTES

KING
PRINCES
NOBLES
WARRIORS

WATER BOYS

KSHATRIYA CASTE

MAIN CASTES
AND SUBCASTES

BIG
MERCHANTS
FINANCIERS
INDUSTRIALISTS
AGRICULTURISTS

LOW RANKING
MILITARY PERSONNEL
AND OFFICIALS

VAISHYA CASTE

MAIN CASTES
AND SUBCASTES

SMALL SHOPKEEPERS
ARTISANS
CRAFTSMEN
FARMERS

SUDRA CASTE

LABORERS AND UNSKILLED WORKERS OTHER THAN AGRICULTURISTS	MAIN CASTES AND SUBCASTES	THE SERVILE CASTES

THE OUTCASTES

THOSE WHO: WORK WITH COWHIDE, WASH DIRTY, PARTICULARLY MENSTRUOUSLY DEFILED, CLOTHES	"UNTOUCHABLES" AND NATIVE TRIBES	THOSE WHO: REMOVE CORPSES; WHO EAT BEEF

Source: John D. Kelley, "The Sociology of Stratification: A Theory of the Power Structure of Society" (unpublished dissertation, Louisiana State University, June, 1961), p. 416. Photograph courtesy of United Nations Organization.

example of a caste system. However, recent trends in that nation indicate that caste barriers have been weakened, especially in the cities. In the past, orthodox Hinduism served as a powerful force to maintain caste lines. Mason Olcott explains that the villager dared to violate one of the many taboos or elaborate ceremonial rules at the risk of being completely boycotted by his fellow villagers. In this way every aspect of his life, including his domestic affairs, his religious practices, his social life, and his work and occupational activity depended entirely upon and was controlled by the caste level in which he was born.[9] The description that follows shows how rigidly status relations were controlled.[10]

It is impossible to exaggerate the extent to which prescription for maintaining the social distance between various castes were proliferated. The whole set of gradations prescribed among castes was based on the idea of purity of the Brahman and the utter impurity of the untouchables. Most fantastic was the belief that the breath, or even the shadow, of an untouchable would pollute another person. In some places untouchables were required to wear cloths over their mouths in order that their breath might not pollute. In Poona they were not permitted within the city walls between 3 P.M. and 9 A.M. because during the early morning and late afternoon sun their bodies cast long shadows. In at least one area there were not only untouchables but unseeables. A caste of washerwomen had to do their work between midnight and daybreak and not show themselves except during the hours of darkness. All castes other than Brahmans were graded in terms of their purity by the extent of provisions to safeguard them against pollution by untouchables. The untouchable who could not, for instance, come closer than 124 feet to a Brahman might come within half that distance to an intermediate caste person and as near as seven feet to some lower caste person. In another area the specified gradations of distance were 96 feet down to 36 feet, the specified distance from Brahmans always being the greatest. Wells were polluted if a low caste man drew water from them. The water of a stream was polluted if a Sudhra was permitted to walk across a bridge over it. A low caste man could pollute an idol in a temple if he came closer than seven feet and if he did not cover his mouth and nostrils with his hands. Even the glance of a man of low caste falling on a cooking pot, would necessitate throwing away the contents of the pot. Public roads which came near temples could not be traveled by untouchables. There were places where untouchables were required to carry sticks or brooms not only so that they might be easily identified but to designate their status.

The list of specifications for physical distance in a caste system are the indicators of social distance. Even the short list given in the above quotation illustrates the fantastic extent to which such rules go. It is understandable why a people who have lived under these rules for generations cannot be expected

[9] Mason Olcott, "The Caste System of India," *American Sociological Review*, Vol. 9 (December, 1944), pp. 648-657.

[10] Carl C. Taylor, Douglas Ensminger, Helen W. Johnson, and Jean Joyce, *India's Roots of Democracy* (London, Longmans, 1965), pp. 48-50.

to quickly rid themselves of the attitudes and feelings which had been engendered by this experience.

No true examples of closed class systems are found in the western nations of the world. However, the position of the Negro in parts of the United States and other countries and the position of some ethnic groups in various western nations have had castelike attributes in the past, if not also presently. So long as it is possible for the individual to move easily from one class to another, a true closed society or caste system does not exist. The whole question of race and ethnic relations will be considered in detail in another chapter.

ESTATE SYSTEMS

The second system of social stratification—the **estate system**—is also essentially a closed class system, but less rigid than the caste system. It flourished during feudal times in Europe and has some rudimentary counterpart in present-day countries maintaining systems of inherited aristocracy or landed gentry. This system derived its name from feudal European terminology.

Like the caste system, the estate system is based on the ranking of positions according to a functional classification. The difference is that functional areas are considered to be complementary and of near equal importance. In other words, the military, religious, government, and economic areas are considered to be equally important to the society. Thus, as can be seen in Figure 10-2, the functional areas assume a vertical rather than a horizontal order of power. Said another way, whereas in a caste system all positions within a given functional area (class) possess the same relative degree of power, in an estate system, each estate contains within itself a completely stratified hierarchy of positions.

Religious and legal sanctions, as in the case of the caste system, provide the ideological support for the estate system. The chief distinction between the two systems is that the estate system permits some legitimate movement from one class to another. In feudal times, the priesthood had to be replenished because of celibacy, and the gifted and ambitious peasant lad thus had an opportunity to move up from his lowly social position. There was also an opportunity in these systems to rise in the military service; indeed even today, successful military leaders in certain countries may be knighted or otherwise moved up socially. Commoner girls had more opportunity to move up the social ladder through marriage than in other ways.

Today, the latifundia-, hacienda-, and plantation-type of land-tenure systems, wherever they are found in traditional society settings, present some features of the estate system. Loomis, Norris, and Proctor describe the status structure of a Costa Rican Hacienda as follows:

The material wealth of the *patron,* consisting of all the property in land, buildings and equipment within the estate, constitutes a virtual monopoly on one

FIGURE 10-2. *Theoretical Model of Estate System Structure.*

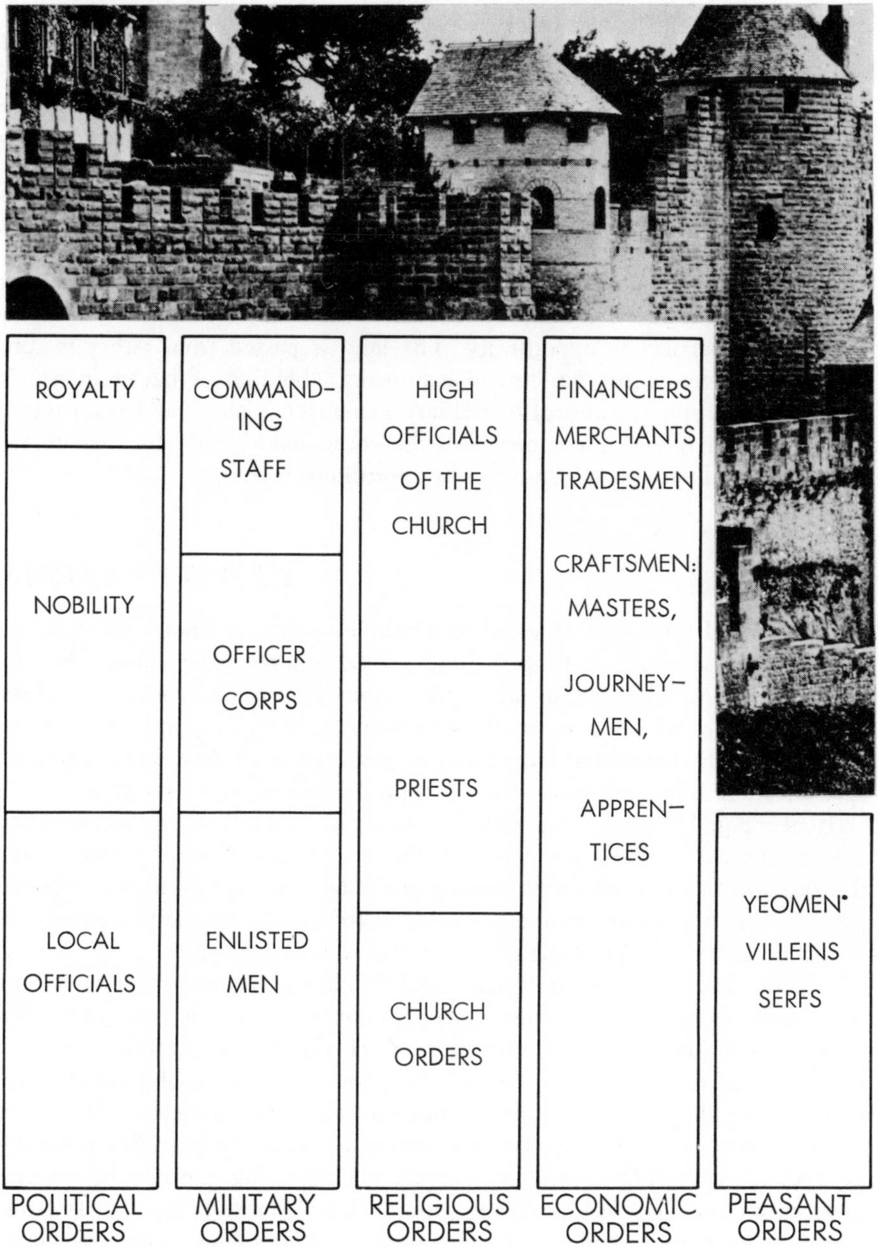

POLITICAL ORDERS	MILITARY ORDERS	RELIGIOUS ORDERS	ECONOMIC ORDERS	PEASANT ORDERS
ROYALTY	COMMAND-ING STAFF	HIGH OFFICIALS OF THE CHURCH	FINANCIERS MERCHANTS TRADESMEN	
NOBILITY	OFFICER CORPS	PRIESTS	CRAFTSMEN: MASTERS, JOURNEY-MEN, APPREN-TICES	
LOCAL OFFICIALS	ENLISTED MEN	CHURCH ORDERS		YEOMEN* VILLEINS SERFS

Source: John D. Kelley, "The Sociology of Stratification: A Theory of the Power Structure of Society" (unpublished dissertation, Louisiana State University, June, 1961), p. 428. Photograph courtesy of United Nations Organization.

of the most cherished values of this segment of Costa Rican population. Consequently his social status is unequaled in the community. The overseer, foreman of
the coffee mill, and foreman of the shop, have sufficient incomes to have invested
in a small farm or two or a small business outside of the estate, and their prestige
varies accordingly. The *colono* or sharecropper whose dominion over a few acres
of land is tentative at best, still enjoys higher status than the ordinary peon whose
claim to property consists of what few animals, clothing and light household goods
he might accumulate.[11]

Mobility is somewhat higher under such a social structure than was
possible under feudal conditions, but remains considerably hampered by institutionalized barriers to opportunity. The land is passed from father to son,
and the chances of the landless of acquiring a holding of hacienda size is
almost nil, except by political or military maneuver. Colono and peon types,
where migration is limited, move up the social ladder only by exceptional
ability coupled with good fortune, or by a fortuitous marriage.

CLASS SYSTEMS

The third and final type of social stratification system is known as the class
system. In one sense, both caste and estate systems have classes, but in
neither one does class stand out as the major identifying criterion. A **class
system** is one in which power is allocated along a politico-economic continuum,
according to the functional importance of positions, with little or no regard to
specialization. Thus, whatever the function performed, those positions which
carry near equal rewards (nominally measured in economic terms, but in other
important ways as well) are placed in the same strata of society. Obviously,
the system of power allocation among positions will vary from one type of
politico-economic society to another, such as from a capitalistic to a socialistic
system. However, the principle of stratification remains the same.

Most class systems do not place rigid limitations on movement from one
social strata to another. The requirement for entrance into a higher (or lower)
strata, in an ideal situation, is possession of the necessary functional importance, that is, ownership or control of the necessary means of production or
possession of the required intellect. This characteristic is why class systems are
usually "open" systems. Class systems are found primarily in highly commer-
cialized, market-oriented societies. Despite claims to the contrary by certain
spokesmen for the so-called democratic societies, most open-class systems
impose at least some—and not always minor—limitations on social movement
on the basis of such factors as regional background, ideology, ethnic background, race, religion, and family. These limitations usually are covertly im-

[11] Charles P. Loomis, Thomas L. Norris, and Charles H. Proctor, "Social Status
and Communication," Chapter III in Charles P. Loomis *et al.*, *Turrialba: Social Systems and the Introduction of Change* (New York, Free Press, 1953), p. 54.

posed, in the sense of informal policies of discrimination, because of their obvious contradiction to the formal values espoused by the society.

It is to be noted that the individual assumes greater importance than the family in open-class societies. Individual initiative and expression become paramount values, since each person is considered to be the "master of his own destiny," and thus has only himself to blame if he does not move upward socially. It is for this reason that family structures differ noticeably in closed and open societies. In closed systems, the family tends to be closely integrated and to maintain control over its members through adulthood, thus effectively holding them to the family social strata level.

Figure 10-3 is an attempt made by Kelley to show schematically the extremely complicated class structure of the United States. In this diagram, Kelley differentiates classes according to *source of income* (the columns) and according to *amount of income or wealth* (the rows). Crossing the diagram, he has drawn lines to represent Acquisition Classes (defined in the Weberian sense of class position being primarily determined by chances of making a profit in the market from goods or services) on the vertical axis, and Property Classes (defined in the Weberian sense of property being the primary factor of one's class position) on the horizontal axis. The model is skewed so that the vertical dimension represents the *degree* of power allocated among the classes. The horizontal solid lines which bisect the angles formed by the intersection of the property and acquisition lines form the boundaries for the three major class groupings—power elite, middle power classes, and low power classes. The reader is cautioned that the boxes formed represent the relative location of occupational positions within the power structure, and not the size of classes.

SOCIAL CLASS IN OPEN CLASS SYSTEMS: DEFINITION AND SIGNIFICANCE

In the preceding discussions of social stratification, frequent reference was made to social strata or social classes. These terms were not defined precisely, since the focus of attention was on the general rather than the specific aspects of social stratification. We turn now to the consideration of social class as it applies to open systems of social stratification.

DEFINITION OF SOCIAL CLASS

The point was made in Chapter 2 that many terms used by sociologists in a technical sense are understood differently by nonsociologists. Social class is one of these words. To the man on the street it is likely to connote some vague

FIGURE 10-3. *Tentative Working Model of Class Structure in the United States.*

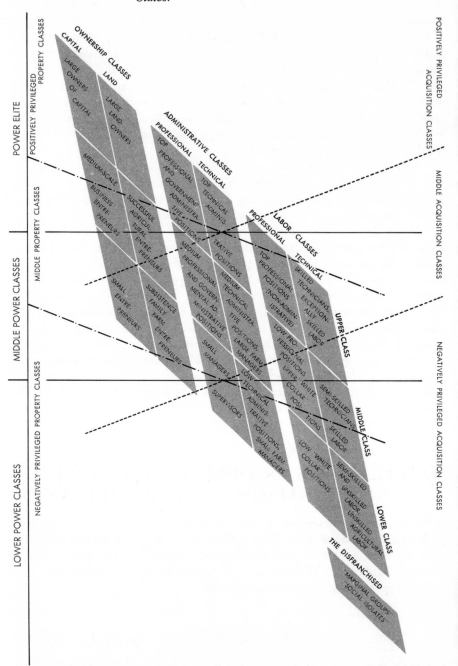

Source: John D. Kelley, "The Sociology of Stratification: A Theory of the Power Structure of Society" (unpublished dissertation, Louisiana State University, June, 1961), p. 454.

notion of the "have-nots," and may generate a mild resentment for fancied or real attitudes of snobbery. To the political activist with a strong Marxist or anti-Marxist view, social class is a cogent word, with overtones of inevitable conflict in the former instance. Variant understandings, such as the above, plus some variations on a theme by sociologists themselves, demonstrate the necessity for adopting a working definition of social class which incorporates the important meanings generally agreed on by social scientists. Hodges, after careful study of existing literature, has produced such a definition. He identifies a **social class** as

. . . a distinct reality which embraces the fact that people live, eat, play, mate, dress, work, and think at contrasting and dissimilar levels. These levels—social classes—are the blended product of shared and analgous occupational orientations, educational backgrounds, economic wherewithal, and life experiences.[12]

Hodge's definition is more complete than definitions which refer to class as groups or stratum of people who occupy a "similar social position," but no more correct.

The sociological concept of social class, then, is far more inclusive than simple aggregates of individuals who enjoy roughly the same economic level and have approximately the same prestige and power in their society. Joseph Kahl makes the point that people who share a given style of life have more contact with one another and this differential interaction leads to a distinctive set of value orientations.[13] The expression *style of life,* which connotes the way people in various classes live as compared to persons in other classes, is the key to social class differences.

SIGNIFICANCE OF CLASS DIFFERENCES

The significance of social class differences in open as well as closed class systems is most dramatically seen in what might be termed the life opportunities of individuals. Many studies have empirically verified the fact that social class is directly related to such things as mortality rates, educational level, incidence of both physical and mental disease, and occupational level. Life opportunity differences are so obvious as to make elaboration redundant. Indeed, it is difficult to think of social class without bringing to mind such differences.

Class differences have significance in other ways which are not so readily seen as those strictly associated with life opportunities. Because of differential socialization, personality is likely to be slanted in one way or another in the various social classes. Although it is difficult to separate personality traits completely from the syndrome of social factors related to class, studies have shown

[12] *Op. cit.,* p. 13.
[13] Joseph A. Kahl, *The American Class Structure* (New York, Holt, Rinehart and Winston, 1957), p. 9.

that delinquency rates, crime rates, divorce rates, school drop-out rates, and like manifestations of personality deviance are closely related to class position. Other personality differences are found in such things as patterns of striving, in feelings toward economic security, and in aspirations generally.

A third way in which social class differences have significance is in attitude and value orientations. It has been demonstrated that, in an advanced society, the social classes differ markedly in political liberalism–conservatism, in their views toward social reforms of particular types, in their feelings about education, and in their outlooks on spending versus saving, not to mention differences in many other important spheres of social life, such as religion.

Finally, social class has significance for social participation. Whether one will attend the opera or go to the corner bar, belong to the country club or to the labor union, take a vacation abroad or head for the nearest amusement park, depends a great deal on his class position. Investigations made in the United States indicate the lower classes read and travel less than the upper classes, but spend more time listening to the radio, viewing television, and going to the movies.[14]

In closing this discussion, it is important to note that it is not always easy to determine why one or another individual in an open class system remains in a lower class position. In most instances, it seems clear that lower class persons are aware of their plight, but that they do not know how to go about bettering themselves. Theories that assume innate lack of ambition or innate happiness with a life of relative hardship are, at best, unprovable. It is more likely, as Hodges argues, that such persons are "culturally deficient," that is, they do not fully comprehend and hence cannot follow the norms of higher social classes.[15] This phenomenon is illustrated by the uneasiness that members of a lower class experience when they have to make an appearance at a function of a higher social class. Outward appearances, in terms of a new suit of clothes may be changed, but speech patterns, topics of conversation, and other mannerisms quickly expose class background. Many marriages outside of one's class fail for the same reason.

SOCIAL CLASS POSITION OR RANK IN OPEN CLASS SYSTEMS

Our discussion up until now has been concerned with social stratification and social class in an overall sense. In studies of concrete open class societies, it is necessary to work out ways to differentiate between social classes and to decide how exclusive or inclusive a given class shall be. The criteria used to

[14] Leo Bogart, *The Age of Television* (New York, Frederick A. Praeger, 1958), p. 91.
[15] *Op. cit.*, p. 15.

rank people into social classes and the theories relating to the number of social classes command our attention here.

DETERMINANTS OF SOCIAL CLASS RANK

In different open class societies, and at different points in time in given societies, various criteria assume major importance as a determinant of social class rank. Presently, in advanced societies, occupation, wealth, property, and income tend to rank highest as measures of class. However, educational, family, religious, and residence factors serve as closely interrelated indicators of social position. In traditional societies, more emphasis is likely to be placed on military, religious, and family factors than on wealth as such. The point is that certain attributes are esteemed in given societies and not looked upon as advantageous in others. This may be illustrated by the prestige awarded the holder of a Ph.D. degree in the United States, as compared to a country such as Korea. In the latter nation the scarcity of Ph.D.'s serves to give persons who have achieved this educational status a high social position. A graduate student acquaintance of the writer returned home to Korea to become one of the few resident nationals to hold such a degree, and his immediate rise in social rank was remarkable, by United States standards, where thousands of persons have earned the highest university degree awarded.

All standards which are used to determine social rank, no matter the particular societal setting, have one thing in common: a close association with what was defined in Chapter 2 as legitimate social power. This concept is so important to the full understanding of the structure of society, that a separate chapter is devoted to it in this text.

The power of an individual or group, it will be recalled, is seen in the ability possessed to control others. It will be shown in Chapter 11 that power can be derived from many sources, including all the measures of social rank listed above. Prestige, which may be defined as admiration, awe, and respect held for an individual by others in his society, is a source of power. Status is perhaps more an indication of degree of power than it is a source of power, but it is both in one sense. The Prime Minister of England occupies a high position which accords him a great deal of prestige and his high status comes from the power inherent in his social position.[16]

If power is interpreted somewhat crudely as measured by one's ability to get what he wants, it may be difficult to construe such achievements as high education or high religious position as sources of power. But, to the degree to which these positions bring prestige, the actors who occupy them can articulate power (as an element in their social systems) to get their ways. Said an-

[16] For a discussion of the interrelation of class, status, and power, see Ely Chinoy, *Society, An Introduction to Sociology* (New York, Random House, 1961), pp. 138-139. John Kelley has developed a whole sociology of stratification based on a theory of the power structure of society (*op. cit.*).

other way, their decision-making roles are enhanced. An educated individual is an expert of sorts, and the less educated defer to him on matters relating to his expertise. Likewise, the priest or minister who is considered to have closer ties with the deity (or deities) worshipped is held in awe by members of his religious social system and thus is given his way (within normative limits) in the matter of religiously important decisions.

In summary, the determinants of social class in an open system can be thought of in two ways. First, those who wish to deal in specific concrete evidence can look for the special symbols and accomplishments which are used by a given society to measure class. These may include obvious manifestations such as material possessions and elite social participation. It may include military prowess, family and kinship ties, political success, educational and occupational achievement, physical beauty or prowess, or it may include any combination of these and other factors. The second, and more theoretical way to look at social class, is in terms of the relative power (including prestige and status) which individuals or groups are accorded by members of their social systems. Actually, as it will be seen, the more thorough investigations of social stratification go into the specific aspects of social rank, and then analyze these findings at a higher level in terms of the social power they afford actors in various social settings.

THE NUMBER OF SOCIAL STRATA; VARIOUS THEORIES

It is much easier to talk in terms of the theory of social stratification than it is to delineate a number of distinct social strata or classes. The difficulties that are encountered are evidenced by the variant number of classes (in open class societies) which various researchers have delineated. In closed caste societies or in estate systems of social stratification, the number of major classes is usually easier to recognize.

Before taking up the categorical theories of social classes it is necessary to consider what some have called the *continuum theory* of social stratification. This theory holds, quite logically, that there are no sharp dividing lines between social classes in truly open class societies. Differences in power, prestige and status are, in fact, so numerous and so widespread as to make for almost imperceptible graduations from the lowest to the highest social rank. Almost all social scientists agree with this interpretation, but there is considerable disagreement as to whether categories of classes should be delineated in the first place, and what arbitrary points on the power, prestige, and status continuum best divide the important classes in the second place. The first controversy poses a neat academic question, but proponents of a "no-category" theory leave the practical matter of class analysis and comparison in a "grey area" at best. The delineation of specific classes is advantageous in terms of the conceptualization of social classes and analysis of class differences as long as the arbitrary criteria used for class distinctions are clearly defined. Three such theories have received widespread attention.

Perhaps the most popular way to approach the study and understanding of the various class strata is in terms of the so-called *"three-class" theory* of social stratification. This theory envisions an upper class composed of a relatively few individuals who hold the top-most positions in society; a middle class composed of persons of lesser status, but of relatively comfortable means; and a lower class of persons who have a bare existence when measured by the given societies' standards. The chief criticism of this theory is that it does not draw a sharp enough dividing line between individuals in complex societies. The middle class, for instance, may run the gamut from semiskilled workers to owners of relatively large business enterprises as well as highly paid professionals. Such criticism has led to the five- and six-class theories of social stratification. The *six-class theory* holds that the upper class is divided into an upper-upper class and a lower-upper class, that the middle class is divided into an upper-middle and a lower-middle class, and that the lower class is divided into an upper-lower class and a lower-lower class.[17] The *five-class theory* generally holds to only one upper class.

Several other approaches to social class rankings have been used, such as the two classes—the business class and the working class—delineated by Robert and Helen Lynd in their study of Middletown.[18] Whatever approach the individual uses in delineating social classes is likely to be dependent on two factors: the relative complexity of the social system under study and the data gathered by the investigator as a basis for the number of ranks he can then define. Class differences are most easily described and compared when they represent wide discrepancies. When rank differences shade imperceptibly from one extreme to another, the precise definitions and careful measurements necessary present a real challenge.

THE MEASUREMENT OF CLASS POSITION IN OPEN CLASS SOCIETIES

Researchers have attempted to identify class position in open class societies in many ways. However, it is possible to classify almost all the methodological approaches to the measurement of class position under five broad headings. The advantages and disadvantages of each of these major approaches are

[17] This approach was popularized by Warner in the Yankee City Series. See W. L. Warner and Paul Lunt, *The Social Life of a Modern Community* (New Haven, Connecticut, Yale University Press, 1941).

[18] Robert Lynd and Helen Lynd, *Middletown in Transition* (New York, Harcourt, Brace & World, 1937).

briefly outlined below. Each approach, as it will be seen, is based on a particular type of data and/or of inquiry.

THE "STYLE-OF-LIFE" APPROACH

One of the most complex and comprehensive measures of class level used by sociologists are indices of what Weber called the *styles of life*. In Hodges' words these indices are devised to gauge ". . . patterns of interaction (who 'mixes' with whom), symbolic possessions (consumption goods and material belongings), and symbolic activities (recreation, speech, and formal affiliations)."[19] The rationale for this approach to the measurement of social class is quite logical. First, it is argued that social intimacy only occurs among people who look upon and treat each other as comparative equals. Second, it is held that the members of different social classes possess and use certain items which set them apart.

The supreme test of social intimacy is intermarriage, although clique relationships, mutual entertainment in homes, common membership in "social" organizations and other types of mutually shared activities also indicate close association. These are the types of things which are observed, recorded, and used to work out indices of social interaction. The so-called socio-economic status scales are designed to measure status in terms of the use and possession of certain items.[20] These scales were popularized on a national level, as previously mentioned, by Margaret Hagood in her work for the U. S. Department of Agriculture. She initiated a continuing program of ranking farm operator families according to level-of-living index by counties. The reader can readily see the utility of such a system for planning national programs of relief and development, such as President Eisenhower's Rural Development Program, President Kennedy's Area Redevelopment Program, and President Johnson's Poverty Program.

The major advantage of style-of-life measures of class position is found in their comprehensiveness. When interactional relations, symbolic possessions and symbolic activities are tabulated, status indices can be computed for individuals or groups which permit ranking on a status scale. The shortcomings of this approach are found in the fact that interaction, even marriage, does not always follow class lines. In addition, possessions quickly lose their status significance in the face of mass production and upper class recreation activity likewise tends to succumb to invasion from the lower classes. Status scales com-

---

[19] *Op. cit.*, p. 81.

[20] Some of the first notable works along this line are V. M. Sims, *The Measurement of Socio-Economic Status* (Bloomington, Illinois, Public School Publishing Co., 1928); F. Stuart Chapin, "A Quantitative Scale for Rating the Home and Social Environment of Middle Class Families in an Urban Community," *Journal of Educational Psychology*, Vol. 19 (February, 1928); and William H. Sewell, "A Short Form of the Farm Family Socio-Economic Status Scale," *Rural Sociology*, Vol. 7 (June, 1943), pp. 161-170.

puted from such indices must constantly be updated to overcome this type of problem.

THE REPUTATIONAL APPROACH

A second way to study social class and to classify individuals and groups into social classes in open systems is to ask knowledgeable persons to rank the members of their communities. There are several ways by which the judges may be selected, but the logic is essentially the same in all instances. The assumption is that members of a community or social system have a first-hand knowledge based on personal experience of the social position of the members of their groups. In other words they know the reputation of each person in the eyes of his fellows. Sociologists who use this approach do not go into the involved statistical methods used by those who compute indexes related to style-of-life and thus save considerable time and effort.

There is no doubt that what people say or think about an individual has important implications for his status position. However, the criticism that is leveled at this approach is that many people will allow personal approval or disapproval of certain types of behavior color their judgment of individuals. An upper class person, for example, may rate down another person because of a supposed snub or breach of etiquette. The reputational approach is also criticized because it is impossible for one individual to know every one in a relatively large community. There are also some rather difficult problems to be solved in the random selection of qualified judges.

THE SUBJECTIVE APPROACH

The third approach to the delineation of social rank in open class systems is termed the subjective approach because the interviewee is asked to rank himself, that is, make himself the subject of class ranking. The logic of this approach is based on the assumption that the individual is in the best position to know where he fits into the class system. This approach has an advantage over the reputational approach in that much larger groups can be studied. The latter is limited by the scope of acquaintance of the judges selected. The subjective approach, like the reputational approach, has advantages of time and simplicity over the style-of-life approach.

The chief criticism that has been raised against the subjective approach is that the man on the street may have a faulty perception, both of his social class system and of his own position in the system. Studies have shown that a substantial number of individuals have difficulty conceiving of class differentiation as more than the rich and the poor, or the haves and the have-nots. Such individuals have little notion of intermediate levels or strata. Also, some persons believe so strongly in a classless society or hold such strong Marxists views toward class, that they will not admit the existence of multiclass systems. With regard to evaluating themselves, some persons for ideological, ego, or other reasons will indicate they belong in lower or higher class categories than they actually hold. These shortcomings can be minimized by careful scholars but do complicate the subjective approach to the study of class position.

THE OCCUPATIONAL PRESTIGE APPROACH

The fourth approach to the study of social class in open systems utilizes occupation as an index to class position. This approach is defended in terms of the rationale that occupation has a "social reality"—it has a direct meaning for status positions. In addition, it is contended that occupation has the advantage of widespread comparability. Occupations, it is argued, are similar in almost all communities as well as in different nations. Perhaps the most popular rating scales of this type are the ones prepared by the National Opinion Research Center at the University of Chicago. These scales (The North-Hatt and the Hodge, Siegel, and Rossi studies of occupational prestige)[21] rank 90 occupations on the basis of prestige as determined by the responses of approximately 3000 interviewees selected at random. Table 10-1 shows the latest ratings to be worked out by NORC.

The disadvantage of this approach is inherent in all single-factor measures of complex entities. Despite the efficiency of occupation as a measure of class position, it becomes somewhat risky to equate occupation precisely with class status and some qualification must always be made if studies are to be taken seriously.

Table 10-1. *National Opinion Research Center Occupational Prestige Ratings, United States, 1963.*

RANK	OCCUPATION	NORC SCORE	RANK	OCCUPATION	NORC SCORE
1	U. S. Supreme Court Justice	94	9	U. S. representative in Congress	90
2	Physician	93	10	Chemist	89
3	Nuclear physicist	92	11	Lawyer	89
4	Scientist	92	12	Diplomat in the U.S. foreign	
5	Government Scientist	91		service	89
6	State Governor	91	13	Dentist	88
7	Cabinet member in the federal		14	Architect	88
	government	90	15	County judge	88
8	College professor	90			

[21] C. C. North and P. K. Hatt, "Jobs and Occupations: A Popular Evaluation," *Public Opinion News,* Vol. 9 (September, 1947), pp. 3-13; and Robert W. Hodge, Paul M. Siegal and Peter H. Rossi, "Occupational Prestige in the United States, 1925-1963," *The American Journal of Sociology,* Vol. 70 (November 1964), pp. 286-302.

Table 10-1. (*Continued*)

16	Psychologist	87
17	Minister	87
18	Member of the board of directors of a large corporation	87
19	Mayor of a large city	87
20	Priest	86
21	Head of a department in a state government	86
22	Civil engineer	86
23	Airline pilot	86
24	Banker	85
25	Biologist	85
26	Sociologist	83
27	Instructor in public schools	82
28	Captain in the regular army	82
29	Accountant for a large business	81
30	Public school teacher	81
31	Owner of a factory that employs about 100 people	80
32	Building contractor	80
33	Artist who paints pictures that are exhibited in galleries	78
34	Musician in a symphony orchestra	78
35	Author of novels	78
36	Economist	78
37	Official of an international labor union	77
38	Railroad engineer	76
39	Electrician	76
40	County agricultural agent	76
41	Owner-operator of a printing shop	75
42	Trained machinist	75
43	Farm owner and operator	74
44	Undertaker	74
45	Welfare worker for a city government	74
46	Newspaper columnist	73
47	Policeman	72
48	Reporter on a daily newspaper	71
49	Radio announcer	70
50	Bookkeeper	70
51	Tenant farmer—one who owns livestock and machinery and manages the farm	69

52	Insurance agent	69
53	Carpenter	68
54	Manager of a small store in a city	67
55	A local official of a labor union	67
56	Mail carrier	66
57	Railroad conductor	66
58	Traveling salesman for a wholesale concern	66
59	Plumber	65
60	Automobile repairman	64
61	Playground director	63
62	Barber	63
63	Machine operator in a factory	63
64	Owner-operator of a lunch stand	63
65	Corporal in the regular army	62
66	Garage mechanic	62
67	Truck driver	59
68	Fisherman who owns his own boat	58
69	Clerk in a store	56
70	Milk route man	56
71	Streetcar motorman	56
72	Lumberjack	55
73	Restaurant cook	55
74	Singer in a nightclub	54
75	Filling station attendant	51
76	Dockworker	50
77	Railroad section hand	50
78	Night watchman	50
79	Coal miner	50
80	Restaurant waiter	49
81	Taxi driver	49
82	Farm hand	48
83	Janitor	48
84	Bartender	48
85	Clothes presser in a laundry	45
86	Soda fountain clerk	44
87	Sharecropper—one who owns no livestock or equipment and does not manage farm	42
88	Garbage collector	39
89	Street sweeper	36
90	Shoe shiner	34

Source: Robert W. Hodge, Paul M. Siegal, and Peter H. Rossi, "Occupational Prestige in the United States, 1925-1963," *The American Journal of Sociology*, Vol. 70 (November, 1964), pp. 290-292.

THE MULTIPLE INDEX APPROACH

The various approaches to the study of social class position described all have rather clear weaknesses when used alone. For this reason, most researchers prefer to use two or more approaches so that they may have multiple indicators of social class positions. Studies which combine the reputational or subjective approach with the style-of-life or occupational prestige approaches are considered more valid and more reliable if high correlation is attained between the measures used. Various researchers have worked out composite indices that are designed to eliminate the biases of single-factor measures of class position and at the same time eliminate the necessity of double-checking by using multiple approaches. However, these new methods are still in the testing stage and it remains to be seen if any one or another will achieve widespread adoption.[22]

AN ILLUSTRATION OF SOCIAL STRATA DIFFERENCES: SMALL TOWN SOCIAL CLASSES IN THE U.S.A.

Numerous studies have been made in the United States of what have been termed typical small towns. These studies, regardless of their regional settings, turned up some impressively similar findings with regard to social stratification patterns. Hodges has summarized the findings of these studies in terms of the characteristics of each class delineated.[23] His discussion is presented in outline form below to illustrate the distinct style of life of persons who belong to, or live their lives out, in particular class situations. It is interesting to note that in each study made, at least one respondent denied the existence of social classes in his community.

THE UPPER-UPPER CLASS

The usual characteristics of the uppermost class, which include no more than one or two percent of the families are:

[22] Examples are the "Index of Status Characteristics" scale developed by Warner, and the "Index of Class Position" developed by Ellis, Land, and Olesen. See W. Lloyd Warner *et al., Social Class in America* (Chicago, Science Research Association, 1949) and Robert A. Ellis, W. Clayton Lane, and Virginia Elesen, "The Index of Class Position: An Improved Intercommunity Measure of Stratification," *American Sociological Review,* Vol. 28 (April, 1963), pp. 271-278.

[23] *Op. cit.,* pp. 66-70.

1. They own sufficient wealth, have sufficient power and social repute and a sufficiently long family history to warrant their position.
2. Their consumption and leisure time behavior is generally quiet, conservative, and "tweedy."
3. They hold reverence for the past and for such visible family trappings as coats of arms and antique heirlooms.
4. They restrict entry into the class to those of proper lineage, with marriage being a rare exception.
5. They educate their children in the highest prestige schools and universities.
6. They wear clothes displayed in *Town and Country* magazine.

THE LOWER-UPPER CLASS

The lower-upper class is constituted of about two or three percent of the typical small town's population. Their important characteristics are:

1. They own adequate or even superior material wealth and power for the upper-upper class status, but have insufficient family history.
2. They are a *nouveaux riche,* with a decided tendency toward conspicuous consumption.
3. They have aspirations to, but are not accepted for, the debutante list, the restricted country clubs, the Junior League, and other organizations of the elite.
4. They eagerly strive to make the grade into upper-upper status, but are constrained to a generation or two of waiting while acquiring the proper "breeding."
5. Like the upper-upper class, they are more likely to attend the Episcopal Church.

THE UPPER-MIDDLE CLASS

The third highest social class, the upper-middle class, usually includes 10 to 12 percent of the population of the average small town. This group is identifiable because:

1. They are made up largely of professional persons (doctors, lawyers, college professors) and successful merchants.
2. They are career-oriented joiners who people the service clubs, such as the Rotary, Lions, and Kiwanis.
3. They consider a college degree a necessity, but accept a bachelors degree from the state university as satisfactory.
4. They wear "Ivy"-styled, men's clothes and women select their wardrobes out of the pages of *Harper's Bazaar* or *Vogue.*
5. They are more likely to attend the Presbyterian church.

6. They are moderate television fans, but frequently forsake television for hi-fi listening.
7. They raise and control their children firmly but easily following a democratic approach to family life.
8. They are relative newcomers to town, generally speaking.
9. They host martini parties with unpuritanical frequency.

THE LOWER-MIDDLE CLASS

Approximately one out of every three persons in the typical small town is a member of the lower-middle class. This group stands out in the following ways:

1. It is made up largely of small business men, salesmen, clerks and foremen.
2. They are not avid joiners, as the upper-middle class, but are active in fraternal, religious, and veterans organizations.
3. They usually have 12 to 13 years of formal schooling (high school graduate with one or two years of college).
4. They make the church and its creed the focal point in their life; they take the Bible and its teachings most seriously.
5. They are rigidly moralistic and almost puritanical in outlook on life.
6. They are faithful followers of the tenets of the Protestant Ethics—they believe in frugality, respectability, thrift, hard work, saving, and the old-fashioned virtues.
7. They are devoutly family-centered and proud of home, town, and nation.

THE UPPER-LOWER CLASS

Just below the lower-middle class and not too well differentiated from it in some ways is the one-third of the population classed as upper-lower class. This group differs from the other classes in that:

1. It is made up mostly of blue-collar workers—employees rather than employers.
2. Like their lower-middle class neighbors, they are considered by the community and consider themselves to be "hard-working" and "reliable."
3. Most have dropped out of high school before graduation and earn less income than lower-middle class persons as a result.
4. They hold no sympathy for the "shiftless no accounts" below them, but feel ill at ease among white collar types above them.
5. They are usually members in good standing of trade unions.

6. They traditionally vote democratic and support social security legislation.
7. They are fervent radio, television, and motion picture fans.
8. They are avid sports fans, with a special interest in fishing. However, they tend to poker instead of the bridge played by members of the classes above them.

THE LOWER-LOWER CLASS

The typical small town in the United States is likely to have about 15–20 percent of its people classed in the bottom strata of society. These persons stand out in the following manner:

1. They are unskilled in an occupational sense, and their employment is marginal and sporadic.
2. They are school drop-outs who quit before the eighth grade.
3. They marry in their teens and have large families, which they cannot support.
4. They have many broken homes (one in two) and a strife-ridden life.
5. They live in cramped, dilapidated quarters.
6. They have a chronic indebtedness.
7. They are hostile and suspicious toward strangers; they see the world as a dog-eat-dog jungle.
8. They are overwhelmed by a pervasive sense of pessimism and resignation; they have no hope for the future.
9. They blame others rather than themselves for their plight, such as businessmen, Jews, politicians, and foreigners.
10. They are seldom religious in the sense of the lower-middle class, but tend to be hell-and-brimstone fundamentalists or Roman Catholic.
11. They are looked upon as innately depraved, slovenly, lazy, and more animal than human by the town's "solid and respectable" citizens.
12. Their main solace is the television set and constant trips to nearby taverns.
13. The men are authoritarians, who believe wives belong in the home, that husbands should rule with an iron hand and that children must be obedient, quiet and subservient.

In conclusion it may be noted that not everyone in the average small town in the United States is aware of everyone else's place in the town's social structure. However, the entire town's social life is subtly geared to those who "belong" and those who do not. Churches, schools, and clubs are all class typed, and in many ways represent inaccessible places for the lower groups. In other words, the citizens of the typical small town in the United States are in Hodges' words ". . . inextricably and overwhelmingly class-bound."[24]

[24] *Ibid.*, p. 70.

SOCIAL MOBILITY

The difference between an open and a closed society was brought out in an earlier section of this chapter. In closed societies there is no opportunity to be socially mobile, but in open societies a greater degree of social movement is in evidence. This phenomenon has greatly interested sociologists, especially in the United States, because of its implications for national values relating to opportunities for getting ahead. The aspirations of almost all persons is but one or another variation on the rags-to-riches theme. This is true despite the fact that most persons move only one or two steps up the class hierarchy during their lifetimes.[25] The important terms and patterns of behavior related to social mobility are reviewed here.

TYPES OF SOCIAL MOBILITY

Two distinct types of social mobility are recognized. Movement up or down from one social strata to another is termed **vertical social mobility.** This is the type of mobility which captures the popular fancy because of its connotations for success and achievement. The second type of mobility involves the movement from one social position to another without changing social strata. This is known as **horizontal social mobility.**

With respect to horizontal social mobility, the term *situs* (see Chapter 9) has significance. It will be recalled that this term was used to designate a set of positions customarily occupied by the same actor in a multigroup structure. For illustration, one may think of a university with its various teaching, research, business, and administrative departments. The professor who is offered an administrative position outside his department which carries approximately the same salary and prestige as his former position has changed his *situs,* but not his class position. Social mobility must then be analyzed in terms of both situs and strata changes.

FACTORS RELATED TO MOBILITY

The amount of social mobility which characterizes a given open society is closely related to the conditions that exist in the society. At least four sets of factors operate to affect the rate of mobility.

THE OPPORTUNITY STRUCTURE: Perhaps the most potent force in setting the stage for mobility is what some have called the *opportunity structure*

[25] See Kahl, *op. cit.,* Chap. IX.

within the given society.[26] Some societies, because of the nature of their social class systems, or because of their simplicity do not provide opportunity for social movement. A caste society discourages almost all vertical social mobility. However, a simple, agrarian, traditionalistic society has little more mobility because, in effect, there is nowhere to go. By contrast, a complex society has elaborate bureaucratic ladders for mobility—in the business world, in the educational world, in the military world, and in many other areas.

DEMOGRAPHIC PROCESSES: The second set of factors which relate to social mobility are demographic in nature. The first of these is immigration. Generally speaking, a strong wave of immigrants serves to push native persons up the social ladder, as the newcomers are willing to take, or at least are required as a rule to accept, lower status occupations. Many examples could be cited, but one has but to take note of the United States where new immigrants for many years literally pushed older settlers up the social ladder. The same thing has happened in many European and Asian countries, where large streams of immigrants have recently entered.

A second way in which demographic factors affect mobility is seen in the impact of internal migration on redistributions of the population. Rural migrants who move to the city to better themselves, that is, raise their social status, are an example. In modern societies, it is not unusual for individuals to move from one region to another to achieve a promotion or raise in pay. In those places where such freedom of mobility is allowed, one finds a continual reshuffling of persons in a social sense.

Differential birth rates also serve to affect social mobility. The upper classes in certain societies have failed to reproduce enough children to replenish their numbers. Thus a sort of vacuum is created which pulls replacements from the lower classes. This phenomenon varies from place to place and time to time, but it is widespread enough to be important in the total picture of social mobility.

THE IMPACT OF AUTOMATION: Today the great societies of the world are struggling with the vexing problems brought on by mass production and mass-marketing techniques. These techniques can loosely be lumped under the umbrella of automation. Automation has two serious consequences for social mobility. On the one hand, it tends to displace blue-collar workers and put them into the ranks of the unemployed. On the other side of the coin, automation tends to increase the number of white-collar jobs and thus opens the door for a certain amount of vertical social mobility. The higher the degree of automation, the more important these trends become.

ASPIRATION LEVELS: A final factor related to social mobility in open class societies is what may be termed aspiration levels. Many studies have

[26] Hodges, op. cit., p. 253.

shown that certain individuals and groups have higher aspirations than others. Why this is true is not our concern of the moment. However, the fact of higher aspirations usually means a willingness to strive harder for social achievement. This explains in part why the middle classes in the United States are the most socially mobile. It also helps explain the relative immobility of the lower-lower class.

It is appropriate to briefly discuss what has been called the *deferred gratification* concept at this point. **Deferred gratification** connotes the postponement of immediate pleasures for future gains. For example, a student may turn down a job with a "decent" salary in order to complete his Ph.D. degree and thus be eligible for a job with an "above average" salary. The several studies done in this area indicate that learning to defer the gratification of one's "needs" is associated with achievement roles. Said another way, such things as good grades and a good "reputation" are gained at some sacrifice of immediate pleasures, but are construed as necessary for attaining an occupation with a high prestige rating and a good salary. Earlier studies indicated that deferred gratification was a peculiarly middle-class pattern. However, a recent study by Straus suggests that it may be a more widespread phenomenon, one that is found to some degree in all social classes.[27]

AVENUES OF SOCIAL MOBILITY

There is a close correlation between the value-system of a society and the ways and means by which a person can legitimately move from one social position to another. However, certain broadly traveled avenues to higher (or lower) social rank can be detected in most open class societies. Each society will, of course, afford specific opportunities for social mobility which are cultural peculiarities. The more nearly universal ways of achieving status are the following.

OCCUPATIONAL IMPROVEMENT: Perhaps the most widespread of all ways to move ahead socially is to achieve a higher status occupation. The wide variation of prestige which various jobs have in the United States was shown in Table 10-1 (pages 180-181). From this list, it can readily be seen that individuals can improve their social status by moving up the occupational ladder.

ECONOMIC SUCCESS: It is difficult to separate occupation from money and education. Yet, the three are often quite distinct. To the extent that one is successful in obtaining money, apart from the amount normal for his occu-

---

[27] See Murray A. Straus, "Deferred Gratification, Social Class, and The Achievement Syndrome," *American Sociological Review*, Vol. 27 (June, 1962), pp. 326-335. Straus presents a well-documented review of the studies of deferred gratification as an introduction to the report of his study findings.

pation, he may enhance his upward social mobility. The near universal esteem of the wealthy is so well known that no elaboration is necessary. The fact that some highly educated persons have low income but high prestige and some occupations have high income but low prestige present exceptions to this rule.

EDUCATIONAL ACHIEVEMENT: Within recent years, as the "race for space" has assumed gigantic proportions, education has come more and more to the front as a key to social mobility. The relationship of education to occupation in the United States is shown in Figure 10-4. Like other complex variables, education as a way to social advancement, has intricate patterns and degrees of importance. In most instances, not only the amount of schooling is important, but also where the schooling was obtained and under whom it was obtained. One who has achieved an advanced degree from a "prestige" school and studied under an eminent scholar has a better chance of rising occupationally and socially.

CONTROL OF POWER: The best way to attain control of social power is debatable. It is also difficult to isolate power from occupation, wealth, and education. However, again using ideal constructs, power may be attained in a political sense, at least, without great initial change in wealth and with no change of formal education. The power exercised by organization men (such as party bosses and managers) is also sometimes divorced from other factors.

MISCELLANEOUS FACTORS: In most open societies there are fairly well defined but less often traveled roads to social improvement. One can name persons whose success stories are attributed to their unusual talent (as musicians, dancers, singers, and actors); their athletic prowess; their physical beauty; or military reputation.[28] It is also possible in some societies to achieve higher status by "exceptional morality," when this behavior is recognized and rewarded by the community or religious group. An important additional factor is that for women marriage has been an important way to rise socially. Many women achieve class levels which their own education, demonstrated ability, and family backgrounds would preclude were it not for the marriage factor alone.

SUMMARY

Social strata are an important structural aspect of all societies. Systems of social stratification—the ranking of individuals on a scale of superiority-inferiority—are based on the differentiation which characterizes status positions and

[28] A recent study demonstrates that a military career is an excellent means of upward mobility in the United States. See Charles H. Coates, "America's New Officer Corps," *Trans-Action*, Vol. 3 (March/April, 1966), pp. 22-24.

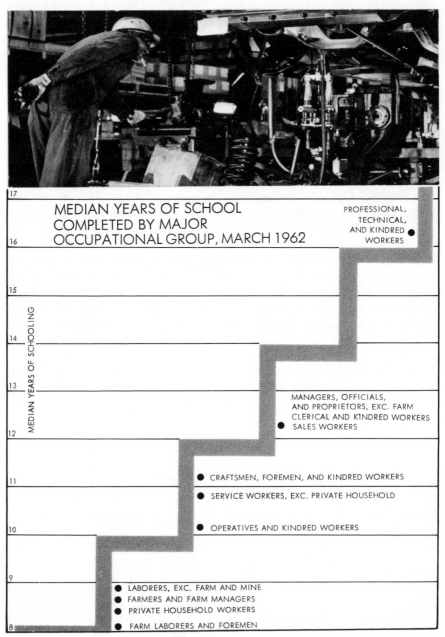

MEDIAN YEARS OF SCHOOL COMPLETED BY MAJOR OCCUPATIONAL GROUP, MARCH 1962

MEDIAN YEARS OF SCHOOLING

17

16

15

14

13

12

11

10

9

8

PROFESSIONAL, TECHNICAL, AND KINDRED WORKERS

MANAGERS, OFFICIALS, AND PROPRIETORS, EXC. FARM
CLERICAL AND KINDRED WORKERS
● SALES WORKERS

● CRAFTSMEN, FOREMEN, AND KINDRED WORKERS

● SERVICE WORKERS, EXC. PRIVATE HOUSEHOLD

● OPERATIVES AND KINDRED WORKERS

● LABORERS, EXC. FARM AND MINE
● FARMERS AND FARM MANAGERS
● PRIVATE HOUSEHOLD WORKERS
● FARM LABORERS AND FOREMEN

Source: *Health, Education, and Welfare Indicators,* U. S. Department of Health, Education, and Welfare, Office of the Secretary (Washington, D. C., U. S. Government Printing Office, April, 1964), p. xxv. Photograph courtesy of Ford Motors.

roles. These systems function to promote a division of labor in society. One system differs from another in degree of freedom which is allowed the individual to achieve higher class status and on ranking of social positions in terms of functional importance.

The placement of an individual in a given stratification system is accomplished through the study of a number of factors like wealth, income, education, and family background. These factors all have a close association with social power and are manifested in terms of material possessions, social participation, prestige ratings, and use of leisure time.

All approaches to the study of social stratification in open class systems must take into consideration the relative complexity of the given social system. When differences between persons and groups shade imperceptibly from one extreme to another, a greater number of classes and a greater complexity of social relations are indicated. Class is more realistically understood in terms of subcultural settings, which account for differences in status symbols and other cultural expressions related to class.

Despite some differences of opinion about class structure and the functions of social stratification, the importance of a person's place in the social hierarchy cannot be overstressed. Every individual lives out every day of his life in the context of situations dictated by his class position. The *real* significance of social class is thus found in the life opportunities which are afforded those who find themselves in one or another social strata.

Supplementary Readings

Bendix, Reinhard and Seymour Martin Lipset, Class, Status, and Power, 2nd ed. (New York, Free Press, 1966).

Clarke, Alfred C., "The Use of Leisure and Its Relation to Levels of Occupational Prestige," American Sociological Review, Vol. 21 (June, 1956), pp. 301-307.

Hodges, Harold M., Jr., Social Stratification: Class in America (Cambridge, Massachusetts, Schenkman Publishing Co., 1964).

Olcott, Mason, "The Caste System of India," American Sociological Review, Vol. 9 (December 1944), pp. 648-657; and also in ROSS.

Presthus, Robert, Men at the Top: A Study in Community Power (New York, Oxford University Press, 1964).

Sjoberg, Gideon, "Are Social Classes in America Becoming More Rigid?" American Sociological Review, Vol. 16 (December, 1951), pp. 775-784.

Straus, Murray A., "Deferred Gratification, Social Class, and the Achievement Syndrome," American Sociological Review, Vol. 27 (June, 1962), pp. 326-335.

Warner, W. Lloyd et al., Social Class in America (New York, Harper & Row, Harper Torchbook, 1960).

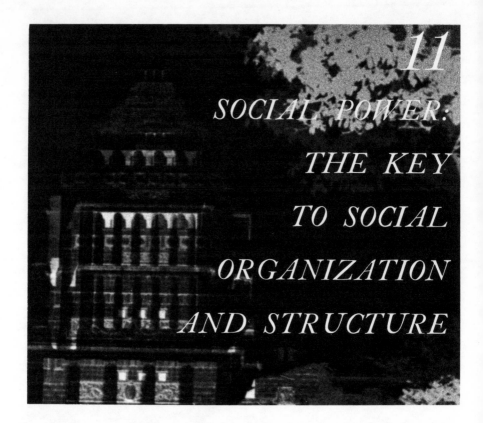

SOCIAL POWER: THE KEY TO SOCIAL ORGANIZATION AND STRUCTURE

Social power was briefly defined in Chapter 3. There it was pointed out that sociologists had only recently achieved something like a consensus of opinion as to how this concept should be defined and used analytically. Studies of power have in the past been left to social philosophers and political scientists. The fact that social systems had come to be seen to include a structural element characterized by the capacity of certain actors to control the behavior of others, forced the attention of sociologists to this phenomenon. Max Weber was perhaps the first whose writings on power were given serious attention. His theories, which provide the basic starting point for modern sociological analysis of power, are set forth in a work which was not translated until 1947.[1] Since Weber's time a large number of theorists, as well as empirical researchers, have seriously addressed themselves to the study of social power. They have conclusively determined that social organization rests to a large extent on a foundation of power. The purpose of this chapter is to acquaint the student with the nature of social power and its importance to the discipline of sociology.

[1] Max Weber, *The Theory of Social and Economic Organization,* translated by A. M. Henderson and Talcott Parsons (New York, Free Press, 1947), Sections III and IV.

THE NATURE OF POWER

POWER AS A CONCEPT

The definition of social power given earlier—the capacity to control others—was worked out by Loomis after careful perusal of the literature on the subject.[2] This definition has advantages of simplicity and clarity. However, there are certain understandings which are necessary for proper use of the term.

The first is that the study of power must be approached, as all sociological phenomena, as objectively as possible. Said another way, power is inherently neither good nor bad. This is not to say that power cannot be used for good or bad purposes as interpreted by the normative standards of a given culture. It is simply to say that power, like status or facilities, has no moral connotation when considered as a structural element of a social system and a vital aspect of social organization.

The second understanding is that social power is a capability. This capability is relative to such things as status position, various facilities and resources, and personal abilities. To illustrate: In a given social system setting, the capability which a given actor has to control the behavior of others rests upon such things as his wealth, his skills, his education, and his outside contacts. This point may be clarified if one thinks of a banker. He has the power to make loans, but has to turn down a large industrial loan representing a sound risk because he does not have the necessary amount of money (facility) at his disposal. His capability to control others, the makers of loans in this instance, goes only so far as the extent of his facilities—here the amount of money available.

A third interpretation which helps clarify the concept of power is that it is a property of social relations, and not the inherent attribute of an individual or group. Power is independent of given persons, and it is technically incorrect to speak of a person as "powerful"—it may only be said that he occupies a powerful position. Emerson points out that the power of one group or individual to control or influence another group or individual resides in the control exercised over the things the other person or group values. Thus he states, ". . . power resides implicitly in the other's dependency."[3] Such a conceptualization permits the study of power in terms of the nature and types of social relations which characterize given social systems rather than on the strength of individuals, groups, and organizations.

[2] From Charles P. Loomis, *Social Systems: Essays on Their Persistence and Change.* Copyright 1960, D. Van Nostrand Company, Inc., Princeton, N.J., p. 20.

[3] Richard M. Emerson, "Power-Dependence Relations," *American Sociological Review,* Vol. 27 (February, 1962), pp. 31-41.

Finally, it should be understood that power is not a simple notion. The approach of an introductory text must necessarily be both general and summary in nature. For this reason, and because the term power is used frequently and glibly in ordinary conversation, there may be a tendency to lose sight of its many intricacies and subtleties.

THE COMPONENTS OF POWER

Social power is generally conceived to have two major components—*authority* and *influence*. Sometimes the distinction is said to be between authoritative and nonauthoritative power, although the term influence is more specific.

Authority is the capability to control others which is established or determined by members of a given social system. This type of power resides in a social position and the actor occupying this position cannot take his authority (power) with him upon vacating the position. The president of a university, for example, cannot retain his decision-making role in student and faculty affairs after retiring to a professorship or accepting a position in the business world. By the same token the members of the university social system expect him to have certain control over students and faculty while he is president of the university. He is delegated such power by virtue of his office rather than by virtue of his individual personality.

In contrast to authority, **influence** is that capability to control others which is independent of the authority vested in a status position. Influence can only come about when one actor, usually in a subordinate position, is willing to, or allows himself to, become controlled in some way by another actor. Actors are able to influence because of advantages in such things as human relations skills, intelligence, wealth, control of mass media, and prestige. Although his authority extends only to the training rules and playing strategy, a football coach can influence his high school team members to be good, clean-living boys with high standards of sportsmanship, or he can influence them to think the important thing is to win at any cost.

In actual concrete social systems the amount of power which may be exercised differs according to certain variables. These variables have been identified by Bohlen, Beal, Klonglan, and Tait.[4] The first is the combination of authority and influence which a given actor is able to bring to a given position. One man may be elected mayor of a town and have great success because he has tremendous influence with other town officials and the citizens of the community. A second man may be a miserable failure because all his power is authoritative, that is, vested in the office of mayor, and he has so little influence otherwise that no one cooperates beyond the limits of necessity. Mod-

[4] Joe M. Bohlen, George M. Beal, Gerald E. Klonglan, and John L. Tait, *Community Power Structure and Civil Defense* (Ames, Iowa, Iowa Agricultural and Home Economics Experiment Station, Rural Sociology Report No. 35, 1964), p. 42.

erately succesful mayors would, presumably, have a certain amount of influence as well as legitimate authority.

The second variable is a function of the fact that the holder of a social position may not exercise his complete authoritative power because he has only a partial knowledge of the power implicit in his office. Many political offices are involved in a tangle of statutes, and the power exercised by a given incumbent depends on his willingness and ability to fathom out what he can and cannot do. In this regard, everyone is familiar with the reports of arrests for certain acts which a previous law officer had tolerated but which were still illegal on the basis of a law passed many years before.

A third variable which accounts for differences in the amount of authority which is exercised at one time or another, is a function of the imperfect socialization of members of a social system. Because they have not been fully informed (socialized) the members of a social system may not know the extent of the power (authority) vested in a given status position in the system. Therefore they either allow the actors who hold these positions to have more power than is legitimate for their positions or they restrain the actors from exercising all the power they are entitled to. Jurisdictional disputes between rival city officials have their origin in this type of problem, as do some civil rights complaints.

LEGITIMATE VERSUS ILLEGITIMATE POWER

Power is considered legitimate as long as it falls within the realm of the culturally sanctioned norms of a society. Thus any power-related action that is in keeping with the folkways, mores, or law is normally approved. This fact has been alluded to when power was said to be invested in the social position rather than in the individual. Illegitimate power, in contrast to legitimate power, is in violation of the standards set up for given positions in a given social system. One very simple example will illustrate the distinction between legitimate and illegitimate power. In American society it is right for a parent to punish his misbehaving child (within reason), but it is not proper or right for a parent to punish someone else's child, regardless of how badly the child might deserve reprimand. The same power is legitimate in one instance and illegitimate in the second instance because social relationships determine which set of norms apply.

Schemerhorn weaves a consideration of coercion into his discussion of the legitimacy of power.[5] He points out that formal power is almost always coercive to some extent. However, he notes, there is an extremely important hazard in the continued use of too much force, even though it may be legitimate. This is because opportunity for cooperation or compromise is thus

[5] Richard A. Schemerhorn, *Society and Power* (New York, Random House, 1961), pp. 36-39.

eliminated. Under such a condition, resistance is inevitable, and a vicious cycle of violence can result. History is full of instances where magnates, rulers, and others have fallen into such an error.

The term **countervailing power** is used to describe the forces which rise in opposition to power organizations that have grown to great power.[6] Thus if one political party, or one corporation, or one labor union grows large enough to wield power against other such organizations in a coercive sense, it can be expected that the other organizations will attempt to check or balance the power of the first party, that is, set up a countervailing power. At the individual level, a similar chain reaction can also be set in motion. In our example of a parent punishing his child, if he abuses the child beyond limits, the second parent, or a neighbor, or a policeman may sooner or later exercise a countervailing type of power.

Schemerhorn has arranged the qualities of power along two axes, legitimacy–illegitimacy and coercion–noncoercion (see Figure 11-1).[7] In this chart, double lines are used to show that sharp distinctions are often impossible to maintain between what is legitimate or coercive. The student should recognize that the diagram is drawn to fit a relatively stable representative government type of society. It could be easily altered to fit other types of societies.

POWER STRUCTURES

At a given time, there are several possibilities for power relations in a social system. Schermerhorn lists what he calls the four logical possibilities for the exercise of power. These are (1) the behavior of an individual may dominate the behavior of another individual; (2) the behavior of an individual may dominate the behavior of a group; (3) the behavior of a group may dominate the behavior of an individual; (4) the behavior of a group may dominate the behavior of another group.[8] In the first instance, a mayor of a town may rule his immediate subordinate with an iron hand, telling him what work to do, where to go, and what to say. In the second instance, the mayor can be seen as extending his power in like fashion over his entire staff. The third situation would be seen when the mayor's assistant and other staff members reach a decision to have more freedom and issue an ultimatum to that effect, backed by a wholesale threat to resign. The mayor must concede or face utter chaos. The last possibility is illustrated when the local restaurant association influences the town council to change certain health regulations.

In each of the above instances one sees that power has a definite structure.

---

[6] This term was introduced by Galbraith in 1952, although its meaning is enlarged upon somewhat here. John K. Galbraith, *American Capitalism: The Concept of Countervailing Power* (Boston, Houghton Mifflin, 1952).

[7] *Op. cit.*, p. 38.

[8] *Ibid.* p. 16.

FIGURE 11-1.   *The Dimensions of Power.*

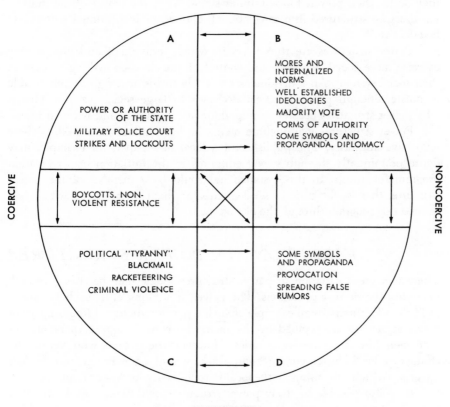

SECTOR A—   LEGITIMATE AND COERCIVE
SECTOR B—   LEGITIMATE AND NONCOERCIVE
SECTOR C—   ILLEGITIMATE AND COERCIVE
SECTOR D—   ILLEGITIMATE AND NONCOERCIVE

Source: Richard A. Schemerhorn, *Society and Power* (New York, Random House, 1961), p. 38.

Said another way, power emanates from a particular type of relationship. It is true that in a real-life situation power may come from several sources at once, but this does not change the fact of power structures.

DEFINITION OF POWER STRUCTURE

The definition of **power structure** generally accepted is *that of a pattern of relationships so structured that individuals possessing social power are able to* *act in concert to impose their decisions on the entire social system.* This definition becomes clearer if one thinks of the power disposed of by individuals or groups as more of a reflection of the interrelationships from which they derive their power. Floyd Hunter states, ". . . the power of the individual must be structured into associational, cliques, or institutional patterns to be effective."[9]

Power structures are thus ways in which individuals and groups may exercise more social power in the control of the decision-making process in their social systems. An individual actor, solely in his own right, rarely is able to muster enough power to affect decisions in large social systems. This is why power structures become so important in community and national life.

Power structures may include men who have influence as well as those who have authority. The publisher of a local newspaper, for example, may figure prominently through strong editorials in the initiation of a recreation program for youth. In this instance he would be a member of the power structure, that is, the civic or service club to which he belonged which had pushed this program through the city council.

VARIATIONS IN POWER STRUCTURES

There is a great variation in power structures. Some may be strong enough to control the destiny of nations. The power of a ruling elite, such as existed in Hitler's Germany, is an example of such a power structure. Other important power structures are typified by the men who control large corporations, or even men who run large universities. However, the persons who control the affairs of a local church congregation also represent a power structure as does the group which runs things in the local Parent–Teachers Association.

It is also possible to study power structures at different levels. In most large social systems, more or less general or overall power structures exist which serve to set broad policy. At lower levels of decision-making one finds other power structures which control lesser issues. To illustrate, the board of directors of a giant corporation decides on how much money is to be spent for a given expansion project, but the specific decisions regarding site, lay-out, and architecture of a new plant are made by lower levels of executives. In government, overall policy for military, educational, health and welfare, and like matters are likely to be set by legislatures, while decisions regarding the implementation of such programs are made at departmental levels.

Power structures, like individuals, derive their power from the control of certain resources and vary in this manner as well. Schemerhorn identifies five types of resources which can be used to advance or to strengthen a power position.

(1) Military, police, or criminal power with its control over violence.

[9] Floyd Hunter, *Community Power Structure* (Chapel Hill, North Carolina, University of North Carolina Press, 1953), p. 6.

(2) Economic power with control over land, labor, wealth, or corporate production.
(3) Political power with control over legitimate and ultimate decision-making within a specific territory.
(4) Traditional or ideological power involving control over belief and value systems, religion, education, specialized knowledge, and propaganda.
(5) Diversionary power with control over hedonistic (pleasure–pain) interests, recreation, and enjoyments.[10]

Each of these power resources is socially controlled and thus those who govern decisions affecting each resource command social power to that extent.

TYPES OF POWER STRUCTURES

Two distinct types of power structures have been recognized. The first type, known as a **monomorphic power structure** is characterized by a situation where the same individuals are the most powerful in all areas of decision-making. Said another way, in a monomorphic power structure, all decisions are made by the same small group of actors. Thus in a town, or even a large city, the same power elite dictates courses of action, whether they be in the realm of business, politics, education, recreation, or other major issue areas. In this regard, it is important to note that even though the same individuals are involved in all decisions, there will likely be a deference to the member of the group considered more knowledgeable or more directly involved in a particular issue. Prominent businessmen, for example, will be relied upon to make a judgment on whether or not to woo a new industry, while educators in the influential group may have first say with regard to school expansion programs. The point is that while business people and educators are part of the monomorphic power structure, they contribute differentially to decisions, depending on the issue.[11]

The second type of power structure is termed a **polymorphic power structure**. As might be expected from the name, this type is characterized by different persons exercising decision-making powers for each separate issue. These persons are not associated in one power elite as in the instance of a monomorphic power structure. They may represent an "elitism" but only in that they are the top persons in their respective groups. This characteristic has led some authors to refer to such power structures as *pluralism*.[12]

[10] *Op. cit.,* p. 17.
[11] For a comprehensive discussion of the types of power structures see Bohlen, Beal, Klonghan, and Tait, *op. cit.,* pp. 49-52.
[12] Robert Presthus defines pluralism as, ". . . a socio-political system in which the power of the state is shared with a large number of private groups, interest organizations, and individuals represented by such organizations." However, most political scientists define the term in a more general sense. Robert Presthus, *Men at the Top* (New York, Oxford University Press, 1964), p. 10.

Polymorphic power structures are on the face more democratic in nature since they allow more actors to have some voice, however small, in decision-making. This is brought about as each power figure relates himself to an organization or electorate from which his power originates. Thus, when different individuals and groups are involved as decision-makers, there is more opportunity for widespread participation in the affairs of a social system.

Power structures are polymorphic when viewed in terms of a single issue as well as when seen in terms of their total operation. For example, in a county educational board, one political faction might control the election of board members, but another faction might have power to pass or defeat school bonds or other measures proposed by the board. In this illustration the social power related to education in the county is distributed between two power groups, a polymorphic situation.

CENTERS OF POWER

Preceding discussions have introduced the student to the nature of power and of power structures. It was implied that power tended to center in certain individuals and groups depending on situational factors. We are now ready to identify and briefly describe the important centers of power which have been recognized.

THE POWER ELITE

Reference was made in the preceding section to monomorphic power structures. It was pointed out that in such structures power tended to be centered in a small number of individuals. The term most often used to describe such a group is the **power elite.** C. Wright Mills popularized this concept. He used the expression to refer to the persons found in every complex society who have extraordinary power at their command. He conceived the elite as being in positions where they could make decisions having major consequences. The power elite is, in his words, " . . . in command of the major hierarchies and organizations of modern society. They rule the big corporations. They run the machinery of the state and claim its prerogatives. They direct the military establishment. They occupy the strategic command posts of the social structure, in which are now centered the effective means of the power and the wealth and the celebrity which they enjoy."[13]

Elitism is a condition which exists when patterns of decision-making are characterized by limited participation of the masses. Since elites are subject to little influence from those outside their select group, elitism always con-

[13] C. Wright Mills, *The Power Elite* (New York, Oxford University Press, 1956), pp. 3-4.

notes the disproportionate control of group affairs by limited numbers. The presence of an elite is usually acknowledged by such references as "the Establishment," "the Brain Trust," and "the Top Brass."

The elite who may be in topmost power positions vary from one community to another. In some instances wealth may be the most important factor in power, in other instances family or educational background may be more important. Not infrequently, occupational prestige looms to the fore and the elite are the executives of large corporations. Pellegrin and Coates found in their study of absentee-owned corporations and community power structure that corporation executives played "preeminent roles" in the life of "Bigtown," the city they studied.[14]

A special term for one type of power elite—**community influentials**—has come into widespread usage since the notable study of Floyd Hunter, previously mentioned. This term is used to refer to the individuals who have more social power to affect community decisions than any one else. The only distinction which can be made between the power elite as a general concept and community influentials as a specific concept is that the power of the latter is thought of and studied solely in relation to decisions which relate to community life, whether it be a rural community, a small town or a large city. The power elite is thought of as having power in corporations, in religious organizations, in politics, in the military, and other more diffuse group structures.

ORGANIZATIONAL POWER

Organizations, as brought out in Chapter 9, are social units or systems deliberately and rationally created to attain certain goals, such as large corporations, professional societies, and labor unions. Modern complex societies are more and more being referred to as *organizational societies*. Amitai Etzioni points out that, "Modern civilization depends largely on organizations as the most rational and efficient form of social grouping known." He goes on to note that, "By coordinating a large number of human actions, the organization creates a powerful social tool."[15] Since organizations have a closer control over the actions of their members than most other social groups, this social tool is more frequently manipulated to gain advantages in terms of social power. The struggle for power between organizations may be the most dramatic social development of our times.

The power of organizations is conceived as somewhat different from the power of an elite. The latter draws its strength from its power positions held within an organizational framework of some kind. By contrast, organizations

[14] Roland J. Pellegrin and Charles Coates, "Absentee-Owned Corporations and Community Power Structure," *American Journal of Sociology*, Vol. 61 (March, 1956), pp. 413-414.
[15] Amitai Etzioni, *Modern Organizations* (Englewood Cliffs, New Jersey, Prentice-Hall, 1964), p. 1.

draw their power from the number of members they can recruit and integrate into an effective course of action. Wealth and facilities enter into organizational power, but take a secondary position to coordinated membership response. Horton and Hunt identify the major source of organizational power as, ". . . the ability to enable people to take *planned, concerted action* to affect social decisions."[16]

The power of organizations is seen in the effectiveness of such groups as the American Medical Association, the League of Women Voters, the American Farm Bureau, and the AFL-CIO. These groups and others like them resort to various tactics to achieve their goals of action. Legislators may be bombarded with letters, telegraphs and telephone calls, threats of boycotts, strikes or other nonviolent types of coercion may be made; propaganda barrages utilizing mass media may be loosed; and occasionally less reputable practices may be employed. Organizational alliances are frequently worked out between the power elite of organizations striving for the same goal. The important understanding is that one can explain certain patterns of behavior and certain aspects of social change in terms of social power that is centered in highly structured organizations.

THE POWER OF UNORGANIZED MASSES

Social power is seen as deriving from one other major area of a societal system. This is in the spontaneous collective action of the unorganized masses of people. From preceding discussions it might appear that the anonymous little man in a large mass society would be totally powerless, except as he might vote for the right man, or belong to a strong organization. The fact is that the actions of the masses, when taken in concert (without conscious collaboration) does represent a very potent type of social power. Sometimes this power goes counter to the decisions of the power elite and the latter fall from grace. This is one reason the elite refrain from active participation in politics or other activities which have a high risk of loss of face.

Many examples of the power of unorganized masses might be given. Among the most obvious are the eccentricities of the mass consumer. What people buy dictates the success or failure of business enterprises. The type of automobile built, the kind of daily newspaper published, the national radio or television program presented, or the music played for the masses is an indication of this power.

At another level of action the masses demonstrate their power by not cooperating with certain laws, or by exhibiting apathy over programs of improvement. In the United States, both the Civil Defense Program and the fluoridation-of-water movement failed initially because of noncooperation by

[16] Paul B. Horton and Chester L. Hunt, *Sociology* (New York, McGraw-Hill, 1964), p. 301.

the public. Another example of the power of the unorganized masses is found in uprisings over certain issues. The voters of several southern states bolted their traditional Democratic party to vote Republican in the 1964 and 1966 elections because they were not happy with certain policies of the party. Likewise many traditional Republicans in the Northeastern part of the nation switched to Democratic candidates because of a dislike for the conservativism of the Republican Party leaders.

SOCIAL CLASS ORIGINS OF THE POWER ELITE

Many of the studies of social power have determined the social background of individuals in power positions. These findings provide an understanding of the recruitment process for elites and help to clarify the pattern of upward social mobility. Drawing on the many studies made in the United States, Suzanne Keller pinpointed the social class origin of various types of elites.[17]

The many studies of *political* elites definitely show that this power group includes a predominance of *middle-class* individuals. Even high offices such as President or senator are filled with middle-class persons. This pattern is apparently tied in with the aspiration levels and achievement orientations of middle-class families. The top power positions in the *military* and in *other government services* are also largely filled with recruits from the professional, managerial, and business levels of society. The evidence available on the *scientific* elite is not as complete as for the above groups, but suggests the same pattern. Leo Moulin, for example, determined from his studies that winners of science Nobel Prizes were *never* of "humble" origin.[18]

The *diplomatic* elite seems to be drawn more from the upper class than other types of elite. Diplomats tend to be drawn from the upper strata of society in countries with a feudal past, while countries like the United States draw many of their ambassadors and ministers from the ranks of the wealthy or otherwise prominent families. This is because the pay received by these top-level foreign-service officials is often not enough for them to fulfill their "social" roles. An independent source of wealth helps overcome this problem.

Studies of the background of *religious* elite are scarce. However, what evidence is available suggests that in recent years a larger percentage of this group has had its origin in the working or lower classes than is true for most other elites. In previous times, however, the religious elite tended to be predominantly from the upper class.

[17] Suzanne Keller, *Beyond the Ruling Class* (New York, Random House, 1963), pp. 392-406.
[18] Leo Moulin, "The Nobel Prizes for the Sciences from 1901–1950—An Essay in Sociological Analysis," *British Journal of Sociology,* Vol. 6 (September, 1955), pp. 246-263.

The information available on the social class background of the members of the various elite stresses that the majority are middle-class individuals from comfortable home backgrounds. However, there is also an indication that recruitment from lower classes is increasing. This trend is seen in Europe and the East as well as in the United States. Recent economic, political, and social developments are no doubt related to this changing pattern. Despite this trend, it is highly unlikely that the lower classes will ever furnish more than a small percentage of the important power figures in any large society.

APPROACHES TO THE STUDY OF POWER

Those persons who have studied social power have used a variety of methodological approaches. Although some of the variation in approaches is more due to conceptual semantics than anything else, basic differences stem from the methods used in locating or identifying community influentials and other personalities. The five approaches reviewed here were outlined by Bell, Hill, and Wright in their study of public leadership.[19]

THE POSITIONAL LEADERSHIP APPROACH

Perhaps the most logical approach to the study of power, in view of the fact that power is vested in social positions to a large extent, is what has been termed the *positional* approach. This approach has two steps. The first is the determination of the positions that carry substantial authority in a given social system. The second step is the identification of the personalities who hold these positions.

This approach to the study of power has the advantage of simplicity. However, despite its apparent rationality, it has one serious disadvantage. This is the fact that those persons who work behind the scenes and who may indeed influence those in power positions, are not identified. Also, sometimes persons who occupy lower echelon positions, but who have more social power than persons in higher positions, are by-passed.

THE REPUTATIONAL LEADERSHIP APPROACH

The second method of studying social power is termed the *reputational* approach and is the same general approach used in the study of stratification. In this approach the investigator interviews knowledgeable persons and asks

---

[19] Wendell Bell, Richard J. Hill, and Charles R. Wright, *Public Leaderships* (San Francisco, Chandler Publishing Co., 1961). The writer is indebted to the summary of Bohlen, Beal, Klonglan, and Tait, *op. cit.*, pp. 60-65.

them to name the influential persons in their communities or other social systems. The questions put may differ in exact wording, but in essence they boil down to, "Who runs this town?" (or community, or corporation, or church).

The reputational approach like the positional approach has the advantage of simplicity and ease of administration. However, it's validity hinges upon the knowledge of the interviewees selected about the true power figures. If enough respondents agree on the top personalities, one can be fairly certain, if not completely sure, that the information obtained is valid.

THE SOCIAL PARTICIPATION APPROACH

The scales used to measure social participation were referred to elsewhere in this text. One approach to the study of social power is to determine who belongs to what organizations and who holds what position in an organization. In a simple subsocial system this is a relatively easy matter to determine, but in larger social systems many organizations, both formal and informal, are involved. The social participation method is very effective in determining who participates, but fails to provide information on persons who are not active in the implementation of action programs, but who may wield great power in other decisions. It is thus seldom used alone.

THE PERSONAL INFLUENCE OR OPINION LEADERSHIP APPROACH

A fourth approach to the study of power is to try to determine who influences people the most. Within a given social system there are opinion leaders at all levels of social relationships. These leaders are not necessarily the elite, nor do they always represent persons in formal positions. These facts and the difficulty faced in determining the real opinion leaders do not encourage the use of the influence and opinion method without other approaches for the sake of validation.

THE EVENT ANALYSIS AND DECISION-MAKING APPROACH

The final method used in the study of social power involves the careful analysis of the process of decision-making in given issues. The researcher may select a current issue and follow it through to a final decision, recording the role each important person played in arriving at the decision. As an alternative, past issues and decisions can be studied to determine who played important parts in bringing about a given course of action.

The limitations of this approach to the study of social power are primarily those of time and resources. It usually takes a long period to follow through until issues are resolved and it is also difficult and time consuming to reconstruct correctly what has happened in the past.

THE USE OF A COMBINATION
OF APPROACHES

In actual practice, it is seldom that a researcher limits himself to one approach to the study of social power. In fact, the various approaches outlined above are not always easily differentiated in a concrete situation. Therefore, they lend themselves to a combination approach. The focus of a given study is the important determining factor in the selection of the combination of approaches to be used.

SUMMARY

Social organization rests to a large extent on a foundation of power defined as the "ability to control others." The two major components of power are authority, which is vested in status positions and stands independent of a given individual, and influence, which is the ability an actor has to affect others' behavior apart from authority. Influence depends on human-relations skills and controls over certain facilities, such as media of communication.

Power is considered legitimate as long as it is exercised in keeping with the norms of a society, even though it may be coercive in nature. The exercise of power is through power structures or patterns of relationships which allow individuals possessing power to act in concert and thus impose their decisions on entire social systems. Such structures are said to be monomorphic in nature when the same individual or group are powerful in all areas of decision-making. They are termed polymorphic when different persons are involved in making the decisions for separate issues.

Several centers of power are recognized. The power elite includes those persons who manage to get extraordinary power at their command, such as men of great wealth, top executives in business and government, and community influentials. Certain organizations represent centers of power because of their ability to mobilize large numbers of people into concerted courses of action such as is done on occasion by large corporations, professional groups, and labor unions. Forces that arise in opposition to power organizations are said to apply countervailing power. Unorganized masses also represent centers of power. The power of the man on the street is expressed through consumer behavior (what he will or won't buy), mass noncooperation, and voting patterns.

The basic approaches to the study of social power focus on the status positions, social reputation, social participation, and personal influence which are characteristic of individuals and groups. Most researchers utilize a combination of the above factors in their efforts to determine the important actors in a given power structure. It is of interest that most bodies of elites, at least in the United States, include a predominance of individuals with a middle-class origin.

Supplementary Readings

Bell, Wendell, Richard J. Hill, and Charles R. Wright, *Public Leaderships* (San Francisco, Chandler Publishing Co., 1961).

Bierstedt, Robert, "An Analysis of Social Power," *American Sociological Review*, Vol. 15 (December, 1950), pp. 730-738; and also in BARRON and BM.

Emerson, Richard M., "Power-Dependence Relations," *American Sociological Review*, Vol. 27 (February, 1962), pp. 31-41.

Mills, C. Wright, *The Power Elite* (New York, Oxford University Press, 1956).

Pellegrin, Roland J. and Charles Coates, "Absentee-Owned Corporations and Community Power Structure," *American Journal of Sociology*, Vol. 61 (March, 1956), pp. 413-419.

Presthus, Robert, *Men at the Top: A Study in Community Power* (New York, Oxford University Press, 1964).

Schemerhorn, Richard A., *Society and Power* (New York, Random House, 1961).

Seligman, Ben B., "The American Corporation: Ideology and Reality," *Dissent*, Vol. 11 (Summer, 1964), pp. 316-327; and also in INKELES.

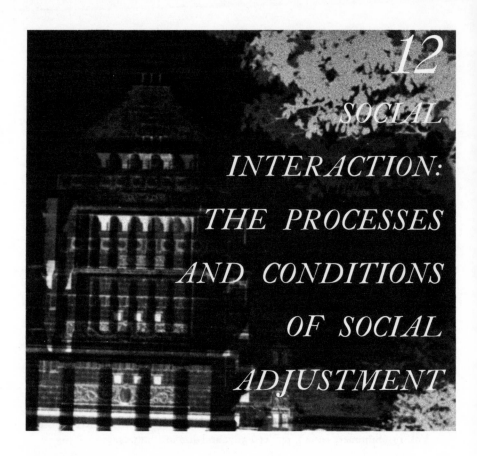

SOCIAL

INTERACTION:

THE PROCESSES

AND CONDITIONS

OF SOCIAL

ADJUSTMENT

Earlier discussions have made it clear that the so-called social processes make up the dynamic element of society. These processes were identified as special *forms of interaction* that occur with great regularity and uniformity. The study of these processes represents another conceptual approach to the study of social structure and organization. This chapter is, thus, devoted to the so-called universal interactional social processes which occur in all societies. They were first identified by Park and Burgess[1] and have since been elaborated by other students of this subject.

The major interactional social processes may be introduced in a relatively simple manner by asking one to contemplate the last meeting he has had with his family, or the last time he or she has worked with others at an industrial or office job, or the last formal meeting which he or she has attended. The usual tendency is to conclude that human behavior is infinitely varied and random in character. However, more careful and prolonged observation will reveal that there is a definite regularity in forms of interaction and further-more, that most interaction can be seen as falling into a relatively few basic

[1] Robert E. Park and Ernest W. Burgess, *Introduction to the Science of Sociology* (Chicago, University of Chicago Press, 1951).

types. These basic types can readily be traced to certain beliefs and under-standings with regard to the appropriateness of selected behavior in speci-fied situations, and widely used, nontechnical words, convey the appropriate meanings.[2]

COOPERATION AS A SOCIAL PROCESS

Cooperation is such a common word in the English language that it hardly needs to be defined. For the sake of formality, we may define this social proc-ess as, *"any form of social interaction involving two or more persons or groups working together to accomplish a common end or ends."*[3] Cooperation and its accompanying values are pervasive in all societies, although some groups stress competition more than cooperation. In fact, no group could exist without a certain degree of cooperation. The nature of the social world is such that none can achieve all of his satisfactions without the help of others. It is thus that individuals can and do foster their self-interests. It has already been demon-strated that social groups are formed to foster mutually sought goals.

Cooperative behavior is generally considered more appropriate in certain group settings than in others. For example, in the family, in the play group, in a neighborhood, and in almost all primary (or *Gemeinschaft*) groups, coop-eration is more likely to be normative than is competition or conflict. In the economic world, this is often not the case. Three major types of cooperative behavior are generally recognized—formal types, informal types, and symbiotic types. In considering each of these, the student should not lose sight of the fact that cooperation always imposes various forms of restraint on the individual.

FORMAL COOPERATION

When cooperation is of a deliberate, contractual nature it is identified as **for-mal cooperation.** In contrast to other types, formal cooperation involves the specific spelling out of the reciprocal rights and obligations of the cooperators. Normally such behavior takes place within the context of a formal organiza-tional structure, that is, a secondary or *Gesellschaft* type of group.

One of the best examples of formal cooperation is seen in the so-called cooperative movement. This movement, in essence, represents a different way

[2] For an excellent treatment of the nature of interaction see Joseph H. Fichter, *Sociology* (Chicago, University of Chicago Press, 1957), Chapter 10.

[3] This definition is that of J. S. Vandiver, although it is essentially the same one used by most writers. The discussions of cooperation, opposition, accommodation, and assimilation that follow are taken largely from Vandiver's work. See Alvin L. Bertrand *et al., Rural Sociology* (New York, McGraw-Hill, 1958), pp. 304-306.

of carrying out business activities in a private-enterprise (capitalistic) system. It involves the formation of an organization for the purpose of serving its owner-members as economically as possible, rather than for making a profit in the usual sense. In contrast to corporations, which distribute profits in the form of dividends on shares (capital invested), cooperatives pay for use of capital at a fixed rate and distribute profits as a patronage dividend in proportion to amount of business done. Consumer cooperatives are organized for joint purchase of goods and services and marketing cooperatives are organized to obtain the highest market prices possible.

The cooperative movement had its beginning in Rochdale, England, in 1844. The movement was initiated by a small group of weavers working in the flannel mills there. They developed a set of principles which appear with slight modification in the internal structure of most modern cooperatives. Cooperatives the world over follow seven general principles: (1) membership open to all, regardless of such things as race or religion, (2) democratic control—one member, one vote, (3) limited interest on share capital at a predetermined rate, (4) profits on savings divided among the members in proportion to their patronage, (5) goods and services to be traded at competitive going market prices, (6) all transactions to be for cash, and (7) continuing education of members in the benefits of cooperative principles.

In the Scandinavian countries over one-third of all business activities involve cooperative enterprises and in Great Britain one-fourth of the entire population holds a membership in consumer cooperatives.[4] An estimated six percent of United States business is done through cooperative organizations. The credit union movement, which provides low cost loans and attractive interest on savings to members, is one example of formal cooperation in the United States. So are the over 9000 farmer's cooperatives with their 7¼ million members.[5] Actually any type of cooperative activity which is expressed through formal bodies such as government agencies, religious organizations, or economic enterprises may be identified as formal cooperation. Many persons are convinced that local, national, and world problems can only be solved through organized cooperative structures.

INFORMAL COOPERATION

Informal cooperation takes place at an entirely different level of behavior than does formal cooperation. It is commonly found in primary or *Gemeinschaft* groups, where daily routines involve mutual-aid practices. Such cooperation has a conscious nature, although it is not as deliberate as formal

---

[4] Ewell P. Roy, *Cooperatives: Today and Tomorrow* (Danville, Illinois, Interstate Printers and Publishers, 1964), pp. 94-102.

[5] Anne L. Gessner, *Statistics of Farmer Cooperatives, 1959–1960* (Washington, D. C., U. S. Dept. of Agriculture, 1962).

cooperation. It is generally spontaneous and does not carry contractual obligations.

In pioneer days in the United States, informal cooperation was more or less the order of life. Such activities as log-rollings, barn-raisings, quilting bees, and husking bees were common. Informal cooperation of this nature made it possible to accomplish tasks that could not have been done alone, and to enjoy a degree of social life as well. These aims are those commonly seen in mutual-aid practices the world over.

It is worthy of note that informal cooperation pervades every aspect of one's day-by-day life. A casual count will turn up numerous instances where one helps another or is helped by another during the course of an ordinary day. These acts are a matter of courtesy or of role definition, but carry no obligation for the recipient, except as he may wish to return a favor. It is also of import that informal cooperation is related to formal cooperation. In fact, within formal group structures there are usually networks of smaller, more intimate groups, as was brought out in Chapter 9, where informal cooperation is in evidence. Studies indicate that informal cooperation is more prevalent in traditional societies and that the trend toward modern social organization is accompanied by increasing formality in cooperative endeavors.

SYMBIOTIC COOPERATION

Symbiosis is defined as a condition in which two organisms live together harmoniously, each benefiting the other in some way. This condition is distinguished from **commensalism,** which is a condition where only one partner benefits, although the second is not harmed. Most everyone is familiar with the symbiotic relationships which occur in the plant and animal world. Ecologists have discovered, for example, that some ants offer protection and solicitous care to certain plant lice. In return, the lice excrete liquids which form an important part of the food of the ants. Humans are frequently involved in similar type relationships. Symbiotic relationships among humans are not planned or deliberately established. In contrast to both formal and informal cooperation, there is very little consciousness of cooperation in the acts that are committed.

The best examples of symbiotic cooperation are found in the market place. Here, producers of goods—such as farmers and manufacturers—bring their products for sale. In the course of processing, transporting, and selling these products, a whole group of people are involved in mutually interdependent relations. They have no deliberate choice in the matter and do not particularly think of their actions as cooperation, yet the one could not accomplish his objective without the other. Similarly, most of us depend on the employees of an electric or water company to provide us with a service. We do not know who they are or care about them in a personal way, although we contribute to their wages by paying for the service we receive. Here another difference between symbiotic cooperation and formal cooperation is highlighted. In formal cooperation, a mutual goal is involved. In symbiotic cooperation, mutual self-interests are served, but a common goal or objective is lacking. In other words, in formal cooperation the actors can be seen as members of the same social system, whereas in symbiotic cooperation, the actors are members of different subsystems, although the cooperation serves to link their separate systems into community or societal systems. (See Chapters 9 and 22.)

OPPOSITION AS A SOCIAL PROCESS

The nature of oppositional behavior is such as to make us more aware of this type of interaction than of cooperative behavior. In this regard, certain classic theories such as the Darwinian theory of the struggle for existence stress oppositional behavior. Darwin's related theory of the survival of the fittest attributes the evolution of innumerable forms of life to oppositional interaction. It is also a common cliché to observe that every person is striving for "his place in the sun." As was brought out in the preceding discussion on cooperation, it is true that there is much striving associated with attempts to satisfy fundamental drives, wants, and needs. However, not all of this behavior is oppositional in nature—many mutually advantageous cooperative arrangements are also seen.

Usually, two types of oppositional behavior are described—competition and conflict. However, a third type, rivalry, can also be distinguished. Each of these three types are considered briefly. Although gross differences may separate certain oppositional behavior it is sometimes difficult to classify behavior as definitely being of one or another type of opposition.

COMPETITION

Competition is recognized as the most pervasive and continuous form of oppositional interaction. Its chief feature is that it is largely impersonal in character. In fact, many times the individual is unaware that he is competing, although he is very definitely striving for a scarce value or object. Young and Mack describe **competition** as ". . . a less violent form of opposition in which two or more persons or groups struggle for some end or goal but in the course of which attention is focussed chiefly on the reward rather than on the competitor."[6] In other words, in competition, the goal is the primary emphasis, the competitor for the goal is secondary.

[6] Kimball Young and Raymond W. Mack, *Systematic Sociology,* 2nd ed. (New York, American Book, 1962), p. 103.

Competition is very intimately bound up with the prevailing culture. Not only do some cultures stress competition, but the rules of competitive behavior are a matter of culture as well. In the United States, for example, competition is regarded as the foundation of economic life and essential to the "American way." Of course, it can readily be determined that governmental restrictions and gentlemen's agreements among business men serve to circumvent true competition in many instances, but this does not negate the fact that competition is a dominant value in the nation.

The rules of competition, whether in the business or industrial realm or in the realm of sports, are a product of culture in a direct sense. In the United States, the professional man, such as a physician or lawyer, dares not openly advertise, because this violates the norms of professional competition. In like manner, one manufacturer does not openly slander his competitor's product. In athletics the world over, all games are played by more or less well-defined rules, the visiting team gets certain concessions, "Good sportsmanship" is encouraged, and so forth. When these rules are not obeyed, it is likely competition will degenerate into conflict.

CONFLICT

On many occasions oppositional behavior is in evidence which does not follow well-defined and generally accepted procedures. In addition it is determinable that the focus of attention is more on the opposition than on the goal. When this pattern of behavior occurs, it is termed conflict. In **conflict**, the opposing parties or groups attempt to thwart, injure, or completely destroy one another, although some secondary goal is usually in mind. Young and Mack refer to conflict as a two-step process, in which the first step is the frustration or elimination of the opposition and the second step is the reward (ultimate goal) which falls to the victor.[7]

Physical violence is not necessarily characteristic of conflict, although there is a tendency to think in this manner. In present-day modern society, some of the most important types of conflict do not involve violence. Later discussions will call attention to psychological warfare, with its propaganda battles, to economic struggles between industrial giants with no holds barred, and to latent but clearly hostile interpersonal or intergroup situations. Espionage activities would also fall under a nonviolent class of conflict.

Conflict, like cooperation and competition, finds expression in practically every avenue of social life. The one important difference is that conflict is necessarily intermittent in nature. This is true because there must eventually be a victor. And, at the time the loser gives up or is destroyed, conflict ceases—perhaps to start again in another quarter; but there is an in-between period of no conflict. Patterns of conflict tend to vary with the cultural and social set-

[7] *Ibid.*, p. 103.

ting in the same manner as other forms of social interaction. Some groups have traditions of violence which lead to much overt conflict between individuals and groups. Prolonged tribal warfare is an example, as is the feuding which was once common in the hill areas of Eastern United States. Race and ethnic relations are often the basis for conflict, as is the difference between town and and country.

Culture also accounts for certain rules or norms for conflict, although they are not as strongly sanctioned as those for other forms of opposition. The Geneva Convention worked out certain conditions for war, and public indignation was aroused when these rules were violated. Even interpersonal conflict is carried on by rules, such as the etiquette of duels, and the mores about shooting a man in the back, or a man hitting a woman.

In closing this discussion, it should be pointed out that conflict may in some instances help in the achievement of a goal or function of a social system. Lewis Coser has addressed himself to this thesis in a book entitled *The Functions of Social Conflict*.[8] The function of conflict may be seen in the effect of increasing social cohesion among the members of a social system when a threat is perceived. This same phenomenon occurs in times of group crisis as is brought out in Chapter 15.

RIVALRY

The third type of oppositional behavior to be described is **rivalry**. This oppositional process has elements of both competition and conflict, but stands apart enough from either of these processes to be considered separately. Rivalry begins as competition, but assumes a personalized nature, which is foreign to true competition. Instead of focusing completely on the goal for which they are competing, rivals consciously strive to defeat one another. In other words, during the time of the interaction, there may be some question about whether more effort is being expended to frustrate the opposition than is being spent on obtaining the supposedly primary goal of the individual or group.

Rivalry tends to be like conflict in that it is more intermittent than competition. But, like competition, it may take place between individuals, groups, or individuals and groups. Rivalry is also more like competition in the adherence to rules of conduct, and because it frequently has an element of fun or sport about it. The rivalry between cross-town high schools in sporting events adds spice to community life. Farmers try to outdo rival farmers in winning blue ribbons at fairs; and women strive to outdo rivals in cooking, grooming, and decorating. A college boy or girl may become the rival of a good friend for the attention of a mutually desired dating partner.

The question sometimes arises as to whether rivalry is good or bad. On

[8] Lewis A. Coser, *The Functions of Social Conflict* (New York, Free Press, 1956).

the one hand, it may be seen as reducing the monotony of ordinary life. On the other hand, it may be seen as setting the stage for vicious conflict. The question is perhaps unanswerable, but it tends to have an unfavorable reply. Rivalry, despite its lighter side, tends to become intense and to require an inordinate expenditure of time and energy as compared with true competitive endeavors. It is also likely to lead to unwise and harmful actions, as one group or individual tries to keep up and best another group or individual. Many high schools, and some universities, lose their educational perspective in fostering athletic rivalries. Price wars put some business enterprises out of business. Vandiver puts it well when he observes that, "In terms of other values held in society, it is apparent that a more satisfactory balance would be attained if some of the less socially beneficial forms of rivalry were less emphasized."[9]

ACCOMMODATION AS A SOCIAL PROCESS

The point was made in the discussions relating to conflict and rivalry that these forms of interaction could not continue indefinitely. Wars can go on only so long, little boys get beat up by other little boys and run home in tears, revolutions succeed or fail, and all other forms of conflict come to a halt. The process of peacemaking, or of halting or avoiding further conflict, is termed *accommodation* in sociological parlance. One of the best formal definitions of accommodation is given by Hornell Hart. He states that **accommodation** ". . . *consists (of) the alteration of functional relations between personalities and groups so as to avoid, reduce or eliminate conflict and to promote reciprocal adjustment . . .*"[10]

From the above definition it is clear that accommodation does not settle issues. It simply replaces conflict with some sort of peaceful interaction, although conflict tendencies may remain as latent and erupt at a later time in overt conflict once more. Sight should not be lost of the fact however, that accommodation does set the stage for cooperation and for peaceful coexistence. The accommodative adjustments which can be made between opponents vary over a range of possibilities. They include adjustments that prevent or minimize conflict as well as those which end existing conflicts. The latter type of adjustment is particularly likely when a potential conflict situation involves one side which has a very definite power advantage over the other side. The weaker opponent may accommodate to the stronger one because he feels he has little other choice.

[9] Bertrand *et al.*, *op. cit.*, p. 317.
[10] Henry Pratt Fairchild, Ed., *Dictionary of Sociology* (New York, Philosophical Library, 1944), p. 2.

DOMINATION

The most extreme form of accommodation occurs when one party to a conflict gains a clear-cut victory. The term used to identify this type of accommodation is *domination,* or sometimes *superordination* or *coercion.* As these terms imply, the loser is forced to submit to the demands and conditions of the winner, because he has no other alternative. It should not be construed that the loser always gives up every right and privilege, however. In many instances the loser is given many important rights and duties, although he must not violate his condition of subordination. Master–slave relationships are a case in point.

COMPROMISE

Sometimes a situation arises between two opponents which makes a clear-cut victory seem unlikely; or the cost of attaining a victory is so high that combatants do not wish to pay the price. The most likely adjustment to such a situation is *compromise,* which involves mutual concessions in the interest of peace. For example, in a wage dispute, management may offer an hourly pay somewhat higher than past pay, but lower than union demands. Nations at war compromise by such acts as ceding territory in the interests of other concessions.

There are special devices for bringing about compromise when the contending parties are unable to achieve a solution. *Arbitration* is a mechanism for bringing in a third party, who is agreeable to both sides and who is given the power to make a decision. Governments sometimes appoint arbitrators to settle labor and other disputes and, in effect, the courts serve in the capacity of arbitrators on many occasions. A second mechanism for bringing about compromise is *mediation.* Mediators serve in the same capacity as arbitrators, but do not have a final word. They simply remain neutral and attempt to bring about a peaceful settlement. *Conciliation* is an attempt to settle disputes by use of some sort of council—such as work, shop or bi-racial—for study of the problem and for working out acceptable recommendations. Many communities settle sticky problems relating to religious conflict, racial conflict, and economic interest conflicts in this manner. The councils, which normally have representation from all parties in conflict, are able to work out satisfactory compromises.

TOLERATION

It happens, on occasion, that compromise is out of the question because the issues involved are not compromisable. This is true when the matters of dispute are related to religious beliefs, political ideologies, and the like. Such values represent the core values of social systems and can only be given up through the disintegration of the particular social system. The latter will occur only under domination, a situation which seldom faces groups such as religious ones. The type of adjustment worked out involves a live-and-let-live policy. In other words an agreement is reached to exclude from the interaction between the two parties the particular bone of contention, although each side is fully aware of their deviance on this point or issue. They simply *tolerate* the existence of this irritation, so long as it is not openly flounted before them. Two professors may intensely disagree on a given theory or procedure, but get along otherwise. By mutual consent they avoid bringing the subject up in their conversations and thus avoid the associated unpleasantries. Toleration does not settle a conflict problem, but does provide a means for peaceful interaction.

TRUCE

The final accommodative device is one which is brought into play when the parties to a conflict become exhausted or for some other reason cannot continue to fight. The conflict is simply stopped under the terms of some sort of *truce*. This form of accommodation settles nothing in and of itself, but does provide an opportunity to work out a more adequate form of accommodation. Unless a compromise or an agreement to tolerate can be worked out, a truce offers little hope for more than a temporary respite from conflict.

ASSIMILATION AS A SOCIAL PROCESS

Assimilation is a second process which serves to bring individuals and groups into closer more harmonious relationships. The original definition of assimilation given by Park and Burgess remains one of the best. They defined **assimilation** as a process ". . . *of interpenetration and fusion in which persons and groups acquire the memories, sentiments, and attitudes of other persons or groups, and, by sharing their experience and history, are incorporated with them in a common cultural life.*"[11] Assimilation is rarely a fast process, because it takes time for people to shed old ways and completely accept new ones.

After a careful study of the assimilation of the Spokane Indians, Prodipto Roy concluded that assimilation could be broken down into three distinguishable and measurable processes—*acculturation, social integration,* and *amalgamation.*[12]

[11] *Op. cit.*, p. 575.

[12] Both acculturation and amalgamation generally are treated in literature as separate cultural and cultural-biological processes respectively. Roy's inclusion of both processes as subprocesses of assimilation appears to the writer as the more logical approach to the discussion of these terms. See Prodipto Roy, *Assimilation of the Spokane Indians* (Pullman, Washington, Washington Agricultural Experiment Station, Bulletin 628, 1961), pp. 3-5.

Acculturation can be defined simply as the adoption of the culture of others, which occurs as a result of continued contact with them. The process may involve almost complete acceptance of the culture of a receiving group by an incoming group, or it may involve different degrees of merging of the cultural traits and patterns of both groups. Acculturation never implies complete acceptance of one group by another, simply the acceptance of the groups learned behavior patterns. This is why acculturation is just the first step in assimilation.

The second step in assimilation, *social integration,* involves complete integration into all social systems—schools, churches, businesses, recreational, and health. This step is not completely realized until all types of segregation and discrimination based on the characteristics of the newcomers or older population disappear. This process is closely related to the third aspect of assimilation, *amalgamation,* but is distinguishable on one basis. The latter term refers to biological fusion, which can legitimately occur only when complete freedom of intermarriage comes about. Sometimes people are willing to associate with others in all types of social life, but are reluctant to intermarry with them. This must occur before complete assimilation is witnessed.

Perhaps the most important factor in assimilation is acceptance of the newcomer. Unless the receiving group permits warm, intimate, personal, face-to-face contact between its members and the incoming group, the pace of assimilation will be slowed down and this condition may never be completely realized. The case of the Negro in the United States and other nations is an illustration of this point. In this regard, physical differences between groups serve to complicate patterns of acceptance, as do certain cultural differences such as language, religion, or politics. Other factors influencing assimilation are the size of the incoming group and its own resistance to assimilation. A small number of individuals usually are assimilated much more rapidly because they are forced into more frequent and prolonged contact with the greater population. However, when immigrant groups resist the native culture, assimilation may be very slow. The Louisiana French in the United States still maintain their language and ways after 150 years. Also, the old-order Amish in Pennsylvania and other states cling tenaciously to their nonconforming ways.[13]

The best example of relatively recent mass scale assimilation is found in the United States of America. The history of this nation is replete with many vivid accounts of the millions of immigrants who came to its shores from almost all countries of the world. Most of these peoples have not only been accultured, but have been completely absorbed into the social life of the nation.

[13] See Alvin L. Bertrand and Calvin L. Beale, *The French and Non-French in Rural Louisiana* (Baton Rouge, Louisiana, Louisiana Agricultural Experiment Station, Bulletin 606, 1965); and John A. Hostetler, *Amish Life* (Scottsdale, Pennsylvania, Herald Press, 1952).

CONFRONTATION AS A SOCIAL PROCESS[14]

Many recent studies of social change have highlighted the fact that individuals, groups, and even whole regions of a national society are confronted with new ways by people with whom they interact. These new ways are presented in the context of massive change which is associated with educational, technological and urbanization trends. The interactional patterns which occur may be identified as manifestations of *confrontation*. As a social process, **confrontation** can be defined as *the process whereby an individual or group is faced with consistent and strong pressure by another individual or group to change his or their values (and ways)*. This process may be illustrated as follows: Rural communities are confronted with urbanism when urban workers move into them or easily accessible lanes of communication are opened from them to urban centers. The confrontation takes place in terms of the increasing contacts which old settlers have with newcomers who espouse urban values. At the small group level, a rural family might be confronted with values alien to its norms by one of its members having migrated to a large city; or a small town family might be confronted in the same way by a son or daughter who has had a year or two away from home at a large university. Representatives of one national society may confront the people of another national society with their politico-economic ideology.[15] It is also a type of confrontation when an individual is faced with the necessity of adopting new ideas and ways because of physiological processes, such as aging and parenthood.

FORMAL CONFRONTATION

At least two types of confrontation may be identified. The first is characterized by face-to-face interaction and may be called **formal** because there is no question about the act of confrontation, and an immediate adjustment reaction is necessary. Many examples of such confrontation may be given, but a few will suffice for illustration. An employer may confront an employee whose skills have become obsolete with the necessity of learning new skills to keep his job.

---

[14] Insofar as the writer knows, this is the first time confrontation has been described as a social process. The confrontation concept is based on extensive pragmatic analyses and was introduced in a paper read at Chicago, Illinois, August, 1965, before a joint session of the American Sociological Association and Rural Sociological Society. See Alvin L. Bertrand, "The Emerging Rural South: A Region under Confrontation by Mass Society," *Rural Sociology*, Vol. 31 (December, 1966), pp. 448-457.

[15] For an example of this kind of study see Justus M. Van der Kroef, "The Sociology of Confrontation," *The Southwestern Social Science Quarterly*, Vol. 45 (December, 1964), pp. 226-238.

A church congregation may be exposed to new "social gospel" views by a newly employed minister fresh from seminary training. The old residents of a community recently invaded by urban families may be confronted at a public meeting with demands for new, updated schools, better-trained government officials, new recreational facilities, all of which represent new norms and values. Finally, persons who have long lived in a subcultural milieu (such as the old-order Amish or a segregated southern community) with strong values which are not shared by the greater society, may find themselves confronted with the enforcement agents of the greater society, who insist on the "proper" way of behaving. The enforcement of tax, crop control, and race-relations legislation are all examples of this type of confrontation.

INFORMAL CONFRONTATION

In contrast to formal confrontation, **informal confrontation** is accomplished indirectly through use of impersonal means of communication. When one learns through reading the newspaper or hearing the radio that something new and foreign to his values and ways is to be introduced, he is being confronted in an informal way. It may be a matter which will be facing him in a formal way at a later time, but for the present moment the confrontation is informal. Examples include a young man reading about or witnessing a movie about ways of thinking and acting which are tabooed in his family or of religiously oriented persons in a community learning of a court ruling that all religious programs in public schools must be stopped, or of the people of a region learning through various news media that new national civil-rights legislation has been passed which will change their previous patterns of interaction. It is also possible for informal or impersonal confrontation to take place in another sense. When a person or group suddenly is faced with a situation where his predefinitions for action are not correct (because of improper or inadequate socialization) there is a situation of informal confrontation. An example is found in the foreign traveller who finds his language, dress, and ways are not "right." Many other illustrations of this type of confrontation could be given.

ADJUSTMENT TO CONFRONTATION

The adjustment which individuals or groups make to social confrontation may consist of acceptance or rejection of the new norms. The more positive the adjustment, of course, the less likelihood there is of conflict, deviance, or revolution. Assuming that the confrontation is being made by individuals or groups in power positions, as is normally the case, varying degrees of coercion may be attempted to hasten acceptance and positive adjustment. Complete acceptance means perfect assimilation, of course. In one southern rural village studied by Raymond Payne, positive adjustment to confrontation by urbanized mass society was made by reviving industry, improving schools, and reopening the bank. However, negative adjustment was seen in the conflict between old leaders and newcomers, and in the reluctance to accept more liberal–progressive ways.[16] The adjustment which rural areas of the United States have made in the face of confrontation by a greater mass society demonstrates the operation of this social process at a national level. The key positive features of this adjustment—an increasing commercialization of farms, and industrialization and urbanization of rural life—are well known. The negative features of the adjustment—problems of displacement, unemployment, and poverty—were much longer in receiving serious attention from both program and policy planners and social scientists.

HOMOGENIZATION AS A SOCIAL PROCESS

In an insightful article published in 1960, T. Lynn Smith contends that the term *homogenization* may be employed to excellent advantage in the designation of a fundamental social process that hitherto has not been adequately described.[17] Using the United States as an illustration, Smith describes this process: ". . . with the passage of time, the various elements (ethnic, religious, demographic, cultural, social, economic, and so forth) of which society in the United States is composed are becoming more uniformly distributed throughout the length and breadth of the nation's territory." He goes on to explain that as one decade succeeds another, local areas within a society tend to become more heterogeneous because of increased division of labor and greater social differentiation generally. However, at the same time, the various major regions of the nation or society definitely show a trend toward greater resemblance to one another. In other words, although various localities in a national society may be growing more heterogeneous, the national society is becoming more homogeneous at the same time.

Smith lists several important forces that operate to bring about a more equal distribution of societal structures and values in a modernizing society. Among these are (1) modern media of communication; (2) rapid and cheap transportation facilities; (3) a very high degree of physical and social mobility of the population; (4) the standardization of educational facilities, programs, requirements, and values; and (5) the large-scale organization of industry. He

---

[16] Raymond Payne, "A Study of Leadership and Perception of Change in a Village Confronted with Urbanism," Proceedings, Agricultural Economics and Rural Sociology Section, *Association of Southern Agricultural Workers* (1961), Vol. I.

[17] T. Lynn Smith, "The Homogenization of Society in the United States," *Memoire du XIX Congress International De Sociologie*, Mexico, Vol. II (1960), pp. 245-275.

holds that, because of these forces, the term **homogenization** is the most accurate designation which can be used for the process whereby, ". . . *all of the social elements come to be more equally distributed throughout all parts of the social body.*"

In the sense in which Smith uses the concept homogenization, it stands at a higher level of abstraction than the processes previously described. He thinks of this process as applying at the societal level of interaction, rather than at the interpersonal or small-group level. However, in its full ramifications, homogenization implies interaction at all levels which reduces cultural differences in such varied respects as diet and food habits, musical tastes, traditional mores, as well as in religion, education, economics, recreation, and government.

SUMMARY

The social processes make up the dynamic element of society. They represent forms of interaction which occur with great regularity and uniformity. Six major processes are recognized as universal, since they occur in all societies.

Cooperation is characterized by joint striving for a given end or goal. When cooperation is deliberate and has a contractual nature, it is termed formal. Informal cooperation is generally spontaneous and carries no formal obligation for the recipient. Symbiotic cooperation differs from both formal and informal cooperation in that there is little consciousness of a cooperative act on the part of those involved, although mutual self-interests are served.

Opposition, defined as the behavior characterized by striving against others, is classified into three types. In competition, the attention is centered on the goal and the competitor is secondary. When the primary attention shifts to the competitor, and opposing parties attempt to thwart, injure, or annihilate one another, conflict is in evidence. Rivalry begins as competition, but assumes a personalized nature.

The process of halting or avoiding further conflict is termed accommodation. This process may come about because one party is able to dominate the other. When a clear-cut victory seems unlikely, a compromise may be worked out as an accommodative process. Toleration is a form of accommodation which takes place when a compromise is out of the question because the issues are uncompromisable. A truce is also an accommodative device, but only provides for a temporary cessation of hostility.

Assimilation serves to eliminate differences between groups. It involves three distinct subprocesses: acculturation, or the adoption of the same body of culture by all; social interaction, or the absence of segregation and discrimination of one group for the other; and amalgamation, or the complete freedom to intermarry between groups.

The interactional patterns which occur when individuals or groups are faced with consistent and strong pressure to change to new ways are termed confrontation. Formal confrontation is seen in face-to-face interaction which calls for an immediate adjustment reaction. Informal confrontation is accomplished through use of impersonal means of commication. Prior knowledge of impending formal confrontation is the key to this type of confrontation. When adjustment to confrontation is characterized by cooperation with the forces of change, it is said to be positive. When conflict with the forces of change occurs, adjustment is negative.

Homogenization, as a social process, comes about over the course of time. It is seen when the various elements of which a society is composed become uniformly distributed throughout the society.

Supplementary Readings

Bertrand, Alvin L., "The Emerging Rural South: A Region under Confrontation by Mass Society," *Rural Sociology,* Vol. 31 (December, 1966), pp. 449-457.

Blau, Peter M., "Co-operation and Competition in a Bureaucracy, *The American Journal of Sociology,* Vol. 59 (May, 1954), pp. 530-538; and also in LASSWELL ET AL. and BM.

Coser, Lewis A., "The Termination of Conflict," *Journal of Conflict Resolution,* Vol. 5 (December, 1961), pp. 347-353; and also in INKELES.

Kercher, Leonard C., "Some Sociological Aspects of Consumers' Cooperation," *Rural Sociology,* Vol. 6 (December, 1941), pp. 311-322; and also in SCHULER ET AL.

Park, Robert E. and Ernest W. Burgess, *Introduction to the Science of Sociology,* 2nd ed. (Chicago, University of Chicago Press, 1924), pp. 506-510; and also in LEE.

Rosenthal, Erich, "Acculturation Without Assimilation? The Jewish Community of Chicago, Illinois," *The American Journal of Sociology,* Vol. 66 (November, 1960), pp. 275-288; and also in LASSWELL ET AL.

Sherif, Musafer, "Experiments in Group Conflict," *Scientific American,* Vol. 195 (November, 1956), pp. 54-58; and also in SCHULER ET AL.

Smith, T. Lynn, "The Homogenization of Society in the United States," *Memoire du XIX Congress International de Sociologie,* Vol. 2 (1960), pp. 245-275.

Van der Kroef, Justus M., "The Sociology of Confrontation," *The Southwestern Social Science Quarterly,* Vol. 45 (December, 1964), pp. 226-238.

SOCIAL

DISORGANIZATION,

SOCIAL

DEVIATION,

AND SOCIAL

CONTROL

After learning how humans organize and structure themselves into groups and why they generally behave according to predictable patterns in these groups, the student is likely to wonder about deviants and nonconformers. The purpose of Part IV is to show how sociological theory allows for and explains such behavior. The four chapters which are included cover the topics of social disorganization (including social deviance) and social control. Chapter 13 provides the groundwork for an understanding of social disorganization and how social deviation is related to this social process. Chapter 14 includes a rather detailed account of the crime and delinquency problem, one of the most serious manifestations of deviant behavior and causes of social disorganization. Disasters are treated in Chapter 15 to illustrate how crisis situations disrupt societal functioning and result in disorganization. The last chapter in Part IV, Chapter 16, is concerned with social control. Its purpose is to explain the various methods by which deviant behavior is kept in bounds or prevented.

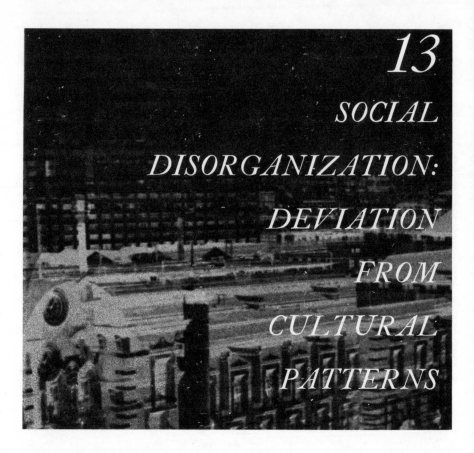

13
SOCIAL DISORGANIZATION: DEVIATION FROM CULTURAL PATTERNS

It was pointed out in Chapter 2 that the stress–strain element of social systems manifested itself in conflict or deviation patterns of behavior which resulted in a process of social disorganization. This chapter is devoted to a general discussion of social disorganization as a social process which is normative to all social systems and to a review of its various causes, characteristics, and classes. In two subsequent chapters a detailed consideration will be given to two important societal manifestations of social disorganization, namely, crime and delinquency and behavior in disaster situations.

THE NATURE OF SOCIAL DISORGANIZATION

There are always some stresses and strains in social systems, regardless of how nearly perfectly integrated they may be. This is why, as pointed out before, a stress–strain structural element is included as a vital part of each system. The behavioral responses of actors in given systems to the stresses which they face are likely to go beyond expected patterns on occasion. When this happens, the behavior of the individual or group is identified as a **deviant** behavior. Such behavior is not inherently bad or even necessarily dysfunctional to a given system; it is merely judged by the members of the system to violate norms.

Deviant behavior always serves to change the rate of progress toward goals, in that the given social system becomes less or better integrated or organized as a result. The moment that goal progress is impeded or speeded (as by deviant behavior which is innovational of higher efficiency) to any extent, the social process of disorganization is apparent. In *Gemeinschaft* systems, where interpersonal relations are ends in themselves, social disorganization is manifest in changes in the amount of harmony in these relations.

In light of the above, **social disorganization** *may be defined as a continuous social process that articulates the stress–strain element of social systems and is characterized by deviation from normative cultural patterns; it results in some degree of change in the goal progress of social systems.*[1]

In some earlier definitions, social organization is conceived as a condition or state, rather than a process. This view not only fails to allow for the transition toward or away from greater social organization as measured by rate of progress toward goals, but it implies that groups of people can actually exist without a definite social structure. The interpretation of social disorganization given in the above definition assumes a social system to be organized, that is, structured to some degree, so long as it may be identified as a system. This means that at any time individuals behave according to some sort of role definitions, there is at least a modicum of organization. Defining social disorganization as a social process also makes it clear that all social systems are characterized by some degree of disorganization at all times. Although disorganization processes are manifested in deviance, nonconformity, and conflict and articulate stress–strain in social systems, these processes are not always associated with deliberate violations of the norms. In some instances, the individual is incapable of understanding the norms, in others he has not had an opportunity to learn them, and in still others his usual cues and symbols are missing.

It is significant that the negative aspects of social disorganization receive more attention than do the positive aspects. This apparent neglect is explained by the fact that, although all social change involves some degree of disorganization, new ways which contribute to greater "progress" are never considered problems. For example, a new factory may completely disrupt a local community by overtaxing all available facilities, such as housing, water, and police

---

[1] The more traditional approach conceives that social systems become "disorganized." This view fails to account for degrees of organization as measured by effective goal progress of social systems. In the writer's analytical scheme, a social system exists until a point is reached where all goal progress ceases. At this point an unorganized state or condition is reached. See Alvin L. Bertrand, "The Stress-Strain Element of Social Systems. A Micro Theory of Conflict and Change," *Social Forces*, Vol. 42 (October, 1963), p. 4.

protection, yet, since disorganization processes in this instance result in change toward the economic goal of more money in the community, the negative aspects of change are overlooked.

Social disorganization is studied at two levels of manifestation. The first level is that of deviant behavior. It is at this level that the specific acts of specific actors are accounted for. The broad aspects of sociological theory which relate to deviant behavior are treated at some length in the discussions that follow. After these discussions, the second or more general level of social disorganization is treated, including a consideration of social problems, community disorganization, and deviant subcultures.

FORMS OF DEVIANCE

Deviance may be defined as failure to behave according to norms. It is possible, on the basis of this definition, to work out a classification of types or forms of deviance. This has been done by Merton, who developed his classificatory scheme in terms of the theory of *anomie*. The latter theory was set forth by the French sociologist, Durkheim, just before the turn of the century.[2] It grew out of his studies of the relation of suicide to social integration and social disorganization. Durkheim conceived of **anomie** as a state of relative normlessness found in societies lacking clear-cut norms to guide behavior and moral conduct. He concluded from his studies that one type of suicide could be traced to individual conditions of anomia. In anomic suicide, the individual's life becomes inadequate and unbearable because group life fails to provide him with controlling standards of behavior and self-discipline.

Merton worked out a fourfold classification of possible types of anomic deviance from approved values which govern goals and the means of attaining goals.[3] In working out this classification he distinguished between group-approved ends and means, pointing out that it was possible to reject one while accepting the other. His various types or forms of deviance are based on combinations of actors' acceptance and rejection of goals and means and are most helpful in an analytical sense. He identified four forms of deviance including: . (1) **Innovators,** who accept goals or ends, but who reject the approved means to attain these ends. The student who buys a term paper in order to pass a course is an example of this type of anomic deviant. (2) **Ritualists,** who are close and strict followers of rules, that is, means, but who lose sight of goals and thus in essence reject them. The eternal student who enrolls for courses year after year, but never fulfills the requirements for a specific degree, is an example of a person with this type of anomia. (3) **Retreatists,** who reject values

---

[2] Emile Durkheim, *Le Suicide* (Paris, Alcan, 1897); English translation and introduction by George Simpson, *Suicide* (New York, Free Press, 1951).

[3] Robert K. Merton, *Social Theory and Social Structure,* rev. ed. (New York, Free Press, 1957), Chapters 4 and 5.

associated with both goals and means. They remain in social systems but are more or less in a state of suspension, since they are not interested in what goes on or what results are achieved. Classic examples are alcoholics, vagrants, and psychotics. (4) **Rebels,** who reject both goals and means, and substitute new goals and means which represent a different system of values. The utopian communities so common earlier in this century are examples of this type of behavior, as are the schisms which develop in religious and political groups. In each instance, rebellion from old ways is apparent but new norms are substituted in each case.

Bredemeier and Stephenson contend that the **overconformer** also represents a type or form of deviant behavior which has some aspects of anomie.[4] Such persons deviate in the sense of too strict conformity with the letter of the law. They push themselves to comply beyond the limits normally expected. Such persons can be found in religious groups, among some new initiates into a given status position, and in some highly structured situations, such as Marine boot camps.

In conclusion, it may be pointed out that the deviant behavior stemming from anomie is usually related to a lack of opportunity or the means for achieving life goals. This fact has been brought out by studies of low-income groups, which show them to have higher rates of anomie. Dan Alleger, after several years of research, concludes that literally thousands of low-income southerners (in the United States) cannot make an adjustment to change because of anomia brought on by abject despair.[5]

The theory of alienation, popularized by Karl Marx in an effort to explain the impact of technology on human relations in industry, also has implications for deviant behavior and anomie. It is used as a concept to explain feelings of powerlessness, of meaningless, of self estrangement, of isolation, and marginality in political, economic, or social life. From a sociological point of view, as Marvin Scott notes, the sources of alienation are to be found in the lack of commitment to values, the lack of conformity to norms, the lack of responsibility in roles, and the lack of control over facilities.[6]

FACTORS RELATED TO DEVIATION

There are several sets of factors which account for individuals behaving according to the patterns or forms of deviance just described. These factors may

[4] Harry L. Bredemeier and Richard M. Stephenson, *The Analysis of Social Systems* (New York, Holt, Rinehart and Winston, 1962), pp. 124-125.

[5] Daniel E. Alleger, "A Southern Rural Paradox: Social Change and Despair," *Research Report*, Vol. XI (January, 1966) (Agricultural Experiment Station, University of Florida), p. 6.

[6] Marvin B. Scott, "The Social Sources of Alienation," selection in Louis Horowitz, Ed., *The New Sociology: Essays in Social Science and Social Theory in Honor of C. Wright Mills* (New York, Oxford University Press, 1964), p. 241.

be thought of as independent from one another for analytical purposes, although they are likely to be interrelated in actual cases. Each class of factors makes up a vital aspect of sociological theory.

INAPPROPRIATE OR INADEQUATE SOCIALIZATION

There is no doubt that the most obvious reason why individuals do not conform to norms is ignorance of the pattern of behavior which is expected. Ignorance of this type stems from two sources: first, the individual has learned ways of acting—definitions of situations—which are inappropriate to the occasion at hand. Second, the individual has not been provided with a socialization experience which gives him a full understanding of the behavior requirements demanded or expected in connection with certain roles.

Inappropriate socialization is frequently in evidence as people move from one cultural setting to another. Persons who move from rural areas to cities, or from one nation to another are likely to react in ways considered strange or deviant by the members of their new cultural groups. For example, the members of a family newly moved to town from the country may insist on visiting with all their new neighbors. The latter receive them with less than enthusiasm, because they prefer both to choose their friends and to live in relative privacy.

Inadequate socialization is sometimes difficult to differentiate from inappropriate socialization. However, it conveys the meaning of not enough knowledge rather than knowledge of the wrong kind. A person may, for example, fail as a football coach, because he lacks coaching finesse, that is, he has not learned the fine points of the game to the extent of other coaches. A businessman or farmer may go bankrupt for the same reason—that is, they are not knowledgeable enough to compete successfully. Likewise, many university freshmen experience frustration and place stresses on their family social systems, because their high school training falls far short of university standards. Inappropriate or inadequate socialization does not preclude one from holding positions in social systems—it simply places stresses on the system, which have implications for social disorganization.

STRUCTURAL STRESSES OR MALADJUSTMENTS

The second major source of deviation is found in the stresses and strains which emanate from the social structure itself. This type of deviation differs from that caused by inadequate or inappropriate socialization in the sense that the individual faces expectations which he understands and knows about but which he does not meet for some reason. How this type of situation comes about can be explained in terms of the behavioral model previously mentioned. This model includes three structural elements in its make-up and is designed to provide a theoretical framework for analyzing the nondeviant as well as deviant behavior of an actor. The first element in behavior is the cultural structure, which has already been explained as made up of the normative patterns of expected behavior. The second element is the personality of the individual, which includes all his attributes, biological as well as psychological, including such things as capacities, drives, and self-conceptions. The third and final element in behavior is made up of all the situational factors over which the individual has no control and range over a wide area of conditions related to the economic, political, geographic, religious, and family aspects of his life. The important matter in this connection is how the given actor defines the particular situation.[7] Figure 13-1 is included to show how the cultural structure, personality and situation relate to one another in a given behavioral situation.

With the above model in mind, it is possible to visualize deviation as a product of maladjustments arising between and within the factors making up the separate elements that account for the behavior of people. Nix and Bates have identified these stresses. Those which occur within the cultural structure —that is, between ideal expectations or norms they term *role conflict* and *role incongruity;* those that occur because of maladjustments between the cultural structure and personality they call *role inadequacy;* stresses that arise from maladjustment between the cultural structure and recurrent situations they classify as *role frustration;* and stresses that involve all three elements in the behavioral model simultaneously they termed *role superfluity.*[8] Each of these sources of deviant behavior is described in turn.

ROLE CONFLICT: On occasion, an actor in a given social system finds that he is confronted with role expectations that are incompatible with other roles he must play. These inconsistencies arise out of the norms that make up the roles of the different social systems in which the actor is a member. The conscientious objector finds himself in such a position in time of war; as does the father who, as a policeman, apprehends his son in the act of stealing an automobile. In the first situation, role conflict develops because the norms of the religious social system of the conscientious objector conflict with the norms of patriotism to his greater society. In the second situation, the norms of the policeman's family system conflict with the norms of his occupation. In each instance deviance or conflict must come about in one or another role. If the

---

[7] For a clear and detailed treatment of the biosocial bases of personality see John T. Doby, *Introduction to Social Psychology* (New York, Appleton-Century-Crofts, 1966), Parts II and III. The importance of "the definition of the situation" is made clear in W. I. Thomas, *The Unadjusted Girl* (Boston, Little, Brown, 1932), p. 42.

[8] Harold L. Nix and Frederick L. Bates, "Occupational Role Stresses; A Structural Approach," *Rural Sociology*, Vol. 27 (March, 1962), pp. 7-17.

FIGURE 13-1.   *Behavioral Model.*

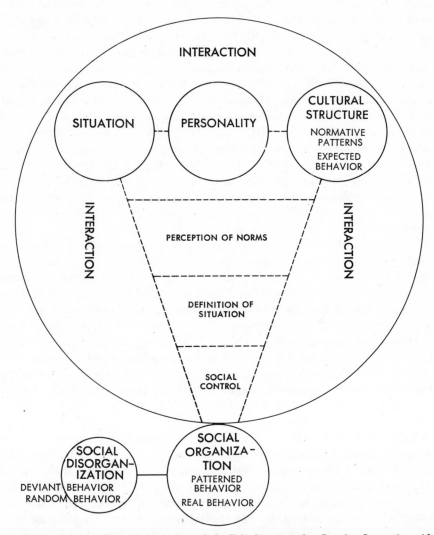

Source: Robert J. Dolan, "An Analysis of the Role Structure of a Complex Occupation with Special Emphasis on the Value and Role Orientations Associated with the County Agent Situs," Vol. 1 (unpublished dissertation, Louisiana State University, June, 1963), p. 146.

conscientious objector remains true to his religion, he is considered unpatriotic, if he joins the armed service, he is considered untrue to his faith. The policeman who arrests his son must answer to his family members for not helping his son get out of trouble; if he does not make the arrest, he violates the norms of his job.

ROLE INCONGRUITY: Role incongruity involves inconsistencies which also arise within the cultural structure.[9] This type of stress is indicated when the formal attributes of a status position—power, prestige, pay—are not in keeping with the informal attributes associated with the status position. This sort of situation was alluded to in the discussion of social stratification. It may be illustrated as follows. Some occupations, such as school teacher and minister have an economic reward that is inferior to their functional importance, power, and prestige. That is, they are paid less than other occupations, such as plumbers and electricians, which carry much lower community prestige. These types of inconsistencies place social structures under stress by creating tensions (strains) within and among actors. Almost everyone has heard teachers and ministers complain of their pay and many seek other occupations, while others press for more economic remuneration. In this sense they represent sources of deviant behavior.

ROLE INADEQUACY: Many times, as mentioned, actors are placed in status positions for which they are not adequately prepared. In such instances, their lack of experience, ability, or their personality traits prevent them from playing the role in the manner expected. This type of situation is exemplified by the persons placed in high bureaucratic positions as a political favor, but who know nothing of the technicalities of their position. It is also seen when a recent graduate is assigned a practical professional task for which he has only "book" preparation.

ROLE FRUSTRATION: It is not unusual for an actor to find that he is unable to fulfill his role in the way others expect him to or in the way he would like. Such occasions arise because of limited facilities, or because of other forms of inadequacy. A teacher, for example, may wish to teach the latest techniques in chemistry but lacks the necessary laboratory facilities. She would experience role frustration to this extent. A mother might likewise be frustrated in trying to be a good mother, because her economic circumstances force her to work and leave her child in a nursery.

ROLE SUPERFLUITY: Occasionally, an actor will find himself in a position or positions where the role expectations are greater than he or his type of actor can fulfill. Such a situation comes about because of inconsistencies in the socio-cultural structure, that is, because communication and other factors have built up expectations which are based on erroneous assumptions. Sociologists often are presented with so-called sociological problems for solution which are outside the scope of the profession. Yet, there is a certain hint of professional incompetence if a ready solution is not provided for the problem.

[9] For an insightful article on role incongruity see Roland J. Pellegrin and Frederick L. Bates, "Congruity and Incongruity of Status Attributes Within Occupations and Work Groups," Social Forces, Vol. 38 (October, 1959), pp. 23-28.

PSYCHOLOGICAL DEFICIENCIES

Some individuals do not perform roles in the expected manner because of mental abnormalities. These individuals do not have the mental capacity to appreciate socially defined standards or they cannot control their behavior at certain times or under certain conditions. Although this area of study is of primary concern to psychologists, it serves a purpose of rounding out our discussion of deviance to include a review of this type of deviation. In terms of the behavior model outlined, psychological deficiencies are among the factors which make up the personality element in behavior.

The stresses and strain produced in social systems by the deviating actions of mentally deficient persons is generally considered in a different analytical context than the deviate behavior of so-called normal individuals. Social control mechanisms and procedures, for one thing, vary for the normal and abnormal individual. For example, the murderer pronounced insane is placed in an institution for mental cases rather than given a prison sentence or put to death. The types and classes of mental abnormalities are as follows.

THE MENTALLY DEFICIENT: Psychologists and other social and medical scientists have been seriously concerned with the measurement of intelligence and the cause of intelligence differentials since the turn of the century. Many tests have been devised to measure such things as "power to reason," "power to comprehend," "time orientation," "power to combine ideas in a meaningful way," "retention of knowledge," and "creative ability." The term I. Q. (Intelligence Quotient) was introduced by Lewis M. Terman in an attempt to provide a convenient index of mental maturity. Terman's procedure was to divide the mental age of an individual as determined by intelligence tests, by his chronological age.[10] During the first years of the use of mental tests, much controversy raged over the relative importance of heredity and environment in determining I.Q. Today there is widespread agreement that I.Q. tests are good indicators of individual differences, but they are considered to measure environmental influences as well as innate ability.

Through use of mental tests, populations are divided into three general classes—the mentally deficient or feeble-minded, the normal, and the supernormal or genius. The feeble-minded have the greatest difficulty in adjusting to social situations. Three types of feeble-minded individuals are recognized: (1) The **idiot** is at the lowest level and has little or no capacity to learn. This type of individual remains unsocialized throughout his rather short lifespan and is incapable of caring for himself. (2) The **imbecile** is just above the idiot in that he may acquire some very elementary socialization, including

[10] Lewis M. Terman, *The Measurement of Intelligence* (Boston, Houghton Mifflin, 1916).

rudimentary speech and certain motor skills. He is not able to manage his affairs or take a responsible position in life, however. (3) The **moron** is at the top of the feeble-minded group. It is not unusual for such individuals to finish elementary school and to perform satisfactorily in uncomplicated social situations, including certain types of gainful occupations. Many morons find a useful place in society and refrain from violation of important folkways and mores.

The above brief description of the feeble-minded makes it obvious why this class of people might deviate from expected norms. They simply do not have the mental capacity to comprehend the full meaning of the roles they are expected to play.

THE MENTALLY AND EMOTIONALLY DISTURBED: In contrast to individuals born with mental deficiencies, there are those who have lost a once-normal mind. The causes for this regression are termed **organic,** if they are associated with some physical deterioration, and are identified as **functional** if no physical defect can be found. Functional disorders are usually explained in terms of an inability to meet the demands of one's social environment. The brainwashing of American prisoners of the Korean War was an attempt to create a functional breakdown of personality. The emotionally disturbed are classed as neurotic or psychotic, depending on the severity of their disturbance.

Persons who suffer from **neurosis** are characterized by undue worries, obsessive fear, extreme fatigue, hysteria, and a general incapacity to participate fully in everyday social life. Neurotics are not usually placed under special care. They are commonly classified under three headings or subclasses: (1) **anxiety neurosis**—identified by symptoms including imaginary ailments, fears, hypochondria, irritability, and fatigue; (2) **obsessional-compulsive neurosis** —which includes symptoms such as obsessive suicidal thoughts, compulsive manias (such as to set fires or steal), and extreme fears (such as claustrophobia, the fear of closed places); (3) **hysteria**—which is characterized by disassociation of thought and action, as manifested in dual or multiple personalities (the Dr. Jekyll and Mr. Hyde model) and other ways.

The **psychotic** represents a more severe mental disturbance than the neurotic. His conduct diverges from normal expectations to such a degree that medical attention is required and institutional attention is common. In contrast to the neurotic, who makes a fighting attempt to live in the real world, the psychotic frequently leaves the real world mentally and his acts may become dangerous. He has no objective insight into his conduct and interaction becomes meaningless to him. Psychotics are divided into two large groups: (1) the **functional psychoses,** whose disturbances cannot be traced to physical conditions but are believed to relate to psychological factors related to the inability to cope with their environment. Included in this group are persons diagnosed as having schizophrenia (a split personality marked by growing indifference to the outside world and hallucinations); paranoia (delusions marked by extreme conceit, suspicion, feelings of persecution, and projection of false intentions and ideas of others); maniac-depressive (who alternately undergoes periods of flightiness characterized by pressure to do things, great energy, and occasional rages; and periods of depression with anxiety, guilt delusions, and melancholy). (2) The **organic psychoses,** whose mental disorders can be related to some brain or neurological damage. The four most common forms of organic psychoses are paresis or brain injury brought on by syphilitic infection and marked by gradual loss of judgment and development of delusions; epilepsy or periodic seizures triggered by the brain and characterized by symptoms ranging from giddiness and momentary loss of consciousness to extended black-outs with violent muscle contractions, foaming of the mouth and changes in respiration; toxic psychoses or disturbances derived from fever, nutritional deficiencies, too much alcohol and various types of poisoning and usually accompanied by delirium, including nightmares, restlessness, and excitement; and senile dementia or the loss of memory, loss of ability to concentrate, insomnia, and other symptoms brought on by old age.

THE UTILITY OF STRUCTURAL DIMENSIONS IN THE ANALYSIS OF DEVIANCE[11]

It is part of the sociologist's charge to predict human behavior within limits. In this regard, questions such as, "At what points in social systems will conflict and deviance most likely occur?" and "What type of role conflict will result in the greatest deviance and consequent system disruption?" are in order. These questions provide the point of departure for the discussion that follows.

LEVELS OF ROLE CONFLICT

Role conflict has already been defined as a type of stress which arises in the cultural structure because the content of one role (norms) played by an actor is in conflict with the content of a second role played by the same actor. Bates distinguishes between two levels of role conflict, and in so doing, helps answer the question of what type of conflict results in the greatest system disruption. He describes **moral conflict** as a role conflict which arises from contradictory values. In other words, one norm calls for behavior which is wrong, improper,

[11] The discussion in this section follows Frederick L. Bates, "Some Observations Concerning the Structural Aspect of Role Conflict," *Pacific Sociological Review,* Vol. 5 (Fall, 1962), pp. 75-82.

immoral, or taboo as judged from the standards of the second norm. An example would be the person whose religious norms forbid drinking, but who finds himself in social situations where alcoholic beverages are normally served, such as in a high level diplomatic gathering.

Behavioral conflict, the second level or role conflict described by Bates, occurs when one norm calls for behavior which is dysfunctional to the behavior called for by a second norm. Said another way, one norm defeats the goal-directed action called for by a second norm which is included in the actor's role. Many examples of this type of role conflict come to mind. In the educational world, it is frequently illustrated by the fact that student positions, such as club president or student body officer, make demands on time that is sorely needed for studying. It is usually true that moral conflict results in the greatest extent of system disruption. This is true because this type of conflict has a severe psychological consequence for the actor, often resulting in feelings of frustration, anxiety, and guilt. Behavioral conflict may impede the efficiency of goal-directed activity but does not involve personal traumas to a great extent.

THE RELATION OF STRUCTURAL DIMENSIONS OF ROLES TO ROLE CONFLICT

A consideration of the structural dimensions of roles also helps answer the questions posed in the first paragraph of this section. Bates has worked out a fourfold analytical approach to determine at what points in given social systems conflict is likely to occur and result in the greatest amount of system disruption. His classification scheme makes it possible to study role conflict as a purely sociological phenomenon.

STRUCTURAL DISTANCE: It is reasonable to assume that the further apart two roles are in a social system, the greater degree of inconsistency can exist between them without causing undue stress in the system. This is true because the perception of inconsistency is much more acute when roles are close and involve intimate relationships. **Structural distance**—defined as the number of "system boundaries" which must be crossed to move from one role to another—is thus closely related to role conflict. Roles played by the one actor toward a second actor in the same elemental group would be as close as it is possible for roles to be. Father's playmate role toward his son and his socializer role toward his son are an example of this type of role relationship. It is clear that these two roles are closer, more proximal, than two roles, one of which is played in another group—such as the father's role of son in his family of orientation (his father's family) and his role of son-in-law in his wife's family. The most distal roles are those which involve the crossing over from roles in one situs to roles in another situs—such as from an occupational role to a family role.

RANGE OF RECIPROCALITY: It is also logical that role conflict is more likely to produce social system disruption when it involves *multilateral roles* than when it only involves *unilateral roles*. A **multilateral role** is one which an actor plays to a number of other actors—such as the husband-father's provider role, which is reciprocal to all family members. **Unilateral roles** are played toward only one actor in the group or system—such as the husband-father's husband role which is reciprocal only to the wife's role. All members of the system are affected by a failure of the father-husband to provide food, clothing, and shelter. However, only the wife-mother is affected if his husband role is not fulfilled. The range of reciprocality increases as the number of roles which are reciprocal increases and this provides a neat way of studying and analyzing conflict and deviance.

ORIENTATION TO GROUP BOUNDARIES: **Extramural roles** are defined as those which require the actor to play another role outside the group of which the role is a part. An illustration would be the father-husband's provider role which necessitates an occupational role. Extramural roles are differentiated from **intramural roles** which are played entirely within a social system, such as the father's playmate and disciplinarian roles. Since both extramural and intramural roles can be involved in conflict, it is a matter of determining which presents the actor with a greater chance for stresses. Bates feels that extramural roles present the greater probability of conflict because of the greater chance for change in role content. In such roles, change may originate in one or both the systems which are linked, whereas in the case of intramural roles, change can only come from one system. This phenomenon is a complicated one, and no doubt particular circumstances will bring about greater or lesser degrees of conflict. However, Bates position is a logical one.

TEMPORAL SPAN OF ROLES: It was pointed out earlier that no role can remain active all of the time and that all roles have active and latent phases. Since highly active roles involve more frequent and prolonged performances by an actor, they provide more chances for conflict to arise. In the case where roles are latent most of the time, not only is there less chance of actors deviating and creating conflict, but the inconsistency between one role and another is more apt to be undetected.

The above discussion was included to demonstrate how the structural qualities of roles can be utilized to study role conflict and deviance. There are many ways in which the four structural dimensions of roles outlined above can be used to study conflict in role systems. The examples given were designed to introduce this analytical approach.

SOCIAL PROBLEMS: SOCIETAL AWARENESS OF DISORGANIZATION

At this point our interest is turned to the more general manifestations of social disorganization. The first topic to be considered is social problems. Such phenomenon are associated with values and norms, as will be seen.

DEFINITION OF A SOCIAL PROBLEM

By definition, a **social problem** *is recognized when a majority or an active minority of the people making up a given society become convinced that certain conditions or customary ways of doing things are wrong.* However, there are several important understandings which must accompany this definition. The first is that the same set of circumstances or behavior patterns might have existed for a long period of time without being identified as a problem. Thus, there is always a question of why a moral significance is now attached to behavior which was considered acceptable before. This may be a matter of change in the value of people, such as took place in the United States with regard to the use of alcoholic beverages. Prohibition was voted in and then voted out again as values changed over the years.

A second implication of the definition of a social problem is that the condition affects a significant number of people in ways which they consider undesirable and about which they believe something can be done. Obviously, a condition which affects only a few people will not receive sufficient attention to be considered a social problem, although it may represent a personal problem to these individuals. For example, the members of a religious group may consider dancing sinful and wrong. However, if the great majority of citizens do not share this view, dancing cannot be called a social problem, except by specific reference to the groups who define this act as a problem.

Some conditions, of course, are such that they are beyond the scope of human control and, although they represent problems, they are not social problems. The weather, for instance, is not considered a social problem because it is largely beyond man's control. Those who suffer from disasters such as hurricanes or floods are said to have suffered a misfortune, rather than to be the victims of a social problem. However, their plight, if it is prolonged, may eventually be called a social problem. The difference is that in natural disasters there is no way to control the phenomenon that caused the problem, whereas a social problem is seen as one which has a solution.

This short discourse on the definition of a social problem can be terminated with the identification of certain specific social problems. Most of us could bring to mind a long list of conditions we consider problems. Perhaps we would be challenged by our fellows on some of the items listed, but for the most part we would have little difficulty in correctly pointing out the conditions considered wrong in our society. Some of the social-problem conditions which come to mind readily are the high auto accident rate, unemployment, mental illness, poverty, race relations, juvenile delinquency, and crime. The specific characteristics of the crime and delinquency problems are presented in Chapter 14.

COMMUNITY PATTERNS OF DISORGANIZATION

Previous discussions have dealt with the social organizational patterns of communities and other social systems. It is now appropriate to outline the important types of breakdown in community organization which may be seen in the malfunctioning of community subsystems at times of stress and which are indicational of social problems.[12]

FUNCTIONAL COMMUNITY DISORGANIZATION

In every community there are a number of subsystems that contribute in a specialized way to the achievement of community goals and functions. The structural linkages between subsystems were outlined in Chapter 9. When any one or a group of subsystems does not function properly, there is a greater or lesser breakdown in the total community structure. This is termed **functional disorganization.** Many examples of situations that bring such disorganization might be given, such as garbage strikes, police intimidation by gangsters, and insufficient funds to pay school teachers. The above types of situation have been grouped by Bernard under two broad headings—*natural disasters* and *man-made disasters*—and identified by her as conditions which give rise to large-scale community disorganization in a functional sense.[13]

Natural disasters are attributed to forces beyond the close control of man. They include hurricanes, tornadoes, typhoons, other storms of various types, floods, fires, wrecks, earthquakes, drought, and epidemics among other things. Disasters represent such an important form of social disorganization that a separate chapter is devoted to the findings of researchers who have studied various phenomenon of this type. For this discussion the important matter is

[12] The organization and discussion of the materials presented follows the excellent treatment of the subject done by Jessie Bernard. Jessie Bernard, *American Community Behavior,* rev. ed. (New York, Holt, Rinehart and Winston, 1962), Part IV.
[13] *Ibid.,* Chapter 23.

that natural disasters destroy property and interrupt normal community processes. In other words, they bring disorganization by making it impossible to conduct the usual activities associated with community life.

Man-made disasters have a somewhat different nature than do natural disasters. One of the more important examples is strikes of all types. When accompanied by violence, strikes immediately disrupt community functions. By closing down plants that provide various services to the community, strikes can affect more people in the long run than many natural disasters. Economic crises also adversely affect community functioning and are recognized as man-caused disasters. Long depressions serve to curtail much activity, but economic booms may also overtax facilities to a point of chaos. Many towns in the United States which became defense centers overnight during World War II found themselves in a virtual social upheaval. The third and final example of a man-made disaster to be given is war. The ravages of an invading army on a community are such as to potentially disrupt every service, not to mention the problems caused by all out mobilization for a war effort. It is almost beyond the imagination to conceive the effect that a thermonuclear war might have on community life.

SCHISMATIC COMMUNITY DISORGANIZATION

Bernard terms the breakdown of relationships within a group as **schismatic disorganization.** This type of situation occurs when the bonds holding people together, such as kinship bonds, race and ethnic bonds, territorial bonds, loyalties of various kinds, and occupational ties, are weakened or broken. The forces which break these bonds may be deliberately employed, or they may be the result of massive forces of change. With regard to the latter, modern complex societies are seen as moving little by little in the direction of more public control of hitherto private matters. For example, in the United States, fraternities and social clubs recently became subject to antidiscrimination norms (as evidenced in statutory regulations).

Several ways are used by those who deliberately wish to break the bonds holding the members of certain subsystems or groups together. One of the most widespread is *hate-mongering.* The hate-monger does not use facts or objectivity, he simply calls names, appeals to fear, plays on emotions, and above all personalizes on someone or some group. The tactics of Hitlerites against Jews, and of race segregationists against integrationists and vice versa, are well filled with hate strategy. *Envy* is also used to split community groups. All communities have groups who are "have-nots" in a relative sense, and the members of these groups can be alienated by expert use of propaganda tactics to play on the resentment they hold for the "haves." Unscrupulous politicians are noted for exploiting such situations. *Fear* is also an effective way of dividing community groups. The so-called witch-hunts which occasionally involve schools and universities evoke a real fear among both teachers and citizens. Informers are used in some societies to create fear and thus curtail freedom of expression. In the above instances it can be seen how fear is used, not only to destroy confidence, but to disorganize normal relationships.

INDIVIDUAL NONCONFORMITY AND COMMUNITY DISORGANIZATION

Previous discussions have treated the process of socialization, including personality formation in some detail. In this chapter, attention has already been given to the types of nonconformity or deviance which characterize individual as well as group behavior. With this information in mind, it may be pointed out that individual nonconformity to community norms leads to a certain amount of disorganization. Criminal behavior, for example, not only involves the expenditure of considerable sums of money that might be wisely spent in other ways, but affects the functioning of one or another institution (the bank that is robbed or the family that has lost its bread-winner, for example). Nonconformists may also succeed in bringing on some disorganization through demonstrations and by flaunting the folkways and mores publicly.

Community social disorganization can often be traced to deviant behavior which has been learned from and encouraged by members of organized groups as approved endeavors. These groups are characterized by a subculture that educates the individual to deviate from the greater society norms. The great majority of delinquents and criminals carry on their activities as members of deviant subcultures. Nonconforming behavior which is short of law-breaking is also found among "beatnik" groups on university campuses and in large cities and in some religious cults that deviate in their beliefs from generally accepted norms. Those who subscribe to deviant subcultures may deviate in but a few ways from approved norms and many apparently cannot repress all guilt feeling, although their deviant behavior represents dominant values.[14] The full character of deviant subcultures will be more evident in Chapter 14 which treats crime in some detail.

VIOLENCE AND COMMUNITY DISORGANIZATION

Social disorders brought on by violence sooner or later come to most communities. Violence is treated independently as a cause of community disor-

[14] Gresham M. Sykes and David Matsa, "Techniques of Neutralization, A Theory of Delinquency," *American Sociological Review*, Vol. 24 (December, 1957), pp. 664-670.

ganization because it frequently is difficult to relate directly to functional or schismatic types of community disruptions. In fact, violence such as fencing or dueling is characteristic of certain cultures, and certain types of violence are condoned in all cultures, such as killing an enemy in war. Bernard classifies violence as "hot" if it is associated with the reduction of tensions (such as a crime of passion) and "cold" if it is the means to an end (such as killing a guard to rob a bank).[15] Because violence is so difficult to control, once started, it has important disorganizational consequences. Mob violence is the most difficult to cope with, as it is likely to be emotionally charged and to spread from a central locale to other areas. Race riots, riots against political leaders, lynching-type mobs, violence against religious or ethnic groups, and gang violence are commonly reported in the daily press. Each such report usually includes strong evidence of temporary or prolonged community social disorganization.

SUMMARY

Social disorganization is a continuing social process that articulates the stress–strain element in social systems. It is characterized by deviation from normative cultural patterns. This deviation may take the form of innovation, ritualism, retreatism, rebellion, or overconformity. The factors related to deviation are of three primary types. First, people may be inadequately or inappropriately socialized to cope with behavioral situations. Second, the social structure itself may present inconsistencies or impose demands that lead to stresses and strains and thus motivate deviance. These stresses are specifically manifested in role conflict, role incongruity, role inadequacy, role frustration, and role superfluity. Third, individuals may have psychological deficiencies which prevent them from completely understanding role requirements. The mentally deficient (idiots, imbeciles, and morons) include persons who have never had normal intelligence. The mentally or emotionally disturbed (neurotics and psychotics) include persons who have lost a once-normal mind.

The structural dimensions of roles provide an approach for the analysis of deviance which has great utility. In this regard, two levels of role conflict can be distinguished—moral conflict and behavioral conflict—which have implications for measurement of the intensity of conflict and the probability of deviance. The consideration of structural distance between roles, the range of role reciprocality, the orientation of roles to group boundaries, and the temporal span of roles provides a convenient and efficient way to analyze role conflict and deviance.

Social problems are conditions that a relatively large number of people in a given society consider wrong. The identification of social problems indi-

---

[15] *Op. cit.*, p. 386.

cates societal awareness of social disorganization. At the community level, when groups or systems do not function properly, social disorganization is considered functional in nature. Schismatic disorganization occurs when the relationships between or within groups break down, and conflict results. Individual nonconformity, such as criminal behavior, and social disorders brought on by violence are other causes of community disorganization.

Supplementary Readings

Bates, Frederick L., "Some Observations Concerning the Structural Aspects of Role Conflict," *Pacific Sociological Review*, Vol. 5 (Fall, 1962), pp. 75-82.

Bernard, Jessie, *American Community Behavior*, rev. ed., New York, Holt, Rinehart and Winston, 1962), Part IV.

Bredemeier, Harry C., and Richard M. Stephenson, *The Analysis of Social Systems* (New York, Holt, Rinehart and Winston, 1962), Chapter 5.

Deutscher, Irwin, "The Social Causes of Social Problems: From Suicide to Delinquency," Publications of the Youth Development Center (Syracuse, Syracuse University, 1962); and also in MIZRUCHI.

Faris, E. L., *Social Disorganization* (New York, Ronald, 1955), pp. 323-382; and also in LASSWELL ET AL.

Merton, Robert K., *Social Theory and Social Structure*, rev. ed., (New York, Free Press, 1957), Chapters 4 and 5.

Nix, Harold L. and Frederick L. Bates, "Occupational Role Stresses: A Structural Approach," *Rural Sociology*, Vol. 27 (March, 1962), pp. 7-17.

Rose, Arnold M., "Theory for the Study of Social Problems," *Social Problems*, Vol. 4 (January, 1957), pp. 189-199; and also in BM.

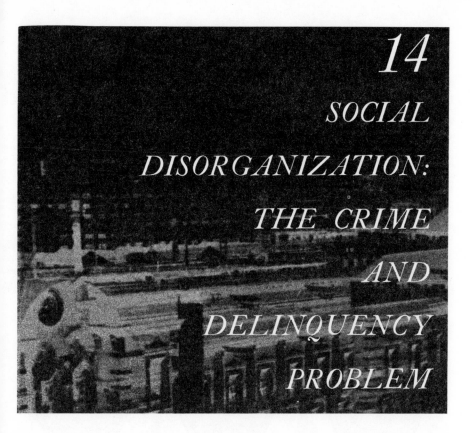

*SOCIAL
DISORGANIZATION:
THE CRIME
AND
DELINQUENCY
PROBLEM*

Both social deviation and social problems were defined in the preceding chapter. There it was also noted that not all deviation from norms was disapproved, although deviation of any type resulted in some degree of social disorganization. It was also pointed out that the members of a social system are usually more concerned with punishing those who deviated in ways which were disapproved, than in rewarding those complying with norms, or deviating in approved ways which might improve the efficiency of their social systems. Perhaps the most important area of disapproved deviation from norms in all societies is crime and delinquency. The view that crime and delinquency represent social problems is universal, despite the fact that what is a crime varies infinitely from one social setting to another. Figure 14-1, which dramatically portrays the "crime clocks" for 1965 in the United States, gives an indication why there is grave concern over this type of social problem. The purpose of this chapter is to briefly introduce the student to the many terms and classifications and the patterns of behavior associated with crime and delinquency. The ways in which the process of disorganization is articulated by this type of deviancy will be evident in the discussions presented. A later chapter will be concerned with social control, including the ways used to curb crime and delinquency.

FIGURE 14-1. *Crime Clocks, 1965.*

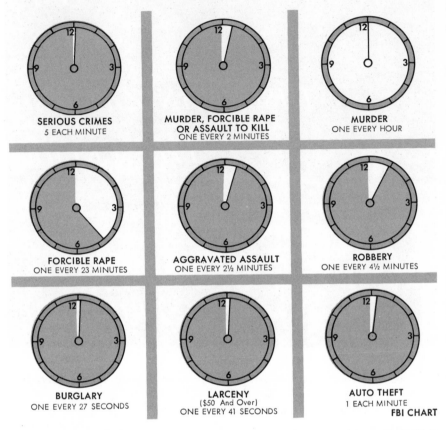

Source: *Uniform Crime Reports—1965*, U. S. Department of Justice (Washington, D. C., U. S. Government Printing Office, 1965), p. 15.

DEFINITION OF CRIME
AND DELINQUENCY

It is a common habit to refer to the behavior of others which we do not like or appreciate, that is, which deviates to a considerable extent from our norms, as crime. However, when any shocking or violent act is referred to as a crime in and of itself, a popular rather than a scientific or technical definition is being used. From a technical standpoint, a **crime** *exists only when behavior is such as to be in violation of a law.* This means that all criminal acts must have a history, that is, represent something that in the past has so aroused public sentiment or concern to cause a law or other formal regulation to be passed. The student will quickly see that there are many acts normally classified as immoral or undesirable that cannot be technically defined as crimes.

This position must be taken despite the fact that some acts that can be engaged in legally are highly injurious to society, such as the selling of useless drugs to people with the impression that all ailments will be cured.

It will also be apparent to the student that many acts legally and technically defined as crime are not considered improper by most persons and go on with little or no censorship. This happens because the laws that apply are outmoded or a greater (dominant) value is served. For example, the father who steals food to feed his starving family has engaged in a criminal act, but is likely to get away with a reprimand because feeding one's family is a paramount value of the greater society. The person stealing purely for profit, a lesser value than feeding one's family, will usually be given some type of jail sentence.

Juvenile delinquency is also arbitrarily distinguished from criminal behavior, in this instance by an age limit. The deviant behavior of persons under a certain age, usually 16 to 18 years, which represents a disapproved violation of important norms is termed delinquent behavior. Delinquency not only includes all violations of criminal law, but many peculiarly juvenile types of deviancy such as truancy, incorrigibility, and vandalism. When apprehended, juvenile delinquents are usually treated differently from criminals. Frequently, for example, they are placed in the custody of their parents or guardians rather than sent to prison. They are also likely to face special courts, rather than the regular criminal courts.

CLASSIFICATION OF CRIME, CRIMINALS AND DELINQUENCY

Crime and criminals can be classified according to various criteria. The descriptions in this section include the generally accepted categories used by criminologists. A working vocabulary of types of crime and types of criminals is a necessary part of the sociologist's intellectual equipment and of prime importance to an informed discussion of the crime problem.

LEGAL CLASSIFICATION OF CRIME

Legal classifications of crime vary from nation to nation, as does the definition of a crime. However, three main categories of crime are recognized almost everywhere: crimes against the person, crimes against property, and crimes against public order. The first type, crimes against the person, includes such deviant acts as murder, assault, and rape. Crimes against property are illustrated by burglary, forgery, and robbery. The behavior of prostitutes, narcotics addicts, and drunks is interpreted as crime against the public order.

In the United States, all crimes are divided into two large groups based on the severity of punishment which is meted out. A **felony** is a crime that is or may be punishable by death or imprisonment in a state or federal prison. A **misdemeanor** is any other crime, but is generally construed to be a petty offense punishable by fine or imprisonment in a local jail. It should be pointed out that there is no universal dividing line between a felony and a misdemeanor. The same act may be ruled a felony in one state and a misdemeanor in another. Of course, such extreme acts as murder and rape are universally regarded as a felony. It should also be noted that some states have laws that automatically make the third or fourth misdemeanor charged to an individual a felonious act.

More elaborate quasi-legal classifications of crime are used in law textbooks and by crime agencies, such as the Federal Bureau of Investigation in the United States. The usual scheme of law books is to segregate crimes as follows: (1) offenses against the person; (2) offenses against the habitation; (3) offenses against property; (4) offenses against the public safety, comfort, and morals; (5) offenses against public justice and authority; (6) offenses against the public peace; and (7) offenses against the existence of government. The F. B. I. reports crimes under 27 headings, which may be found in the *Uniform Crime Reports* published by this agency.

ORGANIZED VERSUS UNORGANIZED CRIME

Criminologists make a distinction between crime that is organized and crime that is carried out on an individual or small-group basis, even though committed by professional criminals. Unorganized crime can and does include much the same type of deviant act as does organized crime. The difference stems from the fact that the former is done by single individuals or casual groups of offenders, who do not stick together for prolonged criminal activities.

Some activities, like picking pockets, swindle games, and robbery cannot be organized on an elaborate scale and remain largely in the province of unorganized crime. However, in instances where the norms are not so clearcut and where deviance patterns are tolerated by the so-called respectable elements in communities, organized crime flourishes. The types of crimes which are most commonly carried out on an organized scale include gambling, prostitution, dope traffic, and racketeering. Organized crime is so important as to deserve some elaboration at this point.

The most important feature of organized crime is a feudal pattern of organization. This type of organization is characterized by a clear-cut hierarchy of power, with each person in a lower status level giving undivided loyalty and service to the person in the power position above him. The organization is held together by powerful leaders who use coercive techniques, including physical violence, to enforce an underworld code of conduct.[1]

---

[1] For a list of the characteristic features of organized crime, see Marshall B. Clinard, *Sociology of Deviant Behavior*, rev. ed. (New York, Holt, Rinehart and Winston, 1963), p. 273.

Individuals who engage in organized crime band themselves together in distinct types of social groups.[2] An **organized criminal gang** is an association of youths or adults bound by intimate ties of friendship and loyalty. **Youth gangs** differ from criminal gangs in the important respect that the latter is organized especially for crime. The youth gangs indulge in violent and other types of criminal activities, but sometimes are motivated by adventure or thrill, rather than profit. All gangs are characterized by strict discipline, with each member having to subordinate his personal interests to the group. Those who threaten the success or safety of the group are violently treated. Some of the more common criminal gang activities are (1) highjacking (thefts of the contents of trucks), (2) armed robbery (on a large scale, such as banks or armored trucks), (3) automobile theft (including the systematic stealing and disposal of autos), and (4) kidnapping (holding someone for ransom).

A second type of group which engages in organized crime is the **criminal syndicate**. The operation of a syndicate is in sharp contrast to that of a gang. The latter is mobile, violent, and engages in sensational crimes; but the syndicate is best characterized as a stable, businesslike organization, whose only violence is likely to be directed against competitors. Syndicates seek control of gambling, prostitution, narcotics, and bootlegging (of whiskey in "dry" areas). Certain characteristics set the syndicate apart from other groups engaging in organized crime. First, it is definitely and primarily a business organization. Second, it depends on an apathetic public which not only permits the deviant behavior, but illicitly demands the services rendered. Third, the syndicate develops through ruthless competition, which may involve the destruction of competitors. Finally, the syndicate tends to operate in larger cities, because of the difficulty of maintaining anonymity in smaller towns.

The third type of organized crime is known as **racketeering**. This term came into use in the United States during the 1920's to indicate an organized scheme to extort money illegally by threats. In contrast to gangs and syndicates, the racketeer groups neither brazenly steal nor offer a service. Rather they force individuals or groups to make periodic payments for nothing more tangible than alleged "protection." Businesses which operate on the border line of the law are especially susceptible to racketeers, although legitimate businesses are by no means exempt. Rackets frequently take the form of control of labor unions, so that the union is operated for those in control rather than the membership. The more powerful among racketeer organizations may control a whole industry or even several industries in a city.

A fourth class of organized crime is **political graft and corruption**. Many elective and appointive offices at various levels of government are associated with the expenditures of large sums of money and with various degrees of authoritative power as well. Political corruption takes many forms, but in an organized sense it is usually associated with the control of these offices by a "machine" under the guidance of a "boss." Various types of disapproved devi-

[2] Ruth S. Cavan, *Criminology*, 3rd ed. (New York, Crowell, 1962), pp. 127-155.

ant behavior on a large scale are in evidence, such as rigging ballot boxes, misuse of public funds for private gain, the performance of normally free services for fees, favoritism for a bribe, and contract kickbacks. It is extremely difficult to control this sort of organized crime because the hands of the law are the hands of the corrupt. Systems of graft usually operate to the benefit of other forms of organized crime as well—for example, police systems become corrupt and give protection to criminals for a fee.

WHITE COLLAR VERSUS BLUE COLLAR CRIME

The investigators of the crime problem in advanced complex societies have discovered that criminal behavior of a particular type can be separated from ordinary underworld activity. This is the type of deviance which occurs among individuals and groups generally thought to be respectable. Such crime follows social stratification patterns to a large extent and lends itself to class differentiation on this basis as *white-collar crime*. This type of crime is committed by persons in the middle or upper social classes in the course of their occupational pursuits.[3] It is often not a criminal activity in the technical sense, because no statute has been violated. It also represents peculiar problems of detection, cessation, and treatment.

Two important types of white-collar crime may be readily identified. The first is characterized by fraudulent practices, including such things as false advertising, short weights, inferior materials, and systematic overcharges. In the United States, home repair frauds have been well advertised, but still take in an estimated $500 million dollars annually.[4] The second type of common white-collar crime is the violation of local and federal laws. Such violations include patent infringements, illegal labor practices such as using unskilled persons in professional roles, illegal rebates to corrupt politicians, and price fixing. During shortage periods so-called black-market practices are common, and in these instances legal price limits are sometimes flagrantly violated. After the second World War, prices of automobiles were set by federal statute, but unscrupulous dealers realized handsome profits by refusing to sell a car unless the customer traded his old car in for grossly underpriced sums ranging down to one dollar.

Blue-collar crime is so designated because it also occurs in connection with occupational pursuits, although at the common labor or worker level. Here it is not usually the customer or client who is the victim, but the employer. Systematic pilferages of small items, such as company materials, or of cargo which is being unloaded may amount to large sums in the course of a year. However, blue-collar crime costs are far below those of white-collar crime.

[3] Edwin R. Sutherland, *White Collar Crime* (New York, The Dryden Press, 1949).
[4] "The Crooks in White Collars," *Life*, Vol. 43 (October 14, 1957), pp. 162 ff.

Neither white- nor blue-collar crime excites great public indignation and this explains why it persists in most societies. More public indignation is generally aroused over an armed robbery of a few thousand dollars than the systematic white-collar robbery of the public of many millions of dollars through short weights or false advertising.

NONPROFESSIONAL VERSUS PROFESSIONAL OFFENDERS

There are many ways in which criminals can be classified, depending upon the criteria selected. The best schemes give insight into the personality of the criminal as seen in the attitude he takes toward his role and the success he achieves. The typology of criminals which follows differentiates between non- or sub-professional offenders and professional offenders, with more attention being given the latter.

NONPROFESSIONAL OFFENDERS: Under the classification of non-professional law violators, it is customary to list offenders who have not developed their criminal roles to a high degree.[5] Examples would include: (1) *The Occasional Property Offender,* who lives out his life with only an occasional theft or forgery to mar his record of abiding by societal norms. (2) *The Habitual Petty Offender,* or the person who habitually commits petty or small crimes. Typically, such offenders compile long criminal records for such deviant activities as vagrancy, disorderly conduct, driving while drunk, shop-lifting, and the like. (3) *The White-Collar Offender,* already identified, who may neatly divide his personality so as to have a personal code of high morality on the one hand and a business code of law violation on the other hand. (4) *The Situational Criminal,* who commits a criminal act under the pressure of overpowering cricumstances, but who otherwise has no criminal inclination. Murders committed by husbands or wives who catch their respective spouses in compromising situations are of this nature. (5) *The Moralistic Offender,* who violates a law that forbids certain vices, but who normally does not harm anyone but himself. The identification of moralistic offenders depends strictly on law norms. Persons such as alcoholics, dope addicts, prostitutes, and homosexuals are moralistic offenders, although they are sometimes said to suffer from a personal pathology.

THE PROFESSIONAL OFFENDER: The most important class of criminals to any society are the so-called career or professional criminals. This class is broad, including persons who pick pockets and work confidence games as well as those who are high-jackers or murderers for hire. However, all professional criminals have one common characteristic. They define themselves as

[5] Clinard, *op. cit.,* pp. 257-266.

criminal and consciously organize their lives around a criminal career. They consider law breaking a professional endeavor and seek competence in their particular line of criminal activity. Actually they look for status and secure prestige among their element through demonstrations of skills in criminal behavior.

Professional criminals are the least likely to get caught of all criminals, because they plan their activities very carefully. Most of the time they have made prior arrangements to protect themselves in such a way that they receive minimum punishment if caught. They seldom engage in acts of violence because this is foolish. When convicted, they are often model prisoners and usually paroled in the shortest possible time because of the connections they have. The outlook of the professional criminal has been likened to that of the professional soldier because of the way in which he takes risks. Risks are calculated and taken only if they can result in something worthy.

The professional criminal operates for the most part in large cities and is likely to be mobile because of his activities. Wherever he goes he becomes a member of the criminal underworld. Roebuck and Johnson point out that confidence men have high prestige in the world of professional criminals. They describe this type of offender as composed of ". . . smooth, adroit, convincing talkers who live by their wits and their ability to manipulate people."[6]

THE JUVENILE OFFENDER: The types of offenses committed by juveniles are much the same as those committed by adult criminals, with at least one major exception, vandalism. For this reason, the latter will be described briefly while other juvenile law-breaking acts are simply listed. The major offenses of juveniles, besides vandalism, are (1) habitual truancy from school, (2) vagrancy (running away from home), (3) incorrigibility (cannot be controlled by parents), (4) stealing, (5) sex offenses (especially among girls), (6) traffic violations, (7) auto theft (usually for joy rides), and (8) burglary (breaking and entering homes).

Vandalism, sometimes referred to as malicious mischief, involves the deliberate destruction of private or public property by some form of defacement or mutilation without the consent of the owner or caretaker of the property. Typical acts of vandalism include breaking windows in schools, destroying school records, mutilating school property such as desks and records, removing street and highway signs, slashing tires, destroying flowers and shrubs in parks, tampering with the seals and contents of trucks and railway cars, damaging public toilets, and tearing up restaurant facilities.

Vandalism tends to have a group nature. Most such acts are committed with companions, often by members of a gang. They are much more common among adolescent boys than among girls. There is an air of bravado in many acts of vandalism which is tempered sometimes with a flavor of spontaneity, triggered by resentment of authority. Vandals seem to have self-conceptions of

[6] Julian B. Roebuck and Ronald C. Johnson, "The 'Short Con' Man," *Crime and Delinquency,* Vol. 10 (July, 1964), pp. 235-248.

themselves as pranksters rather than delinquents, because they do not usually interpret their acts as serious. Acts of vandalism have been classified on the basis of the apparent motivation for the act.[7] **Predatory vandalism** involves acts that are done in the hope of some financial reward, such as from selling parts ripped off buildings to junk dealers. **Vindictive vandalism** is just what the name implies; an attempt to vent one's hatred for individuals or groups by destroying something they own or are associated with. A boy with such a motivation may tear up the room of a teacher whom he dislikes, for example. The third type of vandalism, **wanton vandalism,** apparently has no crystallized motivation except a general rebellion against the world or society. This type of vandalism has no particular focus on individuals or groups and the destruction of property is purely at random, although it may on occasion be associated with the play activity of younger children.

THE SOCIAL STRUCTURE AND CRIME

Social scientists are continually investigating the relationship of crime to various socio-cultural factors. These studies have turned up some interesting patterns, which definitely show that this type of deviant behavior is associated with the cultural structure primarily, although personality and situational factors also have relevance. In this section, an attempt is made to highlight the more important ways in which crime and delinquency relate to social behavioral variables.

RELATIONSHIP BETWEEN SEX AND CRIME

Studies concerning themselves with overall differentials in rate of crimes for men and women inevitably indicate that men have higher rates. For example, in 1964 the *Uniform Crime Reports* published by the United States Federal Bureau of Investigation showed that males were arrested eight times more than females. This pattern holds true in all parts of the world and in all communities for which reliable statistics have been made available. Why this should be true is not altogether clear. The fact that as many girls as boys grow up in slum areas, in conditions of poverty, and in problem homes makes it difficult to account for this pattern, especially when the ratio of male criminals to female criminals is seldom less than 10 to one. Jackson Toby, after doing research on this phenomenon, suggests that this significant difference may be accounted for in large part by differential socialization.[8] Toby's conclusions

---

[7] John M. Martin, *Juvenile Vandalism* (Springfield, Illinois, Charles C Thomas, 1961), pp. 72-103.

[8] Jackson Toby, "The Differential Impact of Family Disorganization," *American Sociological Review,* Vol. 22 (October, 1957), pp. 505-512.

are that girls are supervised more closely than boys and that behavior consist-tent with legal codes is stressed more consistently and uniformly with girls than with boys. Although this study was done in the United States, it seems a plausible basis for a general theory of sex differentials in crime patterns.

RELATIONSHIP BETWEEN AGE AND CRIME

Age is also closely related to both the frequency with which crime is com-mitted and the type of crime committed. The important general pattern, at least in advanced societies, is that crime is more closely associated with youth than old age. This fact is clearly demonstrated in Figure 14-2, which shows the total number of arrests for one year in the United States by age groups. The *Uniform Crime Reports* make it possible to relate crime to age and sex in specific fashion. At least six general age-crime patterns are discernible: (1) The crime rate is highest during adolescence or just prior to adolescence, including the years roughly from 12 to 20. (2) The age of maximum crim-inality varies with the nature of the crime. Auto theft, for example, is associated with a younger criminal than is robbery or murder. (3) Females tend to reach maximum criminality periods at a later age than males, both for offenses in general and specific offenses. (4) The concentration of certain crimes, such as burglary and larceny, in the young-adult age groups is both typical and a long-time phenomenon, dating as far back as statistics are available. (5) There are noticeable residential and regional differences in the age of first delin-quency and the type of crime committed. Environmental differences, such as rural residence, slum residence, and upper-class residence account for these differences. (6) The crime rate for both males and females decreases from the age of maximum criminality to the end of life. The arrests of males begin to drop after age 20 and arrests of females decline after age 23.

There are no clear-cut explanations for the close association of youth with higher rates of crime. The fact that younger persons are more likely to be arrested because of criminal inexperience accounts for only a very minor part of the difference in rates. The evidence suggests that adolescence and early adulthood are maximum stress–strain periods for most individuals, but the problem remains to be studied in much more detail.

RELATIONSHIP BETWEEN
RESIDENCE AND CRIME

Crime rates and patterns of criminality also vary according to residence and occupational factors. This phenomenon is explained more in terms of differ-ential socialization than age variations in crime. For example, the individual growing up in a traditionally oriented rural area will not have the opportunity

FIGURE 14-2. *Total Arrests in the United States by Age Group, 1965.*

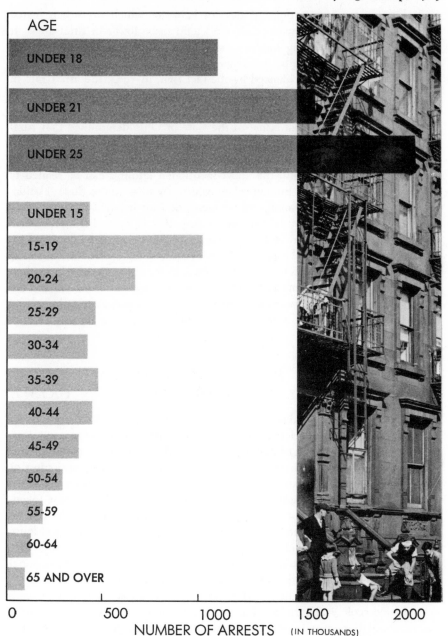

AGE

UNDER 18

UNDER 21

UNDER 25

UNDER 15

15-19

20-24

25-29

30-34

35-39

40-44

45-49

50-54

55-59

60-64

65 AND OVER

0 500 1000 1500 2000

NUMBER OF ARRESTS (IN THOUSANDS)

Source: *Uniform Crime Reports—1965,* U. S. Department of Justice (Washington, D. C., U. S. Government Printing Office, 1965), pp. 112-114. Photograph courtesy of United Nations Organization.

or inclination for certain types of deviant behavior which the urban reared person will have. This is why crime rates tend to be lower in rural areas. It also explains why crimes against property tend to be more prevalent in cities, while rural crime tends to be more against persons. The residence difference in incidence of crime is evidenced by the fact that, in 1964, the arrest rate in urban areas of the United States was 41 persons per 1000 inhabitants, while this rate was only 21 in suburban areas and 15 in rural areas.

A recent study of rural crime in the state of Ohio determined that rural offenders were younger, less intelligent, and more likely to be unmarried than nonrural offenders.[9] They were also less well educated than the average rural male in the state. These and the above-mentioned findings can be related to the normative structure of human relationships. In areas where these relationships tend to be close, personal and frequent, deviant behavior is more likely to be a phenomenon of youth and intelligence—that is, occur before socialization has progressed too far, or because socialization is impeded by mental incapacity. Crimes against the person occur because interaction is at the close, intimate level and breaches of the norms result in more stress at the individual level and it is more customary, because of distance and other factors, to take individual action. If one receives an insult, or if one's property is abused, he is more likely to take direct action against the violator than to resort to the formal processes of law.

REGIONAL AND ECOLOGICAL VARIATIONS IN CRIME

The peculiar cultural conditioning that one receives in a particular region or subregion of a national society also accounts for variances in criminal patterns. Here, such factors as ways of making a living and local codes of morality tend to give crime a certain direction. For example, the cultural conditioning of people in the southern part of the United States, peculiarly prepared them for violation of federal legislation relative to race relations. By the same token, the peculiar business-industrial complex of the northern region of the nation, accounts for the higher rates of labor racketeering and gang warfare. Figure 14-3 shows clearly the use of a gun in murders is more prevalent in the Southern part of the United States. This phenomenon is related both to the regional mores of direct action and the relative rurality of the region.

Crime is also distributed within metropolitan areas according to well-documented ecological variables. For one thing crime rates are correlated with size of population—usually the larger the city, the more crime. Secondly, the central areas of cities tend to have more crime than the outlying districts. Third, highest crime rates are usually found in slum areas, characterized by

[9] Willard T. Rushton and A. R. Mangus, *Rural Criminals and Their Crimes: Ohio, 1956-1960* (Columbus, Ohio, Ohio State University, Department of Agricultural Economics & Rural Sociology Series A. E. 368, September, 1964).

high population density and low income, and with high concentrations of minority race and ethnic groups. This does not mean that crime is intrinsically associated with economic and ethnic factors, but indicates that more criminals of a certain type are apprehended in urban areas with these characteristics. In this regard, Miller puts forth the interesting thesis that the motivation for delinquent behavior characteristics of lower-class "corner" groups is a positive effort to achieve things and recognition highly valued in this cultural milieu.[10]

FIGURE 14-3.   *Murder and Nonnegligent Manslaughter by Gun and Region (percent of United States Total).*

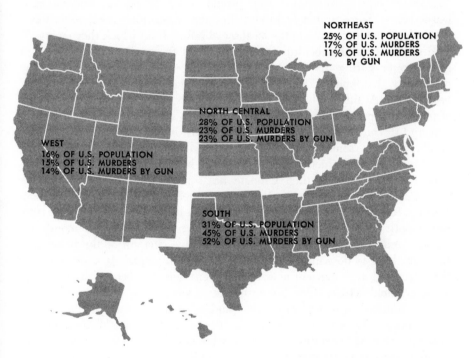

NORTHEAST
25% OF U.S. POPULATION
17% OF U.S. MURDERS
11% OF U.S. MURDERS
BY GUN

NORTH CENTRAL
28% OF U.S. POPULATION
23% OF U.S. MURDERS
23% OF U.S. MURDERS BY GUN

WEST
16% OF U.S. POPULATION
15% OF U.S. MURDERS
14% OF U.S. MURDERS BY GUN

SOUTH
31% OF U.S. POPULATION
45% OF U.S. MURDERS
52% OF U.S. MURDERS BY GUN

Source: *Uniform Crime Reports—1962,* U. S. Department of Justice (Washington, D. C., U. S. Government Printing Office, 1963), p. 10.

OTHER FACTORS RELATED TO CRIME AND DELINQUENCY

Several other factors can be called to attention in connection with the relationship of crime and delinquency to the social structure, although these factors

[10] Walter B. Miller "Lower Class Culture as a Generating Milieu of Gang Delinquency," *Journal of Social Issues,* Vol. 14 (No. 3, 1958), pp. 5-19.

are not as important as residence, age, sex, and region. The first is the economic status of the population. It already has been pointed out that the slum areas of cities apparently breed more crime. This fact can be elaborated to show that poverty and crime tend to go hand-in-hand. Again, it should be made clear that the evidence for this statement comes from arrest rates for particular crimes, and does not in any way rule out the possibility that *actual* crime rates may be quite different. The middle and upper classes tend to be less susceptible to arrest, and this is in itself a cultural factor relevant to the crime problem.

A second factor is the matter of subcultural variations in norms. This type of variation occurs in two ways. The first relates to what is generally referred to as criminal subcultures within the greater society. These subcultures represent special environments, such as slum areas, where criminal models become "significant others" to many young people and a delinquent orientation is learned early. Some writers feel that delinquent subcultures are more or less a direct adjustment response to the local social milieu from which they emerge.[11] The second type of subculture which accounts for criminal behavior has a more specific setting—the family. The influence which the family has on the personality development and general socialization of the child has already been shown. At this level of analysis many factors, such as broken homes, lack of parental supervision, parental rejection, and a home atmosphere of discontent and discord, have to be considered. Many studies have shown that the family setting has some relationship to crime and delinquency.[12]

Other factors which relate to criminal behavior are not as closely related to the cultural setting. Climate has some connection with crime in that crimes of a certain type tend to be committed at certain times of the year. Murder, for example, occurs more frequently in the United States in the summer months, as does aggravated assault. By contrast the peak month for robbery and burglary is December. The effective strength of the police also has something to do with crime, other factors being equal. It is obvious that the larger and more efficient police department will do a better job of discouraging criminal activity. One interesting culturally related thesis is that crime and delinquency is related to wartime and other disturbances in the lives of young people. Wilkins has done research on what he terms "delinquent generations," that is, generations of people who have higher rates of deviant behavior because of such experience.[13]

[11] Richard A. Cloward and Lloyd E. Ohlin, *Delinquency and Opportunity* (New York, Free Press, 1961), pp. 161-186.

[12] For a collection of these studies see Marion E. Wolfgang, Leonard Savitz, and Norman Johnson, *The Sociology of Crime and Delinquency* (New York, Wiley, 1962), Part VI.

[13] Leslie T. Wilkin's "Delinquent Generations," reproduced in, *ibid.*, pp. 170-179; originally published as Home Office Research Unit Report #3 in Studies in the Courses of Delinquency and the Treatment of Offenders (London, Her Majesty's Stationery Office, 1960), pp. 1-10, 14, 19.

CRIMINOLOGY AS A SPECIALIZED DISCIPLINE

With the various classifications and descriptions presented in this chapter in mind, it is appropriate to note that these subjects falls within the scope of the subdiscipline of sociology known as criminology. This field of study is an important one and most university departments of sociology include specialized courses that treat the various aspects of this discipline. Usually three general processes serve as the focus of attention for students of criminology. The first involves questions relating to the nature of crime and to the ways in which an individual becomes a criminal. The ramifications of this process are very broad and they have implications for the whole theory of social organization.

The second process that commands the interest of criminologists is the control of crime and delinquency. Here different patterns of behavior must be studied and it is never entirely clear-cut why some persons persist in criminal behavior despite obvious risks of punishment. The profound questions surrounding the whole process of law making and enforcement are further complicated by social change that causes adjustments in societal norms and values. Many theories of punishment as well as other theoretical models relating to social control are to be found in current literature.

Lastly, criminologists interest themselves in what might be called the correlates of crime. They seek to discover why crime rates are high in certain cultures and at certain times. Such factors as wealth, education, age, race, and religion are related to crime, as are residence and mobility. In short, crime has an explanation in certain social conditions and the hope is to isolate these conditions so as to have a scientific basis for predicting future behavior.

The best tangible evidence available for crime and criminals are the various statistics collected by federal, state, and local governments. These reports give some indication of the crime picture even though they may fall short of a clear, concise picture. The great weakness of most such reports is that they record only the crimes known to the police. Many crimes go unreported because individuals do not want to become involved with the police or because of fear of recrimination or of personal involvement. Many reports of crime are also lost before they are recorded and because of the inefficiency or short-handedness of police departments, or they cannot be used because they lack uniformity. Police records augmented by many thorough first-hand investigations, are the best source of crime data. In the United States, statistics derived from these sources have provided the basis for the present body of knowledge in criminology.

The student interested in this field will do well to consult with a sociologist who has specialized in this subdiscipline. If this opportunity is not available, any one of the many fine criminology texts will give him a perspective of the field.

SUMMARY

Crime and delinquency are manifestations of social disorganization and are considered to be social problems. Crime is defined as behavior which is in violation of a law or laws, and delinquency is defined as violations of laws and certain other norms by juveniles, usually under the age of 18 years. Three legal categories of crime are recognized: crimes against the person, crimes against property, and crimes against public order. A felony is a crime that is punishable by death or imprisonment for a considerable length of time in a federal or state prison. A misdemeanor is a petty offense punishable by fine or imprisonment in a local jail.

Organized crime is characterized by a feudal pattern of organization and held together by powerful leaders who use coercive techniques. The important types of criminal organizations are criminal gangs, criminal syndicates, racketeers, and political groups. Organized crime is in contrast to unorganized crime, which is carried out on an individual or small-group basis. Crime committed by individuals or groups generally thought to be respectable, and in the course of a transaction where the consumer is the loser, is termed white-collar crime. This type of crime is differentiated from blue-collar crime, which is characterized by systematic pilferages by workers from their employers.

Nonprofessional criminal offenders, like occasional property offenders, habitual petty thieves, white-collar offenders, situational criminals, and moralistic offenders, are persons who have not developed their criminal roles to a high degree. They are in contrast to the professional offender, who makes a career out of crime. The juvenile offender has many of the same social characteristics as the adult criminal, but tends toward a different type of crime, vandalism.

Crime and delinquency relate to social behavioral variables in several important ways. First, men commit many more crimes than women; second, crime is committed much more frequently by persons in the younger ages; third, crime is committed more frequently in urban areas than in rural areas—not only is there more crime in the cities, but rural offenders are younger and less intelligent. Regional and ecological variables also account for differences in crime rates, with certain regions of a national society and certain areas in cities having higher rates of crime generally or of particular crimes. Poverty, subcultural orientation, season of the year, and effective strength of police are factors that correlate with rates of crime and delinquency.

Supplementary Readings

Cavan, Ruth S., *Criminology,* 3rd ed. (New York, Crowell, 1962).

Clinard, Marshall B., *Sociology of Deviant Behavior,* rev. ed. (New York, Holt, Rinehart and Winston, 1963).

Cohen, Albert K. and James F. Short, Jr., "Research in Delinquent Subcultures," *The Journal of Social Issues,* Vol. 14 (No. 3, 1958), pp. 20-37; and also in LASSWELL ET AL. and BM.

Empey, LaMar T. and Jerome Rabow, "The Provo Experiment in Delinquency Rehabilitation," *American Sociological Review,* Vol. 26 (October, 1961), pp. 679-696; and also in LASSWELL ET AL.

Roebuck, Julian B., *Criminal Typology* (Springfield, Ill., Charles C Thomas, 1967).

Roebuck, Julian B. and Ronald C. Johnson, "The 'Short Con' Man," *Crime and Delinquency,* Vol. 10 (July, 1964), pp. 235-248.

Simmons, J. L., "Public Stereotypes of Deviants," *Social Problems,* Vol. 13 (Fall, 1965), pp. 223-232; and also in MIZRUCHI.

Sutherland, Edwin H., "White-Collar Criminality," *American Sociological Review,* Vol. 5 (February, 1940), pp. 1-12; and also in INKELES and BM.

Wolfgang, Marvin E., Leonard Savitz, and Norman Johnston, *The Sociology of Crime and Delinquency* (New York, Wiley, 1962).

15

SOCIAL DISORGANIZATION: THE HUMAN BEING IN DISASTERS

It was made clear in previous discussions that processes of social disorganization articulated the stress–strain element of social systems. These processes may be initiated by extreme crisis situations which affect groups of people adversely as well as by deviant behavior such as crime and delinquency. When the mechanisms which normally function to prevent disruption of social systems cease to function, as they often do under extreme crisis situations, social organization is temporarily lost. Disasters serve to introduce what has been called *collective stress situations* which are differentiated from stress situations that do not involve all persons in a given community or society area in an immediate or urgent fashion. This difference may be illustrated by comparing the stress that a delinquent juvenile gang might place on a community with the stress which a vicious hurricane might place on the same community. Both situations are characterized by the processes of disorganization which produce stresses and strains on the structure of the community system, but the hurricane is much more total in its impact. This chapter is designed to show the contrast in social disorganization processes related to role deviancy and social disorganization processes brought on by largely uncontrollable forces that completely disrupt all behavioral patterns.

DISASTERS AS COLLECTIVE STRESS SITUATIONS

To the ordinary person, the term *disaster* connotes some sort of calamity with dire implications. However appealing such an understanding may be for the popular mind, it does not suffice for the technical usage of sociologists. Loomis' definition of a disaster contrasts the difference between what may be called the lay understanding and the scientific understanding. He states, ". . . **disaster . . .** *may be said to exist whenever collective and individual actions that were previously structured and made predictable by the elements and processes (of social systems) are made unpredictable by the impact of either external or internal forces.*"[1]

The above definition needs some elaboration in order that its full implications may be made clear. First, a disaster does not necessarily have to be something which is cataclysmic in nature, although it often is. This point may be illustrated by contrasting the suddenness with which a tornado strikes to the deliberate approach of a drouth condition. Both are forces that paralyze segments of society, but one is much more extended in time. Ketch draws an analogy between cataclysmic disaster and revolutionary change and disaster that occurs over a lengthy period of time and evolutionary change.[2]

The second understanding to be derived from the above definition of disaster is that a considerable segment of society must be involved and near complete disruption of normal activity must occur. This does not mean that the impact must be of a certain scope or type. For example, the first bombardment of a town by enemy aircraft may be defined as a disaster, because the unexpectedness of the attack leaves every facility paralyzed and survivors are unable to carry out normal routines. However, subsequent even larger attacks may find the community well organized, with bomb shelters, emergency

---

[1] From Charles P. Loomis, *Social Systems: Essays on Their Persistence and Change.* Copyright 1960, D. Van Nostrand Company, Inc., Princeton, N.J., pp. 129-130. Harry Moore uses a more "value-laden" definition, but is in essential agreement with Loomis. See Harry E. Moore, *Tornadoes Over Texas* (Austin, Texas, University of Texas Press, 1958), p. 310. Carr also agrees closely with Loomis, as does Wallace, although the latter scholars stress the situational aspects more than the structural aspects in their analyses. See Lowell J. Carr, *Situational Analysis* (New York, Harper & Row, 1948), p. 59; and Anthony F. C. Wallace, *Human Behavior in Extreme Situations* (Washington, D. C., National Academy of Sciences–National Research Council, Disaster Study No. 1, 1956).

[2] Clarence W. Ketch, "A Situational Analysis of the Effects of Drouth as a Disaster on the Mobility of a Selected Rural-Farm Population" (unpublished doctoral dissertation, Louisiana State University, 1961), p. 36.

power plants, fire control devices, and underground medical services. In this instance, since community activities are not disrupted to a great extent, the situation would not be defined as a disaster.

In essence, then, a disaster may be identified as a *collective stress situation*. Such situations are identified when massive forces of stress are placed on a major social system, and involve all of its component subsystems. Barton has delineated three dimensions of collective stress situations which are helpful in studying disasters, although not all collective stress situations are disasters.[3] The first dimension is the scope of the social system primarily affected, which may range from a small community to an entire nation. The second dimension is the speed and duration of the impact of the disaster agent. A range in this dimension may vary from the swift, momentary character of a tornado to the gradual progress of a depression or drouth. The third and final dimension is the degree of institutional (social system) preparation for the disaster. For some disasters, such as economic depressions, there may be considerable pre-planning and preconditioning which blunt the effect of the impact to a certain extent. For others, such as floods or riots, there may be no preparation at all.

The stresses faced in disaster situations are manifest in the following forms of role deviancy, according to Bates and his associates.[4] (1) Role conflict which develops as individuals are faced with conflicting obligations. This may be illustrated by the fireman or policeman who has to decide whether to rescue his family or perform his public duty. (2) Role frustration which comes about because the situations under which normal roles are played no longer exist. This situation may develop because facilities such as roads are no longer usable or homes or businesses are destroyed. (3) Role inadequacy which stems from the inability of individuals to perform roles thrust upon them in emergency situations. Quite frequently medical attention must be rendered by persons not trained in such procedures, for example. (4) Role saturation which comes about because individuals are overloaded with responsibility and the pressure calls forth emotional reaction. The lone doctor who has survived may find it completely impossible to attend to the many needy and end up doing nothing.

The stresses undergone in a disaster result in more or less permanent changes in the affected social systems. These changes (to be discussed later) may or may not involve difficult adjustment for the affected individuals. In this regard, Fritz has proposed a "therapeutic community" hypothesis which

[3] Allen H. Barton, *Social Organization Under Stress: A Sociological Review of Disaster Studies* (Washington, D. C., National Academy of Sciences–National Research Council, Disaster Study No. 17, 1963), pp. 4-5.

[4] F. L. Bates, C. W. Fogleman, V. J. Parenton, R. H. Pittman, and G. S. Tracy, *The Social and Psychological Consequences of a Natural Disaster* (Washington, D. C., National Academy of Sciences–National Research Council, Disaster Study No. 18, 1963), pp. 3-5.

holds that suffering for the individual is lessened when his plight is shared by many others.[5]

TYPES OF DISASTERS

Several scholars have worked out classifications of types of disasters using various criteria. One of the most recent typologies is that of Ketch. He types disasters according to two criteria: (1) their predictability in terms of whether or not they can be anticipated, and (2) the time element involved.[6] Carr utilizes a third criteria, geographic spread, which may be used to expand Ketch's typology somewhat.[7] Table 15-1 was prepared to show the types of disasters generally recognized by students of these phenomenon. No differentiation is made between natural and man-made disasters, since the end result is essentially the same.

In Table 15-1, disasters are typed as unanticipated if they come with little or no warning. They are identified as cataclysmic if they have a short

TABLE 15-1. *Types of Disasters*[a]

Predictability	Duration	Geographic Spread	Illustrative Disaster
Unanticipated	Cataclysmic	Concentrated	Undetected tornado or bombing
		Diffuse	Undetected Hurricane or typhoon
	Extended	Concentrated	Local flood or epidemic
		Diffuse	Sudden large scale riots or war.
Anticipated	Cataclysmic	Concentrated	Bombing during wartime, seasonal flood
		Diffuse	Siege or revolution on national scale.
	Extended	Concentrated	Local strike after negotiations, predicted local drought
		Diffuse	War after period of negotiation, predicted hurricane

a Based on typologies worked out by Clarence Ketch, "A Situational Analysis of Drouth as a Disaster on the Mobility of a Selected Rural-Farm Population" (Unpublished, doctoral dissertation, Louisiana State University, 1961), p. 38, and Charles Loomis, *Social Systems: Essays on Their Persistence* (New York, Van Nostrand, 1960), p. 130.

[5] C. E. Fritz, "Disaster" in R. K. Merton and R. A. Nisbet, Eds., *Contemporary Social Problems* (New York, Harcourt, Brace & World, 1961), pp. 651-694.
[6] From *Tornadoes Over Texas: A Study of Waco and San Angelo in Disaster*, by Harry Estill Moore. University of Texas Press, 1958, pp. 36-39.
[7] L. J. Carr, "Disaster and the Sequence-Pattern Concept of Social Change," *American Journal of Sociology*, Vol. 38 (September, 1963), pp. 207-218.

time span, lasting no longer than a matter of days. Those disasters that affect only local communities at most are classed as concentrated in nature, whereas those which spread over several communities or even larger areas are termed diffuse, in an area sense. A particular type of disaster may thus be quickly categorized in terms of its characteristics of predictability, time duration, and geographic coverage. The student may wish to classify certain disasters with which he is familiar in terms of the above typology.

A brief description of an unanticipated cataclysmic concentrated disaster serves to illustrate both the use of a typology in the classification of disasters and the nature of a specific type of disaster. The account below is from Moore's story of the Waco tornado which hit on May 11, 1953.

A spectator eight miles outside Waco saw a "monster" funnel, but stated, "It was so wide and the rain so heavy, it was impossible for anyone in the city to see the funnel approaching."

Into the area swooped the tornado, dipping down into the Bell's Hill Area on the southwestern flank of the city, bouncing along in a northeasterly direction, and then striking with full force in the very center of the business area. Coincidentally, the heaviest destruction from the tornado was the assumed target in case of enemy attack on the city.

In Waco the final death list contained 114 names. There were 145 others listed as having major injuries, and 952 with less serious ones. More than 2,000 families were reported to have suffered loss of some sort. About 2,000 automobiles were damaged, many of them demolished by falling debris. Fairly careful, but not exact, estimates place the number of homes destroyed at 150, with 250 others seriously damaged, and more than 450 damaged less seriously but requiring repairs. In the business area 196 buildings were classified as "demolished" or so severely damaged that they could not be repaired, and 376 others were placed on the "unsafe" list.

Estimates of damage to buildings and other material possessions run from $21 million to $36 million; total losses, including those resulting from deaths, injuries, unemployment, etc. run from $41 million to $63 million. . . .

The downtown situation during the height of the storm was reported as difficult to believe even by those who witnessed it. Buildings, partly hidden by the driving rain, suddenly lifted and fell into the street in masses of splintered wood, bricks, and plaster; brick walls crumbled across parked automobiles; tons of plate glass flew through the air. Within seconds the former business district was a pile of rubble, its streets obliterated by debris. A survivor said, "I don't think the atom bomb could be any worse."[8]

THE "TIME PHASES" OF DISASTERS

All disasters have certain time sequences that are identifiable. These sequences have been used as the basis for theoretical models. Disaster models not only

[8] *Op. cit.,* p. 5.

provide an analytical frame of reference for the study of disasters, but help explain the nature of disasters as well. The "time phases" presented here are the ones worked out by Wallace[9] and slightly modified by Fogleman and Friedsam.[10] Each phase is described in a general fashion.

THE PREDISASTER "STEADY STATE"

The normal activities that typically characterize an ongoing social system are identified as the "steady state" of the system, when related to a disaster situation. The predisaster steady state finds people engaged in their usual occupations and playing their habitual social roles. These roles may involve stresses and strains, but nothing which is not within the realm of conventional happenings. Individuals faced with personal stresses are largely left to work out their own solutions. Community problems are those that have been confronted to some degree before. In other words, the stresses faced by individuals and some groups are generally anticipated and understood and are not of sufficient import to disrupt usual behavior to any great extent. Life in the predisaster steady state is best described as routine.

THE WARNING-THREAT TIME-PHASE

The first indications of a possible disaster comes as some sort of warning. Warning cues may occur over a long period of time, may barely precede, or may be simultaneous with the impact of the disaster. The cues that are received may be quite uncertain and ambiguous during the first part of the warning-threat time phase because information is based on communication which cannot be tested for reliability. Rumors may or may not be founded on facts that are sound enough for predictive purposes. The second part of this phase is more likely to be characterized by reliable cues. The disaster agent very likely has been identified and its probably course determined. In other words, the threat is real and not just speculative. The warning-threat phase is terminated when the disaster strikes or when it is determined that the danger of the disaster situation is passed.

The warning-threat time phase of disasters is characterized by many social variables. For one thing, warning cues are not interpreted in the same

[9] Anthony F. C. Wallace, *Tornado in Worcester* (Washington, D. C., Disaster Study No. 3, National Academy of Sciences–National Research Council, 1956), pp. 7-12.

[10] C. W. Fogleman, "Family and Community in Disaster: A Socio-psychological Study of the Effects of a Major Disaster upon Individuals and Groups within the Impact Area," (unpublished doctoral dissertation, Louisiana State University, 1958); and H. J. Friedsam, "Memorandum on Formal Organizations in Hurricane Audrey," unpublished report (Washington, D. C., Disaster Research Group, National Academy of Sciences–National Research Council, 1957), p. 12.

way by all individuals. Some may interpret the cues as urgent and take evacuative and security measures, while others pass them off lightly as mere unfounded rumor. In the second place, the actual time that elapses between first warning and actual impact may vary from no time to days or even weeks. Warning threats that are over a prolonged period generally are associated with some relaxation of preliminary planning. Finally, the source of information with regard to disasters has a great deal to do with how warnings are received. A terse communique from a high authoritative source has much more urgency than casual gossip picked up on the street.

THE IMPACT TIME-PHASE

The third time-phase, impact, commences at the time physical destruction by the disaster agent begins. This phase is divided into two periods, including the initial or primary impact when the physical damage is being done and the forces of the disaster agent are rampant; and the secondary impact, which follows after the forces of destruction have receded and continues until all destructive after effects are checked. These two periods may be illustrated as follows. A tornado, during its primary impact may rip apart buildings, break water mains, tear apart electrical circuits, and critically injure many people in a matter of moments, and then pass on. Its secondary impact continues until the water pipes are repaired sufficiently to stop further water damage, electrical circuits are rendered harmless, fires started by "hot" wires controlled, and the wounds and shock of victims adequately treated.

The impact of the disaster agent serves to delineate the ecology of the disaster. The place where death, serious injury and near total destruction occur is termed the area of **total impact.** The surrounding area which undergoes less severe damage is identified as the **fringe impact** area. This area varies in size depending upon the nature of the disaster agent—hurricanes have a fringe impact over a large area while a bombing raid may destroy very little outside the total impact area. That territory just beyond the fringe impact area, where the populace have an immediate awareness of but no damage from the disaster is described as the **filter area.** Filter area residents are usually the first to converge on the scene of the disaster.

THE RESCUE-EVACUATION TIME-PHASE

When the first outside help arrives on the scene of the primary impact area, the rescue-evacuation time phase is begun. Usually, the persons active in this type of activity fall into three groups—impact-area survivors; unorganized, spontaneous volunteers from outside the disaster area; and organized, formally directed groups from the outside. The latter may include Red Cross workers, Armed Services units, Civil Defense groups, and fire or police department units. The chief functions of individuals and groups active during this time phase is to give first aid, extricate and evacuate those hurt, provide food and shelter for the homeless, and to do everything possible to minimize the severity of the secondary impact of the disaster. Some confusion may develop at this stage, unless a strong authority appears to take charge and direct activities in a systematic fashion.

THE REHABILITATION TIME-PHASE

The final time-phase, before resumption of a steady state, is identified as the rehabilitation stage. This period begins when the secondary impact of the disaster has been reduced to the lowest possible point. It normally extends over a relatively long period of time and involves extensive welfare and reconstruction activity. These activities may be under the sole means of victims or they may be sponsored by outside agencies of a charitable or government-supported type. In most instances, the rescue and evacuation groups give over to rehabilitation groups, although some of the former may become involved in rehabilitation activity. This time-phase continues until the disaster area is more or less brought back to a state of normalcy, and is difficult to differentiate from the fringe and filter areas of the original disaster. When building and other activity ceases to be related to the disaster the rehabilitation phase is completed and a steady state is at hand.

PROBLEMS IN PLANNING FOR DISASTERS

Disasters, like crime and delinquency, must be anticipated by every society because of their inevitability. However, despite beforehand knowledge of serious disorganizational consequences, most communities make little or no formal preparation for them. The reason seems to be related to the difficulty of fully comprehending the need for something that is subject to apparently remote chance. Problems in disaster planning are also complicated by the varying conditions which must be coped with at different time-phase sequences. Some of the more serious problems faced under specific situations are reviewed here. As Fritz points out, "The degree of disruption to the society caused by a disaster will be largely determined by the degree to which the society has developed realistic expectations about and preparations for future disasters."[11]

[11] *Op. cit.*, p. 659.

ADVANCED PLANNING PROBLEMS

Advanced planning for disasters involves measures designed to prepare the populace mentally for the ordeal as well as to provide physical rescue and rehabilitation facilities. With regard to the former, Wallace has described what he calls a *disaster syndrome*.[12]

The **disaster syndrome** is a psychologically determined defensive reaction pattern that characterizes individual behavior in disasters. During the initial stage, the person appears to be dazed, apathetic, passive, immobile, or aimlessly puttering around. After some time, the second stage develops. At this time, the individual manifests symptoms of extreme suggestibility, altruism, gratitude for help, and anxiousness to perceive that known persons and places have been preserved. During this time personal loss is minimized and grave concern is expressed for the welfare of family and community. The second stage may last for days but is eventually followed by a third stage, characterized by an identification with the damaged community and enthusiastic participation in repair and rehabilitation enterprises. The final stage is reached when normally ambivalent attitudes return and the expression of criticism and complaints accompanies an awareness of the annoyance of the long-term effects of the disaster. Studies have shown that persons who have been preconditioned to disaster situations do not manifest the symptoms of the disaster syndrome to the extent of those who have not. Fritz quotes a woman who was interviewed shortly after a close relative had been killed in a mine disaster as follows:

"That's your life as a coal miner's wife or daughter. You feel like these accidents are going to happen from time to time. You never know whether the next one will be yours or not. You develop a kind of—not hardness, because we love our men and fathers—but it's more or less a feeling that that's one of the things that goes with coal mining. There's been accidents since the first coal mine and I guess there will be 'till there isn't any."[13]

Persons who have not undergone a recent disaster are extremely difficult to motivate to support programs of disaster preparation, as mentioned. The remoteness and uncertainty of the disaster, when weighed against the pressing problems of immediate existence, is sufficient to breed apathy toward advance preparation. This fact coupled with the lack of present rewards for the personal costs and endeavors involved accounts for the problems that planners for future disasters face.

[12] *Tornado in Worcester, op. cit.,* pp. 109-110.
[13] *Op. cit.,* p. 661.

DISASTER WARNING PROBLEMS

The warning time-phase, in the sense that time should be provided for "securing" and evacuating, is the most important phase of a disaster.[14] Warning problems are amplified when the affected communities have had no recent or previous disaster experience. The first type of problem is at the formal level of communication. Radio announcers, weather forecasters, radar operators, and others in strategic warning positions are usually reluctant to issue a specific warning until detection is no longer questionable. Not infrequently this means waiting until there is little time to prepare, assuming the disaster is not of an instantaneous nature.

The second problem condition is the difficulty of securing public acceptance of warning messages. The tendency is to seize on any discrepancy, vagueness, or ambiguity in the warning message as a reason for discounting it and interpreting the situation optimistically. Even when people take warnings seriously they tend to be optimistic about their personal chances, rationalizing that they can protect themselves or that they will somehow be by-passed. Fritz summarizes the disaster warning problems in these words:

. . . to insure that people are really acting in pursuit of their own safety, the warning agency must also have the capacity to make certain that people are correctly interpreting and acting upon the warning information. The problem of warning, in other words, must be viewed as a total process of communication and organization in which people are informed about the danger, told what to do about the danger, and supervised so that their actions conform to the required protective measures.[15]

PROBLEMS DURING THE PERIOD OF IMPACT AND ITS IMMEDIATE AFTERMATH

The most important problem during the impact period of a disaster is the protection of self. Contrary to popular belief, panic does not seem to be a great danger at the time of disaster impact. Flight may occur, but as a response to danger and in a more or less orderly fashion. It is also erroneous to believe that all people are left in a completely dazed and helpless state immediately after

[14] Moore and his associates stress this point and divide the warning process into seven phases as follows: (1) detection, (2) prediction, (3) dissemination, (4) reception, (5) evaluation, (6) reinforcement, and (7) recall. See Harry E. Moore, Frederick L. Bates, Marvin V. Layman, and Vernon J. Parenton, *Before the Wind* (Washington, D. C., National Academy of Sciences–National Research Council, Disaster Study No. 19, 1963).

[15] *Op. cit.*, p. 667.

the disaster impact. Studies that have been made indicate a great deal of stress, but also show many of the rescue operations are carried out by survivors, most of whom regain their self-control within a short period of time.[16]

The more important problems immediately after a disaster relate to the care and treatment of victims. This type of work is typically hampered by the lack of coordination of activity—a phenomenon typical of social disorganization. Many persons may be attempting some helpful operations, but their actions appear aimless and without direction because there is no central authority with a definite plan of action. At this stage it is likely that role conflict may develop because individuals are forced to decide whether to act in their family roles as husbands, or fathers, or in their occupational roles as public officials (firemen and police officers, for example).

The central problem of coordination and control does not stem from the victim population. Rather, it emanates from what has been termed the "convergence behavior" of persons from outside the stricken area. Immediately after a disaster it is usual for literally thousands of persons to be attracted to the scene, and for those further away to flood all communications channels in an attempt to get word to relatives, friends, and business associates in the impact zone. This behavior must be controlled before effective rescue operations can be initiated. Also, many times the people moving into the disaster area are given to pilferage, and this type of deviant behavior must be controlled.

REHABILITATION PROBLEMS AFTER DISASTERS

Rehabilitation problems are primarily associated with the establishment of a new system of social organization after complete disruption of normal ways of life. These problems may be envisioned as occurring at three levels of interaction. First, when key individuals in the power structure of the affected community have been disabled or killed, there is the problem of finding suitable leaders for the involved status positions. This can be a rather difficult matter, when loss of life has been great and all or almost all qualified persons are casualties.

The second set of rehabilitation problems is related to the physical restoration of the facilities necessary for carrying on normal routines, such as houses, business establishments, and service outlets. In this regard, it fre-

---

[16] The following articles bear out the conclusions presented: Charles W. Fogleman and Vernon J. Parenton, "Disaster and Aftermath: Selected Aspects of Individual and Group Behavior in Critical Situations," *Social Forces*, Vol. 38 (December, 1959), pp. 130-135; Charles E. Fritz and Harry B. Williams, "The Human Being in Disasters: A Research Perspective," *The Annals*, Vol. 309 (January, 1957), pp. 42-51; Harry E. Moore and H. J. Friedsam, "Reported Emotional Stress Following A Disaster," *Social Forces*, Vol. 38 (December, 1959), pp. 135-139; William H. Form *et al.*, "The Persistence and Emergence of Social and Cultural Systems in Disasters," *American Sociological Review*, Vol. 21 (April, 1956), pp. 180-185.

quently occurs that various private and public agencies become involved in a tangle of jurisdiction, competition, and conflicting aims and goals. This type of problem, though serious, is not as serious as the problem of lack of funds or resources to rebuild properly, which makes up the third level of problems. Some notion of rehabilitation problems is gained from the cogent account by Bates and his associates of difficulties after Hurricane Audrey.

When the Cameron civil defense office was opened in Cameron on 9 July, no supplies were on hand for administration or record keeping. There were 1,800 "workers" in the area and several outside contractors and house movers already operating on the authority of Cameron Parish, Cameron civil defense, state civil defense, or just "operating" with no responsible authority. The presence of many of these people was not known to parish civil defense officials until bills began to be presented for payment after 15 July. State civil defense maintained a separate but duplicate office in the courtroom of the courthouse. It was signing up as many as 400 to 500 people to work each day with no foreman to supervise their activities. Entire bus loads of workers signed the work sheets each morning, and immediately reloaded the buses and returned to Lake Charles or other nearby towns. Yet each worker was given credit for 14 hours work and bills were submitted for rental on the buses they rode even though riders were charged as much as $2.00 each per day to ride some of them. House movers picked up several houses near the high-way right-of-way. When the owners, who had been unable to get house movers or were waiting their turn with a mover, asked that their houses be placed on their lots, they were told by the movers to pay them $500 or they would dump the house in the marsh. Several houses were actually carried past their original places and dumped in the marsh. Later court action was taken in several instances of this nature.[17]

POSITIVE EFFECTS OF DISASTER

Until this point, the negative disorganizational aspects of disaster have been stressed. However, as brought out in Chapter 13, processes of disorganization may also have some positive effects, that is, some developments which make for stronger systems of social organization than originally existed. There are several ways in which disasters may be seen as changing patterns of behavior and values in this way. The more important may be grouped under three headings as follows.

INCREASE IN GROUP SOLIDARITY

Perhaps the most obvious positive social organization effect of disasters is to unify people into more cohesive units. Many investigators have reported that

[17] Bates *et al., op. cit.,* p. 33.

persons who have undergone a disaster together tend to forget old animosities, to overlook class and ethnic differences, and in general to work closely and cooperatively in rescue and rehabilitation activity. Barton indicates that the ". . . outpouring of altruistic feelings and behavior begins with the informal mass assault and carries on for days, weeks, and possibly in some cases months after the impact."[18] Fritz discusses what has already been identified as "therapeutic features" in disaster. He cites (1) the reduction of social distance and social distinctions, (2) the reduction of restraints on emotional expression, (3) a high rate of cooperative work to meet the needs of the community, and (4) the allocation of goods and services on the basis of need.[19] These developments are attributed to the fact that many of the worries of the past and anxieties about the future are unrealistic when judged from the perspective of present realities.

It is true that conflict often develops between individuals and between different agencies and groups as a result of disaster. But it is an erroneous impression that widespread hostility and blame develop as people face the monumental and frustrating task of rebuilding. Fritz and Williams maintain that a few vociferous persons in the community who try to use the disaster to secure power and prestige for themselves account for the stereotype of fault-finding and scapegoating often cited. They also note that in some instances local persons are inspired to negative reactions by what they interpret as encroachment of authority and power by outside groups.[20] When representatives of the latter groups are sensitive to local power structures, such situations are avoided. All in all, the net result of most disasters is a dramatic increase in social solidarity.

EXPANSION OF COMMUNITY FACILITIES

It is not uncommon for communities that have undergone a recent disaster to rebound dramatically. Disasters, in this sense, seem to stimulate greater concentration of energy on individual and group projects. The consequence is to carry the community beyond its predisaster level of productivity and interaction. For example, the development of several new facilities in Cameron Parish, Louisiana, was recorded after Hurricane Audrey—including a parish Civil Defense organization along with the necessary communications facilities expanded to include a radio system throughout the area, a library building, and a larger hospital.[21]

The phenomenon of quick recovery and expansion of community facilities after disasters has been called the "amplified rebound" effect.[22] This term is conceptually useful because the great burst of activity expended on re-

[18] *Op. cit.,* p. 126.
[19] *Op. cit.,* pp. 682-693 (summarized in Barton, *ibid.*).
[20] "The Human Being in Disasters: A Research Perspective," *op. cit.,* pp. 48-50.
[21] Bates, Fogleman, Parenton, Pittman and Tracy, *op. cit.,* Chapter 6.
[22] Fritz, *op. cit.,* p. 692.

habilitation carries the level of productivity and growth potential beyond pre-existing levels, much like a ball that is bounced with force will rebound beyond its original height.

IMPLEMENTATION OF SOCIAL CHANGE

Fritz makes the statement that, "Disaster provides an unstructured social situation that enables persons and groups to perceive the possibility of introducing desired innovations into the social system."[23] In essence, this statement indicates that changes that have to be made because of the necessity to accommodate to disaster situations demonstrate the desirability of substituting new ways for old. Several investigators have catalogued lists of changes made as an adjustment to disaster conditions. Ketch lists eight changes made by farm operators in Mills County, Texas, as a result of drouth. The most drastic change was migration to other areas, but other adjustments included a shift to more suitable crops, a change in other farm management practices, and a change in attitude toward federal assistance.[24] Lammers devotes much space to the adjustment problems of refugees from the Holland flood disaster of 1953. He lists, among other things, the tensions arising from the fact that two or more families had to share the same dwelling. Differences in religion, social class, and politics had to be tolerated, but also served to acquaint individuals with new values and ways.[25]

Another way change is promoted is by providing a more or less clean break with the past for individuals. The disaster is such an important crisis situation that it permits a form of "social absolution" from old patterns of behavior and provides an opportunity for experimentation with new ways and for the development of new systems of social organization. After Hurricane Audrey, for example, a public garbage collection and a public water supply were installed in the town of Cameron and social relationships became more formalized with an accompanying increase in secondary group relationships and a loss of family functions, such as recreation, provision of water, and the like.[26] The more drastic the situation, the more change that can be expected.

SUMMARY

Social disorganization may be initiated by extreme crisis situations as well as by deviant behavior. Disasters of all types bring about such a crisis and are

[23] Ibid., p. 685.
[24] Op. cit., pp. 168-189.
[25] C. J. Lammers, "Survey of Evacuation Problems and Disaster Experiences," Studies in Holland Flood Disaster, 1953 (Amsterdam, Holland, Vol. III, Instituut Voor Sociaal Onderzoek Van Het Nederlandse Volk; Washington, D. C., National Academy of Sciences–National Research Council, 1955).
[26] Bates, Fogleman, Parenton, Pittman, and Tracy, op. cit., Chapter 6.

defined as collective stress situations. Disasters result in more or less permanent changes in the affected social systems. The stresses they produce are manifested in several types of role deviancy, including role conflict, role frustration, role inadequacy, and role saturation.

Disasters may be classified according to their predictability, duration, and geographic spread. They are termed unanticipated if they occur without warning, cataclysmic if they last only a short time, and concentrated if only a small geographic area is covered. At the other extreme, a disaster can be anticipated, extended in duration, and diffuse in its geographic spread.

All disasters have time sequences which are identifiable. The predisaster steady state is simply the normal situation; it is followed by the warning-threat time-phase when first word of the impending danger is received. This phase closes with the commencement of the impact time-phase, when the force of the impact of the disaster agent is felt. After this phase there comes an isolation time-phase, which is characterized by loss of contact with the outside world. As soon as help arrives the rescue-evacuation time-phase begins. This phase is followed by the final or rehabilitation time-phase.

The major problems in planning for disasters occur at three time periods. The initial problems come before the disaster. They are associated with the difficulty of getting people to plan in advance for a disaster and with the provision of satisfactory warnings. The problems during impact come next and are related to the protection of self. After the impact, problems associated with the care and treatment of victims are faced. The last of the major disaster related problems are the ones in connection with rehabilitation and the resumption of normal community services.

Disasters have certain positive effects, which are largely overlooked. They usually serve to (1) increase group solidarity, (2) bring about an expansion of community facilities, and (3) to implement social change.

Supplementary Readings

Barton, Allen H., *Social Organization Under Stress* (Washington, D.C., National Academy of Sciences–National Research Council, Disaster Study No. 17, 1963).

Bates, Frederick L., et al., *The Social and Psychological Consequences of a Natural Disaster* (Washington, D.C., National Academy of Sciences–National Research Council, Disaster Study No. 18, 1963).

Fogleman, Charles W. and Vernon J. Parenton, "Disaster and Aftermath; Selected Aspects of Individual and Group Behavior in Critical Situations," *Social Forces*, Vol. 38 (December, 1959), pp. 130-135.

Fritz, Charles E., "Disaster," in R. K. Merton and R. A. Nisbet, Eds., *Contemporary Social Problems* (New York, Harcourt, Brace & World, 1961), pp. 651-694.

Fritz, Charles E. and Harry B. Williams, "The Human Being in Disasters: A Research Perspective," *The Annals,* Vol. 309 (January, 1957), pp. 42-51.

Loomis, Charles P., *Social Systems: Essays on Their Persistence and Change* (New York, Van Nostrand, 1960), Essay No. 3.

Moore, Harry E., *Tornadoes Over Texas* (Austin, Texas, University of Texas Press, 1958).

Moore, Harry E., and Hiram J. Friedsam, "Reported Emotional Stress Following A Disaster," *Social Forces,* Vol. 38 (December, 1959), pp. 135-139.

16
SOCIAL
CONTROL:
THE
MANAGEMENT
OF
DEVIANCE

Frequent reference has been made to the social control process in preceding chapters. Although this term was briefly defined in Chapter 2 its significance in a conceptual and analytical sense has not been presented. This chapter represents an effort to place the term in the proper perspective.[1]

In the broad sense, the importance of studies of social control is found in the concern of every society with problems of order and authority. This concern is evidenced by the fact that few, if any, themes have received more formal attention in the history of mankind. From the ancient Greeks until the present time, social philosophers and social theorists have grappled with problems of conflict, which threatened to disturb order and peace. Essays on the source, organization, distribution, and proper use of social power, essentially

[1] The relative paucity of research attention which has been directed to the broad implications and meanings of social control accounts for the fact that this process is not treated extensively in the literature. The term was first used by E. A. Ross. See *Social Control* (New York, Macmillan, 1901). Since Ross' work, only a few scholars have seriously worked on a definition and theory of social control. The best known works are probably those of LaPiere, Landis, and Roucek. See Richard T. LaPiere, *A Theory of Social Control* (New York, McGraw-Hill, 1954); Paul H. Landis, *Social Control* (New York, Lippincott, 1959); and Joseph S. Roucek, Ed., *Social Control* (Princeton, New Jersey, Van Nostrand, 1956).

the question of social control, are among both ancient and modern classics in philosophy and social science. The discussion which follows is an attempt to present the most general and broadest understanding of social control.

THE NATURE AND IMPORTANCE
OF SOCIAL CONTROL

The point has been made that there is patterned behavior in society which provides the *raison d'etre* for sociology. This patterning must be maintained, otherwise there would be no predictable regularity of social action and as a consequence no social organization. There are at least two major kinds of processes by which individuals are led to behave in ways that are predictable— processes that result in individuals indulging in certain types of actions and refraining from other types of behavior. The first type of process, socialization, has already been discussed at length. Socialization processes promote conformity to expected patterns of behavior by providing a preconditioning for the interpretation of situations in socially acceptable ways. However, for the reasons outlined in the discussions in Chapter 13 on deviance, in real-life situations socialization falls short of preventing all deviation from societal norms. Consequently, the second type of process, social control, must be articulated in order to maintain order in society.[2]

Social control processes are manifested in terms of mechanisms that members of a social system utilize to prevent deviancy from proceeding beyond tolerable limits. In Martindale's words, ". . . the study of social control is the sociology of how social order is maintained."[3] Bredemier and Stephenson present a definition of social control mechanisms which helps clarify the nature of this concept. They include among the latter, "All the social arrangements that either prevent such strains (as may develop because of the individual's place in the social structure) or prevent the strains from leading to deviance. . . ."[4] Martindale goes on to point out that influence and power are necessary to maintain order and that, in this sense, social control may be thought of as "the maintenance of influence and power."[5] However, he is careful to caution that the control of deviance is only one of the functions of power.

At this point, it must be made clear that social control processes are articu-

[2] It may be noted that some authors tend to identify or equate socialization and social control. See Landis, *op. cit.*, and Roucek, *op. cit.* The present writer follows the general approach of Parsons and his students and Martindale in differentiating the two processes. See Talcott Parsons, *The Social System* (New York, Free Press, 1951); and Don Martindale, *American Society* (Princeton, New Jersey, Van Nostrand, 1960).

[3] *Op. cit.*, p. 364.

[4] Harry C. Bredemeier and Richard M. Stephenson, *The Analysis of Social Systems* (New York, Holt, Rinehart and Winston, 1962), p. 146.

[5] *Op. cit.*, p. 364.

lated at what may be roughly classed as four different levels of behavior. First, these processes are in evidence as preventive mechanisms, that is, mechanisms which are designed to prevent situations from developing which might lead to deviance. Second, there is a class of mechanisms designed to manage tensions after an act of nonconformity or deviance has occurred. A third type of social control mechanism is employed to check and change the course of behavior which is deviant in nature and cannot be managed. This level of social control is more direct and thus more likely to be recognized and understood. Finally, there are mechanisms which are designed to control group behavior by molding public opinion in a given way. In such instances, the idea is to persuade people to drop old patterns of behavior which are not in keeping with the patterns desired. Deviancy, in such examples, is promoted rather than blocked; but it is nevertheless "managed."

In summary, social control may be thought of in terms of the processes whereby the individual is made to respond to the behavioral expectations of the members of his social systems. These processes account in large part, as indicated, for the order in society or social organization. The means by which social control is exercised are inherent in the social power vested in the various status positions within given systems and in the institutionalized societal mechanisms which forestall unacceptable deviant behavior or encourage acceptable deviant behavior. In each instance it will be seen that the goal of "pattern maintenance" is clearly in mind. The types of mechanisms employed vary depending on the nature of the social system and the degree of individual motivation to deviance. In the discussions that follow, the reader is cautioned that no attempt is made to differentiate between the legitimate and illegitimate use of social control devices. Rather, the focus of discussion is on the nature and application of such devices.

SOCIAL CONTROL MECHANISMS DESIGNED TO PREVENT STRESS– STRAIN FROM DEVELOPING

The best social control technique is one that anticipates situations conducive to stress–strain and so structures the situation that deviance is forestalled or blocked. As was brought out in earlier discussions, social systems are likely to be placed under stress because of role conflicts related to improper socialization. This is such an important structural aspect of all systems that certain mechanisms are built into each system, that is, institutionalized, to prevent or minimize role conflict. At least three major types of mechanisms are commonly used for this purpose, as follows.[6]

[6] The excellent treatment of the subject done by Bredemeier and Stephenson is followed rather closely (*Op. cit.*, Chapter 6).

SEGREGATION OF STATUS POSITIONS

The first mechanism designed to forestall stress–strain to be considered is the structured segregation of an individual's status position so as to minimize role conflict. Every person usually holds two or more status positions demanding roles that are at least potentially in conflict, and this becomes an important technique of control. For example, a man's role as husband demands certain behavior when he is at home which would not be appropriate when his wife visits him at his office or job site. Segregation of roles is accomplished by allocating certain statuses to certain times, to certain places and to certain persons. Each of these control devices is mutually related, but has an aspect of uniqueness, as will be illustrated.

Place allocations for status positions serve to prevent role conflict by effectively segregating the varying roles an actor has to play to a given location. To elaborate, a student may belong to a social fraternity and play the role of *bon vivant* at the fraternity house, which is expected by his "brothers." However, at the times he is home, or when he goes to church, he plays roles that are rather far removed from his fraternity role. Should he start "living it up" at home or in church, role conflict would likely develop. The ensuing stress–strain placed on his family or religious social system might well lead to the application of sanctions, such as his parents removing him from the "bad" influence of the fraternity. However, so long as he plays one role at home and another at the fraternity, stresses on both systems are forestalled. In this regard, the role of sober, studious, devout, and obedient son, if acted out in the fraternity may well place stresses on this system. It can readily be seen that the mechanism of place allocation serves a real, if subtle, function of social control by segregating potentially conflicting activities; in addition it provides an atmosphere or mood for certain types of behavior.

The second segregation mechanism, *time allocation,* also serves to shield individuals from role conflict. In this instance, the idea is to set apart certain portions of the day, or week, or year for playing one role and other times for playing roles that may conflict with the first role to some degree. This type of mechanism is illustrated in its extreme by the man who plays the role of a tough, Marine sergeant with a "colorful" vocabulary designed to impress and coerce new recruits during the day, but who plays the role of a gentle, doting father to his small children in the evening. Should his children, by chance, see him at the wrong time—that is, during the day—a certain degree of stress–strain on both his family and Marine social systems might arise. It can be seen that there is an element of "place" in this illustration, but the time element assumes greater significance. In actual life situations, a person may regularly shift to several roles "by the clock" during the course of an ordinary day or week. In each role, a stress situation can be created by the appearance of actors who normally play reciprocal roles to the first actor at other times and in connection with other statuses that he holds.

The third type of segregation mechanism, *status allocation by person,* serves to keep certain actors from interacting with two given individuals at the same time, especially actors who occupy somewhat divergent status positions with respect to him. A young man holds an entirely different status for his girl friend than he does for her father. He thus seeks to remove himself from the presence of her father so that he may relax and enjoy his role with the daughter in something less than the dignified, courteous, and aloof role which he must play for her father. The practice of separating actors also serves to avoid tensions that would result were the actors to interact unfavorably with one another with regard to the primary actor. In the above example, the boy may not want to see the father and daughter at the same time because of the possibility of unpleasant exchanges regarding him between these two actors. In places where polygamous marriages are allowed, a man's wives may live in different houses to avoid conflict. In more practical situations, persons who tend to clash in an office may be physically separated by the supervisor to prevent face-to-face association and its consequent stresses.

In conclusion, any device that effectively segregates individuals in such a way as to minimize the opportunity for conflict serves a purpose of maintaining order. When people are segregated from individuals and groups with which they are incompatible, there is less chance for deviant behavior.

INSULATION OF STATUS POSITION

It is often impossible to segregate potentially conflicting status positions in a given social system. When this is the case, certain other mechanisms may be utilized to prevent or minimize stress–strain. This type of mechanism is designed to provide some way of shielding or insulating the actor from the necessity of playing one type of role in its accustomed manner. For example, a man's interaction with women must be so controlled that he will not interact with close female relatives (sisters, nieces) in the same way as he might with nonrelatives. *Insulation techniques,* in this instance, include sexual taboos and other types of "avoidance relationships." The idea, of course, is to prevent conflict that might arise should a man be permitted to consider close female relatives as marriage or sex partners. The difference between segregation and insulation is illustrated by this example, since it is impossible to segregate a man's male status from his kinship status at all times. It is, however, possible to insulate the former status from the latter status by cultural norms that prevent him from acting out the role of male in the same way with a relative as a nonrelative.

Bredemeier and Stephenson point out that in the military establishment, the differential rights and obligations of officers and enlisted men have traditionally been maintained by elaborate mechanisms of insulation.[7] Some of these mechanisms are identified as the salute, use of the third person in communications, and formal forms of address. They also call attention to the study of the social structure of the restaurant done by William F. Whyte. In this study, Whyte found that tension frequently was reduced or eliminated in restaurants by such simple insulating devices as placing a warming counter between waitresses and countermen, and having orders written out and placed on a spindle or rack. In this manner, the men did not have to take orders directly from women, whom they normally would feel should take orders from them.[8]

ESTABLISHING PRIORITIES FOR STATUS POSITIONS

A third mechanism used to prevent order from breaking down in society is the establishment of priorities for status positions. Through cultural conditioning, individual actors are usually given a clear indication as to which of two conflicting roles has greater societal approval. One illustration serves to demonstrate how this mechanism functions. In the service academies of the United States, where future officers for the armed services are trained, stringent honor codes are a part of the structure of the academy. On occasion, a cadet (actor) violates the honor code to the knowledge of his fellow cadets and good friends. The cadet honor code demands that the deviant be reported and clearly places a priority on the so-called citizen role over the friend role. The priority is enforced by definitions of the situation which make the friend who does not report cheating as guilty as the cheater.

In most instances, role priorities are not as clearly defined as in the above example. However, as a general rule social systems are so structured as to include priorities. When an individual is faced with having to reconcile roles in two social systems, priorities are usually not as clearly established. A student may, for example, be placed under considerable stress–strain in trying to decide whether his student role should take priority over his football role. However, to the extent that a role conflict situation is structured (that some notion of priority is prevalent), social control is evident.

SOCIAL CONTROL MECHANISMS FOR TENSION MANAGEMENT

The mechanisms designed to forestall or prevent stress–strain in social systems may be looked upon as the first level or type of social control. It happens quite frequently that the mechanisms employed at this level of defense against dis-

[7] *Ibid.*, pp. 151-152.
[8] William Foote Whyte, "The Social Structure of the Restaurant," *American Journal of Sociology*, Vol. 54 (January, 1949), pp. 302-310.

order fail to prevent conflict situations from developing. When such is the case, there is a probability of deviant behavior unless the ensuing stresses and strains can be controlled. There are, in fact, at least two types of mechanisms which are employed to "manage" tensions so that they do not progress to the point of motivating deviant behavior. These mechanisms, to be described briefly below, represent the second level of social control.

The situses (status-position sets) of most individuals are so varied as to allow the individual to release the tensions that may develop from frustrations encountered in one role by overperformance in a second role. Such behavior is compensating in nature, in that it provides an opportunity for achieving recognition and other satisfactions in one status, which compensates for the lack of achievement in a second status. Many examples of compensatory behavior are commonly cited, such as the boy who cannot make the first team, but achieves recognition as the top team member scholastically. A more common illustration would be the man holding an anonymous position buried deep is a large bureaucratic structure. While he receives no personal recognition in his job situation, he compensates for this frustration by becoming an esteemed, hard-working volunteer Boy Scout executive.

The second way in which tensions are reduced is by providing individuals with the opportunity to change status or retain the same status but change social systems. In one sense, such behavior may be identified as compensatory, but it is something more since it provides for the desertion of a frustrating role. The provision for divorce serves as a way out for unhappy marriages. The prerogative to change jobs or schools serves the same function for unhappy occupational situations.

It is interesting to note that certain status-positions are so fraught with stress–strain that more acceptable alternative statuses are created to reduce tensions. In the United States, considerable resources have been and are being expended on programs for rehabilitating the handicapped, making the adjustment of retirees and the aged in general easier, and for retraining persons whose occupation and skills have been outmoded by automation. It is possible, of course, for a person to assume the initiative for preparing himself for a status alternative. This is done by many individuals, such as retired armed services personnel who go back to school to prepare themselves for positions other than retiree. The point is that status escape mechanisms are provided for in the social structure. These mechanisms serve the purpose of social control by performing a tension-management function.

SOCIAL CONTROL THROUGH THE APPLICATION OF SANCTIONS

When it happens that stress and strain cannot be prevented or managed, a third and more drastic level of social control mechanism must be used in order to suppress tension and to maintain order. This level of control is manifested through the application of positive and negative sanctions. Normally these sanctions are divided into two additional classes, depending on their formality. Those that are applied in keeping with institutionalized structures, that are subject to clear—usually statutory—interpretation are identified as **formal** sanctions. Methods or techniques of social control which are applied at the whim or subjective interpretation of the individual or groups, such as gossip, ostracism, or ridicule are termed **informal** in nature. LaPiere has divided the techniques of social control which he deems basic into three broad groups—physical sanctions, economic sanctions, and psychological sanctions. Each of these broad groups of sanctions is described briefly.[9] In reviewing the techniques that are presented the student should remember that the purpose in mind is to illustrate the basic principles by which members of a social system endeavor to bring deviant members of their system back into conformance with the norms of the group. The descriptions presented are merely illustrative of these broad recurrent patterns of human behavior.

PHYSICAL SANCTIONS AS TECHNIQUES OF SOCIAL CONTROL

The most obvious technique for controlling deviants is the use of force. Since techniques of this nature inevitably involve punishment, they always represent negative sanctions, in contrast to both economic or psychological sanctions, which may include positive (rewards) as well as negative (punishment) measures. In practice there are an infinite number of types and kinds of physical sanctions which may be applied. The range of such sanctions may run from a faint and subtle threat of physical punishment to violent assault and extermination. The more important forms of physical sanctions, according to LaPiere, are expulsion, extermination, and physical punishment. Each may be illustrated as follows.

Some social systems, for reasons relating to their normative structures, will not subject a deviant member to direct physical punishment. For example women's clubs, professional societies (like the American Sociological Association or the American Medical Association), most religious bodies, and many other groups that could be easily brought to mind, would seldom, if ever, report an example of violence in the control of a member. What is generally resorted to in this type of group is *expulsion,* or the rejection of the nonconforming member from group membership. It is, of course, possible that the recalcitrant member may refuse to accept his expulsion and insist on being physically present at group meetings. When this happens, he or she is subjected to total exclusion as a participating member and, if the dissenter becomes belligerent, outside societal control forces may be called upon to en-

[9] *Op. cit.,* pp. 221-245.

force the expulsion. In actual situations, it is generally sufficient to give notice of expulsion. In this regard, most formal social systems have specific methods for expulsion, such as by vote of the membership, failure to send renewal notices for dues, being flunked out, or being given a dishonorable discharge.

Physical punishment is a second type of physical sanction which is often used. In this regard, it must be clearly understood that the person or group administering the punishment is legitimately permitted to do so. In other words, a bully forcing a weaker person to do something is not an example of social control. The person must hold a position of authority, which includes the administration of punishment as part of his role. Thus a father spanking his small son for misbehavior is legitimately using physical punishment as a social control technique, if this act is in keeping with societal norms. Other examples of physical punishment might include enforced labor (on roads, rockpiles, or farms and shops), as done in some prisons, the assignment to do K.P. (kitchen police) duty in the armed services as punishment, or of other distasteful duties, and, in some societies, the application of the whip or lash to an offender by a designated and official person. Physical punishment is closely related to expulsion in that it serves as a latent device of social control. In this respect, the threat of expulsion or punishment hangs over members and may serve to discourage deviance.

A third type of physical sanction, *extermination*, is not as widespread as expulsion or physical punishment, but is found in most societies. It is, of course, the most extreme sanction which can be applied. The death sentence (capital punishment) is still rather widespread, as is the extermination of traitors, informants, and others who might jeopardize the goals of certain military groups, certain political groups, and certain criminal groups. Generally speaking, extermination is only sanctioned by the greater society when it is in keeping with formal (governmental) statutes. Capital punishment, for example, is under the statutory provisions of state or federal governments; and those helping the enemy's cause are shot or otherwise exterminated only after court martial proceedings, which determine guilt and punishment. The accounts of instances when local individuals or groups take the law into their own hands and mete out extralegal "justice" by summarily killing someone, are, however, also examples of the use of extermination as a social control device. The fact that the greater society may discourage such practices by applying certain sanctions to those who perpetuate these acts does not obviate this point. It is only when such acts are without the approval of the subsystem or group that the act would be judged as an interpersonal matter, rather than a social control technique. To illustrate, a man who kills another to commit a robbery does not have group approval, but a man who kills a robber (or cattle rustler) will generally have group approval.

In concluding this short discussion of physical sanctions as techniques of social control, at least two observations are in order. First, such sanctions depend upon the individual's personal reaction to pain and injury, and can be effective only to the extent that he fears being physically hurt. This observation leads logically to the second one, that physical punishment or the threat of physical punishment only serves to restrain behavior. It does not make the individual accept or inwardly approve of the norm for the violation of which he is being punished. It is for the above reasons that LaPiere states that the use of physical sanctions is the least important and least effective (for most purposes) of the social control techniques available to leaders (those in power positions).[10]

ECONOMIC SANCTIONS AS TECHNIQUES OF SOCIAL CONTROL

It is a maxim of social life that every individual is dependent for his well being to a greater or lesser extent on the good will of others. This good will has many facets, but one important manifestation is the ease and efficiency with which he obtains the goods and services normally available to a person of his position in his given cultural milieu. A high-status person with great wealth normally has little difficulty in getting food or clothes, while a poor, lower-class individual may have to "scrounge" for a living. Yet, both the poor man and the rich man can encounter situations that will make their efforts to obtain necessities of life easier or harder. These situations can be associated with and structured by the application of economic sanctions by members of their various social systems. Such techniques are frequently used to control the deviant or nonconforming behavior of individuals and groups. There are several broad classes of negative economic sanctions, such as intimidation, reputational attacks, conspiratorial arrangements, and economic boycotts. Each of these is considered briefly below, as is the general class of positive economic sanctions.

Economic intimidation as a social control technique is based on the fact that most individuals are vulnerable to economic reprisals. Thus a threat that may lead to a loss of or reduction in income may well serve to make one change his behavior, which is considered deviant by members of his groups. Economic intimidation may take many forms, as anyone can imagine. An employer may threaten to discharge an employee, a parent may threaten to reduce a child's allowance, one worker may threaten to report another to the union, a buyer may threaten to take his business elsewhere, a government agency may threaten to withhold funds from a group, and so on. In instances of the above type, the idea is always to bring about conformity by presenting a nonconforming individual with an alternative choice based on his need for economic rewards that are controlled by the person or persons making the threat. If the threat does not succeed in controlling the individual, then the sanction is enforced.

[10] *Ibid.*, p. 221.

One way in which an individual's ability to earn economic rewards may be lessened is through *reputational attacks*. Such attacks take a variety of forms, depending on the status position of the individual under attack, and the cultural setting. For example, a professional person, like a school teacher, physician, or lawyer, may be subtly undermined by well-planted rumors regarding personal morality, professional competency, or mental stability. Attacks of this type are usually traceable to some violation of codes or norms that are considered important to other members of the group. The student should be careful to distinguish between vicious attempts of rivals or antagonists to destroy an individual from the more diffuse impersonal attempts of members of his social systems to control his behavior. To illustrate, one teacher may dislike another for personal reasons of envy or rivalry and attack his reputation for this reason. This would not be an example of a social control mechanism. However, should the same teacher fall into general disfavor with the members of his faculty for obviously courting school administrators to enhance his chances of promotion, he very likely would evoke a general, if subtle, attack on his ethical reputation. The physician who advertises too obviously might likewise draw a rather widespread attack on his reputation by his fellow physicians, and perhaps others aware of the code of ethics which had been violated. LaPiere illustrates this type of control with this example.

> In the academic profession, a man's reputation as a teacher and scholar is largely a function of his status as a person, rather than the other way around. . . . As a consequence, a man who seriously violates academic norms can be punished economically by his associates in a multitude of ways. Through devaluation of his professional abilities they may delay his promotions, through casual but slighting comments they may prevent him from obtaining offers of positions elsewhere, through their advisory role with students they may discourage enrollment in his courses, etc.[11]

Conspiratorial arrangements or agreements are a third way in which individuals may be penalized economically for violation of group norms. This technique may involve reputational attacks, but goes somewhat further. It is more characteristic of close-knit work groups than of loosely organized, diffuse occupational groups. This technique typically involves the withdrawal of the support and protection usually given a worker by his fellows. The "frame-up" may be formally worked out, or may involve no more than a tacit understanding of group members. The tactics employed include the failure to protect the offender from supervisory officials, passing on an excessive share of unpleasant duties, refusing assistance with problem situations, or conveniently misplacing needed records. This kind of a conspiracy, though manifesting itself in petty ways, can eventually result in a repentance on the part of the deviant, or the projection of an image of substandard performer or troublemaker on his part —with eventual discharge. Physicians may treat a member of their profession

[11] *Ibid.*, pp. 233-234.

in like manner by making it difficult for him to obtain important diagnostic services, hospital rooms, or specialist services. In addition, in a conspiratorial arrangement very few patients are likely to be referred to him for treatment.

The fourth type of negative economic sanction, *economic boycott,* is more direct than the first three described, at least in one sense. It simply involves the refusal to patronize an individual or group or the product which he or they produce. This type of sanction may be applied at a local level by the refusal to buy meat from a butcher, who has not cooperated in a community improvement drive, or by the refusal to buy a certain brand of a given product because the company manufacturing the product has sponsored a television show that is considered obnoxious by a certain group. Labor unions, of course, exercise various types of boycotts against various industries, whose labor practices they do not approve. Industries, in turn, attempt to boycott certain labor unions whom they feel make unfair or impractical demands. Many other examples of this type of social control technique could be given, but the above serve to illustrate this type of control mechanism.

Economic rewards are used as positive sanctions to discourage deviance and to demonstrate awareness of exceptional role performance in many cases. The loyal, cooperative, trustworthy worker is lauded and praised to proper officials by his fellow workers so that his promotions come regularly; the civic-minded, charitable merchant gets business (leaving other factors equal); and the professional person who "plays by the rules" enhances his chance for clients. In other words, economic rewards are meted out to those who act out their roles in approved fashion, and in this sense serve as a highly effective social control mechanism.

PSYCHOLOGICAL SANCTIONS AS SOCIAL CONTROL TECHNIQUES

The most important of all techniques used to challenge and check the deviant or nonconforming behavior of individuals are the so-called socio-psychological ones. The importance of this type of technique comes from its universality and the fact that it is the first technique to be brought into play. It is only when psychological sanctions have failed that physical and economic sanctions are tried, as a general rule. Socio-psychological sanctions are imposed entirely through the use of symbols relating to acceptance or rejection of the individual by the members of his group. The symbols used are normally well understood in the particular culture and vary according to the intensity of disfavor or favor meant to be expressed. The effectiveness of this type of control technique is closely related to the satisfaction that one derives from being accepted by the members of his groups. Personal insecurity is traceable to the extent to which the individual feels rejected, that is, to the extent socio-psychological techniques are used to make him feel apart from the group.

There are a great number of ways which can be used to convey approval and disapproval of an individual's conduct. An attempt is made here to classify negative socio-psychological sanctions roughly according to degree of intensity. Three headings are suggested—reproof, ridicule, and ostracism. Positive socio-psychological sanctions are discussed as a whole.

The mildest of socio-psychological sanctions is *reproof*, because it indicates a momentary or short-time span deviancy from the norms, perhaps with a situational significance. Reproof is seen in the good-natured but pointed kidding that the church member receives for going fishing or golfing on Sunday, instead of attending church. It is seen in the sly remarks of the professor addressed to the student who has cut class to attend a ball game and in the teasing that the secretary gets, who drank a little too much at the last office party. The individual subjected to reproof normally does not lose his status, unless his deviant behavior persists and assumes such proportions as to be interpreted as a chronic rather than a temporary matter. In fact, the whole intent of reproof is to gently but firmly call attention to the violation of norms and to suggest that anyone is allowed one or two slips, but not more. It is thus that a church member who habitually plays golf on Sunday instead of attending church may be dropped from the active membership role; the student who continually cuts class for "trivial" reasons may be flunked or dropped from a class; or the secretary who gets drunk at every party may be discharged. In other words, when reproof does not work, other social control measures are brought into play.

The second level of socio-psychological technique, *ridicule*, is somewhat more severe in nature. It involves the use of shaming devices, such as disdain, derision, jeers, and reproach. In instances where ridicule is used, the interpretation is that the violation of group norms is serious and more than just a temporary lapse in behavior. The teen-ager who professes a liking for "longhair" music may well be jeered as a "square" by his peers who consider "rock and roll" or "mod" music the thing worth listening to. The first brave lad to wear bermuda shorts on many campuses was the subject of catcalls, jibes, and other forms of ridicule. Many times pragmatically oriented professors, who insist that knowledge (and science) finds its proof in practical applications are derided by their "pure-science" colleagues who insist that knowledge should be sought for knowledge's sake. The latter are, in turn, taunted as "ivory tower eggheads" who "have trouble finding their way home" by the pragmatists. And so it goes. Each social group attempts to ridicule the individuals deemed nonconformist into coming back into the fold. A wife, for example, may ask her lazy or alcoholic husband, "What will the neighbors say?"; the parents of the flunking student may plead, "Why can't you make as good grades as Tommy?"; and the coach will taunt his losing team with a statement like, "All right girls, let's get ready for the next waltz." In each of the above instances, verbal symbols are used; but nonverbal symbols such as facial expressions may serve the purpose of conveying ridicule as well. The cool, smileless stares that greet the perennial teller of off-color, "inappropriate" jokes is an illustration.

The third socio-psychological mechanism for social control is the most severe. It involves complete *ostracism* of the deviant by members of his group. A good example is the practice of "shunning" used among the Amish and other religious groups. This dreaded punishment submits the violator of religious norms to a life of complete silence, since no member of his family or church may speak to him, although he is shown every other kindness. This treatment is so severe that most deviants make proper amends for their misdeeds in a relatively short while.[12] A less formal example of ostracism would be the failure to invite a "rowdy" couple to the next meeting of a community or other type of club. Ostracism is also manifested in ignoring phone calls, failure to answer letters, and in aloofness on social occasions.

Psychological sanctions may be *positive* as well as negative. In fact, most people are continually striving for this type of sanction. The supreme positive sanction is, of course, complete and warm acceptance into the group. However, other such rewards include praise, invitations to in-group affairs, being trusted with "high-level" secrets, being addressed with warmth and respect, or being given a pat on the back. These types of sanctions are so well known to most persons as not to need further elaboration.

PROPAGANDA AND SOCIAL CONTROL

The fourth and final class of social control techniques to be described goes under the general heading of propaganda. This term is likely to be held in disrepute by the person who is not conversant with its technical meaning. This is true because propaganda techniques have been used by many persons, groups, and governments for obviously ulterior motives. However, in its technical usage, **propaganda** must be thought of as no more or less than a deliberate attempt to control the behavior and interrelationships of members of a social group through the use of devices that are effective in changing feelings and attitudes—that is, values.[13] The distinction propaganda has as a social control technique is found in its obvious attempt to promote rather than to prevent deviance. Propaganda is like other techniques in that it attempts to control or

[12] Walter M. Kollmorgen, *Culture of a Contemporary Rural Community: The Old Order Amish of Lancaster County, Penn.* (Washington, D. C., Bureau of Agricultural Economics, United States Department of Agriculture, Rural Life Studies No. 4, 1942), p. 60.

[13] Harold Lasswell's definition of propaganda emphasized this interpretation some years ago. He stated, "Propaganda may be defined as a technique of social control, or as a species of social movement. As technique, it is the manipulation of collective attitudes by the use of significant symbols (words, pictures, tunes) rather than violence, bribery, boycott." Harold D. Lasswell, "The Person: Subject and Object of Propaganda," *Annals*, Vol. 179 (May, 1935), pp. 187-193.

order human behavior according to predefined standards, although these standards may not be in keeping with old norms. The nature of propaganda is elaborated briefly in the discussions that follow.

WHAT IS AND IS NOT PROPAGANDA

There is an understandable tendency to confuse education with propaganda, because both include attempts to change or manipulate public opinion. However, Leonard W. Doob and others who have carefully studied this phenomenon, make a clear distinction between the two concepts. Doob defines propaganda as, ". . . the attempt to affect the personalities and to control the behavior of individuals toward ends considered unscientific or of doubtful value in a society at a particular time." He then goes on to say that propaganda can be differentiated from education in that the latter includes the kind of information which can be verified, or which is considered to be an acceptable part of the culture, that is, "right," "good," or "necessary."[14] By contrast, "The imparting of knowledge which has not reached the scientific stage is propaganda, as is the teaching of a skill which is not adapted to the situation at hand."[15] This interpretation bases the distinction between education and propaganda on facts (science) and values (cultural interpretations) and thus avoids the meaningless neutrality or strong value interpretations which plague many definitions of propaganda.

The nature of propaganda may be further clarified and its social control purposes brought into sharper focus by outlining certain of its features. First, propaganda represents a conscious attempt to "manage" the minds of others, as William Albig puts it.[16] The goal of the propagandist, whether it be clearly identified or not, is to change the opinion of the individual or group. Such a goal cannot be pursued without a certain degree of conscious effort, especially when it involves the marshaling of materials to support the idea being advanced. In this regard, Doob points out that some individuals may unintentionally serve as propagandists in that they have no formalized purpose for attempting to change someone's opinion.[17] However, this does not preclude their being aware of the fact that they are doing just that.

A second characteristic of propaganda is its one-sidedness. Effective control of public or private opinion can only be accomplished if one side of an issue or product is presented. Thus the propagandist selects the information favorable to his point of view and ignores the information that may be un-

[14] Leonard W. Doob, *Public Opinion and Propaganda* (New York, Holt, Rinehart and Winston, 1956), p. 240.

[15] *Ibid.*

[16] William Albig, *Modern Public Opinion* (New York, McGraw-Hill, 1956), p. 292.

[17] *Op. cit.*, pp. 244-250.

favorable. This approach serves to further differentiate propaganda from formal education, which normally presents both sides to a controversy. In contrast to science, propaganda is not objective and propagandists may deliberately distort information by quoting out of context, or by selection of data. Much of the advertising that touts the merits of one product, fails to mention its demerits, or its poor competitive position.

A third characteristic of propaganda is that it tends to appeal to emotion rather than reason. The propagandist tries to relate his point to some strong value orientation of the propagandee. Wartime propaganda is filled with atrocity stories of the treatment of captives by the enemy for the purpose of building up a war effort. The well-known sex theme of advertising is designed as a subtle play on the emotions, as is the innuendo of politicians on "motherhood" and "corruption."

In essence, propaganda can be thought of as deliberately planned efforts to influence groups or individuals, whether or not a specific goal is in mind. Propaganda techniques vary, but are generally characterized by emotional appeals based on partial evidence.

CLASSES OF PROPAGANDA

There are many ways by which propaganda could be classed or typed. However, for the purposes of a brief presentation in the general context of social control, a fourfold classification based upon the purposes of the propaganda seems most useful. The first general class of propaganda may be identified as *commercial propaganda* or advertising. The purposes of this type of propaganda are obvious and have a definite economic tie. However, the approach to social control varies from "screaming" billboards to subtle suggestions related to status symbols. All mass media are utilized in efforts to gain converts to one or another product, none of which ever have a "fault."

The second general class of propaganda is termed *public relations* propaganda, for lack of a better term. In a sense all propaganda has a public relations motive, but what is intended here is a deliberate attempt to gain public favor for an individual, group, or agency, rather than a product. For example, efforts to promote the candidacy of a given man for high political office involves this type of propaganda. The same general type of propaganda might be used by a labor union to achieve public support. An industrial plant might use such techniques to attract workers, and a university may employ propaganda to enhance its appeal to a certain "well-heeled" class of students. In each instance, given individuals forming a general public are subject to the control techniques.

A third general class of propaganda is broadly termed the *propaganda of prejudice*. This type is also widespread and commonly encountered. Its purpose is to promote a feeling of innate superiority or inferiority, as the case may be.

Race and ethnic as well as religious themes are popular in this type of propaganda. Much of it proceeds informally, in contrast to commercial and public relations propaganda. Since prejudice is likely to lead to discriminatory behavior, this class of propaganda is usually considered more undesirable than other types.

The final general class of propaganda to be identified is *war propaganda*. This type is listed separately for two reasons—it is limited to particular periods of conflict and it is considered by most modern societies as an important part of their military effort. The term "psychological warfare" is used to designate propaganda techniques during wartime. The usual procedures are to spread rumors, myths, and any type of information that will affect the war effort of the enemy adversely and one's own effort favorably. In one sense, nationalistic rivalries and ideological battles are waged in terms of war propaganda.

THE EFFECTIVENESS OF PROPAGANDA AS A SOCIAL CONTROL TECHNIQUE

There is no question that propaganda is effective under certain conditions. The great amount of time, energy, and money spent on advertising, public relations, and other types of propaganda testify to this fact. However, the powers of propaganda are not unlimited—a reassuring thought because otherwise all persons could fall victim to the propagandists with the greatest resources at their command. Horton and Hunt list four basic limitations to propaganda, which relate to the effectiveness of this technique of social control.[18] The first is the amount and type of competing propaganda. When there are many groups competing with radically opposing propaganda, the likelihood of any one "line" becoming all important is much less. Totalitarian states with monopolistic enterprises have, of course, the best situation for using propaganda without competition.

The second limiting factor that affects propaganda is the sophistication of the recipient of the ideas being pushed. The well-educated, well-informed, cosmopolitan individual is less likely to fall prey to a propagandistic attack. On the other hand the poorly educated, relatively uninformed person is likely to swallow a "line" designed to change his opinions. Students, because of their idealism and relative immaturity, are often prey to propaganda skillfully presented by political and other reformers.

The beliefs and values of the individuals to whom the propaganda is directed also present a limitation to its effectiveness. Unless propaganda is so designed as to fit into a "pattern of prejudice" already established, that is, established attitudes and values, it will not be as effective. As Horton and Hunt point out, the Communist propaganda that has been so effective in

[18] Paul B. Horton and Chester L. Hunt, *Sociology* (New York, McGraw-Hill, 1964), pp. 422-423.

certain parts of the world, has not struck a responsive note among middle-class Americans. The latter simply do not "buy" the businessman as a villain, the church as oppressive, or the middle class as proletariat.[19]

Finally, cultural trends limit the effect of propaganda. Anything that goes counter to the general trends of the times just does not catch on as easily. For example, despite much advertising, the compact auto was not successful in the United States when it was first introduced. It is true, of course, that propaganda may speed up or slow down a cultural trend, but it is doubtful if it can halt a development that is national in scope.

SUMMARY

Social control is defined in general terms as the management of deviance. Social control processes are manifested in terms of mechanisms that members of a social system utilize to prevent deviancy from occurring, or to keep deviant behavior within tolerable limits. The mechanisms designed to prevent stress–strain from developing are (1) segregation of status positions, including place allocation, time allocation, and status allocation by person; (2) insulation of status positions; and, (3) establishment of priorities for status positions. Mechanisms for managing tensions created by stresses that have not been forestalled are generally built into social systems. The three most common mechanisms of this type are opportunities for compensatory activity, opportunities for changing statuses, and provision for more acceptable alternative statuses.

When the devices used to prevent or manage tensions do not suffice, social control is accomplished through use of negative sanctions. These may be applied formally or informally and are of three major types. Physical sanctions include expulsion, punishment, or extermination. Economic sanctions may involve intimidation, reputational attacks, conspiratorial arrangements, or boycotts. Psychological sanctions range from reproof to ridicule to ostracism.

Propaganda represents a special type of social control technique in that it is designed to promote rather than prevent deviance. It is differentiated from education in that it includes information that is one-sided. The important classes of propaganda are commercial propaganda, public relations propaganda, propaganda of prejudice, and war propaganda.

Supplementary Readings

Bredemeier, Harry C., and Richard M. Stephenson, *The Analysis of Social Systems* (New York, Holt, Rinehart & Winston, 1962), Chapter 6.
Breed, Warren, "Social Control in the Newsroom: A Functional Analysis," *Social*

[19] *Ibid.*, p. 423.

Forces, Vol. 33 (May, 1955), pp. 326-335; and also in O'BRIEN ET AL. and BM.

Doob, Leonard W., *Public Opinion and Propaganda* (New York, Holt, Rinehart and Winston, 1956).

LaPiere, Richard T., *A Theory of Social Control* (New York, McGraw-Hill, 1954), especially Chapter 9.

Lee, Alfred McClung, "The Analysis of Propaganda: A Clinical Summary," *American Journal of Sociology,* Vol. 51 (September, 1945-46), pp. 126-135; and also in LEE.

Lee, Frank F., "Social Controls in the Race Relations Pattern of a Small New England Town," *Social Forces,* Vol. 33 (October, 1954), pp. 36-40; and also in SCHULER ET AL.

Martindale, Don, *American Society* (Princeton, New Jersey, Van Nostrand, 1960), Chapter 15.

Sykes, Gresham M., "Men, Merchants, and Toughs: A Study of Reactions to Imprisonment," *Social Problems,* Vol. 4 (October, 1956), pp. 130-138; and also in YOUNG & MACK.

MAJOR
INSTITUTION-
ALIZED
SOCIAL
STRUCTURES

The three chapters in Part V are devoted to what have been termed the major institutionalized social structures. These structures are dedicated to goals that are in keeping with the functions served by important social institutions. The latter are conceived as organized ways, clusters of norms, roles, and so on, for fulfilling basic societal needs (functions). Social institutions are social structures and as such are differentiated from the process of institutionalization described in Chapter 2.

A clarification is necessary in connection with the theoretical approach taken. Institutions are construed to represent a higher order of abstraction than groups and organizations. Said another way, when *the family* is thought of as a social institution, what is in mind is a set of behavior patterns related to certain basic functions. This concept is quite distinct from a family considered as a social group (or system) which has as its goals or objectives certain institutional functions. Many separate groups (religious, economic, educational) may include roles whose performances are in keeping with the functions served by *one* institution, *the family*.* However, there are certain types of social systems which are generally associated with specific social institutions because they include the largest clusters of behavior patterns devoted primarily to the functions of the institution. Thus, family groups basically, if not exclusively, serve *the family* as a social institution. It must be remembered, however, that all groups or multigroup systems which are dedicated to institutional objectives come and go, whereas the institution itself persists so long as it represents a societal need.

Two objectives guided the treatment of the five types of institutionalized structures considered. The first purpose was to present a working or operational definition of each major institution and at the same time identify and characterize the major types of institutionalized structures serving a pattern maintenance function for the institution. The second goal was to acquaint the student with the major structural aspects and functions of the social systems within which the institutionalized activity is primarily carried out. Family and kinship systems are considered in Chapter 17, religious and educational systems are described in Chapter 18, and economic and government systems are treated in Chapter 19.

* Frederick L. Bates, "Institutions, Organizations, and Communities: A General Theory of Complex Structures," *The Pacific Sociological Review*, Vol. 3 (Fall, 1960).

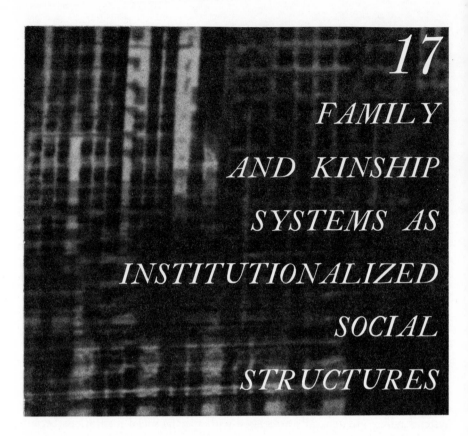

17

FAMILY

AND KINSHIP

SYSTEMS AS

INSTITUTIONALIZED

SOCIAL

STRUCTURES

It has been emphasized that every society includes major structural systems that serve to integrate social interaction. Without such social structures, it is doubtful that a high level of order could be maintained among humans. Family (and kinship) systems are among the oldest and most fundamental of all such systems. As a social institution, *the family may be defined as a system of culturally defined behavioral patterns that serve a definite pattern main-tenance function by providing institutionalized ways for regulating sexual activity and procreation, placing the new member of society in the social structure and introducing the new member to the behavioral requirements necessary for becoming a functioning member of the society.* Our concern in the remainder of this chapter will be with the institutionalized structures—family and kinship systems—through which the functions of the institution of the family are primarily expressed.

MARRIAGE AND FAMILY DEFINED

Even casual acquaintance with the customs in other parts of the world will convince one that there are a great many differences in marriage patterns and family organization. However, if careful study is done, it will be determined that certain aspects of marriage and family are universal. It is this universality, alluded to in Chapter 7, which makes it possible to propose definitions having general application for these patterns of behavior.

DEFINITION OF MARRIAGE

In all societies, marriage is a social affair. It is thus distinguishable from mere mating, which is a biological-psychological matter. The primary connotation of marriage is that of a relatively stable relationship between a man (or men) and a woman (or women) including social sanction for having children. The essential point, then, is what has been called the *principle of legitimacy*. This principle establishes some kind of a socially approved link between the mother and father and the child. Keeping these considerations in mind, Burgess and Locke have formally defined **marriage** as ". . . a socially sanctioned union of one or more men with one or more women in the relationship of husband and wife."[1]

The definition just given must be considered in the light of several possible erroneous interpretations. First, marriage is not to be considered primarily as a way of regulating sexual relations; rather it is a way of legitimizing reproduction. In this regard, although the right to have children implies the right to sexual relations, the reverse is not true. This is a basic distinction in the definition of marriage. Another important point is that the time of pregnancy is a matter of cultural definition. In some societies, an unmarried girl has to prove her eligibility for marriage by demonstrating her fertility—that is, getting pregnant or giving birth to a child. Her children, though conceived out of wedlock, are considered legitimate.

Marital ties do not dictate a single or uniform standard of sexual behavior. For example, many societies permit what is termed by anthropologists as "privileged relationships." Murdock points out that at least 34 societies permit a man to have sexual relations with his brother's wife; 28 societies, with his wife's sister; and six, with his mother's brother's wife.[2] Such privileges are not whimsical. They typically cement a relationship that is close for other reasons, such as the provision of security for the woman whose husband dies. Of course, in some societies such as Japan, the so-called double standard is rather firmly embedded in the culture. This permits a man to have sexual relationships with other women in full cognizance of his wife; but forbids the wife the same privilege.

Under what may be rather loosely termed normal situations, two other conditions are understood as part of marriage. The first is regular and routin-

---

[1] Earnest W. Burgess and Harvey J. Locke, *The Family*, 2nd ed. (New York, American Book, 1953), p. 6.

[2] G. P. Murdock, *Social Structure* (New York, Macmillan, 1949), pp. 202-222.

ized cohabitation of the husband and wife—that is, living together in the same household. The second is economic cooperation in the provision of the mutually needed and desired goods and services. Of course, there are exceptions to the latter in socialist or communist societies, but usually only to a degree.

DEFINITION OF FAMILY

Marriage is the necessary prerequisite to the establishment of a family. In a general sense, a family comprises a unity of parents and offspring. However, this unity has several important characteristics, which serve to clarify its nature as a social structure. (1) Family relationships commence with marriage or with the establishment of kinship ties, and are within the bounds of societal approval. (2) The members of a family are united by ties of marriage, blood, and adoption, according to prevailing custom. (3) Family members typically live together, although there are notable exceptions. (4) Interaction within the family is according to norms, roles, and status positions defined by the greater society. Much of the interaction is associated with the fulfillment of the requirements for living, child bearing and rearing, and emotional security. (5) The role and status identification of family members is accomplished through a system of nomenclature related to the method of reckoning kinship.

With the above listed characteristics in mind, a **family** may be defined as, *a socially sanctioned grouping of persons united by kinship, marriage, or adoption ties, who generally share a common habitat and interact according to well-defined social roles.*

A family can be distinguished from other institutionalized subsystems of society in at least four major ways. First and foremost, it is the first group, under usual circumstances, with which the individual comes into extended contact. It is this experience that accounts for the typical pattern of loyalty and affection characterizing family relationships. Second, the family is one of the smallest of all groups in which an individual will have membership. This is more likely to be true in a family composed of just one married couple and their children. In family arrangements that include several couples and all of their children, the size factor may be a predominant influence, although not as clearly as in the smaller conjugal family. Third, the family group is of importance to the proper functioning of some of the other societal systems and institutions. It is true that other social structures are mutually supporting in terms of systemic linkages, but the support of the family group is almost a necessary prerequisite for the successful functioning of some of the other systems. This is amply illustrated by the many cultures where the family as a social group performs almost all institutionalized educative, religious, economic, and government functions and is true to a lesser extent in the emerging mass societies. Finally, in most societies family systems exercise the most profound control over their members of any social system. There are specific exceptions to this general statement, especially in advanced cultures, but the emotional bonds usually found between family members provide much evidence in support of this contention. In most primitive societies, order is maintained without formal laws or police since the only authority is family authority.

MARRIAGE FORMS AND FAMILY TYPES: THE BASIC STRUCTURAL FEATURES OF FAMILY SOCIAL SYSTEMS

Cultural variation accounts for the fact that marriage forms and family structures vary considerably from one part of the world to the other. The discussion that follows is designed to acquaint the student with the more common practices in both instances. In this regard, it should be remembered that all social systems include the 10 structural elements outlined in Chapter 2. In this instance, and in the discussions in chapters 18 and 19, only the elements that are considered most important are featured. The beliefs, sentiments, norms, and roles that make up the system's structure, should be evident in the material presented.

Variations in Forms of Marriage Relationships. Three major practices are followed with regard to the number of men and women who are parties to the marriage contract. **Monogamy**, the most common form of marriage, involves the union of one husband and one wife. **Polygamous** marriages involve at least two persons of one sex and one of the other. The most important subtype of this type of marriage is termed *polygyny,* and is identified when marriage arrangements include one man and two or more women. This practice is quite common in the Middle Eastern part of the world. A second type of polygamous marriage, *polyandry,* involves the marriage of one woman to two or more men. This is a very rare form of marriage, and the Todas of India provide one of the few examples of societies practicing this custom. Female infanticide is one reason for such a practice. The third type of polygamy is termed "group" marriage for lack of a better term. It involves two or more men marrying two or more women. It is doubtful if true forms of group marriage now exist, although some have been reported in the past. The complicated social roles that would have to be worked out for such arrangements, no doubt account for its lack of popularity.

Societies are usually classified according to the type of marriage considered ideal by most of its members. In this regard, monogamy is the only form of marriage that is universally recognized. It is practiced even in societies where other systems are preferred—usually because most men are too poor to afford more than one wife. In some African tribes, for example, despite the fact that additional wives and their children may represent an economic asset to a man, it is very difficult for him and his kin to raise the necessary price to purchase another bride. Polygynous practices are often related to social status and a politically powerful man may accumulate an entourage of wives to symbolize his high status. In a hunting economy, such as among the Eskimo, a skilled hunter takes a second wife to help prepare his kill and to process his skins and furs, and thus advertises his prowess.

Polyandrous practices almost always denote poverty. Such a practice is a unique social device for conserving limited economic holdings. By marrying one woman, jointly, a number of men can pool their resources and maintain an adequate household. The resources of each individual man, especially of land, generally would not suffice to support a monogamous or polygynous form of marriage.

Variations in Selection Patterns for Marriage Partners. The approved way of selecting a marriage partner (or partners) is also a matter of varied cultural practice. In a general sense, all societies include what are termed *endogamous* and *exogamous* practices. **Endogamy** requires that mates be selected from within certain groups and is more commonly expressed in terms of race groups, religious groups, and social class groups. **Exogamy** refers to prohibitions against seeking a mate within certain groups. Incest taboos forbid individuals from seeking wives or husbands among close blood relatives, for example. In other instances, one must look for a marriage partner in another village, tribe, or clan.

Mate selection patterns also vary in accordance with who has the responsibility for selecting marriage partners. It may come as a shock to some persons to learn that one of the most common practices is for parents or elders to be considered the proper ones to select mates for their children. There is, indeed, a strong logic in this practice in that a choice that affects the welfare of the whole group is not left up to immature, inexperienced individuals. Persons living in societies where "romantic selection" is the rule may argue that such a practice eliminates the romantic adventure of love and courtship. The fact is that in an arranged marriage, love is generally considered as something that should develop after the wedding ceremony, not before it. In this regard, it is interesting to note that this idea was prevalent in early United States. A writer in 1832 reports that, "it is usual for parents to choose a husband for their daughter, and to consult her only for form's sake."[3]

There is, of course, no best way of securing a marriage partner, except in terms of cultural definitions. In some places the approved method of securing a wife is through purchase. Again, this is not a ruthless custom, because it is reasoned that a woman is an economic asset and her family has a right to demand recompense for her loss. The purchased wife is not treated as a piece of property; customarily she has rights in keeping with culturally derived

[3] Quoted in W. F. Ogburn and M. F. Nimkoff, *Technology and the Changing Family* (New York, Houghton Mifflin, 1955), p. 36.

norms. The same general understandings with regard to role, apply to wives stolen from other tribes or clans. The latter is no longer a widely dispersed custom.

William Goode likens the process of mate selection everywhere to a market system.[4] He points out how in upper-class Japanese and Chinese families of the past, all marriage transactions were controlled by the elders; how in traditional Arab societies a man's family paid a bride price for the woman; and how in the Brahmin castes of India a groom price was paid by the bride's family. Turning to advanced cultures, he suggests that romantic love is seldom "true blue," and that systems of courtship are usually quite competitive as well as expensive in the sense of the cost of dates. Furthermore, it is seldom that a young man or woman does not get "coaching" from parents, relatives, and friends on the sideline on how to obtain "a good marriage bargain." In almost every instance, a bargain is measured in terms of whether or not the individual's social and/or financial position is improved by marriage.

Variations in the Reckoning of Lines of Descent. The social placement of children is a problem that arises from marriage. This problem has many facets related to the care and support of the child. Kinship status is most important in this regard, as well as for inheritance and status-succession questions. Three basic ways of reckoning the line of descent of children have been classified. When descent is recognized through the male line alone, the system is called a **patrilineal** one. When, in contrast, descent is only counted through the female or mother's line, the system is classed as a **matrilineal** one. The more common **bilateral** system establishes the kinship of children to a limited number of persons on both the mother's and father's kinship lines. It should be remembered that a person's kinship status provides an important base for determining reciprocal roles in a wide arena of primary group relationships.

Most societies of the western world are characterized by a bilateral system of reckoning descent. In contrast, most societies of central Asia, China, India, and Africa have traditionally had a unilineal system of tracing descent. The latter pattern was preferred because of its advantages in maintaining loyalties to clans or tribes. Since lineage was traced through one parent, the individual was never in doubt about his proper group. Residence and child-rearing practices are more difficult to work out in bilateral societies than in patrilineal societies. In some matrilineal societies, the wife resides in her husband's village, but sends her children to her maternal uncle to be reared. In others, the wife maintains residence in her village away from her husband, but he is allowed to visit her according to certain established practices.

Variations in Rules of Residence. The patterns that are followed with regard to where the newly married couple will take up residence also vary from society to society. Five basic rules of residence seem to predominate, although one, patrilocal residence, is by far the most popular, when judged on the basis

[4] William J. Goode, *The Family* (Englewood Cliffs, New Jersey, Prentice-Hall, 1964), pp. 32-33.

of the number of societies that have this practice.[5] In **patrilocal residence** the newly wed couple simply take up permanent residence with or near the parents of the groom. The couple, in some instances, may temporarily reside with or near the bride's parents and then go to live with the groom's parents. The latter pattern is commonly associated with what is known as "bride service," a custom whereby the groom pays for his bride by working a while for her family.

In **matrilocal residence,** the above custom is reversed and the newly weds go to live with the wife's family. Certain societies are characterized by **bilocal** cultural patterns, which permit the couple to live permanently with the parents of either the groom or the bride. A few societies have a rule whereby the newly married couple go to live with an uncle's family, a rule of residence known as **avunculocal residence.** The practice most common in the United States and certain other western countries is known as **neolocal residence.** Under this rule, the married couple establishes a residence separate from either of their parental households.

Again, it is clear that practices with regard to residence are not whimsical. Murdock associates patrilocal residence with societies characterized by polygyny, warfare, slavery, political integration, and a hunting economy. He states that matrilocal residence is encouraged by the introduction of agriculture and the ownership of land by women. Bilocal residence is seen by him as associated with migratory life in unstable bands and approximate equality of the sexes in property rights. He relates neolocal residence to monogamy, about equal contribution of the sexes to subsistence, extensive poverty, territorial form of government, and individualism, as in private property.[6]

In reviewing the above classification, the student should be aware that it is seldom that only one custom will prevail in a given society. It is usual that two or more of the above described practices exist side by side within a given cultural group, although the one pattern will tend to predominate.

Variations in Authority Patterns. The **patriarchal** family, in which all or most family authority is vested in the husband or father has traditionally been the most widespread in time and space. The power of the patriarch has varied according to the cultural setting, but has on occasion been extended to include the right to sell a daughter or son into servitude and the right to condemn members of his family to death. In modern societies, this practice has tended to be superceded by what has been called an **equalitarian** or "egalitarian" family structure. Under the latter, the wife and the husband have more or less equality in family decision-making.

The literature on family structures occasionally includes a reference to **matriarchal** families. However, the evidence that the wife ever assumes complete authority does not seem to be conclusive. The most quoted example of

[5] Murdock sampled 250 societies and found that 146 of them followed patrilocal practices (*op. cit.*, p. 17).

[6] *Ibid.*, p. 202.

modern-day matriarchal arrangements is that found among many lower-class Negro families in the United States. This practice is attributed to circumstances related to slavery and its aftermath and is reinforced by loose man–woman ties among many lower-class Negroes generally. At best, matriarchal authority is an informal practice, and it tends to vary widely.

This discussion of what is perhaps the oldest and most extensively used criterion for categorizing family types would not be complete without a strong word of caution. It is unrealistic to conceive of power in family systems as being completely monolithic and undifferentiated. There has always been what is termed "spheres of power." Even in societies like the traditional Chinese or Indian societies, where the patriarchal pattern was strongly emphasized, other family members had certain power prerogatives in given situations. In the Hindu family, for example, the grandmother wielded such power that a father would not address his daughter before the grandmother, because this was presumed to show disrespect to the grandmother. It is, of course, a general rule that men have more power than women. However, as Nimkoff points out, certain types of marriage forms encourage particular patterns of power. Monogamy tends to foster equality between the sexes, whereas polygyny encourages patriarchal rule.[7]

Variations in Kinship Groups and Family Types. Kinship relations are the basis for many types of social relationships as well as for family identification. Consanguineal kin relations—including "blood" relatives, however these may be defined—are the basis for what are termed "extended" families. An **extended family** normally includes all those persons defined as being kin and their several nuclear families. A **nuclear family** is made up of an immediate conjugal unit, that is, a husband and wife plus those children they identify as their own and for whom they assume the role of parent. As indicated, a nuclear family may well be but a part of an extended family.

Kinship ties and relationships are further distinguished according to which of an individual's two nuclear families they involve. The family into which a person is born or adopted is known as his **family of orientation.** The family that he establishes through marriage is termed his **family of procreation.**

There are, of course, many variations of the ideal types listed above. For one thing, extended family organization sooner or later faces problems of size and space, as well as complicated questions of inheritance and emigration. Population pressures have led to customs like infanticide and delayed marriages.

Yang describes the organization of the traditional Chinese family as follows:

In traditional social life there is the term *liu ch'in,* or "six kinship relations," which suggests a delimitation for the larger kinship circle as a functioning unit.

[7] Meyer F. Nimkoff, Ed., *Comparative Family Systems* (Boston, Houghton Mifflin, 1965), p. 30.

Interpretations vary as to what constitutes the "six kinship relations," but a commonly accepted version is that they are the relations (1) between husband and wife, (2) between parents and children, (3) between brothers, (4) between the children of brothers, (5) between brother's grandchildren, and (6) between brother's great grandchildren. In actual social life, however, the first four categories of relations are comparatively more intimate, and the last two types belong more to the organization of the clan than to the intimate kinship circle of the extended family.[8]

In the United States, a version of the extended family seems to be evolving which has been termed the *modified extended family*.[9] The modified extended family differs from the classical extended family in that it does not require that family members live in geographic proximity to one another, and does not have a hierarchal authoritarian pattern. It does, however, provide for significant and continuing aid to the nuclear family. Studies conducted to date reveal kin systems involving a network of mutual aid, patterns of visiting, and socio-psychological ties that extend through several generations.

The modified extended family is apparently more commonly found in metropolitan areas than in rural settings. In contrast, the *joint family system* of India which is as universal as the caste system, is the product of an agricultural economy.[10] The principle feature of this **joint family system** is its three-dimensional depth, its characteristic of all members living under one roof, and that property of whatever kind is shared by all. It typically includes a father, his grown sons and their wives and children, as well as unmarried sons and daughters; it serves as the center for social, recreational, and religious activity of all its members. Essentially, the stability of the Indian joint family depends on the strength of the father–son and brother–brother relationships. These relationships are established to guarantee the continuity of land ownership, through inheritance, from one generation to the next. Customarily, all sons inherit equally at birth, but the land is kept in one holding through the joint family system.

THE FUNCTIONS OF FAMILY SYSTEMS

The preceding section was devoted to the structural aspects of families—that is, to the institutionalized patterns of behavior relating to the formation and functioning of this type of social system. In this section, attention is focused on the human "needs" that are generally served by these structures.

[8] Reprinted from *Chinese Communist Society: The Family and the Village* by C. K. Yang by permission of The M.I.T. Press, Cambridge, Massachusetts. Copyright © 1965.
[9] E. Litwak, "Geographical Mobility and Extended Family Cohesion," *American Sociological Review*, Vol. 25 (June, 1960), pp. 385-394.
[10] Carl C. Taylor, Douglas Ensminger, Helen W. Johnson, and Jean Joyce, *India's Roots of Democracy* (London, Longmans, 1965), Chapter 4.

The functions of family systems presented below are the ones that apply in moderately advanced and advanced cultures. Other functions, such as physical protection, religious instruction, recreation, and taking care of the aged and other dependent members are often times of primary concern to the family in less advanced societies. In such instances a family system might well be said to primarily serve another institution besides the family.

THE PERPETUATION OF THE GROUP

All societies must perpetuate themselves if they are to survive. This basic need is almost universally met (legitimately) in family groups, which provide an ideal setting for procreation. The nature of this setting is such that conflict over sex drives is minimized and necessary patterns for rearing dependent young over a long period of time is facilitated. The two reinforce one another as a rule. Also, a family provides an ideal structure for the implementation of rational programs designed to increase or decrease birth rates. Other structures might function in response to positive or negative sanctions to promote a higher or lower birth rate, but inducements such as cash bonuses and praise, and negative sanctions such as gossip or social stigma tend to work more effectively at the family level.

THE CARE AND TRAINING OF THE YOUNG

As brought out before, the human child remains helpless for an extremely long period of time. For a matter of several years it is necessary that most of his needs be administered to by adults. It is generally within the family group that this care is given. Besides food, clothing, and shelter, a family normally furnishes whatever accoutrements are necessary for various types of social participation. The latter would include such things as costumes, toys, and ritualistic articles. Also, a certain degree of protection is afforded the young from dangers they do not comprehend because of immaturity or inexperience.

THE INITIAL STATUS ASCRIPTION OF THE YOUNG

In every society, certain social statuses are initially fixed for the individual by his family. These ascribed statuses may or may not remain with the family member throughout his lifetime, depending on factors of social mobility and class structure. The important positions initially ascribed are family social-class reputation, family economic level, and family religion. Most persons never completely lose the initial statuses they acquire from their families.

PROVISION FOR AND REGULATION OF
THE SEXUAL AND PARENTAL DRIVES

Two of the strongest drives that characterize humans are the sexual and parental drives. Without some sort of institutionalized social structure, within the framework of which these drives can be controlled, problems would tend to develop or be aggravated. These important functions are relegated to families in most societies. The performance of these functions serves both to legitimize offspring and to provide for felt needs to care for and socialize the young.

THE PROVISION OF AN INTIMATE CIRCLE
FOR AFFECTION AND COMPANIONSHIP

Part of the nature of man as a social being is a fundamental need for love and affection. This need is fulfilled for most people (to an extent at least) within their family groups, as a part of, or as a consequence of, the intimate circle of interactional relations. The family, ideally, protects the individual from psycho-social isolation as well as providing him with needed love and affection. In actual fact, the opposite can and does occur and, in many concrete examples, family relationships serve more to promote hate and insecurity than anything else. However, here we are more concerned with the idealized patterns found in most cultures.

THE PROVISION OF A BASIS FOR ECONOMIC
INHERITANCE OF PRIVATE PROPERTY

There are societies in which the institution of private property is not important, since nearly everything is held by the state or group. However, there are always some personal effects or mementos that are held by individuals in a private sense. A family provides each of its members with a kinship status which in turn places him in a definite order for the inheritance of property held by other family members. In a democratic society characterized by fee simple ownership of property in such things as land and houses, this function becomes very important indeed. Without precisely worked-out lines of inheritance, the division of the economic substance of the deceased family member would likely develop into a real source of conflict.

THE SOCIALIZING OF THE INDIVIDUAL

Since, in most cases, his family is the first social group for every individual, it must universally perform a function of introducing the newcomer to his society. The socialization process has already been described in detail, and needs no elaboration here. However, it is impossible to stress too much the importance of the family in this process. The individual could not become a functioning member of society, that is, learn the cultural requirements necessary for survival, were it not for the experiences derived in his family—or a substitute primary group.

DIVORCE: INSTITUTIONALIZED ARRANGEMENT FOR DISSOLVING FAMILY GROUPS

It is logical that there should be institutionalized structures for dissolving families as well as for bringing them into existence. These structures are of two types, separation and divorce. Separation simply involves the desertion of one spouse by the other, and the cessation of normal family relations. Separation may or may not be sanctioned by the greater society, but is institutionalized to the extent that it is condoned as a way out of an undesired marital contract. This is most clearly seen in societies where divorce is not legally possible. Although separation does dissolve the family group in a *de facto* sense, it is generally not considered a permanent (that is, legal) breaking up of this group.

Divorce is the socially sanctioned arrangement whereby marriage is terminated and the family group broken up. It is practiced in most societies, but varies from one place to another in terms of conditions that must be met, the sanctions that it implies, and the frequency with which it is used. Further variations center around such questions as (1) disposition of and responsibility for the care of children, if any; (2) disposition of family property and effects; (3) placement of divorced persons in other societal structures such as occupations and generalized social states. In addition, the rituals, procedures, and ceremonies which legitimize divorce differ in rather extreme ways as one moves from one group or society to another.

The conditions under which divorce is granted vary, as mentioned, from quite painless procedures to long, drawn-out, traumatic experiences. As a general rule, in consanguineal family structures, where the individual is surrounded by a large group of kin and his status is well-defined and protected, divorce may mean little change in regular behavior and hardly any emotional experience. In a society where there is a strong emphasis on attachments within the conjugal family unit, divorce is quite likely to mean emotional shock, social stigma, and economic problems to at least one, if not both spouses, as well as to children.

The grounds or reasons for divorce also depend on the given culture. In some countries, as Spain, Italy, and Ireland, divorce is not permitted under

FIGURE 17-1. *Marriage and Divorce Trends in the United States.*

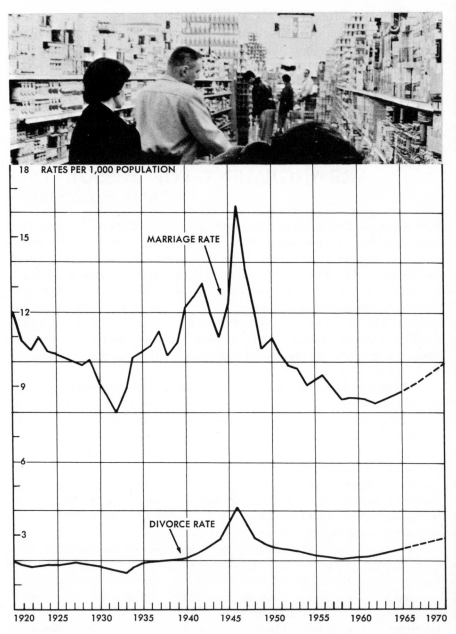

Source: *Monthly Vital Statistics Report,* Vol. 14 (February, 1966) Public Health Service, U. S. Department of Health, Education, and Welfare, Washington, D. C. (Note: Author of text has extended trends from 1965 to 1970 for the sake of illustration.) Photograph courtesy of United Nations Organization.

any circumstances. In other societies, like the pygmies of the Ituri forest, divorce is extremely casual—the woman simply gathers her personal belongings and moves out. Among the Ruwall Bedawin nomads, a man may divorce his wife by merely telling her that he is doing so. It appears that divorce is generally more difficult in advanced societies, although there are notable exceptions. Divorce laws vary radically from state to state in the United States.

The causes of divorce are difficult to assess properly. Of course, divorce rates are related to the ease with which divorces may be obtained. However, this is far from the total picture. Usually there is some sort of incompatibility between husband and wife, ranging from sexual maladjustment to broad cultural and intellectual differences. Studies of marital adjustment indicate that personality factors (ability to make allowances for others and to face frustrations) and socialization factors (coming from a happy home) are important to marital success. Crisis periods such as wars also affect divorces. This is dramatically illustrated in Figure 17-1, where it can be seen that both marriage and divorce reached all-time highs in the United States during World War II (in the mid-1940's).

The complicated nature of the types of factors which contribute to divorce rates can be seen in the list of causes of divorce in contemporary United States prepared by Johnson:[11]

(1) Religious tolerance of divorce or a decline in the influence of "strict" religions.
(2) Legal tolerance of divorce.
(3) Increased industrialization which reduces the importance of the family as a producing unit.
(4) Urbanization—urban neighbors exercise less control over one another's conduct.
(5) Birth control—childless couples are more likely to obtain a divorce.
(6) Greater geographic mobility—moving from place to place reduces the influence of the local group.
(7) High vertical social mobility—marriage partners seldom adapt equally as well to new social environments.
(8) Heterogeneity of population—increases chances of culturally and socially incompatible persons getting married.
(9) High demands on the intimate affectional side of marriage—too high "romantic-love" expectations since marriage is no longer a prerequisite to comfortable living.

It is interesting to note that divorce may or may not have implications for remarriage. In some cultures a divorced man or woman is stigmatized to such a degree that remarriage is almost out of the question. In others, divorce may enhance chances of remarriage. It is a commentary on culture change in the United States that divorce has only recently become common, if not fully

[11] Harry M. Johnson, *Sociology: A Systematic Introduction* (New York, Harcourt, Brace & World, 1960), pp. 171-173.

accepted. Close to one-third of all marriage licenses issued are to couples including at least one divorced party. In fact, national statistics indicate divorced persons have a better chance of marriage than persons never married—well over 90 percent of persons between the ages of 20 and 35 who lose a spouse through divorce or death remarry. This is in sharp contrast to certain upper-caste groups in India. Among these groups the religious codes look upon marriage as a spiritual union and the souls of husband and wife are said to reunite after death. Remarriage is thus not encouraged.

THE EMERGING AMERICAN FAMILY SYSTEM: A CASE ILLUSTRATION OF CHANGING FAMILY PATTERNS

Social structures undergo changes at a greater or lesser pace among the societies of the world. Changes in highly institutionalized structures like the family are usually slower to come about than changes in less well-established areas of interaction. The direction and degree of change of a given social structure varies with the cultural milieu. Thus, it is hazardous to generalize from one cultural setting to another. Nevertheless, it serves a purpose of illustrating the type of change that can come about, to review what has taken place in one society. For this reason the most significant emerging patterns in the organization of the United States family are presented here. The reader from another national society may or may not find the patterns described helpful in understanding changes in family patterns in his social setting.

The following list of changes that have or are taking place in the United States is based on the findings of a multitude of studies done within the past few years.[12]

(1) *The status of women has improved.* Perhaps the most far-reaching and important change related to the family in the United States is the recent improvement in the status of women. This change is manifested in more-equal educational opportunities, in increasing job equality, in a trend away from patriarchal-family authority patterns to equalitarian patterns, in an increase in the range of social opportunities and contacts for women, and in increasing male–female equality under the law. Perhaps the best indicator of the above trend is the increasing number of women who are gainfully employed, that is, work outside the home. One-third of all workers in the United States are women and the number is increasing. Figure 17-2 shows the percentage of all women, by age group, expected to be in the labor force by 1970.

(2) *Division of family tasks is becoming less stereotyped.* In keeping

[12] See Lee G. Burchinal, "The Rural Family of the Future," Chapter 5 in James H. Carp, ed., *Our Changing Rural Society: Perspectives and Trends* (Ames, Iowa, Iowa State University Press, 1964).

FIGURE 17-2. *Percentage of Women Expected To Be in the 1970 Labor Force.*

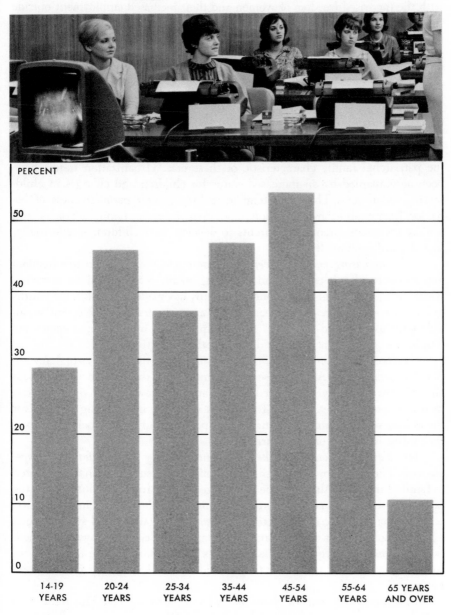

Source: *Converging Social Trends. Emerging Social Problems*, U. S. Department of Health, Education, and Welfare, Welfare Administration, Division of Research Bulletin No. 15 (Washington, D. C., U. S. Government Printing Office, 1966), p. 49. Photograph courtesy of Socony Mobil Oil Corporation.

with the increased freedom of women and their increased employment outside the home, family chores and tasks are becoming increasingly accepted by husbands in the United States. In other words, the household division of labor is more likely to be based upon the particular work situation of the family members than on traditional patterns that assigned domestic duties exclusively to women.

(3) *Children are receiving higher status and child-rearing techniques are becoming more permissive.* During the pioneering days of the United States and so long as the nation was primarily a rural one, children were construed as an economic asset. However, they occupied an inferior position in the patriarchal family characteristic of these eras. Urbanization trends have been accompanied by an increased status for children and changes in child-rearing techniques. The latter tend to include greater permissiveness of behavior, freer expression of affection, more involvement in family decisions, and a more conscious attempt by parents to develop their children intellectually, socially, and emotionally.

(4) *Increasing personal freedom in mate selection.* The greater freedom and mobility of adolescents and changing mores with regard to marrying within religious, social, and economic groups has made it possible for youths to have a wider choice of prospective marriage partners. Mate selection standards tend to be based on "love" and companionate interests, and mates are sought anywhere in the nation and even in other countries.

(5) *Sex norms are becoming increasingly permissive.* A virtual revolution has occurred in American sexual norms within the past 50 years. These changes are primarily manifested in the attitudes toward the right of both men and women to expect satisfactory sex relations, in lessening support for the double sex standard, in an increase in petting, and in less societal support for continence before or after marriage.

(6) *Family functions are becoming increasingly differentiated and specialized.* The trend toward the nuclear family has resulted in changes related to family functions. Although the generalized family functions outlined in the preceding section remain, important functions are developing in connection with the maintenance of interactional patterns with other social systems, such as the school, work or occupational group, and other economic systems. These "systemic linkages" require specialized roles and account for the trend toward specialization. At the same time they provide a broader base for role differentiation.

(7) *Increasing concern about marital and parental roles.* This trend is so well known as to need little elaboration. Marriage preparation classes are common in secondary schools, as well as colleges and universities. Many groups, such as Parent–Teachers Associations, local public health agencies, and women's clubs promote and support activities designed to improve the individual's performance as a marriage partner and parent. In this regard, there is an increasing number of scientific studies of marriage and family life, and

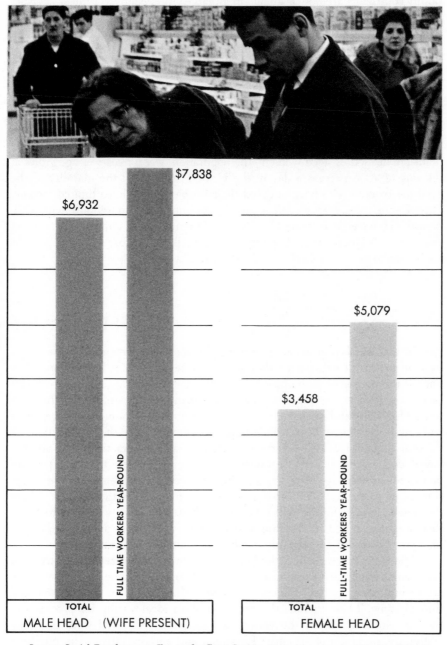

FIGURE 17-3. *Median Income in 1964 of Intact and Female Head Families in the United States (March 1965).*

$7,838

$6,932

$5,079

$3,458

FULL-TIME WORKERS YEAR-ROUND

FULL-TIME WORKERS YEAR-ROUND

TOTAL

TOTAL

MALE HEAD   (WIFE PRESENT)

FEMALE HEAD

Source: *Social Development: Key to the Great Society,* U. S. Department of Health, Education, and Welfare, Welfare Administration, Division of Research Publication No. 15 (Washington, D. C., U. S. Government Printing Office, 1966), p. 49. Photograph courtesy of United Nations Organization.

family counselors are now available in all large cities. Many volunteer agencies also provide marriage counseling services. This trend is occurring in the face of a long-time trend to smaller family size. The average family in the United States is, statistically speaking, between one and two children. (In 1965 the average family population included 3.71 persons.)

(8) *The Growing Number of Households.* A final trend is worth mentioning, although it relates to households (the people who live as a family-type group under one roof) rather than families in the usual sense. This is the growing number of manless households. Since the turn of the century, there has been a 50 per cent increase in this class of household. Many of these households are headed by aged women—the population over 65 years of age grows at the rate of 1000 persons a day in the United States, and the majority of the aged are women who have outlived their husbands and have limited income. (See Figure 17-3.) However, a growing number are households with children which have been created by divorce. The number of children born out of wedlock is also increasing. (See Figure 17-4.) All in all, more and more women are having to play the role of household (or family) head.

SUMMARY

Family and kinship systems are among the most fundamental of the major societal structural subsystems that serve to integrate social interaction. Marriage is the necessary prerequisite to the establishment of a family, which can be looked upon as a group or system whose members are united together as a unity of parents and offspring in a socially approved manner. Marriage forms and family types vary over a wide range and demonstrate the ramifications of cultural variability. These variations include specific practices that are followed concerning (1) the number of men and women who are primary parties to the marriage contract; (2) the approved way of selecting a marriage partner or partners; (3) the patterns that are followed with regard to where the newly formed family will take up residence; (4) the way in which authority is distributed in the family structure; (5) the way in which kinship lines are traced; and, (6) the way in which the family is organized.

The functions served by the family as an institutionalized social structure vary somewhat from society to society and change over time. However, there are several more or less universal functions that persist in all societies and through time. These include the provision of an ideal setting for procreation; the care and training of the young; the ascription of initial statuses to the young; the provision of an outlet for sexual and parental drives; the provision of an intimate circle of companionship and affection; the provision of a basis for economic inheritance; and the socializing of the individual.

All cultures include some sort of structure for dissolving family groups,

FIGURE 17-4. *Illegitimate Birth Trends in the United States.*

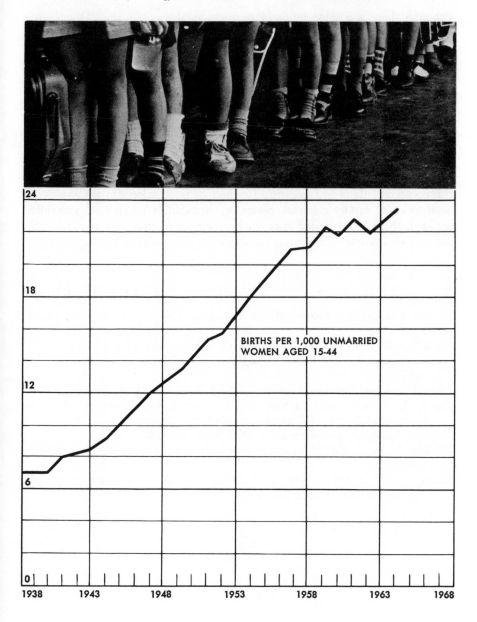

BIRTHS PER 1,000 UNMARRIED WOMEN AGED 15-44

Source: *Health, Education, and Welfare Trends,* 1965 Edition, Department of Health, Education, and Welfare (Washington, D. C., U. S. Government Printing Office, 1965), p. S-7. Photograph courtesy of United Nations Organization.

although there is a wide range of practices in this connection. Divorce is a socially sanctioned arrangement for terminating the marriage contract. The conditions under which divorces are granted are interrelated with a host of questions such as disposition and care of children, disposition of property, and remarriageability. Causes of divorce are difficult to trace, but generally involve some sort of incompatibility between husband and wife.

The family in the United States is undergoing rather rapid change. For this reason it may be studied to determine the types of trends that one can expect in modern advanced societies. The changes taking place may be summarized as follows: the status of women is improving, the role of men and women is becoming less clear-cut; child-rearing techniques are becoming more child-centered; there is increasing freedom in mate selection; sex norms are being relaxed, family roles are becoming increasingly specialized and differentiated; there is increasing concern over proper marital and parental roles; and more households are coming into existence without male heads.

Supplementary Readings

Blitsten, Dorothy R., *The World of the Family* (New York, Random House, 1963).

Davis, Kingsley, "The Early Marriage Trend," selection in LASWELL ET AL.

Goode, William J., *The Family* (Englewood Cliffs, New Jersey, Prentice-Hall, 1964).

Lewis, Oscar, *Five Families* (New York, Wiley, Science Editions, 1962).

Litwak, E., "Geographical Mobility and Extended Family Cohesion," *American Sociological Review*, Vol. 25 (June, 1960), pp. 385-394.

Murdock, George P., *Social Structure* (New York, Macmillan, 1949).

Nimkoff, Meyer F., Ed., *Comparative Family Systems* (Boston, Houghton Mifflin, 1965).

Stroup, Atlee L., *Marriage and Family: A Developmental Approach* (New York, Appleton-Century-Crofts, 1966).

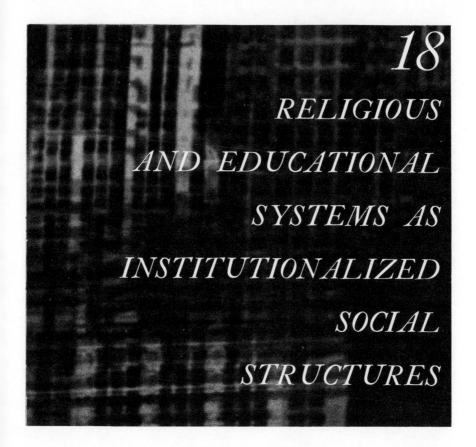

18

RELIGIOUS
AND EDUCATIONAL
SYSTEMS AS
INSTITUTIONALIZED
SOCIAL
STRUCTURES

The significance of culture in conditioning human behavior is stressed throughout this book. Perhaps there is no better way of emphasizing the important role in human affairs which culture plays, than to point out that a number of very basic human needs are culturally derived. Two such needs that have universal expression are the "need" for explaining the nonempirical universe and the "need" for explaining the empirical universe. The explanations, in each instance, have been worked out in terms of societal structures (socal institutions) that serve to integrate and transmit these explanations according to patterns of thought and action which are culturally fitting. In other words, a body of folkways, mores, and law (norms) is developed which applies specifically to the fulfillment of these needs and provides role definitions for social interaction in the fulfillment of the needs.

Here, it may again be emphasized that *religion* and *education* as social institutions have a structural nature which is separate and distinct from the structure of a given religious or educational social system, such as a given church or a given high school. The latter are simply institutionalized social structures dedicated primarily, but not exclusively, to serving the functions of the respective institutions.

In a broad sense, **religion,** as a social institution, *is a system of culturally defined behavioral patterns that serves a definite pattern-maintenance function by providing institutionalized ways for man to understand and relate himself to the nonempirical aspects of his world.* **Education,** as a social institution, is *a system of culturally defined behavioral patterns that serves a definite pattern-maintenance function by providing institutionalized ways for man to come to understand the empirical aspects of his world and to transmit this knowledge to others.*

This chapter has as its main objective the presentation of religious and educational systems as institutionalized social structures, so that the beginning student of sociology can see how these systems fit into the broader spectrum of social organization. For those who have an interest in reading beyond the introductory statements provided here, there are many detailed works in the fields of the sociology of religion and educational sociology.

RELIGIOUS SOCIAL SYSTEMS

Some form of religion appears in all known societies. The universality of religion is attributed to the social functions that such belief systems fulfill, namely relating man to the unknown world. Specific functions of religious systems are variations on this general institutional theme, and will be outlined after the nature of religious systems is described.

NATURE OF RELIGIOUS SYSTEMS

One of the most often quoted definitions of religion (by sociologists) was formulated in 1912 by Emile Durkheim. He defined "a religion" as ". . . a unified system of beliefs and practices relative to sacred things, uniting into a single moral community all those who adhere to those beliefs and practices."[1] This definition needs only slight elaboration to fit our concept of **religious social systems.** The latter may be *defined as socially sanctioned groupings of persons united together by a set of mutually shared beliefs and practices relative to the nonempirical world, who interact according to well-defined roles.*

From this definition, it is clear that members of religious groups share a common concern about the unknown and unexplainable things in the world. In this regard, the author agrees with Hertzler that, "Religion seemingly grows out of the fact that man lives in an atmosphere of uncertainty, insecurity, and incompletion."[2] This atmosphere logically leads to the attributing of

[1] Emile Durkheim, *The Elementary Forms of the Religious Life* (New York, Free Press, 1947), p. 47. (First published in 1912.)

[2] J. O. Hertzler, "Religious Institutions," *The Annals,* Vol. 256 (March, 1948), pp. 1-13.

things that cannot be understood to the supernatural or at least the extrahuman. The range of such "entities" covers many types of perceivable and nonperceivable items including god(s), animals, planets, living persons, dead ancestors, fire, storms, creeds, and volcanos. Some persons, as will be seen, also think of ideologies, such as nationalism and communism, in the same manner.

MAGIC AND RELIGION: Many writers agree that all religious systems have an element of magic, and that it is difficult to distinguish where religious beliefs end and magical belief begins.[3] Both relate to the mysterious and unknown, but at least one rather neat distinction can be made between the two. Magic is generally defined as a technique for controlling these unknown forces in such a way as to produce a desired result. The magician, in effect, is a manipulator of these forces, and produces effects automatically once he learns the correct secrets. Magic thus has an empirical goal, even though the means of attaining the goal are supernatural. For example, a medicine man may say incantations over a sacred object for the purpose of healing a member of his tribe or winning a tribal war. The goal in each instance is empirical, that is, it can be determined at a later date whether the man became well or the war was won.

In contrast to magic, members of religious groups tend to regard supernatural powers as voluntary in nature. Thus religious practices are designed to establish friendly relations with the supernatural powers by showing devotion, allegiance, and obedience. Since many religious goals cannot be tested, the element of trust or faith is important. This fact also serves to further differentiate religion and magic. For example, praying that a dead man may go to heaven cannot be classed as magic, because one does not have a way to prove that the supernatural has or has not complied. The close relationship between religion and magic is seen, when one contemplates the many prayers said (by advanced peoples) for purely empirical goals—such as to pass an exam, win an athletic contest, or to be cured of an ailment.

Some further distinctions between types of magic are helpful in understanding its general nature. "White" magic is never used to do harm within the group of the person practicing the magic, although it may harm an enemy. "Black" magic always does harm and frequently is directed against members of one's society, such as rivals in love affairs, or persons with whom one has had disputes or quarrels. Magic is also classified according to the mechanisms by which the magical act is produced. *Anthropomorphism* is a type of magic which imputes human qualities to spirits, gods, or inanimate objects, so that they can be handled in the same manner as human beings. For example, one may command the winds to blow, or to stop blowing; or one may command ancestors to do favors, such as showing the location of hidden treasures. Non-

[3] J. Milton Yinger, *Religion, Society, and the Individual* (New York, Macmillan, 1957), p. 42.

anthropomorphic magic emphasizes word or act "spells." To illustrate, one may repeat certain incantations to heal the sick or afflict an enemy. Or, he may take some action like stuffing a piece of his enemy's clothing down a dead snake's throat to bring the enemy death. Voodooism is noted for sticking pins into dolls made to represent persons one wants to harm.

One of the most fascinating magical beliefs involves human–animal relationships. There are different variations of such beliefs, but most can be classed under (1) transmigration—that is, beliefs that a personality can pass into a different body that already exists or can be reborn into a different body; and (2) transformation—the assumption that a person or animal can take the other shape for a period of time, or that animals can be controlled or directed by men, that is, follow the will of a man without the man changing his identity. The belief that dead persons can establish connections with animals and direct their activities is also related to transformation. Lindskog gives detailed and interesting accounts of the African Leopard Men in which he describes their belief of this nature.[4] He cites stories, such as this one found among the Asaba. A leopard was sighted and wounded by gunfire; it was followed and the bloody tracks were found to change to human tracks, which led to a hut where an old woman with a wound in one foot was lying. He also cites stories of transformation such as those found in the history of the Bambara. In this tribe it is recorded that there were found the so-called uarraninkalla, who were persons who could transform themselves into leopards by eating different powders. Quite frequently, in these accounts of transformation, the animal would become dangerous to man. All such stories have an element of witchcraft in them, since enemies or rivals and even innocent persons are often attacked.

FAITH AND RELIGION: The fact that religion (and magic) are founded on the belief in supernatural force—often called *mana*—logically raises the question of faith. Men, in other words, must believe in what they cannot verify by their senses. The difficulty in believing in an unseen power is evidenced by the fact that most individuals tend to personify this force, through use of idols, statuettes, or pictures. Yet most men believe in these forces, and give tangible evidence of their faith. Faith usually involves a combination of goals, ideals, aspirations, and emotions, all of which have a cultural base. This is why there are so many "faiths" and why religious groups take so many forms and include such widely variant beliefs. In the United States alone, there are over 250 different religious groups.

SCIENCE AND RELIGION: Throughout most of recorded history, religion and science have clashed, or said in a better way, the adherents of certain religious beliefs have clashed with those able to marshal empirical evidence in

---

[4] B. Lindskog, *African Leopard Men* (Uppsala, Sweden, Almqvist & Wiksells Boktryckerie Ab, 1954), pp. 146-148.

contradiction to these beliefs. The story of how Galileo, in the middle of the seventeenth century, had to disclaim his defense of the Copernican theory that the earth and other planets revolved around the sun, is an example of such controversy. Modern times have seen a shift in view to a position that science and religion can and must be reconciled. This new view holds that science properly deals with what is known or potentially knowable and that religion deals with those things that cannot be proved nonexistent. In other words, religion deals with a supernatural world that lies outside the range of scientific observation and analysis.

THE STRUCTURAL FEATURES OF RELIGIOUS SOCIAL SYSTEMS

The important structural characteristics of religious systems have been catalogued by many scholars. The features listed here are the ones most often identified. It is in these features that one finds the great proliferation of activity which characterizes religious groups.

THEOLOGIES AND CREEDS: Most religious groups have some authoritatively established "reasoned" interpretations of their views and practices. These beliefs are systematized in the form of theologies and creeds. The latter include not only ideas and beliefs, but doctrines, dogmas, articles of faith, ideals, and ideologies as well. Theological knowledge encompasses two kinds of answers—explanations of "how things work" and of "why things work." The theologies of various religious groups range over a wide variety of interpretations, as might be expected. However, in each instance, the theology serves to bring a degree of order and understanding and social integration for the group. The cosmic beliefs and beliefs about salvation, which characterize the major religious groups in the world, are given in Table 18-1.

RITUALS, CODES, PRACTICES, AND TECHNIQUES: There must be some way of communicating with, and serving or placating, the supernatural or unknown powers, and each religious body has standardized ways of so doing. These ways may normally involve certain types of actions (rituals); bodies of law, such as The Ten Commandments (codes); music or dances (practices); and patterns of worship, ways of instructing the uninitiated, methods of proselyting (techniques). The types of activities which fall under the above classifications make up one of the most fascinating chapters of human experience. Accounts run from human sacrifices and torture to more or less passive acceptance of rituals and incantations whose origins are lost in history. The rituals known as *"Rites de Passage"* (rites of transition) are often referred to. In the Catholic church, for example, there are five such rites—Baptism, Confirmation, Extreme Unction, Ordination, and Matrimony.

TABLE 18-1. *Some Examples of Religious Beliefs.*

Religion	Cosmic beliefs	Beliefs about salvation
HINDUISM (Includes cults and sects of Vishnu and Shiva, as well as orthodox Brahmanism.)	*Karma* and *samsara* (transmigration). Gods are essentially different symbols of impersonal pantheism. Endless wheel of incarnations, even for gods.	Fulfilling one's *dharma* will lead to a better incarnation, perhaps as a god. The especially devout may hope to merge with the "All-One" (thus losing personal identity forever). Asceticism and mysticism common.
BUDDHISM (Originally a revolt from Hinduism and a "purification" of Brahman doctrine. Caste *dharma* is meaningless. Many subsequent developments.)	Reincarnation. Evil is the result of unrealistic desires. The world is guided by Buddhas ("Enlightened Ones").	Escape from the eternal wheel of *karma* and *samsara* by following the "Noble Eightfold Path." Monastic mysticism. Much popular (uncanonical) magic.
CONFUCIANISM ("Official" religion of precommunist China. Largely a social ethic, with much tolerance for popular magic.)	Shadowy gods; virtual pantheism. *Tao* is the harmony that pervades all things unless it is disturbed by wrong conduct. The cosmos is essentially unchanging.	Happiness through following ethics of Confucius. Gods need sacrifices in order to keep the world in harmony. Ancestor worship. "Worldly" religion; No asceticism; no mysticism.
JUDAISM (The characterization is of the main stream and ignores certain sects; e.g., Hassidism.)	One supramundane god of power, justice, and mercy. The world does not pass through cycles but is passing through a history that will eventually come to an end.	Salvation of mankind at the end of the world, after the coming of the Messiah. Stress on ethics and (in Orthodox Judaism) on ritual acts, pervading life. Nonascetic; little mysticism.

TABLE 18.1. (Continued)

Religion	Cosmic beliefs	Beliefs about salvation
CATHOLICISM (Largest Christian church. Proclaims itself to be the only true church as an organized body.)	One perfect God "in Trinity, and Trinity in Unity": Father, Son (Christ), and Holy Spirit.	Salvation achieved by the Spirit and sacrifice of Christ, especially with the help of the seven sacraments of the Church. Little concern for this world except as theatre for creating saints and saving souls. Ascetic monasticism. Little mysticism.
PROTESTANTISM (Great variation in belief; therefore, present characterization mentions tendencies.)	Most churches accept Trinity. Some are unitarian.	More emphasis on the love of God and on the saving power of faith, less emphasis on sacraments. Most churches now nonmystical and nonascetic, but some exceptions.
ISLAM (Mohammedanism. Partly grew out of Judaism and Christianity, partly had a common source with them.)	One supramundane god, called Allah. Mohammed is his prophet. A Day of Judgment is to come.	By following Mohammed and taking a pilgrimage to Mecca if possible, men attain Paradise after death. Hell for the wicked. Some asceticism (fasting), but little mysticism in the main tradition.

Source: Harry M. Johnson, *Sociology: A Systematic Introduction* (New York, Harcourt, Brace & World, 1960), pp. 402–403.

SACRED OBJECTS, SYMBOLS, AND PHYSICAL EQUIPMENT: Rituals, practices, codes, and techniques normally are carried on in given physical settings and involve symbols or sacred objects which have religious significance. Major religious groups may own vast holdings of land and buildings, including arrays of shrines, altars, musical instruments and furniture. In fact, it would be unusual to find a religious group that did not claim ownership of certain physical equipment. No group is without certain sacred objects and symbols. The Cross of the Christian religion is well known, as are the sacred cattle of the Hindus and the shrines of the Buddhists.

THE ORGANIZATIONAL CHARACTER
OF RELIGIOUS ENTERPRISES

The "body of believers" of all religious groups is organized in such a way as to promote their beliefs, to enhance their opportunity for "salvation," and to carry out other objectives in the group. Religious organizations vary in size and complexity from small localized groups to global operations held together by extended means of communication. Regardless of size or scope the membership of most religious organizations can be divided rather easily into two broad groups of status-positions: the priesthood or clergy and the laiety or the rank and file of devotees. Graduations of intermediate status positions differ from one religion to another and may be identified by specialized study. Normally the number of such positions varies with the complexity of the given organization. Four basic types of religious systems have been classified and this classification is helpful in understanding the social structure of various religious bodies.

(1) *The Church.* Although most English-speaking persons refer to the members of a religious group as belonging to a church, this is not a correct technical usage. In its more restricted sociological sense, this term is used to designate a religious group that is well established and highly institutionalized in its operation and that is integrated fully into the social and economic order. Clark makes the important point that "the church" stresses order rather than separation in society and accepts responsibility for the problems of secular society.[5]

Many writers distinguish two subclasses of the "the church." The *ecclesia* is seen as a church that attempts to completely enmesh itself with the rest of society, seeking universal membership and a unity with the state. By contrast, *denomination* is a church that has more restricted membership, and contents itself to exist and be compatible with other religions. Denominations openly approve the separation of church and state. The ecclesia type of church is clearly represented by the Roman Catholic Church of the Middle Ages,

[5] S. D. Clark, *Church and Sect in Canada* (Toronto, Canada, University of Toronto Press, 1948), p. 249.

while the denomination type of church is well illustrated by the major church bodies found in the United States today.

(2) *The Sect.* The second type of religious organization is known as a sect. Normally sects are smaller than churches and more fundamental in their approach to doctrinal matters. Also, more demands are made on the time and commitments of members. Several persons have differentiated between sects and churches or denominations. The list of distinctions prepared by Anderson is reproduced in Table 18-2, and serves to make clearer the difference between these two types of religious organization in a modern setting.

Several interesting studies have been made, such as Clark's and Anderson's, of the transition from sect to denomination in the United States and Canada. The trend is for the sect to increase in membership size and at the same time lose some of its militancy. Sometimes a reverse process takes place, with a splinter group breaking away from an established church or denomination to become a new sect.

The Pillar of Fire is an interesting sect which can be used as an example of this type of group. It is a quasi-Methodist organization which owes its existence to the zeal and labors of Mrs. Alma White.[6] Not only was Mrs. White its founder, but she became its bishop and controlling personality. A Kentuckian, Mrs. White early came under the influence of the Methodist holiness preachers. While still a young woman, she migrated west and married a Methodist pastor in Colorado. She used his pulpit to exhort her holiness views and eventually branched out by organizing missions and preaching at camp meetings. This activity brought her in conflict with the authorities of the established church, and led her to found her own sect. Her first group was organized in 1901 in Denver and was known as the Pentacostal Union. In 1917 the name of the sect was changed to the Pillar of Fire.

The Pillar of Fire sect is strongly fundamentalist and insists on a literal interpretation of the scripture. Its members oppose all forms of intellectual modernism. They are intensely devoted to "second blessing" holiness and premillenarianism. The Pillar of Fire includes forty-five churches with approximately 4,000 members. This sect also has a college, an academy, a training school, a publishing plant, a radio station, and a large camp-meeting tabernacle, plus several other types of schools and operations.

(3) *The Cult.* Still a third type of religious organization is known as a cult. Cults differ from both church and sect in at least four important ways: (1) they normally open their membership to all who would join or participate; (2) they tend to focus on one doctrine above all others; (3) they have a very loose organization, permitting members to come and go and to participate in other groups if they wish; and (4) they are held together by strong emotional attachment to a leader, to a special ritual, or to a unique belief. In the United States, cults are illustrated by such groups as The Father Divine Peace Mis-

[6] Described in Elmer T. Clark, *The Small Sects in America* (New York, Abingdon, 1949), pp. 78-79.

TABLE 18-2.   *Identifying Characteristics of Sect and Church Types of Religious Organizations.*

Sect	Denomination
1. Small membership	Large membership
2. Exclusive	Inclusive
3. Economic poverty	Economic wealth
4. Principal concern for adults	Equal concern for adults and children
5. Unprofessional, unspecialized part-time ministers	Professional, specialized full-time ministers
6. Members received through regular services	Members received through special services
7. Membership voluntary and by confession only	Membership based on ritual or social prerequisite
8. A moral community excluding unworthy members	A social institution embracing all who are socially compatible in it
9. Direct methods of social control	Indirect methods of social control
10. Intolerant and suspicious of those holding different doctrinal beliefs	Tolerant and cooperative with those holding different beliefs
11. Little cooperation and organizational affiliation to reach common objectives	Much cooperation and organized affiliation to reach common objectives
12. Organizations for fellowship (*Gemeinschaft*)	Organizations to promote objectives (*Gesellschaft*)
13. Limited and local religious interest	Broad and world-wide religious interest
14. Education of minor concern	Education of major concern
15. Renunciation of, or indifference toward, prevailing cultural patterns	Affirmation of and acceptance of prevailing cultural patterns
16. Emphasis on Evangelism and conversion	Emphasis on religious education
17. Primary interest in the next world	Primary interest in a future in the world

Source: Maurice John Anderson, "Social Change and the Transition from Sect to Denomination: A Study of the White Baptists in Lincoln County, Mississippi, 1815-1910" (unpublished Master's thesis, Louisiana State University, 1952), pp. 20-21.

sion Movement, The Theosophical Society, The Buchmanites, I Am, and The Moorish Science Temple of America.

Studies indicate that in modern societies cults tend to develop in large metropolitan areas where there are special environmental factors of diversity, complexity, loose social controls, and social distance. It seems that cults attract individuals who have no "roots" and are "floating" about. Their members are characterized as being somewhat disassociated from *Gemeinschaft* or primary-group relations and looking for some sort of personal involvement in close-knit groups. The same pattern is witnessed in more primitive settings, where groups of people have been dislodged and greatly frustrated. Yinger makes this point in describing cults that appeared among the American Indians and the people of Melanesia. The so called "Cargo cults" of the latter are explained and described in the manner following.

> For a great many years the European-dominated economy created hardships for many of the residents of the islands of Melanesia. The demand for laborers drew a great many of them, some after harsh recruiting methods, to the mines and plantations run by the white man. Here, barracks life, low pay, newly created wants for food, clothes, and drink, and forceful domination set the stage for the development of religious movements. Many of these movements developed into what has been called the "Cargo" cults. The theme of these cults was that the white man received his vast supplies of goods by steamer or plane from unknown lands. He did not manufacture the goods, or work for them but merely sent back scraps of paper. The natives believed that the goods were made by their own ancestors and stolen by the whites, who had control of some secret for acquiring the cargoes illicitly. Native prophets appeared to reveal the way to secure the cargoes and to reestablish native supremacy by defeat of the white man and forcing him to reveal the secret of how to obtain the cargoes. The Cargo cults often led to conflict situations with white landlords, and also the neglect of native gardens and work, because of a strong belief that the prophesied cargo of fruit, tinned goods of all types, cloth, drinks, and every desirable commodity would be arriving soon.[7]

THE FUNCTIONS OF RELIGIOUS SYSTEMS

The above definitions and discussion of religion makes it clear that religious social systems provide certain answers to some of the most difficult questions that face man. These answers, once they have become institutionalized—that is, become a fundamental part of a social structure—serve a general function of pattern-maintenance and contribute to social organization to this extent. The specific functions of religion or religious social systems elaborate this general function. It will be noted from the list of major specific functions given below that the foundations of religion reach into psychology as well as sociology.

FACILITATE THE QUEST FOR MORAL IDENTITY: Man is eternally seeking to find himself. In his quest for a "moral" identity he inevitably goes outside himself for some principle of the universe which will explain his strivings and help him rationalize his frustrations and suffering. Religious systems, by providing explanations that derive from divine (not necessarily supernatural) powers, put a consistent meaning into life and prevent man from

[7] Reprinted by permission of The Macmillan Company from *Sociology Looks at Religion* by J. Milton Yinger. © J. Milton Yinger 1963.

being psychologically alone in the universe. His successes, his inner desires, his failure and his suffering can all be met with greater equanimity. In this sense religion provides all types of integration for the individual's personality. A man's worth as a person is continuously reaffirmed through participation in religious communities.

PROVIDE INTERPRETATIONS FOR MAN'S ENVIRONMENT: Despite the advances of science, indeed perhaps *because of* the incredibility of much scientific achievement, there is a strong element of incomprehensibility in the world. The unknown troubles man, and religious beliefs restore comprehensibility, making his life more familiar and meaningful. In this regard, religion serves to relieve much of the fear and anxiety which stems from the precariousness of life. For example, one can experience a great deal of anxiety about grades, about promotions, about how others feel about him, about thwarted ambitions; but this anxiety is lessened or relieved completely for the religious person who attributes adverse circumstances, failures, or loss of "face" to "God's will." Religious explanations for the vicissitudes of nature (floods, tornadoes, hurricanes, and droughts) are more readily acceptable, as a rule, than social or more "human" disasters like wars. However, religion functions to provide explanations at both these levels of the unknown.

PROMOTE SOCIAL COHESION AND SOLIDARITY: The core values in almost every society find their validation in religious teachings and beliefs. It is no accident that mores are by and large expressions of religious precepts. Since these values are so important in social life, they provide the basis for social control and for social cohesion. In this regard, religious groups function to train individuals to accept these values on faith and to behave according to norms they imply without question. This may be illustrated by citing such norms as these: married people should remain faithful to their spouses; men should not kill other men, except under certain circumstances; students should not lie and cheat; and women should observe "decent" standards of dress—all of which have a religious implication.

Religious beliefs, with certain exceptions, serve to promote social solidarity in another way. By presenting the individual with an ever-present threat of jeopardizing his existence after death, more or less effective control is maintained over deviant behavior (sin). In fact, without some sort of a reward to look forward to, religious support for moral behavior would be seriously weakened. This fact poses the interesting question of whether or not a completely atheistic society could survive, since all social control would have to be based on rational and admittedly man-inspired rules. When "God" makes the rule, one is more likely to accept it.

OTHER FUNCTIONS: Religious groups serve many more specific functions in one society or another depending on cultural factors. For example, in some places religion and government are so closely allied that much of the legislative and judicial work is in the hands of the "ecclesia." Many charitable, recreational, and educational functions are maintained. In the United States, many hospitals are operated by church groups. The student of a given religious culture will do well to look into such types of activity in order to determine the full role of religious systems in the given society. In each instance, however, it must be remembered that the functions of this type being served are not the functions of religion as a social institution, even though the given social system is primarily a religious one.

SOME FEATURES OF RELIGIOUS SYSTEMS IN THE UNITED STATES

The structural and functional characteristics of religious systems outlined in the preceding sections of this chapter are general in nature and designed to give an overview of these institutionalized structures everywhere. However, religious expressions follow broad cultural patterns for every society.

For example, in the Hindu areas of India the total life of the individual has long tended to be oriented to religion, since caste position affects all social relationships. In a nation like England, where the major church is supported to a considerable extent by government funds, church officials do not feel the necessity to develop a large number of "extracurricular" activities to attract people, and church attendance is relatively low. In the United States, the independence of church from state, the protestant-congregationalist tradition, and a rapidly changing society have given religion and religious systems still another direction. A brief summary of the rather unique structural aspects of religious systems in the United States serves two purposes: (1) it makes clear that religion conforms to some degree to the broad cultural framework of a society; (2) it highlights problems that religious systems face in a rapidly changing and technologically and materialistically oriented social milieu.

DIVERSITY OF BELIEFS AND PRACTICES: It has already been pointed out that there are over 250 different religious bodies in the United States. Many of these groups differ very little from one another in theology and doctrinal practice, yet they maintain distinct organizations. Judged on the basis of this fact and the fact that an estimated three-fifths to two-thirds of the people of the nation hold membership in one church body or another, the United States can be called a religious nation. Of all church members, well over half belong to protestant churches, with Baptists and Methodists predominating; close to two-fifths are Roman Catholic and about one-twentieth belong to Jewish congregations.

Membership in a church does not, of course, mean the same thing for all people. It may mean no more than a token or tacit support for the church, or it may mean a devout and fervent support of the program and doctrines of the church. Fichter made an intensive study of selected urban Catholic parishes, and, on the basis of his findings, classified church members into four general classes[8]: (1) the *nuclear* member who is the most active participant and most faithful believer; (2) the *modal* member, who is the "normal" practicing member and who constitutes the great mass of laymen; (3) the *marginal* member who conforms to a bare minimum of the patterns and activities expected of a church member; (4) the *dormant* member, who has his name on the books, but who does not participate in church life. This pattern of practice seems to pervade throughout the various larger church bodies in the nation.

At this point, the whole question of why people go to church in a modern advanced society can be raised. This in fact has been a question that has faced social scientists as well as religious leaders of all faiths for some time. There is no doubt that the functions listed in the first part of this chapter are primary motivations for most church members. However there is also evidence that many persons go to church for other purposes, only peripherically if at all related to the usual functions. Besides those who go just to be seen (women with new clothes, men who have selfish business interests), there are many members who go to church because they are involved with secular activities supported by the church, such as Boy Scouts, summer camps, or athletic events. Others go to the church because they are involved in charitable enterprises, such as ministrations to the sick, the orphaned, or the mentally deficient. For these classes of membership the church is something in addition to a place of worship. The question of whether or not such members provide a source of strength or weakness to the church is much debated. The important point for our purposes is that this kind of activity is gaining prominence in the United States and is now quite characteristic of religious social systems.

RELIGION IS FACING CHANGE: The cleavages that characterize the structure of religious social systems in the United States are well known and documented. Ideal ways long considered the standard of behavior are in conflict with real behavior necessary for "survival" in the new world. These cleavages can be accounted for in large part by contradictions that come about in time of rapid change. Harvey Cox puts this dilemma into sharp focus:

> Our doctrines of the church have come to us from the frayed-out period of classical Christendom and are infected with the ideology of preservation and permanence. They are almost entirely past-oriented, deriving their authority from one or another classical period, from an alleged resemblance to some earlier form of church life, or from a theory of historical continuity. But this will no longer do. A church whose life is defined and shaped by what God is *now* doing in the world

---

[8] Joseph H. Fichter, S. J., *Social Relations in the Urban Parish* (Chicago, The University of Chicago Press, 1954), p. 22.

cannot be imprisoned in such antiquated specifications. It must allow itself to be broken and reshaped continuously by God's continuous action; hence the need for a theology of social change.[9]

Many examples of cleavages both within church bodies and between church groups trace directly to changing times. Questions such as those relating to separation of church and state; those relating to racial integration; those relating to practices such as drinking, dancing, eating certain types of meat, and birth control; those relating to religious education in public schools —all are controversial. On many of the above issues, and on other issues as well, church members do not know the stand of their church group or do not adhere to the stand if they know it. This fact, and the fact that religious groups have a definite competitive relationship with other institutionalized social groups (namely the family) for the loyalty and support of individuals,[10] are what inspired Cox to call for a theology of change. This call, and the fact that religious systems are in a definite period of transition that heralds sweeping changes, suggests that religious social systems of the future everywhere may exhibit a nature quite different from what exists now.

THE ROLE OF THE MINISTER REPRESENTS A CLEAR SOCIAL IDENTITY:

With regard to the roles played by officials of religious groups, the minister is one of the most socially visible participants in the life of most communities in the United States. He has a social identity that in general projects an image of a man of God, and therefore a man who acts in an exemplary fashion at all times. This means his personal behavior is a matter of common concern and is continually under close scrutiny. Vidich and Bensman list the criteria commonly used to judge ministers by the people in a small town they studied.[11] It is logical to assume that similar criteria would be used in most communities in the United States.

(1) The minister must be able to "get along with people." This means that he not only must be a "good fellow," but he must keep himself from involvement in controversial topics and must not take political sides.

(2) The length of the minister's sermons are more a matter of critical appraisal than the contents of the sermon, so long as no controversial topic is treated.

(3) The minister's wife must associate with all church members on a broad basis, or she will be considered snobbish. At the same time she must be a "helpmate" to her husband, a Sunday school teacher, and a fund raiser. But at all costs, she must not give the appearance of trying to "run the church."

[9] Harvey Cox, The Secular City (New York, Macmillan, 1965), p. 105.
[10] See Gerhard Lenski, The Religious Factor (Garden City, New York, Doubleday, 1961), Chapter V.
[11] Arthur J. Vidich and Joseph Bensman, Small Town in Mass Society (New York, Doubleday, Anchor Books, 1958), pp. 244-245.

(4) A minister must have good administrative ability—he must keep things going, initiate programs, take a deep but impersonal interest in finances, and keep all workers, volunteer or paid, happy.

(5) The minister must not give the impression of being too intellectual. "High-blown" ideas make for dull sermons, and too much concern with books doesn't leave time for visitations and other necessary activities.

A consideration of the above criteria makes it clear that in many religious systems, as is true in other institutionalized structures, the major functions being served can be, and are, diverted to issues of personality and behavior.

SUPERNATURAL AND SECULAR RELIGIONS (IDEOLOGIES)

Before closing this brief discussion of religious social structures, a word needs to be said about what some identify as secular religions and others term ideologies.[12] The distinction is necessary because there are powerful movements and belief systems in the world which do not emphasize supernaturalism. Yet these systems have all the other characteristics of religion. Most have an economic-political-ideological base, as socialism, communism, and fascism; but some are more properly classed as systems based on nationalism.

In attempting to decide whether these systems are truly religious ones or not, one must take into consideration the generally accepted definition of religion. This definition, as brought out, refers specifically to beliefs in the "sacred" and the "unknown." Those who interpret the "unknown" as exclusively supernatural would necessarily rule out as religions those systems that attempt to explain injustice and suffering empirically. However, if one sees no supernatural implication in the "unknown" and interprets religion as characterized by a sacred attitude along with a "faith" in an ideology, then it is possible to speak of secular religions.

The writer is inclined to the view that ideologies represent religious forms. The justification for this view derives from the fact that those who subscribe to ideologies, such as Communism, demonstrate a faith that is as real as a faith in a deity. Just as believing Christians hold that an all-seeing God works out the course of events for mortals to achieve life everlasting, the Marxian dialectic is seen by the Communist as something that will eventually produce a classless society (looked upon as a sort of heaven on earth). In this sense, the so-called secular religions fulfill essentially the societal functions as the supernatural religions. In nationalism, the state is seen as above individual self-interests and the only true salvation to human ills.

[12] Elizabeth K. Nottingham, *Religion and Society* (Garden City, New York, Doubleday, 1954), pp. 10-11, and H. Bredemeier and R. Stephenson, *The Analysis of Social Systems* (New York, Holt, Rinehart and Winston, 1962), pp. 209-302.

EDUCATIONAL SOCIAL SYSTEMS

Man is constantly seeking ways to enlighten himself to the world in which he lives. This quest for enlightenment and the practical value of being knowledgeable, leads almost universally to institutionalized social structures known as educational social systems. In this section, such systems are formally defined and their structure and functions are described.

NATURE OF EDUCATIONAL SYSTEMS

There are probably as many definitions of education as there are of religion. However, as in the case of religion, the technical sociological meaning of education can be stated rather precisely.

Educational systems *are socially sanctioned groupings of persons who are united for the purpose of formally and consciously providing a systematic training experience to members of the society relative to the empirical world, and who interact according to well-defined social roles.* It may be seen from this definition that educational systems emphasize teaching rather than learning, although the contrary view is popular. It is also clear that many learning processes, such as a father teaching his son certain skills or a student learning how to do something by watching television, take place outside of educational systems. Here again the point may be emphasized that a given system may include interaction designed to serve functions for two or more social institutions.

Educational systems, as pointed out, deal primarily with the empirical world, or at least with the rational world. Even in religious schools, teachers devote their time to systematic teaching of the meaning of ritual, or the analysis of church history and doctrine, or the more mundane considerations of the fundamental aspects of church management and administration.

EDUCATION AND SOCIALIZATION: The socialization process involves education; and to avoid confusion, it is of importance to understand the nature of this involvement. Actually, socialization is an inclusive concept that takes in all ways by which individuals come to acquire the cultural patterns in their societies. Educational systems, in contrast, provide only one way (the formal way) by which these patterns may be acquired, and they serve a socialization function to this extent. The schools tend to assume the responsibility for transmitting the more technical (scientific) parts of the culture, although this varies from one society to another. Among preliterates, for example, learning may be entirely outside formal educational structures.

STRUCTURAL FEATURES OF EDUCATIONAL SYSTEMS

The social structure of educational systems varies over a wide range, but universal patterns can be detected. Two factors seem always to be taken into account in formal education: age and time. Both provide a basis for organizing activity; and age, in addition, provides a basis for an authority structure. Generally school systems have the following structural features.

THE ORGANIZATIONAL CHARACTER OF EDUCATIONAL ENTERPRISES: All educational systems include a hierarchy of status positions and role definitions. Normally, at least three levels of functionaries are found in modern school systems: teachers, administrators, and governing bodies. Teachers and administrators are usually professionally trained, whereas board members or other governing bodies may or may not be recruited from outside educational circles.

Corwin's list of possible measures of bureaucratic characteristics in a particular modern school indicates the range of this type of structural feature.[13] Under the size factor, he notes that both the number of teachers and the number of students are relevant. Under the centralization factor, he cites the ratio of administrators to teachers, the number of administrative levels between teachers and the top administrative position, and the authority and power of each position relative to specific decisions on curricula, materials, and budgets as important measures of the bureaucracy. Under the specialization factor, he lists a host of measures such as percentage of line to staff personnel, percentage of teachers not teaching their subject of specialty, the level of education of personnel, and percentage of classes with limited or total ability groupings. Under the standardization factor, he names the following things as having significance in the understanding of the structure of the given school system: the uniformity of tests, of curriculum, of textbooks; the proportion of required courses to elective courses; and dispersion of, and choice of, elective subjects.

LEVEL AND TYPES OF INSTRUCTION: Each educational system has a more or less specialized operation. Specialization is based on the level of instruction, that is, the age groups taught and the subject matter or level of subject matter taught. Thus, in modern situations, we find elementary or primary schools for the first years of instruction; secondary schools for older youths; and colleges and universities for young adults. Vocational and technical schools emphasize skills rather than a general "liberal" education. Re-

[13] Ronald G. Corwin, *A Sociology of Education* (New York, Appleton-Century-Crofts, 1965), pp. 42-43.

gardless of designation, various types of schools are found in all societies where educational institutions flourish.

TYPE OF SUPPORT AND CONTROL: There are many possibilities for financial support and overall control of educational systems. Again, in modern societies the more common practices are for these systems to be sponsored by private or public organizations. Private operation may be by any one of several arrangements, by private "trust fund" or individuals, by church bodies or by corporations. Public schools are supported and controlled by public bodies such as a state or city. The percentage of the cost of all formal education which comes from public sources tells much about the value placed on education in a given society. In the U.S.A., approximately four-fifths of total annual expenditure for education of close to 30 billion dollars comes from public sources.

COMPULSORY NATURE: Depending on cultural norms, educational systems may be voluntary or compulsory in nature. For example, in the United States, school attendance is (in effect, if not legally) compulsory for every mentally and physically capable child until approximately age 16. However, in many countries, schools are limited in number and attended by only those who can afford the rather high cost involved. Such an educational system does not guarantee that everyone will obtain an education, as does a compulsory system.

FUNCTIONS OF EDUCATIONAL SYSTEMS

The fact that institutionalized social structures develop in response to societal needs has already been noted. The specific functions that educational institutions fulfill are several and vary somewhat from one society to another. However, there are major functions that have more or less general application, regardless of the relative complexity or simplicity of the given culture. In a general way, as has already been stated, the overall function of education is socialization. Said another way, educational institutions serve society by further preparing individuals to get along in the society. However, this general function is accomplished through the more specific functions that are listed as follows.

SYSTEMATIC TRANSMISSION OF CULTURAL HERITAGE: Almost every person has some interest and pride in the cultural history of his society. This interest stems from the close association between ethnic pride and civic and patriotic responsibility and from a strong human nostalgia for the past. Educational systems devote much of their time and effort to historical themes, including the traditional cultural expressions such as music, poetry, prose, and philosophy. In addition, the given nation's past is glorified and national heroes, national shrines, and other highly venerated traditions are treated in detail in the schools. All in all, it is normally a part of the educational process to transmit in systematic and detailed fashion what can be broadly termed the cultural heritage.

ACQUAINTANCE OF INDIVIDUALS WITH DIVERSE ROLES: The individual learns about certain roles in his family and in other noneducational social systems. This experience is primarily related to his own status and the reciprocal statuses to his in these systems. It is a function of the school to teach him the ideally required behavior in a larger number of different status positions. In a modern school system, for example, the curricula for the various grades include not only instruction in how to be a good citizen, but also provide knowledge relating to almost every economic, political, vocational, and professional role known in the society. The importance of this function is in the preconditioning of individuals for understanding the many behavioral situations that might be encountered in the course of a lifetime. Although a person may never be president or prime minister of his country, or a physicist, or a bricklayer, or a waiter, the chances are that he will learn of the requirements of these roles in school. This is why an educated person normally is more at ease than an uneducated person in strange groups.

PREPARATION OF INDIVIDUALS FOR SPECIAL ROLES: Educational systems not only serve to acquaint one with other roles in his society, but they also prepare him for specialized roles by making him an expert of sorts. Specialized-role training is achieved at two levels. First, the schools train so as to make one an "educated" more knowledgeable person in a broad sense. One can easily detect the person who is "educated" and contrast him to the less sophisticated person or the illiterate. Second, the schools train for a specific task or skill like teaching, working as an engineer, or even homemaking. This is probably the best known function of educational systems in the United States, but not necessarily elsewhere.

PROVIDES A BASIS FOR EVALUATING STATUS: In preparing persons for such specialized roles, as listed above, education serves what has been called a "status sifting" function in two ways. First, students in pursuit of education are sorted out for special status positions on the basis of grades, mentality, and application—such as members of Phi Kappa Phi honor society, "C" students and "goof-offs." Sifting is also done according to specialty training, such as sociology major or music major. Finally, the school confers various degrees or certificates such as B.A. in mathematics, M.S. in poultry science, and a Ph.D. in education, which serve to sift people into status position categories after leaving educational systems. This is the second way these systems function to permit status evaluation.

PROMOTION OF CHANGE: Not only does education serve to make one more knowledgeable about new things and ways, but in a very real sense it makes one more susceptible to change. The many studies of diffusion of culture indicate quite clearly that persons with more schooling accept change more readily. Many schools also engage in research, although this is not an educational activity in and of itself. Research awareness functions to condition one toward change.

It should be noted that while formal educational processes speed the process of cultural change, in so doing cultural "discontinuities" between generations may be created. Green suggests that education "drives a wedge" between generations by turning the child of a peasant into a clerk, the son of a farmer into a lawyer, and the son of the Italian immigrant into a typical American teen-ager.[14]

EDUCATIONAL SUBCULTURES AND ORGANIZATIONAL COMPLEXES

It is difficult to generalize about the various subcultures and organizations which are associated with educational systems because of the vast differences between advanced, developing, and underdeveloped societies. However, the point can be made that certain subcultures and certain systems of social organization will probably be found linked to or closely associated with educational activity in all societies. The type of social interaction and activity which may be expected can be illustrated with examples from the United States. In reviewing the picture in the United States, the reader should keep in mind that parallel cases might be worked out for the whole school systems in their communities.

STUDENT SUBCULTURES IN THE UNITED STATES: By the time students reach junior high school (their eighth or ninth year of formal education) they are usually well entrenched in a world of their peers. Parents and teachers assume a secondary place as a source of "important" values, and what looms important is what one's "crowd" thinks. Since, at this age and on through high school, one's crowd is found among one's fellow students primarily, behavior is carried on in direct reference to the school. Burton R. Clark identifies three types of subcultures to which almost every junior and senior high school student belongs.[15] The first is the so-called *fun subculture*, which places utmost emphasis on having a good time. In this subculture, one must have a "good personality," must have *savoir faire* in the realm of clothes, autos, "hanging out" places, and sports, both as spectator and participant in the local

---

[14] Arnold W. Green, *Sociology*, 4th ed. (New York, McGraw-Hill, 1965), p. 499.
[15] Burton R. Clark, *Educating the Expert Society* (San Francisco, Chandler Publishing Co., 1962), Chapter 7.

school rivalries. Books and learning represent drudgery and low status. The second subculture is described by Clark as the *academic subculture*. Those who participate in these groups place high value on being a good student, on discussing serious questions and interests of the day, and on high educational achievement. This subculture tends to be considerably less popular in secondary schools than the fun subculture. The least popular, but the most apparent, student subculture is termed the *delinquent subculture*. Members of such groups are known for their overt expression of contempt for the school and its faculty; their defiant attitude toward any form of regulation; and a general rebellion against anything and everybody not condoned by their crowd.

The collegiate world also has subcultures.[16] They tend to be advanced editions of the high school subcultures. The *collegiate subculture* stresses the social and secular world. Its routines are dates, parties, sports, and fun. Its stars are the football and basketball heroes and various beauty queens. The members of collegiate subculture exhibit great loyalty to their school, but are quite content to barely get by in their studies. The *vocational subculture* is made up of students who are single-mindedly preparing themselves for a career or profession. The passing scene makes little impression on this group and they in turn, develop little school loyalty. Their intellectual commitment is limited to the necessary courses, credits, and skills which will lead to the occupational goal in mind. Not infrequently students of this subculture are engaged in full or part-time employment off campus. The *academic subculture* is one that includes the serious, hard-working, "concerned" students. The library and the stimulating teacher are sought, and classroom topics and assignments are debated endlessly. Honor classes, colloquia, and seminars are the gathering places of members of this subculture, and ultimate goals are advanced and professional degrees. The *nonconformist subculture* marks the rebellious element among college students. The intellectual or pseudo-intellectual student who is consumed with one or another "idealism" and who resents the mundane, "practical" decision-making of college administrators is a member of this subculture. Nonconformity is expressed in sloppy dress, and disdain of other "middle-class" standards. It is probable that this group tends to be the most *conforming* of all student subcultures because, in their great desire to be recognized as nonconformists, they tend to adopt a completely standardized uniform. In the 1960's a beard or long hair, and an unwashed, unpressed look became faddish. The members of this subculture have been described as "somewhat detached from the college as a whole," but often deeply concerned with the *ideas* of the classroom and current issues.

PROFESSIONAL, SEMIPROFESSIONAL, AND ALUMNI ORGANIZATIONS: Again addressing ourselves to the total school picture, rather than

---

[16] Burton R. Clark and Martin A. Trow, "Determinants of College Student Subcultures," selection in Leonard Broom and Philip Selznick, *Sociology*, 3rd ed. (New York, Harper & Row, 1963), pp. 453-454.

just to advanced systems, we can call attention to organizations associated with, but not structurally a part of, the given school. These organizations, in effect, set the policy and programs for educational social systems, although their voice is indirect rather than direct. They include not only local and state teachers associations, but national organizations like the NEA (National Education Association) and AAUP (American Association of University Professors). Added to these organizations are the many subject-matter societies and associations, such as those in mathematics, biology, agriculture, and history, and so on. At another level of operation, semiprofessional organizations like the Parent–Teachers Association wield influence on school systems by tying the local community to the school. At a third level of organizational influence, almost all secondary and advanced educational systems in the United States have alumni organizations of one kind or another. These organizations concern themselves with every type of activity imaginable, from raising funds for employing "professors of distinction" to buying equipment for the football players. The influence of alumni groups is literally untold in the total support and control they provide their alma maters in the realm of politics, economics, and educational policy.

SOME FEATURES OF EDUCATIONAL SYSTEMS IN THE UNITED STATES

The characteristics of educational systems in general have been noted. It serves a purpose of illustrating how these structures operate in a specific setting to review a few salient features of education in the United States.

IDEOLOGICAL FOUNDATIONS OF THE EDUCATIONAL SYSTEM: Through the years, the formal educational system of the United States has rooted itself in at least three ideologies or value orientations. This is not to say that all persons have agreed on these tenets, but that education in general has taken a turn in these directions. The first is a *faith in education* which almost approaches a religious fervor. It is a near unanimous belief that the welfare and progress of both the individual and the nation depends on education. This belief is so strong that one would be hard put to find a dissenter. The second major belief is that all should be given the opportunity to become learned. It has been called the ideology of *mass education.* This notion is so entrenched in the nation that attendance in a tax-supported or comparable school is compulsory (in most states) until an age when a capable child has had an opportunity to achieve functional literacy. The third basic orientation of education in the United States is *vocational education.* It is widely felt that schools should include courses of study leading to specialized training for particular jobs—engineer, home economist, teacher. Emphasis on vocational education is found throughout the educational system, from the secondary schools to the great universities.

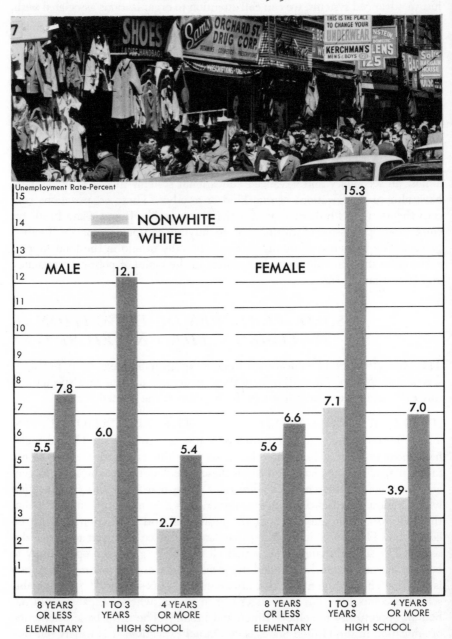

Source: *Social Development: Key to the Great Society*, U. S. Deartment of Health, Education,
and Welfare, Welfare Administration, Division of Research Publication No. 15 (Washington, D. C.,
U. S. Government Printing Office, 1966), p. 29. Photograph courtesy of Chase Manhattan Bank.

RECENT ENROLLMENT TRENDS: Increased school attendance at all levels has continued in the nation to the point where it is appropriate to speak of an enrollment explosion. In 1965 there were some 56 million school children and college students attending classes. During the 1960's, the country's high schools are expected to add an average of 640,000 students a year to their enrollment and the colleges and universities will add some 270,000 students a year. Gains in elementary schools are expected to average 350,000 annually. It is estimated that by 1970, there will be well over 60 million students of all kinds in the nation.

ECONOMIC BENEFITS OF EDUCATION: It was pointed out in Chapter 10 that education is oftentimes closely related to both occupation and economic success. This relationship is clearly demonstrated in the United States. Dollar returns on educational investment are tricky to compute in the sense that many well-educated people such as housewives never enter the labor market, some people with little formal education achieve great economic success, and the worth of the dollar fluctuates a great deal. However, it has been calculated (by a distinguished economist, Dr. T. W. Schultz of the University of Chicago) that for each dollar spent for all education there is a return of about 17 cents each year. It is also possible to demonstrate that a four year college diploma in the United States is worth as much in pay as 20 years' experience without a diploma. What the future will mean in terms of the relation of education and employment opportunity is drastically shown in Figure 18-1. Here it can be seen that persons without a high school education will literally be unemployable in the near future. At the present time (1965) slightly less than half of the adults in the nation are high school graduates.

THE DROPOUT: EDUCATIONAL DILEMMA AND CHALLENGE: Despite the fact that almost three-fourths of the young people of the United States will have at least a high school education in 1970, more than 7.5 million pupils will drop out of school in the preceding decade. The grades from which they will drop out are shown in Figure 18-2. Most of these dropouts will be from lower socio-economic families. Many of these families will be broken and the majority will offer only limited cultural opportunities. A high percentage of the dropouts will be members of minority groups and migratory farm workers. Although dropouts tend to have a lower than average IQ and are more likely to be delinquents, tests have proved that most of them can become productive members of society. This is the challenge that the educational systems of the nation must meet, since dropouts can be considered, partly at least, as a dysfunction of these systems.

SCHOOL DESEGREGATION: A STATE OF TRANSITION: In 1954, the United States Supreme Court ruled that racial segregation in public schools was unconstitutional. This ruling had far-reaching effects for the school systems of all southern states and many systems in other parts of the nation as well. In every instance where a school system has been confronted with the necessity of adding Negro children, it has meant some adjustment

FIGURE 18-2.   *Dropouts by Last School Grade Completed.*

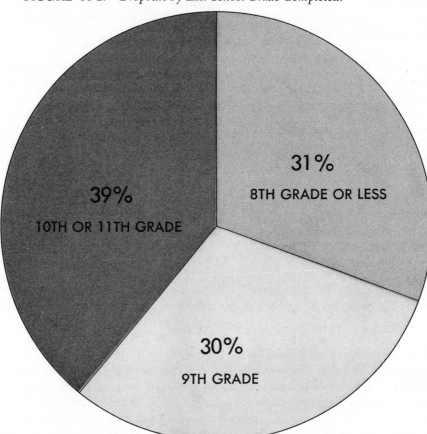

Source: *Converging Social Trends, Emerging Social Problems,* U. S. Department of Health, Education, and Welfare (Washington, D. C., U. S. Government Printing Office, 1964), p. 42.

on the part of members of the system. In many places violence occurred and compliance did not come until court decrees were handed down. It appears that the problem has been worked out in some communities but others remain the scene of resistance. The best that can be said is that the current state is a transitory one fraught with many role stresses and strains.

HIGHER EDUCATION IN A COMPLEX SOCIETY: In closing this very brief outline of some of the features of education in the United States, it is fitting to show the extent to which higher education in the nation has become a most complex operation. Such systems are usually divided into four major divisions of activity. First, and usually the most important, is the education division. Broadly speaking this division is charged with instruction and research, both of which can be far-flung activities. State universities, for example, maintain agricultural extension and agricultural experiment station personnel in all sections of a state. Other types of extension teaching, including correspondence work, may extend the operation of a given university to far countries of the world, where armed forces are stationed. Contracts with the federal government or with large foundations may send university personnel almost anywhere to do almost any type of research imaginable. In this regard, many university professors serve as part-time consultants to government agencies and private concerns, and in turn many employees of private or public agencies teach courses at various colleges and universities. The registrar's office with its vital record-keeping function is an important part of this division.

The second division of systems of higher education is concerned with student life and extracurricular activity. This is a social control operation of a rather unique type. Housing arrangements, including the working out of regulations, feeding arrangements, all types of entertainment, the matter of societies and social organizations, plus all of the activity associated with athletics, where this type of activity is prevalent, makes this division of the university a very involved activity indeed.

The third division of vital importance to an educational system is the business division. Since most colleges and universities have enrollments in the thousands—some are anticipating as many as 50,000 or more in the near future—it takes a very complicated social and mechanical machinery to pay the necessary salaries, do the necessary banking, and in many instances, do the vital solicitation of funds. In addition, when large-scale research activity is in the picture, there is the matter of keeping track of many independent funds.

The fourth division of most advanced educational systems is more or less a miscellaneous one. Normally such activities as those of alumni organizations, university presses, directors of short courses and conferences, and campus police would fall under such a division. All of these activities are important, both in terms of public relations and in terms of a well-rounded program.

It is interesting to note that the findings of a recent study indicate that the complexity of a major state university in the United States is such that even state-level public leaders are ignorant of many of its activities. It is also significant that their concept of the mission of the university and their reactions toward its programs and problems vary considerably.[17]

[17] Eugene C. Erickson, *Higher Education in a Complex Society* (Pullman, Washington, Washington Agriculture Experimental Station, Bulletin 659, 1964).

SUMMARY

The "need" that humans have for explaining the nonempirical and the empirical world in which they live gives rise to the social institutions of education and religion. In each instance, these needs are served by institutionalized social structures (groups and systems) that contain roles related to fulfillment of the specific need. Systems in which a majority of the roles are dedicated to either religious or educational goals are termed religious or educational systems, respectively.

Religious systems are unique in several ways. They differ from magic systems in that supernatural powers are not considered manipulatible; rather it is believed they act according to their own volition. Science and religion differ in that the latter deals with a supernatural world that lies outside the range of scientific observation and analysis and involves faith (or belief in what cannot be verified by the senses). The structural features of religion are seen in the theologies and creeds subscribed to, the rituals, codes, practices, and techniques used, the sacred objects, symbols and equipment utilized, and in the organizational character of religious enterprises. The functions of religion are, in a broad sense, facilitation of man's quest for moral identity; provision of interpretations for man's environment; promotion of social cohesion and solidarity; and many specific other things such as charitable, recreational, and educational activity.

Educational social systems provide a formal approach to socialization by explaining the empirical world. Their structural features include their organizational character, levels and types of instruction, type of support and control which is in evidence, and whether they are compulsory or noncompulsory in nature. These systems function primarily to transmit the cultural heritage, to acquaint the individual with diverse roles, to prepare the individual for special roles, to provide a basis for evaluating status, and to promote change.

Supplementary Readings

Bertrand, Alvin L., "School Attendance and Attainment: Function and Dysfunction of School and Family Social Systems," *Social Forces*, Vol. 40 (March, 1962), pp. 228-233.

Clark, Burton R., *Educating the Expert Society* (San Francisco, Chandler Publishing Co., 1962).

Coleman, James B., "Adolescent Subculture and Academic Achievement," *American Journal of Sociology*, Vol. 65 (January, 1960), pp. 337-347; and also in LASSWELL ET AL. and O'BRIEN ET AL.

Corwin, Ronald G., *A Sociology of Education* (New York, Appleton-Century-Crofts, 1965).

Fichter, Joseph H., S. J., *Social Relations in the Urban Parish* (Chicago, University of Chicago Press, 1954).

Gross, Neal, "The Sociology of Education," selection in Robert K. Merton, Leonard Broom and Leonard S. Cottrell, Jr., Eds., *Sociology Today: Problems and Prospects* (New York, Basic Books, 1959). Chapter V.

Noss, John B., *Man's Religions,* 3rd ed. (New York, Macmillan, 1961).

Philips, Derek L., Ed., *Studies in American Society* (New York, Crowell, 1965), pp. 1-199.

Wilson, Bryan, "An Analysis of Sect Development," *American Sociological Review,* Vol. 24 (February, 1959), pp. 3-15; and also in O'BRIEN ET AL.

Yinger, J. Milton, *Sociology Looks at Religion* (New York, Macmillan, 1961).

19

ECONOMIC

AND POLITICAL

SYSTEMS AS

INSTITUTIONALIZED

SOCIAL

STRUCTURES

By now the student should be aware of the general nature of social systems as institutionalized social structures. It is the purpose of this chapter to review the important aspects of the economic and political systems which are more or less universally found in all societies. These systems operate primarily to satisfy the needs that people have for dividing available resources and controlling themselves. The latter are the respective general functions of the economy and government social institutions. We speak here of the economy as a social institution for the sake of consistency. *The* **economy,** *as a social institution, may be defined as a system of culturally defined behavioral patterns that serves a pattern-maintenance function by providing institutionalized ways for the allocation of scarce resources*—those things that people cannot have all they want of when they want it. **Government,** *as a social institution, is a system of culturally defined behavioral patterns that serves a pattern-maintenance function by providing institutionalized ways for members of a society to work out and control their relationships with one another.*

ECONOMIC SOCIAL SYSTEMS

NATURE OF ECONOMIC SYSTEMS

DEFINITION: Every person who has had an introduction to social science has probably had to learn a definition of economics. Most such definitions imply that economics is concerned with how people obtain and share scarce resources. Here we must seek a more encompassing understanding of an economic social system. In keeping with our previous definitions of institutionalized social structures, *an economic system may be defined as a socially sanctioned grouping of persons united for the purpose of producing, distributing, or consuming scarce goods and services, who interact according to well-defined roles.*

IMPORTANCE OF ECONOMIC SYSTEMS: The importance of economic systems is easy to demonstrate, especially in highly advanced societies. This importance is based on the inability of individuals to supply the things they want for themselves. The greater division of labor, the more importance economic systems assume. Other systems, such as families, schools, government agencies, and even churches, survive because of, and participate to a degree in, economic interaction.

Besides production and distribution activity, economic groups also encompass the services needed by members of a society. Some common services such as entertainment, education, spiritual guidance, financial help, and the repairing of many items are associated with everyday life. All activity related to the production of goods and the rendering of services in turn is directly associated with the social-psychological "wants" that motivate humans, including the following. (1) Physical needs—the need for food, shelter and clothing. In this regard it should not be forgotten that many of the specific forms of these needs are determined by the particular culture. What we eat, the houses we build and the clothes we wear are largely matters of prevailing customs. (2) Power—that is, the control of resources which enables one to exercise power. Wealth is one source of power in most societies and since economic success is measured in terms of wealth, there is a definite tie with power. (3) Recognition and approval—in most societies, economic possessions such as automobiles, houses, swimming pools, or whatnot are a basis of social status. Therefore, individuals are motivated to economic activity in order to achieve status or approval. (4) Welfare or noneconomic motives—many times economic activity is a means toward a noneconomic end. Most of the noneconomic ends are sociological in character. One example is seen when people work hard so as to leave sums of money for other people to use; as is true in philanthropies. Other times people pursue economic activity simply because they wish to pursue a career intrinsically; they work, though not obliged to, in order to support themselves.

STRUCTURAL FEATURES OF ECONOMIC SYSTEMS

The structural aspects of economic systems are not as clearly identified as are the structural aspects of systems devoted to certain other types of institutionalized goals. In this discussion, an attempt will be made first to outline the more or less pervasive patterns of relationships that exist in all systems relative to economic endeavors, and then the specific characteristics of a particular type of economic social system will be described.

PROPERTY RIGHTS, DIVISION OF LABOR, AND EXCHANGE: Moore points out that "the institutional controls within which any economic system operates must include those governing the division of labor, the disposition of property rights, and the methods of distribution." He goes on to say that, ". . . the social order must provide answers to the questions: who does what, who controls what (and whom), and who gets what?"[1] Each of these structural conditions for social institutions will now be considered in some detail.

(1) *Property Rights.* The word property has its origin in the language of the ancient Romans. This term was used by them as *propter,* a Latin adverb meaning "according to custom." The word gradually spread to France, and from there followed the Norman conquerors into England. Here is was anglicized as *proportie* and *propriete,* and associated with feudal privileges or relationships. In the eighteenth and early nineteenth centuries, about the time of the Industrial Revolution, the word assumed its present connotation. Today, there is common agreement that property is, "the system of rights of persons or other social units in 'scarce' values."[2]

In a general sense then, property may be viewed as defining the relationships between persons which relate to scarce values. As Moore states, "a value is meaningless unless there is potential challenges to that right."[3] In this context, property must be understood to organize the power relations, real or potential, between persons holding such rights and those persons who do not have these rights. Property rights always appear in economic systems, and the actors in these systems align themselves, that is, rank themselves, according to

---

[1] Wilbert E. Moore, *Economy and Society* (Garden City, New York, Doubleday, 1955), p. 9.
[2] *Ibid.,* p. 12.
[3] *Ibid.*

the property rights they hold. This fact makes clear the structural foundation that the concept of property has for these systems.

(2) *Division of Labor.* From the time of Adam Smith the concept of division of labor has been a popular one in social science analysis. Although economists and sociologists continue to view this concept in somewhat different ways, it refers to differentiation of role within economic systems in both disciplines. Economists point out that division of labor explains how the allocation of useful work is accomplished and what is causally involved in specialization. The sociologists, by contrast, look upon labor as only a basis for assignment of status and roles, and make an association between occupation and work and such personal criteria as age, sex, race, and education. Taken together the two views provide an explanation for division of labor as a universal structural element of economic social systems.

(3) *Exchange or Distribution.* The structural implication that exchange or distribution has for economic systems is more abstract. Traditional economic theory tends to assume economic rewards are assigned according to merit, that is, according to the economic contribution of the actor. This interpretation is too narrow to explain fully the distribution principle, even in a "free" market, but it does make obvious that each person in an economic system has a certain claim upon the system's wealth. Wealth is in turn translated into power and rank.

At this point a note on money is appropriate. Money is the so-called "catalyst" that serves to facilitate exchange. Money creates greater freedom for both buyers and sellers of goods and services, since it removes the necessity of a barter system and depersonalizes the relationship between the two parties to the transaction. It also creates a common denominator of economic value so that a certain worth may be assigned to the scarce values sought. In addition, money gives rise to certain other economic activity and this gives rise to additional economic systems such as banks and other credit operations.

TYPES OF GOVERNMENT CONTROL
EXERCISED OVER ECONOMIC ACTIVITY

Another broad structural aspect of economic systems is found in the kind of government control that is exercised over economic activity. Five types can be readily listed. In this regard, it should be remembered that no type of government control is ever found in "pure" form in advanced societies. As the population of countries becomes larger and their culture becomes more complex, it is difficult to adhere to ideal patterns. In the United States, for example, it was necessary to increase controls to regulate increasing economic activity made possible by advancing technology. The invention of automobiles required driving regulations and the invention of radio and television required control of the airwaves. In each instance the lack of control would have meant chaos. The automobile and radio and television enterprises, therefore, had to be placed under regulation. Thus the term "regulated capitalism" is used to describe the type of government control that exists over economic activity in the nation. In the definitions below, only the ideal picture will be portrayed, that is, features of pure capitalism, pure socialism, and so forth.

(1) *Capitalism.* This is a type of politico-economic system which permits very great, though not unlimited, freedom of use of capital by private owners. Usually, under capitalism the state reserves the right of *eminent domain.* This right permits the confiscation of privately held property for uses declared to be in the greater public interests. Normally, however, compensation is given to the owner of the property. Under capitalistic systems it is also customary for certain properties related to public services to be held and/or controlled by the government; this includes public utilities and public facilities, such as roads and harbors.

(2) *Socialism.* Socialism, as a politico-economic system, permits private ownership and operation of smaller economic enterprises, but holds the major industries and economic activities under public control. For example, public utilities, transportation systems, health, education, sources of fuel and power such as coal mines or oil fields, and iron and steel industries are likely to be under government operation.

(3) *Fascism.* Under fascism, the politico-economic system is characterized by rigid governmental regulation. The distinction between fascism and socialism lies in the *purpose* of the government control and the *interests for which it is maintained.* In fascist countries control of major economic enterprises is in the hands of a small group of persons who control these enterprises for their own purposes and interests. In other words, the mass of citizens have little or no voice in the determination of how economic systems will be operated.

(4) *Communism.* Under pure communism there is very little if any private ownership of property. The theory is that everything belongs to the people and that all should share alike in wealth. Such a system is difficult to maintain in a modern society because certain individuals must be accorded greater or lesser power over certain forms of wealth. When this happens, it follows that some members of the society become privileged and the original ideology is lost or at least compromised.

THE ORGANIZATIONAL FEATURES OF BUSINESS AND LABOR ENTERPRISES

All modern societies include some kind of business and labor organizations. These organizations all exhibit structural patterns that are more or less institutionalized. In business, for example, owners are separated from managers and top managers are separated from lesser managers, who in turn are separated from workers, and so on. In labor groups, there is a hierarchy of officials as well. These hierarchies indicate that *economic systems may be studied as bureaucracies.* While this is not the place to describe bureaucratic structures in detail, it is appropriate to view some of the problems of a modern bureaucracy because they indicate the types of structural relations, including the resultant stresses and strains, which characterize business and labor in economic systems.

One such list of problems was worked up by Arnold Green.[4] (1) *Personality Manipulation.* This problem stems from the fact that in a bureaucratic structure it is necessary to manipulate personalities (rather than things) for the achievement of goals and objectives. The problem arises when status relations become confused with personal relations and friendships and other "nonobjective" considerations enter into the decision-making process. (2) *Communication.* In a bureaucracy, the problem of communication relates to the degree of depersonalization of communiques. Office memoranda and other nonpersonal messages often are not as meaningful to workers or lesser functionaries as face-to-face orders or explanations. Also, the channels of communication can and do break down when there are many steps from the higher echelons in the bureaucratic hierarchy to the lower echelons. (3) *Impersonality and Responsibility.* Because of the fact that impersonality rules in large bureaucratic structures, the fixing of responsibilities is either difficult or impossible. Each person in the rank hierarchy tends to pass the blame for whatever goes wrong on to the next person—up or down the line of command. (4) *The Place of Initiative.* It is generally conceded that bureaucratic structures tend to dry up individual initiative since employees mainly get ahead by going along with the system and serving the necessary number of years. In this regard, those who demonstrate too much productivity are likely to be subtly or not so subtly, "brought into line" by their fellow workers. (5) *"Latent Structures."* Almost all bureaucratic organizations develop what are called "latent structures." These structures, composed of groups or individuals who have the opportunity to usurp power, serve to efficiently block action that is not condoned by those persons included in the structure. An example would be an old army sergeant who has a close personal relation with the general in command, perhaps because of past campaigns together. The sergeant can literally bypass many officers, and thus forces everyone to get on his good side. In many offices, the secretaries hold such power with the boss, and in effect, "rule the roost." (6) *Program Unification.* A final problem that occurs in bureaucratic structures is the difficulty of collating or integrating the various subunits of the organization. Many illustrations could be given where some department of the government or business in a large organization is actually working at cross-purposes with other departments. This situation arises because there is no overall planning that coordinates and integrates all activity.

In closing this brief discussion, it may be noted that, despite the problems

[4] Arnold W. Green, *Sociology,* 4th ed. (New York, McGraw-Hill, 1964), pp. 307-323.

that arise in bureaucratic structures, no better way has been devised to organize and implement the activity of large economic-political systems. The giant industries, the large labor unions, and all other economic systems are structured to include top levels of policy and decision-makers, intermediate levels of functionaries, and lower levels of workers and related followers. The intent of a bureaucracy is to efficiently weld these various groups into a smoothly functioning organization.

THE FUNCTIONS OF ECONOMIC SYSTEMS

It was brought out earlier in this chapter that social institutions come into existence because they serve to satisfy certain human needs. Economic systems function to meet both biologically and culturally derived needs. In the first instance, physical survival makes it mandatory that man eat and be sheltered against weather. In the second instance, man *develops* a need for a particular kind of food, or certain type of house, or a particular mode of transportation, because of cultural experience. These needs must be met in the face of a degree of scarcity of the goods and services which are demanded. As pointed out before, the functions of economic systems, in a broad sense, are to fulfill these demands. Specific functions can be elaborated to a great extent, but boil down to three major goals.

ECONOMIC PRODUCTION: Somewhere, somehow, the goods and services that humans demand must be created. This type of activity, which involves the manipulation of natural resources or the development of skills, is the first function of economic systems. Many classifications have been developed to help in the analysis of production. One such classification distinguishes between (1) the primary production industries—those devoted to the processing of natural resources (mining, fishing, and agriculture), (2) the secondary production industries—those engaged in the processing of materials so as to enhance their usefulness (weaving, mills, automobile assembly plants), (3) the tertiary production industries—those represented by some sort of service activity (entertainment, education, health care).

DISTRIBUTION: Economic systems also function as institutionalized social structures for the division and transfer of economic resources. The way economic resources are divided has already been noted. The transfer function is necessitated because it is seldom that natural resources occur at the place where consumers of these resources can and do congregate. These resources must therefore be transported from their source of origin to various places for further processing as well as ultimate consumption. Transportation systems, plus the many allied "parasite" organizations are important in this process. With regard to the latter, the advertising business is designed largely to increase demand, which in turn promotes more production and wider distribution.

CONSUMPTION: Once goods are produced and distributed they must be disposed of, or else they will lose their scarce character and cease to be economically worthwhile. Here, then, we can see that the "using up" of goods and services is in and of itself an economic function. Man cannot consume without producing, any more than he can long continue to produce without consumption.

SOME FEATURES OF THE
UNITED STATES ECONOMY

Again, it serves a purpose of illustration to review some of the more important characteristics of a specific institutional setting in an advanced society. The following are some of the more important features of the United States economy.

IDEOLOGICAL FOUNDATIONS AND TRADITIONS: Through the years certain ideological standards have been used as frames of reference for economic activity in the United States. These standards apparently had their origin in the so-called Protestant ethic, which is related to the rise of capitalism —the prevailing economic system in the nation.[5] The Protestant ethic is characterized by (1) Private enterprise, backed by a philosophy that through competition and with a free market to sell one's labor or produce, individuals rise to their deserved positions of power, prominence and wealth. (2) The pursuit of profits, backed by a belief that the taking of a profit is both ethical and accounts for national economic growth and expansion. (3) Doctrine of work, backed by a great respect for the self-made man and "honest" toil. (4) Non-interference by government, backed by a philosophy that government should support and protect business but should refrain from too much interference with the operation of business men.

At the present time the standards mentioned above are tending to give way in the face of massive change. However, they still provide the broader normative structure for economic endeavors.

AN AFFLUENT SOCIETY: The gross national product (GNP) is the sum total of all the goods and services a nation produces. This total hit 700 billion dollars in the United States in the mid-1960's. It is continuing to climb at a rather sharp rate and expected to reach 960-970 billion dollars by 1975. Family and personal income has followed the same trend and the growing affluency

[5] Max Weber, The Protestant Ethic and the Spirit of Capitalism, translated by Talcott Parsons (New York, Scribner, 1930).

of the society is attested by increased use of many pleasure items and of growing leisure time. Consumption of such items as radios, television sets, boats, and phonograph records is skyrocketing, as is the purchase of tickets for spectator sports and other forms of amusement. (See Figure 19-1.) Affluency has had a close relation to an increasingly complex system of producing goods and services. However, this very complexity has resulted in the appearance in rather large numbers of people who are aptly called "other Americans." These are the people who are found in city slums, mountain cabins, farm shacks, and labor camps because they have not been able to keep up with the cultural demands of a complex world: they are now poverty groups. They represent a problem that has aroused considerable concern and activity from the more fortunate elements of the society.

AN EMERGING MASS SOCIETY: The United States exhibits all the characteristics of an emerging mass society that were described in Chapter 7. It has an urban-industrial population of large size, mass techniques are employed in manufacturing and marketing, automation is the order of the day, and people are brought together for all types of collective action on a large scale. Since this picture has been described in some detail before, there is no need of extensive elaboration here. These trends need to be reviewed, however.

(1) *Rapidly Changing Labor Force.* The labor force of the United States is expected to increase by 18 percent from 1960 to 1970 and to reach an all-time high of nearly 86 million people at this time. This increase will represent a greater rate of increase than that of the population as a whole—and a 50 percent greater increase than that experienced by the labor force in the preceding decade. At the same time that the labor force is increasing rapidly, there is a changing picture in terms of what is required in the way of a laborer—more and more education and experience are being demanded. Another striking development is the increasing number of women working. Almost two out of every five women are already in the labor force. It is also of great significance that the labor force is increasing in mobility. A study in the early 1960's showed that 8 million workers made over 11 million job changes in one year. The big question for the future is whether the tremendous number of new workers which will enter the labor force in the 1970's and 1980's will be able to obtain the necessary education and reeducation to hold on to employment. In this regard, the fast pace of change means that one *must* keep up. For example, General Motors annually retrains more than 7,000 of its employees for new jobs.

(2) *Unions, Management, and Government Becoming Increasingly Interrelated.* Not many years ago labor unions were bitterly fighting the management of industrial and business operations for what they considered their rightful place in the United States' social and economic structure. Government agencies were kept busy and agitated in an effort to effectively use the power of the state to prevent economic disorder. Trends in keeping with an emerging

FIGURE 19-1. *Millions of Dollars Buy Pleasure.*

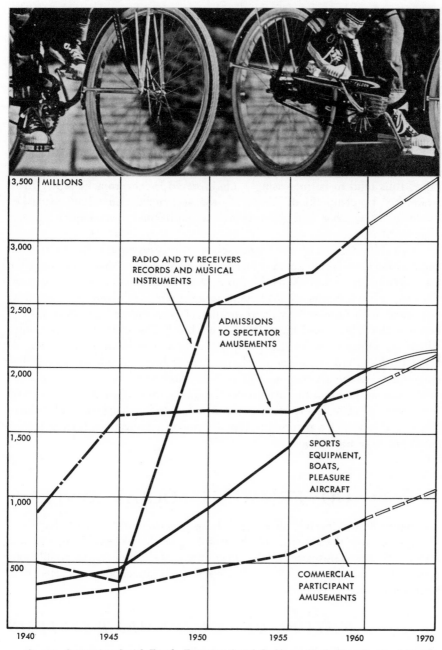

3,500 | MILLIONS

RADIO AND TV RECEIVERS
RECORDS AND MUSICAL
INSTRUMENTS

3,000

2,500

ADMISSIONS
TO SPECTATOR
AMUSEMENTS

2,000

SPORTS
EQUIPMENT,
BOATS,
PLEASURE
AIRCRAFT

1,500

1,000

500

COMMERCIAL
PARTICIPANT
AMUSEMENTS

1940   1945   1950   1955   1960   1970

Source: *Converging Social Trends Emerging Social Problems,* U. S. Department of Health, Education and Welfare (Washington, D. C., U. S. Government Printing Office, 1964), p. 17. (Note: Author of text has extended trends from 1960 to 1970 for the sake of illustration.) Photograph courtesy of American Machine and Foundry Company.

mass society, such as diversification and automation, have changed this picture to a remarkable degree. Great corporations and labor unions alike now maintain lobbies in Washington and in state capitals to secure favorable legislation. Governmental organizations, as a result of this pressure, distribute defense and other contracts in ways designed to pacify these power groups. In turn, government legislation, such as fair employment practices and minimum wages, is designed to minimize labor conflict. At another level of action, unions are less involved in squabbles among themselves because of the merger of unions, a strategic move in the face of unending change that makes jurisdictional lines hard to maintain. Also, business organizations increasingly divide the market among themselves, rather than engage in competitive wars. Prices thus tend to be increasingly administered by government rather than established by competition. All in all, the accommodation taking place between industry, labor, and government may be likened to a complex balance of power structures.

(3) *The Advent of the Organization Man Personality.* In the face of encroaching mass society, man is faced with many devices that tend to shatter his individuality and to reduce him to a pawn in an organizational structure. This trend has led men like Whyte to write extensively about "the organization men" who form intermediate stratum of corporation leadership, falling between the "elites" and the masses of workers.[6] The social ethics or norms which are imperatives for this group include at least three propositions: A belief in the group as the source of creativity, a belief in what is called "belongingness" as the ultimate need of an individual, and a belief in the application of science to attain the latter stage. To follow these tenets is to place one's "organization" above every other group in which one participates. The emergence of this sort of a personality type has many ramifications for the future development of the nation.

GOVERNMENT SOCIAL SYSTEMS

No matter how primitive, all societies have governmental systems that exercise control over the activities of the members of the society. The structural forms of these systems vary widely, depending on factors of size of population, value orientations, and historical developments. This section is devoted to a brief overview of their characteristics.

NATURE OF GOVERNMENT SYSTEMS

Historians have traced the origin and development of governmental systems of given societies. The legal systems, the law enforcement patterns, and the

[6] William H Whyte, Jr., *The Organization Man* (Garden City, New York, Doubleday, 1957).

political ideology of most nations have been traced in this manner and are somewhat familiar to all. Historical treatises provide validation for the fact that government systems derive their organization or structure from society. In this regard, the question often arises, When does a "government" exist? The answer provides a definition of government systems at the same time that it clarifies the nature of government institutions. **Government systems** exist *when a socially sanctioned grouping of persons unite together to establish means and methods for the adjustment and control of their relationships, and interact according to well-defined roles.* Johnson elaborates this definition somewhat. He contends that a government (system) exercises imperative control within a definite territory and that it successfully claims or exercises a monopoly or use of force in this territory. He points out that there are some governments that claim a monopoly of force only with respect to certain rules while other governments enforce other rules within the same geographic area. He notes that government may condone the use of force by persons or groups who are not associated with the government.[7] Respectively, these two points may be illustrated as follows: the federal government of a nation has certain jurisdiction over the behavior of all peoples in a nation, but local governments within the nation maintain certain other powers, such as regulation of schools, and some police functions. In the second instance, parents may well exercise power or control over their children without being a part of, or having specific permission from, the federal or local governments.

GOVERNMENT VERSUS STATE

In order to fully understand the nature of government, it must be made clear how government as a concept is distinguished from "state" as a concept. The *state* is generally conceded by social scientists to arise out of the centralized power manifested by some, but not all, forms of government. To illustrate, in a patriarchal family or nomadic group, the essential elements of government are to be found, but no one would attempt to classify such families or tribes as states. Before a state would be recognized, three ideas must exhibit full development. (1) The notion of state above all else is manifested in patriotism or love of country, as is the idea of national self-determination, or state sovereignty. Green believes this type of national consciousness in part develops as a substitute for the *mystique* of a church that is no longer accepted as universal.[8] (2) Conscription in time of war. Before the development of nation-states, wars were fought by professional armies. It was not until the time of the French Revolution that conscription became widespread. Napoleon conscripted citizens for his army and in doing this, forced others to do the same. (3) The third idea that is important to the concept of state is that

[7] Harry M. Johnson, *Sociology: A Systematic Introduction* (New York, Harcourt, Brace & World, 1960), pp. 313-315.

[8] *Op. cit.*, pp. 356-357.

of individual liberty. Before the rise of the nation-state, the feudal system with its fixed classes was the prevailing pattern in much of the world.

The essential characteristics of a state are (1) citizens, that is, a population that recognizes itself as part of a political body and is willing to submit to the authority of an established government; (2) a fixed and definite territory—in other words, a geographical area within which the above control is maintained; (3) a supreme authority over the actions of the people who make up the citizenry within the territorial boundaries of the state.

There are many theories as to the origin of the state. Most students are familiar with these. They run from the Divine Right theory which held that a king was a divinely appointed ruler, to the Social Contract theory which held that men at some unspecified past time recognized the value of a stable government and formed a contract by which certain individuals were granted the power of ruler. Some hold to the belief that force (conquest by an outside enemy or by an aggressive internal group) is the basis for the development of a state. In actual fact, it is impossible to trace the development of a state to any one origin or single cause or factor. The modern sovereign state has become the principal instrument of public order and reflects the need that peoples have for some agency of control. Actually, the control is vested in governments, which fluctuate and are temporary, although the state tends to persist over time.

THE STRUCTURAL FEATURES OF GOVERNMENT SYSTEMS

The structure of government systems is manifested at various levels, as is true of other types of social systems. At the broadest possible level, classifications vary according to the criteria that are selected. The different structural bases listed are the ones readily identified.

AUTHORITY AND POWER STRUCTURE: Authority and power vary in two general ways in government system. The first is seen in the relations that exist between the central government and the local subdivisions of government. The unitary state is one in which the local government branches exercise power through delegation from the central authority. By contrast, the federal state is one in which the local subdivisions of government have a relatively large extent of independent legal existence such as is found in the various states of the United States. The second is the basis on which governmental authority rests. In democratic states, the authority rests in officials elected by qualified voters to represent the remainder of the citizens. In the so-called totalitarian states, the power is vested in one man or a small group of individuals who do not owe their position to or hold themselves responsible directly to the citizens of the nation.

LEGISLATIVE, EXECUTIVE, AND JUDICIAL STRUCTURES: At another conceptual level, the structure of government may be seen as revolving around certain institutionalized activity. In almost all governments there are groups who make the rules and laws, or at least standardize these relations. Such groups are known as the *legislative structures of the government*. Secondly, there are always groups who have the power to enforce the regulations made. These groups become the *executive or administrative structures of the government*. Finally, some group in government is responsible for judging the exact meaning and application of the laws that have been made. This is the *judicial structure of the government*.

THE ORGANIZATIONAL CHARACTER OF GOVERNMENT ENTERPRISES: The structure of government is also seen in terms of a *bureaucratic structure*. In all modern governments, there are many special departments and sections, whose job it is to take care of special functions or special jobs. In a highly advanced society, government bureaucratic structures are likely to be very much elaborated. Every office and position is defined precisely in legalized jargon, and qualifications for office, duties, salaries, and powers are detailed in literally tons of directives, memoranda, tables of organization, and job descriptions. Figure 19-2 shows the table of organization of the United States Department of Health, Education, and Welfare and illustrates this aspect of the structure of government.

FUNCTIONS OF GOVERNMENT SYSTEMS

Government social systems are institutionalized for the purpose of performing several major functions, which are more or less universal. The way in which these functions are performed varies according to the complexity of the given society's social structure and the political ideology to which its members subscribe.

THE INSTITUTIONALIZATION OF NORMS: This function is primarily accomplished by the legislative bodies of governments. In democratic societies, legislators are elected and are vested with the responsibility and duty to pass laws, which in turn become the guides for normative behavior. Whether or not government legislators are elected, appointed, or simply assume power, the fact remains that they function to make laws and other types of regulations. Most students are thoroughly familiar with this function, as it is basic to social organization.

ENFORCEMENT OF NORMS: A second function of governments is the enforcement of norms. This is simply a manifestation of the necessary social control for putting into effect the laws that have been made. Normally, this type of power is vested in the head of state, the tribal chief, or other government head.

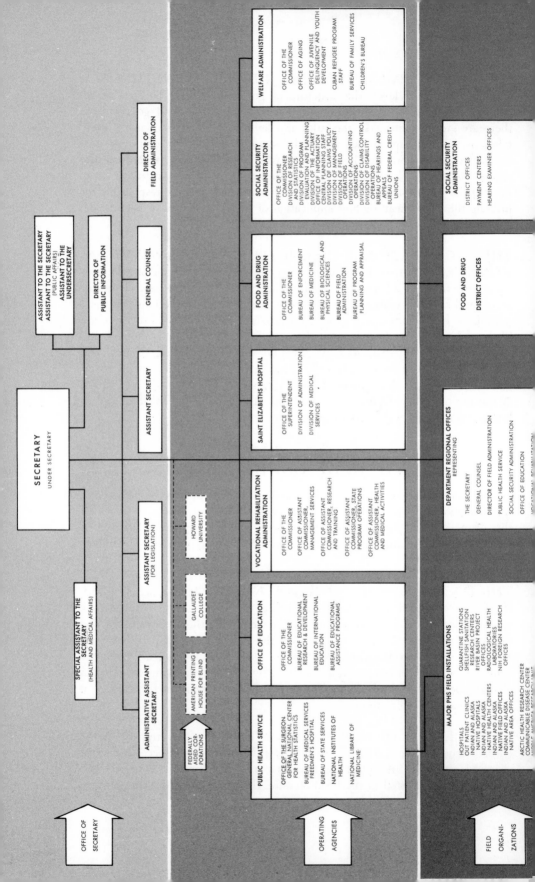

OFFICE OF SECRETARY

SECRETARY
UNDER SECRETARY

SPECIAL ASSISTANT TO THE SECRETARY
(HEALTH AND MEDICAL AFFAIRS)

ASSISTANT TO THE SECRETARY
ASSISTANT TO THE SECRETARY
(PUBLIC AFFAIRS)
ASSISTANT TO THE UNDERSECRETARY

ADMINISTRATIVE ASSISTANT SECRETARY

ASSISTANT SECRETARY
(FOR LEGISLATION)

ASSISTANT SECRETARY

DIRECTOR OF PUBLIC INFORMATION

DIRECTOR OF FIELD ADMINISTRATION

GENERAL COUNSEL

OPERATING AGENCIES

FEDERALLY AIDED COR- PORATIONS

AMERICAN PRINTING HOUSE FOR BLIND

GALLAUDET COLLEGE

HOWARD UNIVERSITY

PUBLIC HEALTH SERVICE
OFFICE OF THE SURGEON GENERAL
NATIONAL CENTER FOR HEALTH STATISTICS
BUREAU OF MEDICAL SERVICES
FREEDMEN'S HOSPITAL
BUREAU OF STATE SERVICES
NATIONAL INSTITUTES OF HEALTH
NATIONAL LIBRARY OF MEDICINE

OFFICE OF EDUCATION
OFFICE OF THE COMMISSIONER
BUREAU OF EDUCATIONAL RESEARCH & DEVELOPMENT
BUREAU OF INTERNATIONAL EDUCATION
BUREAU OF EDUCATIONAL ASSISTANCE PROGRAMS

VOCATIONAL REHABILITATION ADMINISTRATION
OFFICE OF THE COMMISSIONER
OFFICE OF ASSISTANT COMMISSIONER, MANAGEMENT SERVICES
OFFICE OF ASSISTANT COMMISSIONER, RESEARCH AND TRAINING
OFFICE OF ASSISTANT COMMISSIONER, STATE PROGRAM OPERATIONS
OFFICE OF ASSISTANT COMMISSIONER, HEALTH AND MEDICAL ACTIVITIES

SAINT ELIZABETHS HOSPITAL
OFFICE OF THE SUPERINTENDENT
DIVISION OF ADMINISTRATION
DIVISION OF MEDICAL SERVICES

FOOD AND DRUG ADMINISTRATION
OFFICE OF THE COMMISSIONER
BUREAU OF ENFORCEMENT
BUREAU OF MEDICINE
BUREAU OF BIOLOGICAL AND PHYSICAL SCIENCES
BUREAU OF FIELD ADMINISTRATION
BUREAU OF PROGRAM PLANNING AND APPRAISAL

SOCIAL SECURITY ADMINISTRATION
OFFICE OF THE COMMISSIONER
DIVISION OF RESEARCH AND STATISTICS
DIVISION OF PROGRAM EVALUATION AND PLANNING
OFFICE OF THE ACTUARY
OFFICE OF INFORMATION
CENTRAL PLANNING STAFF
DIVISION OF CLAIMS POLICY
DIVISION OF MANAGEMENT
DIVISION OF FIELD OPERATIONS
DIVISION OF ACCOUNTING OPERATIONS
DIVISION OF CLAIMS CONTROL
DIVISION OF DISABILITY OPERATIONS
BUREAU OF HEARINGS AND APPEALS
BUREAU OF FEDERAL CREDIT UNIONS

WELFARE ADMINISTRATION
OFFICE OF THE COMMISSIONER
OFFICE OF AGING
OFFICE OF JUVENILE DELINQUENCY AND YOUTH DEVELOPMENT
CUBAN REFUGEE PROGRAM STAFF
BUREAU OF FAMILY SERVICES
CHILDREN'S BUREAU

FIELD ORGANI- ZATIONS

MAJOR PHS FIELD INSTALLATIONS
HOSPITALS
OUT PATIENT CLINICS
INDIAN AND ALASKA NATIVE HOSPITALS
INDIAN AND ALASKA NATIVE HEALTH CENTERS
INDIAN AND ALASKA NATIVE FIELD OFFICES
INDIAN AND ALASKA NATIVE AREA OFFICES
QUARANTINE STATIONS
SHELLFISH SANITATION RESEARCH CENTERS
RIVER BASIN PROJECT OFFICES
RADIOLOGICAL HEALTH LABORATORIES
NIH FOREIGN RESEARCH OFFICES
ARCTIC HEALTH RESEARCH CENTER
COMMUNICABLE DISEASE CENTER

DEPARTMENT REGIONAL OFFICES
REPRESENTING
THE SECRETARY
GENERAL COUNSEL
DIRECTOR OF FIELD ADMINISTRATION
PUBLIC HEALTH SERVICE
SOCIAL SECURITY ADMINISTRATION
OFFICE OF EDUCATION
VOCATIONAL REHABILITATION

SOCIAL SECURITY ADMINISTRATION
DISTRICT OFFICES
PAYMENT CENTERS
HEARING EXAMINER OFFICES

FOOD AND DRUG
DISTRICT OFFICES

THE ADJUDICATION OF CONFLICT: Governments not only have the function to make and enforce laws, but to interpret the behavior of its citizens with regard to the law as well. In advanced societies the courts serve as the adjudicators of conflict between members of the society. In less advanced groups, more informal means are used, but some person is always delegated the authority by the government to resolve conflicts. This is usually done by assigning guilt or declaring the accused not in violation of the norms.

THE PROMOTION OF THE GENERAL WELFARE: The more or less residual functions of government may be designated as the promotion of the general welfare. This can take a variety of forms. It tends to become more complex with increasing technology and with population increases. Included under this general function are the establishment and control of school systems, the provision for health care, regulations designed to improve communications and other public services, the promotion of certain types of social change, and broad welfare functions. The specific activity of this type varies with political ideology. In the so-called socialistic countries, governments assume many more such functions than is normally true elsewhere.

PROTECTION FROM EXTERNAL ATTACKS: The final function of government to be listed is obvious. On occasion, it becomes necessary for one society to defend itself against another. Such defense may involve physical resistance, as in the case of war. However, it may involve educational programs designed to counter propaganda attacks as well. Even though diplomacy may be used to settle differences, this is still a form of protection.

SOME FEATURES OF THE GOVERNMENT OF THE UNITED STATES

The important features of the United States government again serve as an illustration of the functioning of an institution and its various systems in a particular societal setting.

IDEOLOGICAL FOUNDATIONS AND TRADITIONS: The United States has, from its beginning, been characterized by a democratic tradition—that is, regular institutionalized means have been provided for periodic change of government officials. The notion that this should be done, and the use of specific political procedures for selecting contenders for political office, is deeply ingrained in the traditions of the nation. Other ideological bases for government are that the powers of officials be specifically defined in terms of

FIGURE 19-2. *Department of Health, Education, and Welfare: 1963.*

Source: *New Directions in Health, Education and Welfare Background Papers on Current Emerging Issues* (Washington, D. C., U. S. Government Printing Office, 1963), p. 38.

constitutional by-laws and that the power of one official or branch of government be limited and separated in such a way that the power of another official
or branch serves to check and balance it. There is also a strong feeling which
persists, even though the exigencies of mass change have pointed in another
direction, that the central (federal) government's powers should be limited
to those specified under the Constitution. These beliefs continue to form the
structural foundation for overall political activity.

THE POLITICAL STRUCTURE: By any measure, the political structure
of the United States is large and complicated. To begin with, it encompasses
a population of approximately 200 million people. Only three national entities
have larger populations—China, India, and the Soviet Union. In the second
place, there is an elaborate bureaucratic structure, with literally thousands of
jobs neatly described in terms of necessary qualifications, term of office, pay,
and duties. It is significant that most basic positions remain after a change of
government, although there is considerable shuffling of personalities. In the
third place, government in the United States is the most important employer
in the nation. The vast programs relating to health, education, welfare, and
research, plus support and control of agriculture, industry, public utilities, and
the armed forces literally spreads government employees throughout the nation and world. Finally, it is most important that the political structure of the
nation is a very stable one. In this regard, it is difficult to define what is meant
by political party, or to characterize a party by a distinct set of principles.

PARTICIPATION IN NATIONAL ELECTIONS: It is a paradox of sorts
that citizens of the United States place a high value on the right to vote, but
then do not exercise this right. Voting is heaviest in presidential elections,
with one of the largest votes ever turning out in 1964 when Lyndon Johnson
and Barry Goldwater were candidates. An estimated 69 percent of the civilian
noninstitutional population of voting age cast a ballot in the election, according to United States Census reports. Figure 19-3 shows that there was a substantial difference in voter participation by age. This phenomenon is consistent with younger and older persons not voting in the same relative degree as
middle-aged persons. It is also a pattern that women do not vote as faithfully
as men, and whites vote in considerably larger relative numbers than nonwhites.

POLITICAL POWER IS DIFFUSE: There is a recurrent theme in the
United States that the country is run by a "power elite" which functions quite
effectively at the national level. However, despite persuasive cases, such as
the one made by the late sociologist, C. Wright Mills, in his controversial
book, *The Power Elite,* empirical evidence for such a statement is lacking.
This is not to say that power elites do not exist at lower levels of political

FIGURE 19-3. *Voter Participation in the National Election November 1964.*

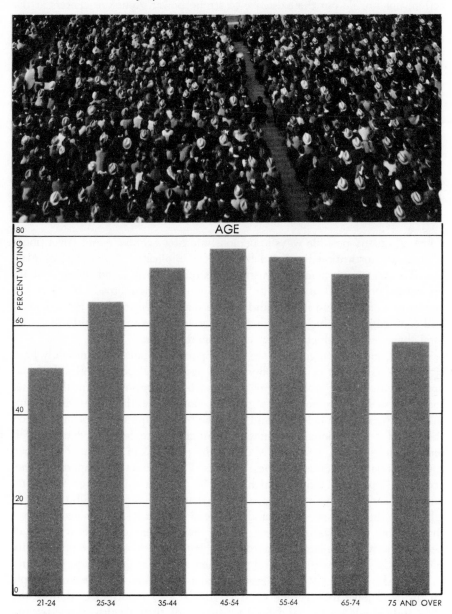

Source: *Current Population Reports,* U. S. Bureau of the Census (Washington, D. C., U. S. Government Printing Office, 1965), Series P-20, No. 143, cover. Photograph courtesy of United Nations Organization.

action, nor to rule out the existence of strong power groups or centers at the national level. It is simply to recognize that the political structure of the nation is so large, complex, and changing that one group would have great difficulty gaining and holding power for an extended time.

LAND TENURE SYSTEMS: AN ILLUSTRATION OF THE RELATIONSHIP BETWEEN ECONOMIC AND GOVERNMENT SYSTEMS AND SYSTEMS OF SOCIAL ORGANIZATION

There are many possible ways to demonstrate how economic and government systems are institutionalized and have direct implication for social organization. Land tenure systems demonstrate this relationship. Land tenure systems are related to agricultural activity and so have as their broad objectives the production of food and fiber. **Land tenure** may be defined as, "the customary and codified rights which individuals and groups have to land and the behavioral characteristics which directly result from this right."[9]

Land tenure arrangements are very important because they not only have significance in terms of the production of agricultural commodities, but also are closely tied to the well-being of persons who till the soil and for the greater society as well. There has been a growing concern over land tenure problems in recent years and much time and considerable resources have been spent on the part of many national governments in an attempt to develop what has been termed, "ideal tenure systems." Many of the problems of the underdeveloped countries relate very closely to these systems. There are several important socio-economic aspects of tenure which must be kept in mind when reviewing tenure arrangements: (1) property rights—that is, the rights which the people who work the land have to use and dispose of the land; (2) personal liberty—that is, how much control is exercised by government over the activities of people who work the land; (3) freedom of enterprise—that is, the opportunity provided those who work the land to try new things, to exercise initiative and to take risks; (4) freedom to contract—that is, the degree of freedom people on the land have to negotiate contracts freely; (5) inheritance—that is, the right individuals on the land have to dispose of their wealth, property, and lands as they wish after their death.

---

[9] This discussion is a summary of a previous work by the writer. See Alvin L. Bertrand and Floyd L. Corty, Eds., *Rural Land Tenure in the United States* (Baton Rouge, Louisiana, Louisiana State University Press, 1962), Chapters 2 and 3.

MAJOR TYPES OF TENURE SYSTEMS

The particular tenure forms found in any society are closely related to the social and economic well-being of the people.[10] Six major types of tenure systems are described.

RESTRICTION OF RIGHTS TO THE USE OF "FREE" LAND: This is an emergent form of tenure found only in societies that have not progressed beyond a hunting, fishing, and gathering economy. When people are nomadic and range over large areas in search of food and other necessities, they have little cause to attach value to a specific piece of ground. The social organization of such groups is usually simple. Their laws, for the most part, are uncodified and familistic in nature. They live in tribes or clans under the leadership of a chief or elder and social differentiation is at a minimum. Yet, even in these societies, some claims are made on certain parcels of land. Usually these parcels have religious significance, as with burial sites, or they represent choice hunting and fishing grounds. To the extent that claims are made on land, there is a tenure system, which in turn can be recognized as an institutionalized social structure.

COMMUNAL ARRANGEMENTS FOR THE USE AND CONTROL OF LAND: Communal farms are differentiated from the so-called collective farms which are managed or operated by state governments. Under communal tenure patterns, the inhabitants usually are grouped into villages and bound by a series of social-economic-political ties. Since everyone is considered a co-owner of the land, social differentiation is relatively slight and community members are a fairly homogeneous group. Such communities are usually self-governing. True communal systems can only operate in relatively simple societies where a subsistence agriculture suffices. In advanced societies, the problems of social control and land division are so difficult that it is impossible to maintain impartiality in distribution of lands and other commodities.

It has been observed that communal communities exhibit a greater sense of cooperativeness than found in communities characterized by other forms of tenure. However, these communities do not appear to have as high a level of living as those where private ownership exists. Seemingly, the incentive to work and save is not as strong in communal communities.

CONTROL OF LAND BY INDEPENDENT CLASSES OF SMALL OWNERS OR TENANTS: Under this system, characteristically, each landholder operates a parcel of land which is approximately the size that he and

[10] Pitrim A. Sorokin, Carl C. Zimmerman, and Charles J. Galpin, *Systematic Source Book in Rural Sociology*, 2 vols. (Minneapolis, Minnesota, University of Minnesota Press, 1930), Vol. I, pp. 558-645.

the members of his family can take care of. The decision-making function is largely retained by the operator. There are many examples of such holdings, but possibly the family farm system in the United States is the best known. Such a tenure system provides maximum freedom for the individual. In no other tenure form is individualism, initiative, and rationalism so well developed. There is a tendency for more social differentiation and social stratification, because the farm operators control their own destiny to a large extent.

COOPERATIVE ARRANGEMENTS FOR THE USE AND CONTROL OF THE LAND: Within recent years, a cooperative form of land tenure has been adopted on a national scale in Mexico. This system, known as the *ejido* system, was the outcome of the agrarian reform movement which began with the Revolution of 1910.[11] Each ejido is a legal entity that comes into being when at least 20 adults, actual or potential heads of families, form a committee and apply for land to the central government. Once the land is provided, local authority is vested in a general assembly of the *ejidatarios,* with administrative functions delegated to two local committees. All ejido authorities are independent from other local, state, and national authorities. Each member of the ejido receives a parcel of the ejido land which he can work and care for as he and his fellow ejidatarios see fit. He cannot sell his land but it can be inherited by his closest and ablest beneficiary. All affairs affecting the ejido are handled by vote, and ideally are supposed to be both cooperative in nature and designed to promote democracy and freedom. This idea of cooperative arrangement for the use and control of land is not altogether new, but does not seem to have been tried on a national scale before. It remains to be seen whether the ejido system, which was designed to combine the best features of the communal and private types of small holdings, will accomplish those goals.

CONTROL OF LAND BY OWNERS OF LARGE PRIVATE ESTATES: Most persons are familiar with words like "plantation," "latifundia," and "hacienda." They refer to large properties managed as single units. When these properties are owned privately, a particular type of land tenure system is recognized. Under this system, generally the landlord controls the land, not particularly for the welfare of his cultivators, but rather for the income and other gains that he may derive from this operation. It is interesting to note that almost always the masses who serve as laborers on such holdings manifest an element of discontent. They see their lot as a disadvantaged one and want to change to a better social order, which they do not always see clearly. Typically, large holdings have a greater efficiency because they are run more expertly. All decisions are made by the owner or his managers.

---

[11] For a recent account of the functioning of ejidos see Pedro F. Hernandez, "An Analysis of Social Power in Five Mexican Ejidos" (Ames, Iowa, Ph.D. Dissertation, Iowa State University, 1965).

This system of large holdings is conspicuously characterized by a high degree of social stratification. Strong and vigorous social institutions are not encouraged. Churches and schools are likely to be poor if not totally lacking for the mass of workers; but for the elite, they may be excellent in quality, as examplified by the American South before the Civil War.

LARGE ESTATES OWNED AND CONTROLLED BY CHURCH, STATE, OR OTHER PUBLIC BODY: Publicly owned estates are similar in many ways to private estates. The major difference is in control, which is vested in some public body. One of the best contemporary examples of such a system is the collective farms in the socialistic countries of Eastern Europe. According to some authorities, the independent peasants who go to collective farms become subordinated manual laborers who serve in much the same role as the workers do on a private estate. The feudal systems of earlier years in Europe and elsewhere were also good examples of this type of tenure system. Social organization tends to follow the patterns that develop in areas where large private holdings exist.

SUMMARY

Economic and government systems serve the social institutions of the economy and government and function primarily to provide ways of allocating scarce resources and of controlling relations between members of the society. Economic systems find their importance in the inability of individuals to satisfy their wants. Their structural bases include varying patterns of property rights, division of labor, and patterns of distributing economic rewards (or exchange), as well as types of government control exercised over economic activity and the organizational nature of business and labor enterprises. Economic systems have many specific functions, but most of these can be typed under three broad goals: economic production, the distribution of economic production, and the consumption of what has been produced and distributed.

Government systems derive their structure from society and can usually be traced to a specific beginning date. They are differentiated from "states," which arise out of the centralized power exercised by governments. The structure of government systems is manifested in several ways: their authority and power structure, their legislative, executive, and judicial structures; and the organizational character of government enterprises. Governments usually function to institutionalize norms, enforce the norms, adjudicate conflict, promote the general welfare, and to provide protection for citizens from external attacks.

Land tenure systems demonstrate how economic and government systems have implications for social organization. Six major types of tenure systems are found: (1) restrictions of rights to the use of "free" land, (2) communal arrangements for the use and control of land, (3) control of land by independent classes of small owners or tenants, (4) cooperative arrangements for the use and control of the land, (5) control of land by owners of large private estates, and (6) large estates owned and controlled by church, state, or other public body.

Supplementary Readings

Bertrand, Alvin L. and Floyd L. Corty, Eds., *Rural Land Tenure in the United States*. (Baton Rouge, Louisiana, Louisiana State University Press, 1962), Chapter III.

Dahrendorf, Rolf, "Conflict and Liberty: Some Remarks on the Social Structure of German Politics," *British Journal of Sociology* (1963), pp. 197-211; and also in MIZRUCHI.

Galbraith, John K., *The Affluent Society* (Boston, Houghton Mifflin, 1958).

Lipset, Seymour M., *Political Man* (Garden City, New York, Doubleday, 1963); also an exerpt appears in INKELES.

Miller, Delbert C. and William H. Form, *Industrial Sociology*, 2nd ed. (New York, Harper & Row, 1964).

Mitchell, William C., *The American Policy* (New York, Free Press, 1962).

Shostak, Arthur B. and William Gomberg, *New Perspectives on Poverty* (Englewood Cliffs, N.J., Prentice-Hall, 1965).

Smelser, Neil J., *The Sociology of Economic Life* (Englewood Cliffs, New Jersey, Prentice-Hall, 1963).

Whyte, William H., Jr., *The Organization Man* (New York, Simon and Schuster, 1956); also an exerpt appears in CUBER & HARROFF.

PART VI

THE DEMOGRAPHIC AND ECOLOGICAL ASPECTS OF SOCIAL DIFFERENTIATION

The chapters included in Part VI are devoted to phenomena that relate closely to all sociological analyses. The subject matter is demography and ecology. **Demography** can be defined as the study of population including its distribution, composition, and other characteristics. Ecology has to do with the spatial distribution of populations.

The first chapter, Chapter 20, emphasizes the importance of population size and describes methods for determining rates of growth and change. Chapter 21 is intended to show the student how the make-up of the population has important implications for social interaction. Sex, race, and residence differences and the resultant patterns of behavior which relate to these differences are described. Chapter 23 attempts to acquaint the student with the important ecological principles of human interrelationships. It is hoped that the student will, after completing his study of this part, comprehend how population and ecology studies are important in understanding the organization of given societies and the relationship between societies.

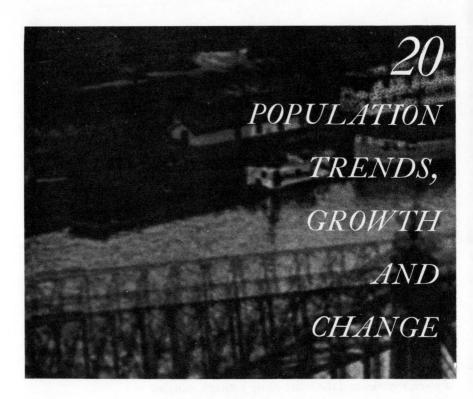

20
POPULATION
TRENDS,
GROWTH
AND
CHANGE

This chapter deals primarily with the quantity aspects of population. As here used, quantity simply refers to number, whereas quality refers to the composition or make-up of a population. In reading the material presented in this chapter, the student should keep these two important facts in mind. First, population changes have immediate implications for a society in the sense of problems to be solved, and long-term implications for culture in the sense that new patterns evolve in the solving of these problems. Second, population studies not only provide objective indexes to human behavior, but point the way to more exhaustive and rewarding sociological inquiry into causally related factors.

WORLD POPULATION TRENDS

The total number of people in the world and in most nations is at an all-time high. No one knows how large population aggregates may eventually get, but demographers are convinced that present-day trends have many implications for the future.

Estimates of the world population to 1975 are shown in Table 20-1. Estimates have to be made because there are large areas where no census has ever been taken. Harold Dorn points out that the world's population reached a

Table 20-1. *Estimated Population of the World and the Number of Years Required for it to Double*

Year (A.D.)	Population (billons)	Number of years to double
I	0.25(?)	1650(?)
1650	0.50	200
1850	1.1	80
1930	2.0	45
1975	4.0	35
2010	8.0	?

Source: Harold F. Dorn, "World Population Growth," in Philip M. Hauser, Editor, *The Population Dilemma*, © 1963 by The American Assembly, Columbia University, New York, New York. Reprinted by permission of Prentice-Hall, Inc., Englewood Cliffs, New Jersey, p. 10.

quarter-billion people some 2000 years ago, and required 16 more centuries to grow a second quarter billion in size. By contrast, the second half-billion was added to the world population in just two centuries.[1] Since this time the rate of growth of the number of people has accelerated rapidly. In 1964 the world population was estimated at 3.3 billion and the rate of growth was placed at 65 million persons a year—as many people as make up the populations of England, the Netherlands, and Switzerland combined.[2] The population of the different regions of the world is shown in Table 20-2.

Table 20-2. *Estimated Population of the World and its Major Regions, 1900, 1960, and 2000 (Millions)*

Area	Population Estimated			Projected Population	Increase	
	1900	1950	1960	2000	1900 to 1950	1950 to 2000
World	1,550	2,518	2,995	6,907	968	4,389
Africa	120	209	254	663	89	454
North America	81	168	199	326	87	158
Latin America	63	163	206	651	100	488
Asia	857	1,389	1,679	4,250	532	2,861
Europe (incl. USSR)	423	576	641	987	153	411
Oceania	6	13	17	30	7	17

Source: Harold F. Dorn, "World Population Growth," in Philip M. Hauser, Editor, *The Population Dilemma*, © 1963 by The American Assembly, Columbia University, New York, New York. Reprinted by permission of Prentice-Hall, Inc., Englewood Cliffs, New Jersey, p. 21.

The question arises as to the reason for the phenomenal rise in the number of people in the world in recent years. After all, man is known to have

[1] Harold F. Dorn, "World Population Growth," selection in Philip Hauser, Ed. *The Population Dilemma* (Englewood Cliffs, New Jersey, Prentice-Hall, 1963), p. 11.
[2] Report of The Population Council (July, 1965), p. 8.

existed for thousands of years, and it is clear from the above-quoted statistics that his numbers increased extremely slowly during most of this time. The "explosive" growth in population in the last 300 years has been attributed to several factors: (1) improvements in food production, (2) improved health knowledge and practices, (3) improved means of transportation, (4) general technological advances, (5) generally improved living conditions, and (6) the opening up of new continents. Since the above factors have not operated equally for all nations, growth has been uneven from one place in the world to another. However, it seems likely from present-day trends that both the industrial and agricultural revolutions will spread to all corners of the globe before many years. When this happens, the world population can be expected to grow even faster, unless certain checks are brought into play.[3]

The implications of a rapidly increasing population are the concern of many persons. Perhaps the most immediate problem is the imbalance between the rate of population growth and the natural resources and technical know-how necessary to feed, clothe, and otherwise provide for the increasing numbers of people. Questions of "standing room only" are also raised as are those of a decreasing level of living. These problems make it worthwhile to review the important factors in population growth and change.

FACTORS RELATED TO POPULATION GROWTH AND CHANGE

Population change is dependent upon the interplay of the *vital processes* of birth and death and of in-migration and out-migration. In other words, if migration is held constant, a determination of the net product of the difference between the birth and death rates of a population will make possible accurate predictions of its potential growth. The importance of these processes is such that most governments require that births, deaths, and migrants be registered.

The factors affecting population change can be understood easily in terms of the following formula:[4] $P_2 = P_1 +$ Natural increase $+$ Net migration. In this formula P_2 is the future population and P_1 is the present population. *Natural increase* is determined by subtracting the number of deaths from the number of births over a given period of time. *Net migration* is computed by subtracting the number of persons leaving an area from those coming into it in a given time.

It can readily be seen that any factor, physical, biological, or social, which influences one or more of the above-mentioned variables affects the size of

---

[3] For an excellent account of population trends the world over, see Ronald Freedman, Ed., *Population: the Vital Revolution* (Garden City, New York, Doubleday, Anchor Books, 1964).

[4] George A. Lundberg, Clarence C. Schrag, and Otto N. Larsen, *Sociology* (New York, Harper & Row, 1954), p. 81.

population. Demographers are thus concerned with studying and measuring these variables in their efforts to predict population changes. The techniques and terms used and certain findings and trends related to each variable are described briefly in the discussions that follow.

FERTILITY

There are several terms relating to the birth rate which are part of the demographers' vocabulary. *Fecundity* refers to the capacity for having children or to potential reproduction. Women, from a biological standpoint, can generally produce more children than they do; they do not primarily because of the cultural and other environmental influences impinging upon them. Some of these influences will be enumerated later. The term *fertility* is used to refer to actual reproduction, and this is what demographers are primarily concerned with measuring. It should be noted that in modern industrialized populations fertility and fecundity are usually far apart.

MEASURES OF FERTILITY: Through the years students of demography have developed several objective methods for measuring the fertility of human populations. The simplest of these procedures relates the new births in a population to the total population for a given period of time. This index is known as the **birth rate.** The crude birth rate is computed by dividing the population at midyear (or the average population for the year) into the number of births during the year and multiplying the product by 1,000.

Although it is possible to make predictions of the growth of a given population with only a knowledge of the crude birth rates, some refinement of this rate is usually necessary for valid comparisons of the fertility of two or more populations. One practice followed by demographers, when comparisons are desired, is to make allowances for differences in the age and sex composition of the different populations so that the populations will be comparable. The index so computed is known as the **standardized birth rate.**[5] Sometimes the purpose in mind makes the **nuptial birth rate** preferable. This is determined by relating number of births to the number of married women. For some uses, it is necessary to measure fertility in terms of the reproduction in certain age groups. This measure is known as the **age-specific birth rate.**

A second common method of measuring the fertility of a population is the **fertility ratio.** The determination of the fertility ratio is quite simple. Customarily the number of women in the child-bearing ages (15 to 44 or 49 years of age) are divided into the number of children under 5 years of age and the product multiplied by 1,000, so that fertility can be expressed in terms of children per 1,000 women. The advantage of the fertility ratio is that it can

[5] See Warren S. Thompson and David T. Lewis, *Population Problems,* 5th ed. (New York, McGraw-Hill, 1965), pp. 253-254.

be computed directly from census data, without the necessity of birth registration. Thus the fertility of all countries where fairly accurate censuses have been taken can be compared. Its disadvantage is that no allowance is made for children who die before they reach the age of four.[6]

One final index needs mention in this section, although it is not strictly a measure of fertility. The **net reproduction rate** balances fertility against mortality to indicate the degree to which a given population is growing or declining. The net reproduction rate is determined by applying prevailing birth rates and death rates at each level to 1,000 female infants beginning life together and determining how many daughters they will have in their lifetime. A net reproduction rate of 1,000 means the population is just replacing itself, whereas a figure higher or lower indicates the population is growing or declining. This is an extremely reliable technique, although somewhat complicated. It effectively allows for most factors influencing natural increase in a given population.

FERTILITY DIFFERENTIALS: There are some patterns of fertility differentials which are fairly well established. These differentials follow cultural patterns and values prevalent in a given country. The major differentials found vary somewhat from society to society, but in general, are as follows.[7]

The first and most obvious differential in birth rate is that between the urban and rural populations. Actually the phenomenon of larger families in rural areas is world-wide, with few exceptions. The usual pattern is for rural-farm areas to have higher fertility than rural-nonfarm areas and for the latter to have higher fertility than urban areas. It is generally the case that the larger the city the lower the fertility, although certain exceptions have been noted.

A second important differential in fertility is that between the socioeconomic classes. Although this phenomenon is by no means true of all individual families, it is true in most societies that upper-class families generally have fewer children than lower-class families. This holds true whether class status is equated to income or education. Interestingly, however, the well-educated elements in the United States apparently shared disproportionately in the increased fertility associated with the baby boom of the mid-twentieth century.

Other fertility differentials are not as universal, but indicate interesting patterns. As a group, manual workers' (those working with their hands) wives have more children than white-collar workers' wives. Race and ethnic differences and religious affiliation tend to be associated with fertility in some places. For example, in the United States, nonwhites have larger families than whites and Catholic fertility tends to be higher than Protestant fertility.[8]

[6] *Ibid.*, pp. 241-242.

[7] For a detailed treatment of differential fertility, see Dennis H. Wrong, *Population and Society*, 2nd ed. (New York, Random House, 1961), Chapter 5.

[8] This was brought out again in the Indianapolis Studies. See Charles F. Westoff, Robert G. Potter, Jr., and Philip C. Sagi, *The Third Child: A Study in the Prediction of Fertility* (Princeton, New Jersey, Princeton University Press, 1963), Chapter VIII.

The question arises as to what sociological importance the above-mentioned differentials in fertility have. There are several significant consequences as follows: (1) The groups with large proportions of children in nonsocialistic countries have disproportionate burdens of education, feeding, and clothing, usually at the same time that they have less economic and other resources. (2) The differential fertility between groups also provides cues regarding future size relations between different groups in a given population, which may have political and other implications. (3) A third consequence is that certain groups (such as large urban centers) have to depend on other groups for their continued survival and growth. This is also true of the upper classes, which continually have to dip down to the lower classes to replenish their numbers. (4) The study of fertility patterns provides an important basis for estimations of future population growth, and consequent societal needs.

MORTALITY

As mentioned earlier, mortality is the second of the vital processes basic to the growth of a society. The death rate is measured in much the same way as the birth rate. The two principal indexes used in measuring mortality are the death rate and the life table. The **crude death rate** is determined in essentially the same way as the crude birth rate. That is, the number of deaths in a population in a given year is divided by the total population at midyear or by the average population for the whole year, with the product being multiplied by 1,000.

Crude death rates are subject to criticism because they reflect differentials in age structure. In this regard, it is apparent that relatively young populations would show up to advantage against relatively old populations in a comparison of crude death rates. This will happen even though the older population may be a healthier one.

Age-specific death rates are calculated to avoid the criticism mentioned above. These rates show the number of deaths per 1,000 persons of specified ages. It can be seen how particular measures such as infant mortality rates and maternal mortality rates can be computed for certain usage also. In other words, by computing specific rates for different subpopulations it can be determined where the highest rates persist, and where research attention should be directed.

Everything considered, some scholars feel the life expectation table to be the most useful yardstick for the study of mortality.[9] These tables indicate the theoretical duration of life of persons born at the same time. They are computed by taking age-specific death rates of a population and determining the expected longevity of persons of a given age. Life tables are used by life insurance companies to compute premium rates, as they indicate the average

[9] T. Lynn Smith, *The Sociology of Rural Life,* 3rd ed. (New York, Harper & Row, 1953), p. 149.

number of years that individuals of any given age may expect to live. Since male and female mortality rates tend to differ somewhat, it is common to construct separate life tables for the sexes. This can also be done for race or other component elements in a population.

MAJOR MORTALITY DIFFERENTIALS: Longevity is not shared equally by all the people in any society. Different age, sex, race, and socio-economic groups have unique mortality experiences.[10] Level of medical and other types of technology also account for differences in death rates. Normally, persons in the older ages have higher death rates than younger persons (with the exception of infants under one year of age). It is noteworthy that, although death rates have decreased for all age groups in most countries, the large reductions in mortality have been registered in the younger ages. This is because contagious diseases have largely been brought under control. In fact, childhood diseases are now under such good control that some scholars feel the next significant reduction in mortality will be among the older persons. They base their beliefs on the studies being made in the treatment of certain chronic diseases and on the breakthrough of such terminal diseases as cancer and heart disease.

Data vary somewhat from country to country, but it is generally found that in advanced societies, women live considerably longer than men. (In 1965 there were only 96.4 men for every 100 women in the United States, despite the fact that 105 males are born for every 100 females.) Explanations for the higher mortality of males are partially found in the higher death rates for males in accidents, because of certain diseases (such as heart disease, tuberculosis and cancer), because of greater occupational stresses and strains, and because of less frequent consultation of physicians.[11] Part of the difference is thought by some scholars to reflect a biological advantage of females. Mortality differences also vary with race and other factors in given societies. To illustrate, the mortality rate of nonwhites in the United States has decreased substantially in recent years, but is still significantly higher than that of whites. In the years 1900–1902 white infants had a life expectation of approximately 49.6 years while nonwhite infants could only be expected to live an average of 33.8 years. By 1963, the respective life expectations of these two groups was 70.8 and 63.6.

MIGRATION

Throughout history, migration has been an important source of population change. Of course, a given migration does not affect the total population of the world, but it can have a drastic effect on the population of a given country.

---

[10] "Life Grows Longer," *Population Bulletin,* Population Reference Bureau, Inc., Vol. XI (December, 1955).

[11] "Health and the Sexes," *Health Information Foundation,* Vol. VI (December, 1957).

Migration in ancient times was, for the most part, by small groups such as tribes or clans. In contrast, modern migration is generally by individuals or families.

The motives for migration can be divided into two broad classes. On the one hand, there are forces that exert a "pull" on individuals and populations because of their attraction, such as job opportunities or certain freedoms. "Push" factors are in contrast as they exert certain pressures that more or less force persons and groups to leave one place for another. An example of the latter kind of migration is the situation in an authoritarian state where people are shuffled about or made to flee to serve the purpose of those in power.

Five important causes of migration are recognized:[12] (1) the desire to improve economic status (by far the most important cause for the movement of people); (2) the desire to be free from political oppression on the part of minority groups; (3) maladjustments of individuals to family or community life; (4) the wish to secure freedom of belief and worship; (5) pressure associated with military and national considerations.

Two additional factors besides push and pull have a definite association with migration. The first is means of transportation. It can readily be seen that an individual or group can never realize ambitions to move unless there is some means of travel. It is also true that the easier it is to travel, the greater migration streams can become. For illustration, the era of the steamboat made possible a tremendous migration of Europeans to the United States. This migration would have been greatly curtailed had dependence on sailing vessels been maintained.

Migrations are also closely related to restrictive laws which prohibit movement of people. The Immigration Quota laws of the United States are a good example. It is certain that the movement of people into this country would have continued at a fast pace had not such laws been passed in the early 1920's. Restrictive laws are also used to prevent people from leaving a country, such as the ban on travellers in certain totalitarian regions.

There are two major types of migration, which the student should be aware of. International or external migrations include all movements from one nation to another, while internal migrations involve movements within a particular nation. In this regard, immigration and emigration are the terms used to designate migration into and out of a nation, respectively.

RECENT WORLD MIGRATION: The history of the world is filled with accounts of political upheavals that have been responsible for migrations. These historical migrations are well known to most students and need not be repeated here. Recent migrations involving international movement, those coming in the wake of World War II, are not so well known, although the movement of people was unprecedented in history.[13]

[12] Thompson and Lewis, *op. cit.*, pp. 479-480.
[13] There have been some notable internal migrations, such as the urbanization

Approximately 50 million persons migrated from their homelands during the period from 1946 to 1955.[14] Around 20 million were Eastern and Central Europeans and about the same number were Asians. Most of both groups of migrants were displaced persons of one kind or another. The remainder were largely persons leaving overpopulated lands. The United States, Great Britain, and France were on the receiving end of many migrations of the latter type and in each instance citizens of the respective nations were involved. The migration to the United States was from Puerto Rico, that to Great Britain from the British West Indies, and that to France from Algeria.

It is revealing to review the estimated net overseas migration from Europe from 1946 to 1955. The principal receiving countries were the United States, which received some 1,200,000 persons; Canada which received about 900,000 persons; Australia which received about 800,000 persons; Israel which received about 360,000 persons; New Zealand which received about 100,000 persons; and Latin America, which received about 1,300,000 persons altogether. This later migration has an entirely different character from the spontaneous, unrestricted migrations prior to World War I. Recent migrants have been generally controlled and directed by both the country of origin and the country of destination. Screening for matters of health, political belief, and professional competencies are quite common. There has been no comparable movement of Asians because of restrictive immigration policies on the part of western nations. Many writers feel that a removal of these barriers would see a literal swarming of the peoples of these nations to other parts of the world.

RECENT INTERNAL MIGRATION IN THE UNITED STATES

Recent movements of the peoples of the United States serve to illustrate a specific case of internal migration. These movements have resulted in phenomenal increases in population in some parts of the nation and almost complete lack of growth in other parts. The main currents of migratory movements can be seen in Figure 20-1. From March 1964 to March 1965, about six million people moved from one state to another and half this number moved from one region to another. The volume and rate of migration reflected in these figures are typical of what has happened in the previous decade and a half. The western part of the nation experienced a ratio of five in-migrants to three out-migrants and continued its attraction for people which began in

movement in the United States and the relocation of peoples in China. See Amos H. Hawley, "Some Observations of Changes in Metropolitan Population in the United States," *Demography*, Vol. 1, No. 1 (1964), pp. 148-163; and H. Yhay Tien, "The Demographic Significance of Organized Population Transfers in Communist China," *Demography*, Vol. I, No. 1 (1964), pp. 220-226.

[14] "World Migration, 1946-55," *Population Bulletin*, Population Reference Bureau, Vol. XIII (No. 5, 1957).

FIGURE 20-1. *Flow of Migrants between Regions, Annual Average (thousands): 1960 to 1965 and 1955 to 1960.*

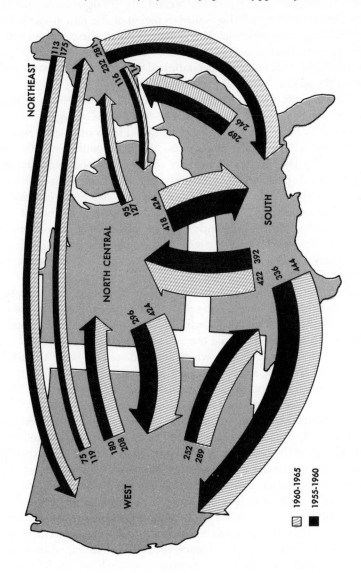

Source: *Americans at Mid-Decade*, U. S. Department of Commerce (Washington, D. C., U. S. Government Printing Office, 1966), p. 17.

the late 1930's and early 1940's. The second largest migration stream joined the North Central region and the Southern region of the nation—with a virtually equal exchange of population. Movements between these two regions and the Northeast were smaller in volume but also represented about equal exchanges of people. California and Florida continued to be the fastest growing of the 50 states for the second decade in succession.

The race, age, and residence composition of these streams of migrants is changing somewhat from past years. The two Northern regions of the nation had losses of whites and gains of nonwhites. The South had a nominal gain of whites and a heavy loss of nonwhites. The West gained in both whites and nonwhites. By far the largest number of long distance migrants are in the younger ages (25-29 years). However, the South lost disproportionately in these age groups and the West gained disproportionately. In contrast, the gain in the white population of the South was due to the in-movement of middle-aged and older adults—apparently seeking places to retire. There is still a movement of people from rural areas to cities, but this stream has lost its once great magnitude. Rural migrants to cities are more likely to be southern and nonwhite.[15]

Moves between states and regions, despite their significance, make up only a fraction of the total moves taking place in the United States. In the 12-month period from March 1964 to March 1965, 38 million persons changed their residence. This meant that one out of every five persons changed residences in this period, a rate of change which has persisted for some time. Of course, most of these changes, about two-thirds, represented a local move that did not involve crossing a county line. Nevertheless, it can be stated that the citizens of the nation are much on the move.

The motivation for migration of the people of the United States has been difficult to study because of lack of data. Shryock, utilizing data collected in the mid-1940's, gives the best answers available.[16] His analyses show that "primary" migrants—those persons who made the basic decisions either for themselves alone or their families as well—moved primarily for economic considerations, either to take a job or to look for work. Miscellaneous reasons such as retirement, losing a job, or a search for adventure prompted the second largest number of movers. Housing problems, indicating that younger married couples were seeking larger and better homes, ranked next in importance as a reason for moving. Next was change in marital status, which can be accounted for in large part by the breaking away of newly-weds from parental homes. A smaller number of movers are prompted by the need to find more healthful locations.

[15] Gladys K. Bowles and James D. Tarver, "The Composition of Net Migration Among Counties in the United States," *Agricultural Economics Research,* Vol. 18 (January, 1966) pp. 13-19.

[16] Henry S. Shryock, Jr., *Population Mobility Within the United States* (Chicago, Community and Family Study Center, University of Chicago, 1964), Chapter 12.

CULTURAL VALUES AND POPULATION GROWTH

Although population growth is basically the function of fertility, mortality, and migration, these processes take place within the context of culture.[17] Cultural practices relating to population growth can be classified as restrictive or expansive, depending on the goal in mind. Restrictive practices include infanticide, abortion, sexual taboos, killing or abandonment of the sick or aged, passive acceptance of disaster, continuous warring, marriage restrictions, migration, traditional orientation, and contraception. Expansive practices are calculated to increase the population. They include such things as public policies toward use and development of resources, felt need for defense and the belief that defense potential is heightened by increased numbers, nationalistic ambitions for larger numbers of peoples, religious beliefs and practices that discourage contraceptive practices, and high technology. The more important cultural factors relating to population growth are described here.

(1) *Technology.* Food production is closely linked to the stage of technology in a society, and technology is, in turn, related to the number of people who can be provided with food, clothing, and shelter. A case in point is the United States. At the time of the discovery of America there were less than a half-million Indians in the nation; yet it has been estimated that this number was near the limit of people who could be supported by the primarily hunting and gathering technology of the time. Today the nation is faced with surpluses as a result of an advanced technology.

T. Lynn Smith has pointed out that the level of living of a society is directly related to the system of agriculture practiced.[18] The relationship is shown to be inherent in value systems that set limits to food production by blocking or retarding technological change. Smith contends that output per worker is the important factor bearing on level of living and demonstrates that labor input per productive unit decreases as one moves up the ranks of the following agricultural systems: (1) river bank plantings, (2) fire agriculture, (3) hoe culture, (4) rudimentary plow culture, (5) advanced plow culture, and (6) mechanized farming.

(2) *Values Related to Levels and Standards of Living.* Level-of-living values are a factor in the balance reached between food production and numbers of people. The lower the level of living a society is willing to accommodate, the more people a given system of agriculture can support. Thus, if a

---

[17] See G. William Skinner, "Cultural Values, Social Structure and Population Growth," *Population Bulletin of the United Nations,* No. 5 (July, 1956), pp. 5-12.

[18] T. Lynn Smith, *op. cit.,* Chapter 14.

group is willing to live at a bare subsistence level, its numbers will be greater than if a level commensurate with a "chicken in every pot" is demanded. Studies have shown that many families in the United States faced with an alternative will forgo a large family so that they may enjoy higher levels of living. This practice is carried out in terms of a cultural orientation that places higher social value on certain material possessions than on children.

Levels and standards of living are differentiated in that the former is what one has and the latter is what one would like to have. Most of us have a medium-priced automobile level of living, but a standard of living which tends toward a high-priced limousine or sports car. Higher standards may be a matter of quantity of children versus quality of opportunities open to children. A middle-class family, for example, may practice planned parenthood in order to assure that the family can afford a college education for the children it has. The significant fact is that standards of living can effectively reduce the numbers of the total population.

Each society works out for itself the balance it will strive for between levels and standards of living and numbers of people.

(3) *The valuation placed on children.* Naturally a society cannot survive without placing positive values on children. However, there is wide variation from one society to another in the intensity of this valuation. It is possible to have ranges of values from the one extreme where the child may be regarded with dismay or near hostility, to the other extreme where children are received with great joy.

Cultural valuation may favor male or female children, depending on such things as the division of labor between the sexes, economic arrangements of marriage, inheritance patterns, and ritual duties. Where a strong preference for the one or the other sex is manifest, there will generally be a high fertility. This is true because it requires proportionately more births to satisfy requirements relative to one sex. In other words, if the cultural ideal is at least two sons, some families may have to have a large number of daughters before acquiring the desired number of sons.

Various techniques are used by different cultures to encourage or retard the birth of children. Religious sanctions of one kind or another are commonly applied. For example, in Arabia, having as many children as possible is said to be the will of Allah. According to the Hindu Shastras, only a man who marries and produces a son can ascend to Heaven. Most Americans are familiar with the Biblical passage "be fruitful and multiply and replenish the earth" (Genesis 9:1) which is often quoted in Christian circles.

(4) *The social regulation of sex.* All societies control sex to a greater or lesser degree. Some of the common cultural controls include taboos on extramarital sexual relations, age of marriage, remarriage of widows and divorced persons, celibate groups, and proscriptions relating to continence.[19]

[19] Judah Matras, "The Social Strategy of Family Formation: Some Variations in Time and Space," *Demography*, Vol. 2 (1965), pp. 349-362.

Age of marriage is one of the most important of the above factors in controlling birth rates. When cultural practices are such that marriage is generally consummated in the early teens, as in many parts of rural India, the total number of births is likely to be high. On the other hand, when marriage is generally delayed to the early twenties, as in rural Japan (and reportedly in Communist China) the number of children is likely to be relatively fewer.

In Tibet, an illustration is found of the effect of celibacy on child rearing. Here the highest prestige is reserved for the men in the Lamaist orders, with the result that a high proportion of men enter the monasteries. Tibetan fertility is clearly depressed in consequence.

Cultural practices regarding widows, widowers, and divorced persons vary from outright prohibition of remarriage to encouragement of it. The Jains of India, with a strict prohibition of widow marriage, have definitely affected their natural increase, as a fifth of their women in the 15-39 age groups have been relegated to widowhood in recent years.

(5) *The Post-Conception Regulation of Child Survival.* This type of cultural regulation regarding child survival may take several forms. Attitudes toward pregnant women and induced abortion, and knowledge of maternal care, are cultural variables which offset survival. In some societies, for instance, a pregnant woman is entitled to special diet considerations because of her condition. Several cultures (such as the Japanese) not only contain knowledge of efficient abortion techniques, but sanction their use and effectively control fertility through this measure. In other places, like Chile where one of every three or four pregnancies is deliberately interrupted, there is a public health problem because of unsanitary conditions.[20]

Infanticide is another means of controlling child survival and this practice helps explain the sex ratios in some pre-modern Asiatic societies.

Infant survival is also regulated indirectly by certain cultural practices related to their care. There are the contrasts of the highly sanitary medical practices in advanced nations and the crude unsanitary practices in primitive societies.

Finally, survival of children is conditioned by cultural values placed on boys and girls. This phenomenon is apparent in certain parts of the world, where girls are denied the same subsistence and health advantages given to boys. It can be imagined that social change in the direction of sex equality in these areas will increase fertility.

(6) *Attitudes and Practices Regarding Health and Mortality.* Although it is safe to assume that all cultures place a high value on survival, there are cultural practices that either shorten or prolong life. Dietary practices, such as the preference of many Asians and Americans for polished rice, often explain nutritional deficiencies. Some societies have bans on the consumption of certain foods that are highly nutritious, such as those on eggs, poultry, and meat

[20] Mariano B. Requena, "Social and Economic Correlates of Induced Abortion in Santiago, Chile," *Demography*, Vol. 2 (1965), p. 33.

in certain Indian castes. Personal hygiene falls in the realm of cultural practices and people who do not take regular baths probably have shorter lives. The use of "night soil" in agriculture by certain Asians has tremendous health implications. Other practices, such as the facilitation of the spread of disease by pilgrimages and the placing of a positive value on suicide, also have significance for population growth.

MALTHUSIAN THEORY AND THE MEANING OF OVERPOPULATION

Thomas Malthus is called the father of modern population study.[21] He gained lasting fame with his recognition of and concern with the problem of overpopulation. Malthus' concern, as outlined in his early writings, stemmed from his belief that an unchecked human population would grow at a geometric ratio, (1,2,4,8,16,32, . . .) while food supplies would only increase at an arithmetic ratio (1,2,3,4,5,6, . . .). He felt that because of differential rates of growth, population would soon catch up with food supply and prevent rises in levels of living. In his later works, Malthus recognized that certain positive checks (such as hunger, disease, war, and vice) and preventive checks (such as deferred marriage and celibacy) would keep population growth from achieving a geometric progression.

Malthus' conclusions were perhaps unduly pessimistic because he could not foresee two important developments. The first was the widespread use of contraceptive techniques as a measure of birth control. He regarded the use of such techniques as a "vice" utilized by individuals to avoid the sanctions applying to extramarital intercourse and did not anticipate their present popularity as a preventive check on births within marriage. The second development not foreseen by Malthus was the great technological revolution which has taken place. Nations characterized by advanced technology have been able to produce food and fiber far in excess of what Malthus foresaw and there are yet many food frontiers, such as the ocean, to be exploited.

Although Malthus' predictions have as yet not come about for the world as a whole, there are certain scholars who feel it is but a matter of time until we "have standing room only." These persons have been called "neo-Malthusians," as their arguments and outlook follow the Malthusian model.[22] They have found a hearing in many quarters, as is evidenced by the programs inaugurated by various agencies in certain "developing" countries where recent

[21] For a comprehensive discussion of Malthusian theory, see William Petersen, *The Politics of Population* (Garden City, New York, Doubleday, Anchor Books, 1965), pp. 26-45.
[22] See Robert C. Cook, *Human Fertility: The Modern Dilemma* (New York, William Sloane Associates, 1951), and certain articles in Philip M. Hauser, Ed., *The Population Dilemma* (Englewood Cliffs, New Jersey, Prentice-Hall, 1963).

declines in death rates have not been matched by declines in the birth rate. The Population Council, a private foundation, spent $20.4 million dollars for work on problems of population from 1953 to 1964.

The writing and predictions of the neo-Malthusians logically lead to a question of the meaning of overpopulation. Overpopulation, quite clearly, is a relative term. The people of the United States are not overly concerned with such a problem, although the nation has a higher population density than some countries that have such a concern. The difference, of course, is the technological base. In other words, overpopulation refers to the ability of a given people to supply themselves with the necessities for life. Figure 20-2 shows how much faster the so-called underdeveloped countries are expanding their populations as compared to the developed countries.

There is another dimension of what has been called the Malthusian problem. This is the threat to international peace which population pressure poses.[23] It is a matter of serious conjecture as to whether or not the over-populated countries may be tempted to invade their more sparsely settled neighbors in search of "living room." It is precisely this question which leads Dennis Wrong to state that the political and economic transformation of the highly populated nonwestern world is the central issue of contemporary history.[24]

SUMMARY

Studies of populations provide information necessary for understanding many facets of human behavior and at the same time make it possible to plan for the future. The total number of people in the world is at an all-time high and is increasing at an unprecedented rate, as is the population of most nations. The explosive growth of population in recent years has been attributed to improvements in food production, in health knowledge and practices, and in technological advances generally.

Three factors, birth, death, and migration, account for population growth and change. Fertility differentials follow definite patterns with the following predominating: higher birth rates in rural areas than in urban areas, higher birth rates among the lower socio-economic classes, and higher birth rates among certain ethnic, racial, and religious groups. Mortality differentials indicate that women live longer than men; and that residence and race are related to longevity. Migration in recent years has been by individuals and families rather than whole groups of people. Recent trends show that international migration is slowing down because of many national restrictions.

[23] Katherine Organshi and A. F. K. Organshi, *Population and World Power* (New York, Knopf, 1961).
[24] *Op. cit.*, p. 115.

FIGURE 20-2. *Development Problems are Intensified by Soaring Populations.*

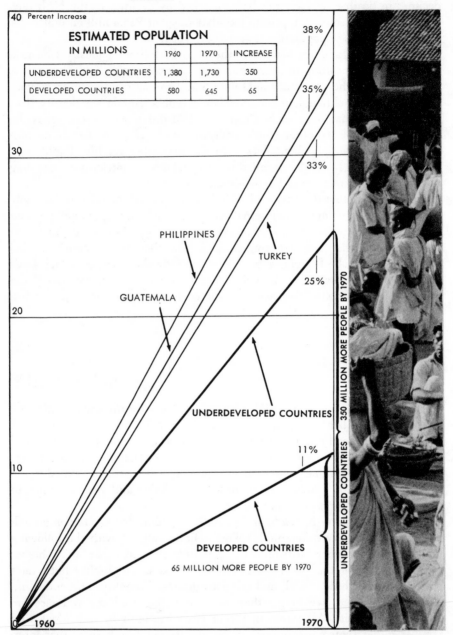

ESTIMATED POPULATION IN MILLIONS	1960	1970	INCREASE
UNDERDEVELOPED COUNTRIES	1,380	1,730	350
DEVELOPED COUNTRIES	580	645	65

40 Percent Increase

38%

35%

30

33%

PHILIPPINES

TURKEY

25%

GUATEMALA

20

UNDERDEVELOPED COUNTRIES

11%

10

DEVELOPED COUNTRIES

65 MILLION MORE PEOPLE BY 1970

350 MILLION MORE PEOPLE BY 1970

UNDERDEVELOPED COUNTRIES

0 1960

1970

Source: *A New Program for a Decade of Development for Underdeveloped Areas of the World,* Bureau of Public Affairs (Washington, D. C., 1961), p. 12. Photograph courtesy of United Nations Organization.

However, within the United States, people continue to manifest a desire to rove, and the average person changes residences once every five years. Economic motivation provides the primary reason for changes.

Cultural values are closely related to population growth. Such factors as technology, levels and standards of living, valuation placed on children, sex regulations, regulations relating to child survival, and health practices have important implications for population increments.

Modern-day concern with problems of overpopulation recall the writings of Malthus, who was concerned about the differential rates of growth between the population and the food supply. This type of problem makes clear the social significance of population growth and change and also indicates that such questions have political implications.

Supplementary Readings

Freedman, Ronald, *Population: The Vital Revolution* (Garden City, New York, Doubleday, 1964).

Hauser, Philip M., *The Population Dilemma* (Englewood Cliffs, New Jersey, Prentice-Hall, 1963).

Petersen, William, *The Politics of Population* (Garden City, New York, Doubleday, 1964).

Shryock, Henry S., Jr., *Population Mobility Within the United States* (Chicago, Community and Family Study Center, University of Chicago, 1964).

Simpson, Hoke S., Ed., *The Changing American Population* (New York, Institute of Life Insurance Graduate School of Business, Columbia University, 1962).

Thompson, Warren S., and David T. Lewis, *Population Problems*, 5th ed. (New York, McGraw-Hill, 1965).

Westoff, Charles F., Robert G. Potter, and Philip C. Sagi, *The Third Child: A Study of the Prediction of Fertility* (Princeton, New Jersey, Princeton University Press, 1963).

Wrong, Dennis H., *Population and Society*, 2nd and enlarged ed. (New York, Random House, 1961).

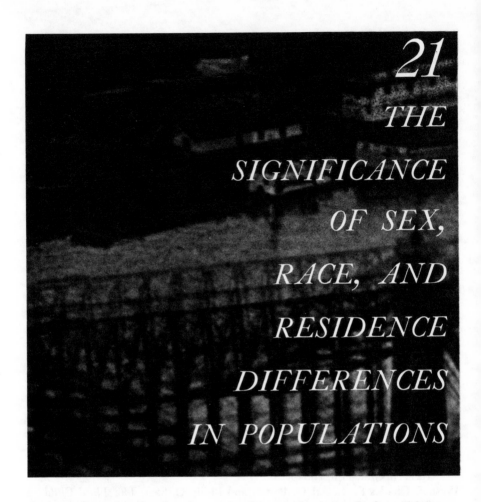

21

THE SIGNIFICANCE OF SEX, RACE, AND RESIDENCE DIFFERENCES IN POPULATIONS

It was indicated in the introduction to this part that a knowledge of the number and characteristics of a given population is basic to most types of sociological inquiry. The discussion in this chapter is designed to acquaint the student with some important specific implications that the composition of the population has for human interaction. Special emphasis is placed on the biological categories of sex and race, and the social category of residence. Emphasis is placed on these three aspects of population composition because they are, perhaps, the most prevailing and universal basis for social differentiation.

THE SEX FACTOR IN SOCIAL DIFFERENTIATION

It is appropriate to begin this discussion on the demographic aspects of social differentiation with a consideration of sex differences. Nowhere can one find a situation where the same standards of behavior apply with equal force to men and women. The culture of all societies designates different generalized roles and status positions for men and women, not to mention different standards of dress and grooming. In this discussion various methodological approaches to the study of sex differences will be introduced, and a review of the implications that these differences have for human interaction and the prediction of behavior will be given.

THE SEX RATIO: ITS UTILITY AND APPLICATIONS

When describing the sex composition of a population, social scientists generally utilize the sex ratio as a summarizing device. The **sex ratio** is simply a statement of the number of males per one hundred females. It is calculated by dividing the total number of males by the total number of females and multiplying the result by 100. A sex ratio of 100 indicates there are equal numbers of males and females in the population, a smaller figure shows that there are more women than men, and a larger figure indicates that males are in the majority. An extremely low or an extremely high ratio indicates a serious imbalance between the sexes.

The sex ratio affects the social and other conditions in a given society in a number of ways.[1] The most obvious is in connection with the birth rate. If there are a disproportionate number of males in what are generally thought of as marriageable ages, there will be smaller percentages of persons married. The birth rate will be affected to this extent. In many European countries one can find a relatively large number of unmarried women because of the out-migration of males and the high number of male war casualties.

The sex ratio also has an important implication for the death rate of a population. This is true because women normally live longer than men. Thus if the sex ratio is low, the death rate will be correspondingly lower. In the United States the sex ratio was down to 96.4 in 1965, and overall, there were 3.6 million more women than men. Since women outlive men an average of three or four years, life expectancy in the nation is improved by this low sex ratio.

Sex ratios also tell much about what one can expect concerning social activity. For example, in communities where women predominate, the whole social climate reflects the women's point of view. Studies have shown that subdivisions or communities located near large urban centers tend to be women dominated because so many men commute to work to the central city.

Finally, marriage and family customs often trace back to the sex ratio of the population. In communities where women are scarce, such as mining or frontier communities, women tend to be placed on a pedestal and to get exag-

[1] Warren S. Thompson and David T. Lewis, *Population Problems*, 5th ed. (New York, McGraw-Hill, 1965), pp. 78-84.

gerated attention from men. Contrariwise, where men are in the minority, as is true in certain large cities, women are much more aggressive in the courtship process.

Enough has been said to demonstrate the utility of the sex ratio and the implications that an imbalance of the sexes may have. We turn now to other aspects of sexual differentiation.

THE SEXUAL DIVISION OF LABOR

Sexual division of labor is fairly uniform in most cultures. This is true because it is women who must bear and nurse babies and because men have greater physical strength and endurance. There are, of course, some cultural variations. In this regard, the Russians and the Israelites used women as combat troops, something of an innovation in the modern world. However, in each instance there were certain limitations to the tasks performed by the woman soldier.

It is fairly easy to observe the tasks which primarily are relegated to women in a given society. This is as true for the advanced societies as for the more primitive societies. The occupational characteristics of women of the United States illustrate this point. In the mid-1960's women made up just over one-third of all the workers in the United States, but over 70 percent of all clerical workers were women. Women were also an overwhelming majority (97.5 percent) of all workers in private household jobs. By contrast, women made up a minority of the blue-collar workers (15.2 percent).[2]

From the statistics just quoted, it can be seen that working women in the United States tend to be occupied in a few professions and to concentrate in a few occupational groups. It is likely that similar patterns could be determined for other countries, although the specific professions and occupations might vary.

THE QUESTION OF A SUPERIOR SEX

Many arguments have been launched as to which of the two sexes is superior in a specific sense or in general. At times, beliefs along these lines have been strong enough to serve as the basis for special privileges or honors. For example, it has not been unusual for women to be denied voting privileges or decision-making rights in higher societal councils, because they were not considered as capable as men.

Recent developments associated with the so-called emancipation of women, suggest that cultural patterns based on what has been considered the innate superiority of men are changing. However, since this question

[2] Monthly Report on The Labor Force, U.S. Dept. of Labor, January, 1966.

keeps cropping up, it is worthwhile to examine some of the more relevant facts.

The first reference usually made in debates on the superiority of one or the other sex is to physical maturity. Beliefs (and facts) in this regard are the basis for various cultural patterns. For one thing, the age at which a boy is considered a man or a girl is considered a woman varies from one place to another. In the United States, it is possible in some states for a girl to marry without consent of her parents at a younger age than a boy. This is because the girl is considered to mature faster physically. However, it is almost universal in the United States that both men and women have to be 21 years of age before they can vote. From this pattern, one can infer that a distinction is made between physical and intellectual maturity. If one uses marriage criteria, then women may be judged superior.

Another basis for comparing men and women is on the basis of physical strength. Here the evidence is more clear-cut. Women normally do not play rough contact sports, such as football and hockey. Nor do they excel in any activity demanding great physical strength.

A third criteria frequently used to base arguments of sex superiority is intelligence. It is probably fortunate, for the sake of amicable relations, that no clear-cut pattern persists. Studies of intelligence tend to indicate that boys are superior to girls in mathematical and mechanical reasoning. But girls show superiority in color perception and manual dexterity. Whether these scores are related to particular socialization factors rather than intelligence is not clear. When one studies the list of so-called geniuses in history, men appear in far greater numbers than do women. This finding is also difficult to disassociate from cultural factors, which clearly favor men. Since women are generally excluded from military and political offices as well as discriminated against in other professional fields, their chances of attaining notoriety are reduced, to say the least.

After considering the above factors, and in light of other considerations not presented, the only statement that can be made is that the double standard of conduct that exists for the sexes makes it difficult to clearly evaluate the differences between men and women. The fact remains, and must be reckoned with, that women are generally considered the "weaker" sex. This leads us directly to what has been referred to as the "woman problem."

THE WOMAN PROBLEM[3]

The limitation that biological processes place upon women has direct implications for her cultural aspirations. A woman can never forget that she is a woman, because her life is punctuated, in Margaret Mead's words, with a

[3] For a lucid discussion of this topic, see Robert Bierstedt, *The Social Order*, 2nd ed. (New York, McGraw-Hill, 1963), pp. 370-372.

series of specific events that vividly remind her that she is a female.[4] These events include the beginning of physical maturity at menarche, the end of virginity, pregnancy and birth, and menopause. Men do not have these periodic interferences with their careers, which might interfere with their ability to command an army or to guide a giant corporation.

There is no doubt that the "woman problem" can and has been exaggerated by both men and women writers. For this reason, there is no attempt here to take one or another position, simply to note one reason why women are not considered seriously for some positions. This "fact of life" relates back to the importance of sexual differentiation.

THE RACE FACTOR IN SOCIAL DIFFERENTIATION

It can be said without fear of contradiction that no major nation of the world is racially homogeneous. Only a few nations have discouraged immigration so thoroughly that their populations do not include peoples with diverse racial origins. Race, in fact, almost universally serves as a social selector and is a wide-spread basis for differential statuses and roles. This is why race has been associated with dramatic historical themes, some involving great human tragedies.

WHAT "RACE" MEANS

Despite much concern over race problems, there is still a tremendous amount of ignorance on the subject. In everyday conversations, one can hear examples of the type of confusion which exists over this concept. Perhaps the most common error is to confuse race with nationality or with religious affiliation. One is likely to hear such statements as "He is a member of the German race" or "He belongs to the Jewish race." Race, in its biological sense, is based upon a combination of physical traits and not on nationality or religion. In this regard, social definitions that concentrate on one lineage are of great interest to sociologists because they represent definitions of a situation.[5] For example, very few Negroes in the United States are racially pure and many so-called Negroes have more white than Negro ancestors. Yet in many places a person is considered a Negro if he has any trace of Negro ancestry.

[4] Margaret Mead, *Male and Female* (New York, New American Library, 1955), pp. 127-128.
[5] For a very forceful presentation of what race means sociologically, see Edgar T. Thompson and Everett C. Hughes, Eds., *Race: Individual and Collective Behavior* (New York, Free Press, 1958), Part I.

In this discussion we are not concerned primarily with a classification of racial groups. However, it may serve a purpose of review to name the major races of mankind. The major racial divisions recognized by anthropologists are shown in Table 21-1.

RACE AND PREJUDICE

The one indisputable fact that is associated with race is that it creates a consciousness of kind, or if one wishes, a consciousness of difference. This consciousness is directly related to group membership and types of social interaction. People who have similar physical traits recognize in one another something kindred and thus often tend to seek one another out and to form groups. This process may occur unconsciously, but the fact that one belongs to a different race is always a matter of consciousness. Consciousness of racial group leads quite understandably to a certain type of prejudice known as race prejudice.

DEFINING PREJUDICE: Before elaborating on race prejudice, it is well to define what is meant by this term. Prejudice is simply a prejudgment, regardless of the basis on which it is made. A prejudiced person is one who holds rigid, deeply internalized feelings toward the members of a group to which he does not belong. Some prejudices derive from direct experiences while others stem from socialization experiences and are "inborn," so to speak. Prejudice can be both positive and negative. It is positive when one is egocentric or ethnocentric and considers himself or his group to be superior in all ways. It is negative when it is against someone or some group. Positive prejudice is closely associated with pride, patriotism, loyalty, and other sentiments which are considered both normal and worthwhile. Negative prejudices are more likely to be considered "bad" because they elicit behavior based on consideration other than the usual or normal one. To illustrate, a Jewish student may be denied admission to a medical school, although he is better qualified scholastically than non-Jewish students who are admitted. Much of race prejudice is of this type.

MANIFESTATIONS OF PREJUDICE: Robin M. Williams outlines two basic manifestations of prejudice.[6] The first manifestation that he identifies is social distance feelings. These feelings are described as feelings of willingness among members of a group to accept or approve a given degree of intimacy in their interaction with members of certain other groups. Williams lists some specific aspects of social distance feelings: (1) feelings of group differences,

---

[6] Robin M. Williams, Jr., *Strangers Next Door* (Englewood Cliffs, New Jersey, Prentice-Hall, 1964), pp. 29-43.

TABLE 21-1. Outline Racial Classification of Mankind

Primary Stocks and Races	Texture of Hair of Head	Hair of Body and Face	Head	Nose	Prognathism	Skin Color	Stature	Remarks
CAUCASIAN OR "WHITE"								
Nordic	Wavy	Abundant	Narrow	Narrow	Slight	Very fair	Tall	Often blond, eyes light
Alpine	Wavy	Abundant	Broad	Narrow	Slight	Fair	Above aver.	Hair brown, eyes brown
Mediterranean	Wavy	Abundant	Narrow	Narrow	Slight	Dark white	Medium	"Regular features," graceful
Hindu	Wavy	Abundant	Narrow	Variable	Moderate	Brown	Above aver.	Dark admixture espec. in S.
MONGOLOID OR "YELLOW"								
Mongolian	Straight	Slight	Broad	Medium	Medium	Light brown	Below aver.	Broad face, Mongolian eye
Malaysian	Straight	Slight	Broad	Medium	Medium	Brown	Below aver.	Broad face
American Indian	Straight	Slight	Variable	Medium	Medium	Brown	Tall to medium	Broad face
NEGROID OR "BLACK"								
Negro	Woolly	Slight	Narrow	Broad	Strong	Dark brown	Tall	Everted lips
Melanesian	Woolly	Slight	Narrow	Broad	Strong	Dark brown	Medium	Some aquiline noses
Pygmy Black	Woolly	Slight	Broadish	Broad	Strong	Dark brown	Very short	
Bushman	Peppercorn	Slight	Narrow	Broad	Slight	Yellowish	Very short	Wrinkles, steatopygy, thin lips, Mongolian eye
OF DOUBTFUL CLASSIFICATION								
Australoid	Wavy	Abundant	Narrow	Broad	Strong	Dark brown	Medium	Negroid traits preponderate, some Caucasian resembl.
Veddoid (Indo-Austral.)	Wavy	Moderate	Narrow	Broad	Medium	Brown	Short	Generalized proto-Caucasian, some Australoid resembl.
Polynesian	Wavy	Moderate	Variable	Medium	Medium	Brown	Tall	Mongoloid and Caucas. traits, with local Negroid admixture
Ainu	Wavy	Abundant	Narrow	Medium	Medium	Light brown	Medium	Prob. generalized Caucasian

Hair and eyes are "black" unless otherwise stated.

(2) dislike of the outgroup, (3) feelings of inappropriateness, (4) fear of anticipated reactions of the ingroup, (5) aversion to and fear of anticipated responses of the outgroup, (6) generalized feelings of shyness or discomfort, regarding unfamiliar social situations. Williams goes on to indicate that the source of social distance feeling can usually be traced to the primary groups in which the individual has membership. These feelings reflect conformity to the expectations and demands of ingroups rather than attitudes toward the members of the outgroup against whom the prejudice is expressed. By expressing prejudice, the individual is actually showing a positive desire to be associated with and to be approved by the members of his group.

The second manifestation of prejudice is the use of stereotypes. Stereotypes are simply labels or identities which are commonly used to show what is believed about the behavior of a person and group. The stereotype is a generalized technique for classing all members of an outgroup into one class. It obviates the need for personal experience or observation, since personal traits of members of the stereotype group are divested of any originality or individuality by the fact that they are labeled as a Jew, Negro, or whatever the case may be. Stereotypes, of course, are a part of all cultures. They thrive on a combination of interest and ignorance. This explains why all nationalities have stereotypes applied to them by members of other nationalities. These stereotypes serve propaganda purposes as well as form the basis of much humor. In this regard, it is significant that hostility between groups tends to serve both to cause and perpetuate stereotyping.

PREJUDICE AND DISCRIMINATION

Prejudice often leads to discrimination, and thus there is a tendency to confuse these terms. Actually they are two different concepts. Prejudice is a matter of belief, discrimination is a mode of behavior. E. Franklin Frazier wrote cogently about discrimination some time ago and made the point clear that to discriminate means to deny an individual or a group a privilege or an opportunity granted other members of the society.[7]

The relevance of a consideration of discrimination to a discussion of racial differentiation is that race is often used as a basis for discriminatory behavior. A man may possess all of the qualifications for voting, but may be denied this opportunity because he happens to be a Negro or Oriental. Racial discrimination procedures may involve physical segregation, as when restaurants or hotels do not serve Negroes. In this regard, a distinction must be maintained between racial and other types of discrimination. Segregation on the basis of social class, religion, or other factors is sometimes confused with racial discrimination.

[7] E. Franklin Frazier, *The Negro in the United States* (New York, Macmillan, 1949), pp. 671-678.

"MISLEADING TRAILS"[8]*:*
RACIAL PREJUDICE IN PERSPECTIVE

Because of the great concern in certain parts of the world over race relations and because of many misconceptions about patterns of prejudice related to race, it seems appropriate to include a short note at this point on what have been called "misleading trails."

The first and foremost pitfall that entraps the less experienced person who becomes aware of prejudice as a social problem is the temptation to overly emphasize race relations problems. The usual case is to forget about other patterns of prejudice and to become a crusader for race equality. Such a tendency may be natural, because of the great publicity over racial injustices but it indicates an *a priori* judgment that race problems are more serious than other problems of prejudice. This point, at best, is an unsettled one.

The second "misleading trail" is often taken by persons with high motives to eliminate prejudice. They simply deny that races exist or look upon race differences as being of little importance and accuse those who argue differently of harboring a delusion. Some adherents of this school base their claim on the fact that there is no "pure" race, because of widespread miscegenation. The fact is that race does exist, from both a biological and sociological viewpoint. Acknowledging this does not in any way condone patterns of discrimination. It simply acknowledges that differences in humans do exist and are used as a basis for specific behavior patterns. Despite the greater or lesser differences between one person or another, his or her social participation depends, in many instances, on the race with which they are identified. A Negro doctor in the southern United States until recently could not become a member of many local county medical societies. It is still difficult for Negroes to move into many northern subdivisions. One must understand the importance of such racial differences in order to understand the nature of patterns of prejudice.

A third common error is to associate prejudice with minority groups and to assume all minority groups are subjected to prejudice. As a matter of fact, many minority groups experience no prejudice at all. Indeed, they may be accorded higher esteem than majority groups. This is especially true where a powerful elite exists and perpetuates itself, as the whites in parts of Africa.

Another fallacy, which occasionally is committed by a professional social scientist, is to take the point of view that prejudice can only be understood by studying those against whom it is directed. For example, a good many studies of race prejudice in the United States focus solely on the Negro. The findings of such studies cannot help but be one-sided. Rightfully the subjects of prejudice should be studied as intensively, if not more so, than the objects of prejudice.

[8] The writer is indebted to Bierstedt for this title: *op. cit.,* p. 478.

Finally, the person who would study prejudice, must understand that almost all individuals, groups, and members of any society experience some prejudice for or against some group. Although it is faddish, and even fashionable, to point the finger at others who are very obviously prejudiced and by inference imply that one is free from such a human frailty, this is seldom the case. This pitfall is illustrated by the experience of a professor friend of the writer who taught in one of the universities in California. Students in his classes were righteously indignant over the patterns of prejudice against the Negro in the southern region of the United States. They were ready to engage in direct action to right this evil. The professor subtly switched the discussion to Orientals, Spanish Americans, and the southern white immigrants to California. Immediately voices were heard deploring the existence of these groups in California cities because they were given to criminality, were shiftless, and did not have good health and sanitation standards. Perhaps the most prevalent prejudice of many of us is against those whom we consider prejudiced because they do not share our views.

IMPLICATIONS OF RACE DIFFERENTIATION

This brief discussion on the racial aspects of social differentiation is intentionally more analytic than descriptive. It is intended to provide the student with an understanding why the racial make-up of a population is important. Those who wish detailed descriptions of the race problem in any particular social setting are referred to the many excellent works on this subject.[9] Here the point that must be again emphasized is that so long as society exists, there will be certain patterns of interaction which are based on racial characteristics. This is true because race always gives way to a certain pride of race, which generally is translated into a form of prejudice against other races. When such prejudice is the basis for discrimination, the existence of a social problem depends on whether or not these patterns of behavior are judged right or wrong. The frightening thought is that although prejudice of one type may be eradicated, another type will likely crop up.

THE RESIDENCE FACTOR IN SOCIAL DIFFERENTIATION

Given societal populations are not only differentiated on the basis of race and sex, but also on the basis of where one lives. Residence, rural or urban, is

[9] For two good examples, see Lewis Killian and Charles Grigg, *Racial Crisis in America* (Englewood Cliffs, New Jersey, Prentice-Hall, 1964), and Elaine Burgess "Race Relations and Social Change," selection in John C. McKinney and Edgar T. Thompson, Eds., *The South in Continuity and Change* (Durham, North Carolina, Duke University Press, 1965), Chapter XVI.

important in the socialization of an individual, and accounts for the significance of residence differentials in the make-up of a given population. In this section we review the nature of environmental factors that account for these differences. The purpose in mind is to demonstrate how life in a rural or an urban setting is related to patterns of behavior.

THE RURAL-URBAN CONTINUUM[10]

Sociological classifications can seldom be worked out so that they have extreme precision. The words "rural" and "urban" are no exception. Rural-urban differences occur over a wide range of characteristics extending from the two polar extremes of completely rural and completely urban. The student should keep this understanding in mind when he reads the materials in this section. Rural-urban differences can be thought of as varying in degree along a scale that can be termed the rural-urban continuum. This view does not weaken or otherwise invalidate the basic position that rural-urban differences are real and definite and can be studied.

THE ENVIRONMENTAL INFLUENCES THAT ACCOUNT FOR RURAL-URBAN DIFFERENCES

The importance of certain environmental influences in the socialization process was brought out in Chapter 4. Here these same influences are reviewed to show how they may account for the difference in behavior between two relatively distinct population groups.

THE GEOGRAPHIC ENVIRONMENT: The major aspects of the geographic environment—location, climate, topography, and natural resources—account for rural-urban differences in at least four different ways: (1) *Physical setting*—Rural persons usually face nature in its unmodified extremes and must wrest their living directly from nature. In so doing, they develop ways of life compatible with their struggle with nature. The urbanite seldom comes face-to-face with the extremes of nature. He thus is at a loss to understand some of the basic personality traits of ruralites. (2) *The capriciousness of nature*—In rural areas one is dependent upon the vicissitudes of weather, including major disasters on occasion. Because he has to struggle against the capriciousness of nature, the ruralite tends to be a more practical man (in terms of fatalism and stoicism) than his urban neighbor. At the same time he is more religious and more superstitious for the same reason. (3) *Close communion with nature*—Because he deals with nature constantly, the ruralite is likely to

---

[10] Alvin L. Bertrand *et al.*, *Rural Sociology* (New York, McGraw-Hill, 1958), p. 24.

develop a special feeling for plants and animals which his city neighbor has difficulty understanding. He is more at ease with the outdoors and, in contrast to the urbanite, is generally ill at ease and uncomfortable if he has to remain cooped up for indoor work. (4) *Relative isolation*—Perhaps one of the most obvious geographic features of rural life is the low density of population. This isolation or semi-isolation has implications for his personality and social life. He is generally not as closely attuned to national and international developments nor is he likely to be as sophisticated about new ways and things as his urban cousin.

THE SOCIAL ENVIRONMENT: The social environment accounts for rural-urban differences in four ways as follows. (1) *The predominance of primary group contacts*—In rural areas the person is likely to have most of his experience in groups that are close-knit and primary (*Gemeinschaft*) in nature. The family, for example, predominates in the lives of its members in rural areas, more than in urban areas. This is true because it is a producing unit as well as a consuming unit. Associations within a neighborhood or local community are generally with friends and neighbors and are on a personal basis. This is seldom true in an urban setting. (2) *Social differentiation*—The city contains a great heterogeneity of groups. There is much division of labor, and a great deal of social stratification. In contrast, in rural areas, homogeneity tends to be the key to social integration—that is, everyone tends to work and live in similar fashion. (3) *Social stratification*—Generally, there are fewer strata or classes in rural society, and the social extremes are not as differentiated as in the city. (4) *Social mobility*—Social mobility is not as prevalent in rural areas as in urban society. This pattern is related to the fact that there are fewer social classes and fewer occupational groups.

THE CULTURAL ENVIRONMENT: Culture patterns exist independent of the social structures that make up the social environment. The cultural influences that impinge on rural individuals as contrasted to urban persons are as follows. (1) *Simplicity of cultural expressions*—It is usually true that cultural expressions tend to be simpler and less embellished in rural areas than in urban areas. Expressions of this type include songs, dances, clothing, and language. In addition, the basic moral and ethical standards tend to lose their rural forthrightness when they are transported to the city. (2) *Social control*—In rural areas, generally speaking, order is maintained through means which tend to be informal in nature, such as gossip, ostracism, and ridicule. In the urban setting, social control is likely to be more in terms of formal law-enforcing institutions. (3) *Variety of knowledge and skills required*—The ruralite usually has to have command of a large variety of knowledge and skills to be occupationally successful. This is true because he does not operate in a specialized setting. A farmer, for example, must have knowledge of soils, plants, and animals as well as machinery and equipment. In contrast, the city person is much more likely to be highly specialized in his occupational endeavors. (4) *Levels and standards of living*—The home, to a great extent, reflects cultural participation. Normally speaking, ruralites enjoy much lower levels of living as measured by such items as refrigerators, washing machines, bathrooms, and types of clothes worn. This factor counts in some measure for urban attitudes of superiority which are almost universal. The orientation of rural culture does not bring to the attention of the ruralite many of the advanced goods and services which are known to the urbanite. Consequently, the standard of living of the latter group as well as the level of living is considerably higher.

RURAL-URBAN POPULATION DIFFERENCES: The sociologist is quite concerned about the population differences that exist between rural and urban people. These vary somewhat from society to society. However, some indication of the types of differences which do exist can be gleaned from the situation in the United States. (1) The rural population has fewer persons in the productive ages, but more people in the dependent ages. The productive ages are normally construed to be between 20 and 65 years. It is interesting to note that elderly people are comprising an ever-increasing proportion of the total urban population. This is a part, of course, of the increasing longevity of life. (2) There are more women in the city and more men on the farms. This pattern has been more exaggerated in the past in the United States than it is now, but continues to hold true. Discovery of this fact leads to the assumption that women leave farms in greater numbers than men, which is also generally true. There are important implications in this pattern for marriage and other types of social interaction. (3) Generally speaking, the urban population is characterized by considerably higher formal educational attainment than the rural population. This finding is in keeping with the greater educational advantages to be found in urban centers. (4) Marital stability tends to be greater in rural areas than in urban places. A higher divorce rate in urban places is accounted for by the greater social differentiation.

OTHER DEMOGRAPHIC ASPECTS OF SOCIAL DIFFERENTIATION

This chapter may be concluded with a brief review of other important components of population which normally are used to analyze social differentiation.

Little reflection is necessary to become aware of the many important ways in which age influences social action. Age thus represents another important demographic differential. The most commonly used device for showing the age composition of a given population is the population pyramid. Population pyramids give the age and sex characteristics of the population in summary form at a given time. They are constructed in such a way that a vertical line separates the percentage of males (on the left) from the percentage of females (on the right) in given age groups. (See Figure 21-1.) Whether a given population is relatively aged or not is quite significant. In an aging population a smaller proportion of the population is in the productive ages and a larger proportion in the dependent ages. One illustration discloses the significance of this fact. Taxes are paid in the main by the adult population of ages from 25 to 65 years. At the same time older persons must have the same government services, and in addition, provision must be made for their security. Aging is also related to conservativeness in politics and in business and industrial endeavors. It also affects consumer patterns, as there is a greater demand for such things as medical services, conservative clothing, certain foods, and special recreational items.

Marriage also has many social and cultural implications and is considered still another important characteristic of populations. It is for this reason that most sociologists are interested in the percentage of any given population which is married, which has been married, or which intends to be married.

Education is also closely associated with social interaction. This fact is so well known that no elaboration is necessary.

SUMMARY

Each criteria that separates one individual from another in a given population is a potential basis for differential patterns of behavior. A knowledge of the composition of a population is thus of great importance to the sociologist. Three criteria have been of primary interest to social scientists: sex, race, and residence.

Sexual division of labor occurs in all societies and is related to the physical differences between men and women. However, the cultural setting is important in terms of the specific tasks considered appropriate for men and women. No clear-cut evidence can be presented that men or women are superior in intelligence, although the one sex or the other shows superiority in certain types of performance. In this connection, the limitations that biological processes place on women tend to interfere with their embarking on certain types of careers.

The racial differences that characterize mankind are also related to social differentiation and particular patterns of interaction. While the technical meaning of race is restricted to physical traits, social definitions may extend to individuals with any trace of ancestry from another racial group. The importance of race to sociologists is found in the patterns of prejudice which often accompany racial differences. These patterns result in types of behavior,

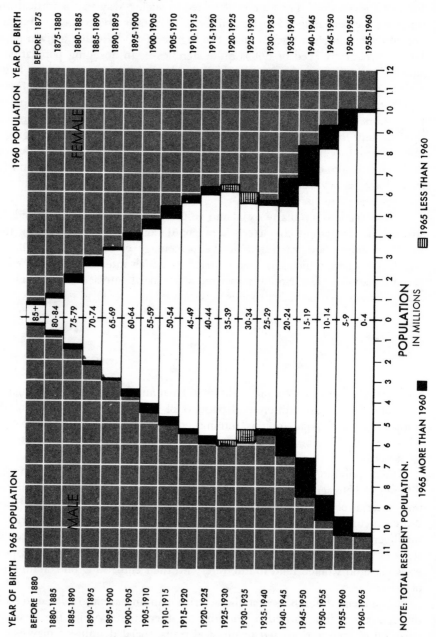

FIGURE 21-1. *Pyramid Constructed from Estimates of the Population of the United States, by Age, Color, and Sex: July 1, 1960 and 1965.*

Source: *Current Population Reports, U. S. Bureau of the Census* (Washington, D. C., U. S. Government Printing Office, 1965), Series P.25, No. 321, cover.

such as discrimination and segregation, which lead to social problems. In this regard there are many myths and fallacies which account for patterns of relations between the races.

Not only can populations be differentiated on the basis of varying physical traits, but on the basis of socio-cultural differences as well. Everywhere, people who live in urban centers are differentiated from people who live in rural areas. The differences in social organization between these two residence groups is accounted for in terms of the different way in which the geographic, social, and cultural environment impinges on people from the respective setting. Not only do rural populations tend to be less sophisticated and have lower levels of living, but they tend to have different population characteristics of age, sex, and education.

There are many other ways in which the composition or make-up of a population has significance for sociological purposes. The age composition of the population, the educational make-up of the population, and the marital make-up of the population are some of the more meaningful classes of this type which are studied by sociologists.

Supplementary Readings

Bertrand, Alvin L., Ed., *Rural Sociology* (New York, McGraw-Hill, 1958), Chapters 2-5.

Mead, Margaret, *Male and Female* (New York, New American Library, Mentor Books, 1949).

Rose, Arnold M. and Caroline B. Rose, Eds., *Minority Problems* (New York, Harper & Row, 1965).

Segal, Bernard E., Ed., *Racial and Ethnic Relations* (New York, Crowell, 1966).

Simpson, Richard L. and Ida Harper Simpson, Eds., *Social Organization and Behavior* (New York, Wiley, 1964), Chapters 9 and 13.

Taylor, Lee and Arthur R. Jones, Jr., *Rural Life and Urbanized Society* (New York, Oxford University Press, 1964), Parts I and II.

Thompson, Edgar T. and Everett C. Hughes, *Race: Individual and Collective Behavior* (New York, Free Press, 1958).

Thompson, Warren S. and David T. Lewis, *Population Problems*, 5th ed. (New York, McGraw-Hill, 1965), Part II.

Williams, Robin M., Jr., *Strangers Next Door* (Englewood Cliffs, New Jersey, Prentice-Hall, 1964).

22

COMMUNITY AND REGION: THE BROADER ASPECTS OF HUMAN ECOLOGY

It has been stressed throughout this text that humans group themselves into subsocial systems (groups) which are linked together to form master societal systems. In a concrete sense, every level of social organization, from the smallest recognizable group to the largest societal system, has to have a geographic location. This does not mean that a specific territorial base is a prerequisite for a community or other social system. The prime requirement for a system, as mentioned before, is a certain type of structural make-up. This is why social systems can be thought of in the abstract without reference to geographic space. However, a given concrete group is always related to certain geographic (locational) variables, many of which can be determined and classified. Locational characteristics are so persistent in human behavior that they represent an important basis of social differentiation. The purpose of this chapter is to acquaint the student with the classifications and conceptual language which has been developed by sociologists and other social scientists in their study of the locality aspects of actually existing human groupings. The branch of sociology within which studies of this type fall is termed human ecology.[1]

[1] This interpretation is in keeping with the views of Hawley and Quinn. Hawley states, "Human Ecology emerged as and remains primarily a sociological concern" [Amos

THE NATURE AND IMPORTANCE OF HUMAN ECOLOGY

SYMBIOTIC NATURE OF HUMAN INTERRELATIONSHIPS

Human ecology as stated, centers in the study of the relationship between man and his environment. Said another way, human ecology is concerned with how man distributes himself in geographical space. Ecological units are formed when men distribute themselves in relation to land areas in order to realize some social organization advantage. These advantages may range from economic considerations, such as to be near the source of certain natural resources like water, to health needs and recreational activity which can only be satisfied in specific types of climate.

The way in which humans distribute themselves in particular habitats has been likened to symbiotic relations among plants and animals. There are, however, at least two important differences between human and subhuman symbiosis. The first difference stems from the fact that men relate themselves to one another more in an occupational sense—what social scientists term the division of labor. Since this is true, interdependence is primarily between men, rather than between men and plants and animals. Human symbiosis is thus best described as intraspecies in nature. By contrast, subhuman symbiosis is chiefly interspecies, that is, between plants and animals.

The second difference between human and subhuman symbiosis is that humans always react to geographic influences in terms of their cultural conditioning. Plants and animals cannot deliberately alter their physical environment nor can they exert systematic control over their kind. Man does both, and his relations to land are strongly conditioned by his customs, beliefs, and knowledge. To illustrate, the development of a given community in a remote part of the world can often be explained by the presence of a highly valued commodity, like diamonds. In another sense, man creates ecological areas deliberately by introducing new uses for the land. There are many examples of the latter: irrigating arid lands, clearing jungles, and developing new strains of plants and animals that can survive in places where they were not adaptable before, are but a few. Man also develops certain preferences for such things as food items and recreational activity, and this helps explain why he will settle in one place and not another.

H. Hawley, *Human Ecology* (New York, The Ronald Press, 1950), p. 67]. Quinn holds that a sociological investigation is ecological ". . . to the extent that it examines any aspect of the spatial-functional-cultural complex of a community or region" [James A. Quinn, *Human Ecology* (Englewood Cliffs, New Jersey, Prentice-Hall, 1950), pp. 10-11].

Despite the fact that man adapts to the geographical environment in terms of his culture, his patterns of settlement are definitely arranged so as to implement symbiotic relationships. The student can readily verify this pattern of behavior by observing and studying the intricate and complex web of inter-action and interdependence which develops and exists between persons and groups located in different places. This fact provides us with a sound basis for defining and delimiting the field of human ecology.

DEFINITION OF HUMAN ECOLOGY

With the preceding discussion in mind, the following definition is appropri-ate. **Human or "sociological" ecology** *is the study of the symbiotic relationships between human beings and of the spatial patterns of settlement, land use, and social organization forms which result from these relationships.*[2] In reviewing this definition the student should not forget that plant ecology and animal ecology represent entirely different disciplines, although all ecological studies are based on symbiotic relationships of some sort. It should also be kept in mind that the study of human ecology is justified in terms of the vast amount of important social planning—for communities (urban and rural), regions, and national societies—which is dependent upon a knowledge of ecological facts and theory. In this regard, not only must one know the nature of "natural" ecological entities (those that are not deliberately planned), but he must be-come acquainted with the entities that have been rationally planned and created. Some four classes of ecological entities or forms are usually recognized and studied, including major composite regions, subregions, communities, and neighborhoods. Since sociologists have given special attention to regions and communities, these are considered in some detail in the remainder of this chapter.

THE COMMUNITY CONCEPT

The term community is a very old one in the English language and one which is used often and in many contexts in ordinary conversation. It is thus not surprising that ambiguous and varied meanings are attached to this concept, by professional as well as lay persons.[3] The lack of agreement about what a community is does not invalidate the notion of community, which is over-whelmingly accepted. It simply prescribes the necessity for each scholar to

[2] This definition follows the definitions of McKenzie and others. See R. D. Mc-Kenzie, "Human Ecology," *Encyclopedia of the Social Sciences* (New York, MacMillan, 1930), Vol. V., p. 314.

[3] See, for example, George A. Hillery, Jr., "Definitions of Community: Areas of Agreement," *Rural Sociology*, Vol. 20 (1955), pp. 111-123, and Thomas R. Ford and Willis A. Sutton, Jr., "The Impact of Change on Rural Communities and Fringe Areas: Review of Decade's Research," in James H. Copp, Ed., *Our Changing Rural Society: Perspectives and Trends* (Ames, Iowa, University of Iowa Press, 1964), Chapter 6.

carefully define his use and understanding of the concept. The research of many eminent scholars furnish the sources for the understandings which are given.

DEFINITION OF COMMUNITY

A community as mentioned, is generally looked upon by sociologists as a particular class of social system.[4] As a social system, a community has a structure of interrelated parts. It is also characterized by a certain type of relationship to other social structures—groups, organizations, and societies.

Keeping these points in mind, it is possible to attempt a definition of community which is consistent with a systematic theory of social organization. A **community** *is a social system that encompasses a sufficient number of institutionalized social structures for individuals, groups, and organizations to satisfy their needs through the formation of symbiotic role relationships that cut across the total system structure. It is the smallest unit of social structure within a society which can maintain itself.*

The above definition makes it quite clear that a community is an ecological entity. This is to say the members of the community play roles that are significant to the system in terms of symbiotic relationships. Long has called this a type of game relationship, where ". . . the banker makes use of the newspaperman, the politician, the contractors, the ecclesiastic, the labor leader, the civic leader—all to further his success in the banking game—but, reciprocally, he is used to further the others' success in the newspaper, political, contracting, ecclesiastical, labor, and civic games."[5] Since these symbiotic relationships bear a definite connection to a particular place, members of a community identify themselves with this place. This identification—"I'm from New Orleans" or "I live in Plainville"—has an important significance. It indicates that the individual holds a position as community member, and that this position includes a role that is reciprocal to all other community members in the sense of an identification with a member of a mutual social system. It will be noted that this is a sociological (or structural) tie, although psychological bonds also tend to be present in identification processes.

The definition of community given also gets around such questions as those of size, type of activity, shape, number of people, and location. It also rules out smaller social entities, which may or may not be thought of as ecological in nature, such as families and neighborhoods. It also makes clear that a community is a self-sufficient unity insofar as it provides the institutionalized structures that are normally demanded by members of the community in their routines designed to accomplish the functions of social institutions. In this regard, the student will no doubt question why a community can be said

[4] See Irwin T. Sanders, *The Community: An Introduction To A Social System* 2nd ed. (New York, The Ronald Press, 1966).

[5] Norton E. Long, "The Local Community as an Ecology of Games," *American Journal of Sociology,* Vol. 64 (November, 1958), p. 254-255.

to be self-sufficient when a given manufacturing plant or a department store must go outside the community for its needed raw materials or its stock. The point here is that the plant and the store exist in the community and provide structures that allow residents to work and buy—functions of economic institutions. The fact that systemic linkage is maintained with outside systems does not change the fact that a resident of the community can obtain work, can buy the essentials of life, can worship, and can obtain an education within the community. Systemic linkages are, of course, closely related to the efficiency and extent to which these functions are performed.

The nature and type of role relationships are what separates one community from another and from other groups and organizations. Community level roles, as brought out in Chapter 9, tend to be conjunctive in nature; that is, they are played toward a class of actor holding generalized positions rather than toward a specific actor holding a specific position. To illustrate, in a community housewives and store clerks regard one another generally as customers and clerks and not as *the* wife-mother or *the* shoe clerk, as they are considered in their respective family and store groups. It may be, of course, that they are personally acquainted and even belong to the same family, church, or neighborhood. In these systems their relationships would be at a different level of role interaction. In this regard, when the housewife and clerk interact in terms of their community level roles, they are pursuing separate goals—the goals of their respective groups. Yet, in the broader sense, they also serve the functions—customer and supplier—necessary for the community to exist. It may help to understand community level roles to think of how social stratification patterns work. A person's class status remains the same, within the community (or society) even though he is associated with particular groups within the total system.

One final advantage of the definition given above is its emphasis on the fact that communities consist of interactional relationships rather than upon people as units.[6] This understanding is important because individuals move in and out of communities, as well as being born and dying within a community. Yet, the communities persist because they are systems of behavior—one or another individual's action is simply a part of the total community action system.

THE COMMUNITY VERSUS
THE NEIGHBORHOOD

The distinction generally made between the neighborhood and the community helps to clarify the community concept. A neighborhood is also a structural entity, but is usually characterized by a smaller size than a community.

[6] Harold Kaufman has elaborated an interactional conception of community. See "Toward an Interactional Conception of Community," *Social Forces*, Vol. 38 (October, 1959), pp. 9-17.

There are two distinguishing features of the neighborhood which set it apart from the community. First, all actors are intimately acquainted with one another. It is expected that everyone will not only know every one else's name, but his life history as well. Thus at one level all members of a neighborhood interact as members of a primary or *Gemeinschaft* group, although at another level their interaction is in terms of the generalized roles characteristic of the community. In contrast, the community is usually characterized by a much greater variety in interactional patterns and is likely, although not necessarily, to afford a degree of anonymity.

The second important distinguishing feature of the neighborhood is that it is not a self-sufficient entity. It does not include the major institutionalized structures listed above as characteristic of communities. A neighborhood may provide for educational or religious needs or both. However, it never provides for the whole range of basic needs of its inhabitants. In this regard, it is helpful in clarifying the difference between a neighborhood and community to think of a community as usually encompassing several neighborhoods. It is possible, however, for the two to be coincident in situations where everyone is closely acquainted and all needed services are available.

In concluding this discussion, it may be noted that two questions regarding neighborhoods are currently under serious investigation by sociologists. The first pertains to whether or not a neighborhood can survive in a rapidly urbanizing society. Evidence to date from the United States indicates that some rural neighborhoods are disappearing at the same time that newer communities with somewhat different characteristics are appearing.[7]

The second question pertains to the nature of neighborhoods in urban places. Since the criteria of intimate, primary group relations does not hold for many city people who live as close as adjoining apartments or residences, many locality groups that might otherwise be identified as neighborhoods are ruled out. Some authors refer to these areas as special types of neighborhoods. However, there remains a serious question as to how this type of area should be classified.[8]

THE DELINEATION OF COMMUNITIES

The community has been identified as a unit of social structure above the level of group and organization which exists in geographical space. Such an identification could not be made if it were not possible to map or delineate communities. Actually, although delineational procedures must vary with size and type of community, these procedures are not too difficult. The two meth-

---

[7] Alvin L. Bertrand, "Rural Locality Groups: Changing Patterns, Change Factors, and Implications," *Rural Sociology*, Vol. XIX (1954), pp. 174-179.

[8] Nels Anderson, *The Urban Community* (New York, Holt, Rinehart and Winston, 1959), pp. 32-34.

ods most commonly used are known as the *identification method* and the *neighborhood cluster method.*[9]

The **identification method** of community delineation assumes that individuals living in the peripheral areas between communities not only identify with a given community but participate more fully in the social life of the community with which they identify. Thus, it is a matter of selecting a sample of these persons and asking them to name the community to which they belong, or if one wishes to be more methodologically sound, asking each person where he goes most frequently for the services he needs. In an abstract sense, this method involves the determination of the number and intensity of roles that are played. The responses given make it possible to draw a line on a map, which separates the people who "belong" to one community, that is, interact most frequently with a certain group in the fulfillment of their life activities. Sometimes a zone of transition appears between two larger urban communities, where the residents do not seem to clearly belong to one or another of the communities. However, this does not occur frequently enough to be a problem.

The **neighborhood cluster method** of delineating communities works especially well in rural areas, where many neighborhoods dot the countryside. The procedure followed is to determine the location of each neighborhood, and then to find out what trade center most of the residents in the given neighborhood identify with and use. After this is done for the neighborhoods around several trade center towns, a line can be drawn encompassing the neighborhoods which "belong" or make up a part of one or the other community.

The question may be asked, "What purpose does it serve to delineate communities?" Although many business purposes might be named, the most important reasons relate to community planning and development. Unless representatives from all areas of the community are involved, realistic planning programs cannot be worked out. In fact, the stage is set for conflict situations. To illustrate, it frequently happens that the people from a segment of a community without representation on councils will vote against bond issues for improvements that would benefit them as well as the rest of the community.

TYPES OF COMMUNITIES

Communities are classified according to various criteria, including location, history, economic function, size, and space-occupancy (arrangement of houses, for example) patterns. However, most scholars consider that two general types of communities emerge, when social organization criteria are used as a basis for delineation. These two types can be identified broadly as rural and urban communities, respectively.[10] Many typologies of rural and urban communities

---

[9] These methods are described by Irwin T. Sanders, *op. cit.*, pp. 68-76.

[10] Alvin Boskoff, *The Sociology of Urban Regions* (New York, Appleton-Century-Crofts, 1962), p. 13.

have appeared and the classifications presented here are designed to acquaint the student with the more popular classifications for each resident group.

RURAL COMMUNITIES: **Rural communities** are usually distinguished from urban communities on the basis of size and the occupational activities of their residents. In the United States for example, communities of less than 2,500 persons are usually classed as rural. Rural classification based on the economic base of the community is also common. If most employment is related to agriculture, forestry, or the extractive industries, the community is normally classed as rural. Interactional patterns also serve to make rural communities distinctive. In this regard, the presence of a predominance of *Gemeinschaft* (or primary group) relations closely interwoven with powerful kinship loyalties serve to differentiate rural communities from urban communities. The two major types of rural communities listed below are found in various parts of the world.

(1) *Village communities.* The most common type of village community is the **nucleated village.** In this type of community, the homes of the residents are clustered together, while the land which is cultivated is located away from the village area. It is not uncommon to have animals quartered in the village and to have small garden plots as well. The nucleated village may take many shapes—round, rectangular, or irregular.

A second type of rural village community is identified as the **line village.** Here, houses are built in a row along a stream or road and the farm land is in long, narrow strips extending behind each house. This pattern of settlement is designed to retain the advantages of living on one's land holdings at the same time that the social advantages of residential propinquity are maintained.

A third type of rural village community is known as the **plantation** (or hacienda, or latifundia) community. These communities are differentiated because the land is all under the ownership or control of one or a few men or a public body and the residents are workers on the land. Typically, the homes are located with respect to the "big house" of the owner or manager in such a way as to show social rank. That is, the homes of the overseers, supervisors, and specialists are larger and better than those of ordinary laborers. Plantation communities are typically nucleated, although sometimes homes are scattered around for the purpose of caring for livestock, or to protect crops.

(2) *Town-country communities.* In a town-country community, the families live both in a central location or trade-center and in the surrounding area. The dispersed nature of settlement makes community boundaries harder to delineate than in village types. However, through the procedures outlined in the previous section, neighborhoods that group together to form the community can be determined. The town-country community must be distinguished from a totally open-country community where the various service facilities, such as schools, churches, and stores are not located in one place but distrib-

uted throughout the community.[11] It is usual, however, to have some grouping of such facilities.

URBAN COMMUNITIES: Boskoff defines an **urban community** as, "characterized by a dominance of commercial, industrial, and 'service' occupations; an extensive division of labor and its corresponding social complexity; an accompanying and underlying high density of population; and the development of coordination and social controls on a nonkinship basis."[12] This definition clearly sets urban communities apart from rural communities which, as pointed out, are dominated by agriculture and characterized by familial type relationships.

The classification of urban communities presents a somewhat more difficult problem because of diversity, than does the classification of rural communities. Generally the so-called functional classifications of cities are more descriptive of the type of activity which sets one city apart from another. The classification shown below was worked out by Chauncy D. Harris for the cities of the United States and is more or less typical of classifications of urban community types.[13]

(1) *Manufacturing communities (including two subclasses).* The first subclass is made up of cities where 74 percent of total employment is manufacturing, wholesaling and retailing, but about 45 percent of all workers are in manufacture and mechanical work. The second subclass includes those cities where 60 percent of total employment is in manufacture, wholesaling and retailing, but 30 to 45 percent of all employed persons are in manufacture or mechanical work.

(2) *Retail communities.* Those communities where 50 percent of total employment is in manufacture, wholesaling and retailing, but the number in retailing is at least 2.2 times greater than in wholesaling.

(3) *Diversified communities.* Those communities where 60 percent of total employment is in manufacture and 20 percent in retailing, or 50 percent is in retailing. Manufacture and mechanical work would usually make up 25 to 35 percent of all employment in these centers.

(4) *Wholesale communities.* Cities where at least 20 percent of total employment is in manufacture, wholesaling and retailing, but at least 45 percent is in retailing alone.

(5) *Transportation communities.* Those places where 11 percent of total employment is in transportation, and this number is one-third the number in manufacture and two-thirds the number in trade.

(6) *Mining communities.* Cities over 25,000 having 15 percent or more of all employment in the extraction of minerals.

[11] See Allen D. Edwards, "Types of Rural Communities," in Marvin B. Sussman, Ed., *Community Structure and Analysis* (New York, Crowell, 1959), pp. 39-41.
[12] *Op. cit.,* pp. 13-14.
[13] Chauncy D. Harris, "A Functional Classification of Cities in the United States," in T. Lynn Smith and C. A. McMahan, *The Sociology of Urban Life* (New York, The Dryden Press, 1951), pp. 97-161.

(7) *University communities.* Cities of 10,000 or more having 25 percent of their total population occupied as students or teachers.

(8) *Resort and retirement communities.* Cities serving these functions especially, but with no other special criteria for identification.

ECOLOGICAL PROCESSES CHARACTERISTIC OF URBAN COMMUNITIES

Through time crucial changes occur in all communities. These changes almost always have important implications for ecological organization, especially in urban centers. Some aspects of change are seen in growing or declining populations; others are seen in the change in relationships of areas within the community—that is, the relative decline of some residential or business areas and the growth of others. Still other aspects of change are seen in visible shifts of functions from one area to another, as when a school, church, or industry moves to a new site. Ecologists have applied certain terms to the processes of change in urban centers which are worthy of attention here.

(1) **Aggregation** refers to the growth of the population base within a definite area over a specified period of time.

(2) **Concentration** refers to the process whereby certain areas get more people through higher rates of aggregation.

(3) **Centralization** refers to the process of accumulating important functions and services in one or another subarea. This process does not necessarily involve concentration.

(4) **Segregation** refers to the conscious or unconscious process whereby certain categories of population—racial groups, other ethnic groups, working classes—come to have heavy concentrations in specific areas.

(5) **Invasion** refers to a noticeable shift of population or function of an area due to encroachment from adjacent areas. Residential areas become slums or succumb to commercial activities, for example.

(6) **Succession** refers to the process whereby invasion becomes complete and the transition to a new population class or new function is realized.

(7) **Decentralization** refers to the process whereby population and functions are dispersed from areas that have become overcentralized or lost appeal for other reasons. The movement to the suburbs from central residential areas is an illustration.

ECOLOGICAL UNITS AND PATTERNS OF URBAN COMMUNITIES

The great diversity of urban communities accounts for the fact that they display much more complex ecological organization than rural communities. It also provides one explanation for the many studies that have been done of these communities. Boskoff quite logically points out that an accurate and useful description of urban ecological organization rests ultimately on the way in which ecological parts or units are selected. The most common approaches to the delineation of urban ecological units are as follows.[14]

USE OF NATURAL AREAS: A natural area is defined as an unplanned area within a city which is marked off by some definable feature, such as a street, railroad, stream, or hill, and which exhibits a high degree of uniformity. In other words, it is an area where the population and the activity of the population are distinctive. Natural areas do not usually correspond to political subdivisions, but usually are given descriptive names by local residents—such as Skid Row, Little Italy, Irish Channel, French Quarter, or Gold Coast.

CONCENTRIC ZONES: One of the classic approaches to the study of ecological units of cities is to delineate circular zones that radiate from the central business district. The zones may vary in width, but each is considered to include a central distinctive aspect of the structure of the city. This approach was worked out by Professor Burgess and others at the University of Chicago.[15] In his original work, he included five zones as follows: Zone I, in the center of city, which contained the central business district. Zone II, the zone of transition which immediately surrounds the business district, and which includes older residential areas converted into cheaper boarding houses or into second-hand stores, pawn shops, and so on. Some homes of poorer working classes are in this area. Zone III shades off from Zone II into better working-class homes. Zone IV is where the most modern homes, larger yards, and middle-class way of life is evidenced; Zone V includes the fashionable suburbs in which we find economic abundance and plenty and some industrial development.

The disadvantage of using concentric zones as ecological units is that urban development is not uniform. However, this approach does provide a useful orientation to the ecological organization of cities.

SECTORS: A scheme for studying the ecology of cities utilizing radial sectors was developed by Hoyt in an attempt to supplement and modify the zone scheme presented above.[16] His view was that ecological units radiated from the center of the city in sectors more often than they followed a concentric pattern. Each sector tended to follow major transportation routes and to reflect segregation of population groups according to such things as income and social class.

[14] *Op. cit.*, pp. 103-107.
[15] Ernest W. Burgess, "The Growth of the City," in Robert E. Park, *et al.*, *The City* (Chicago, University of Chicago Press, 1925).
[16] Homer Hoyt, *The Structure and Growth of Residential Neighborhoods in American Cities* (Washington, Federal Housing Administration, 1939).

NUCLEI: Since both the zone and sector theories tend to oversimplify urban ecological patterns, many researchers prefer to use other ecological units. One such unit is the nucleus. Nuclei are clusters of population and activities (city functions) which appear at various places in almost all cities—such as shopping center areas, central business districts, dormitory suburbs, and industrial areas.

CENSUS TRACTS: Within recent years, as a result of increasing concern over convenient ecological units as a basis for planning in such areas as urban problems and development, many cities in the United States have been divided into census tracts. These are small, clearly defined areas within a city which contain a homogeneous population, and for which census information is reported. Although certain problems of size and arbitrariness have not been worked out, census tracts offer one solution to the need for detailed information on ecological units.

SOCIAL AREAS: Perhaps the most systematic sociological approach to the study of urban ecology is seen in the utilization of social area as ecological units. This approach uses census tract information to group populations showing similar characteristics into inclusive areas, designated social areas. In this way the number of census tract units are reduced to manageable proportions and only the significant characteristics of the population are used for delineation purposes.

What has been called the "Orthodox Ecological Structure of Cities" by Boskoff is shown in Figure 22-1. It incorporates the concentric zone, the sector and the nuclei concepts to show the structure of typical cities.

THE REGIONAL CONCEPT

Sociologists are constantly being confronted with social problems that relate to areas larger than communities but smaller than total societies. These larger ecological units, as pointed out before, are identified as regions. The regional idea has long been recognized, but it was not until the 1930's that Howard Odum and his associates at the University of North Carolina began calling the attention of sociologists to this highly promising and relatively unexplored area of study. Prior to this time, the regional frame of reference was used for the most part by geographers, who dealt primarily with areal differences in the facts of geography—differences such as weather, topography, and temperature. The approach and understandings of regional sociology are briefly summarized here in order to give the beginning student an orientation to this subdiscipline of sociology.

FIGURE 22-1.   *The Orthodox Ecological Structure of Cities.*

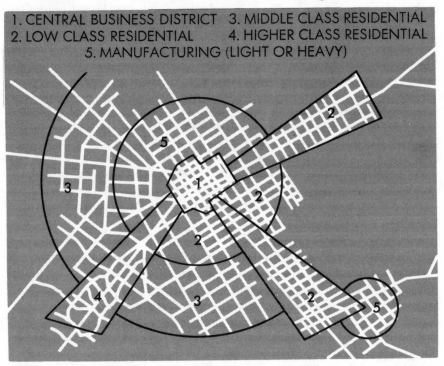

1. CENTRAL BUSINESS DISTRICT   3. MIDDLE CLASS RESIDENTIAL
2. LOW CLASS RESIDENTIAL   4. HIGHER CLASS RESIDENTIAL
          5. MANUFACTURING (LIGHT OR HEAVY)

Source: Alvin Boskoff, *The Sociology of Urban Regions* (New York, Appleton-Century-Crofts, 1962), p. 111. Reproduced by permission of Appleton-Century-Crofts, Division of Meredith Publishing Company.

DEFINITION OF A REGION

There are several criteria that must be met before regions can be differentiated from other areal entities of fairly large size. The following definition takes these criteria into account. *A* **region,** *from a socio-cultural standpoint, is an area larger than a community within which historical and environmental factors have combined to create a relatively homogeneous social structure.* The several conditions that set regions apart are implicit in this definition. First, the region must exhibit homogeneity in several significant ways related to social life. It is possible to delineate certain subregions on the basis of a single factor, but never a major region. The second important fact about a region is that the people within the region are aware of its uniqueness and consciously identify themselves as having distinctive ways. Finally, it is clear that a region is normally an area which does not have distinct boundaries. One region is typically separated from neighboring regions by broad zones of transition where it is difficult to classify customs and practices as belonging in one region or another. The general attributes of regions listed by Odum and Moore elaborate these understandings and help clarify the concept of a region.[17] They are

1. The region is first of all an area, a geographic unit with limits and bounds. Regionalism is therefore an areal or spatial generalization.
2. The region differs from the mere locality of pure geographic area in that it is characterized not so much by boundary lines and actual limits as it is by flexibility of limits by extension from a center, and by fringe or border margins which separate one region from another.
3. The third attribute of the region is some degree of homogeneity in a number of selected characteristics. (geographic, cultural, economic, etc.)
4. The fourth attribute of the region is some structural or functional aspect or aspects through which the region is to be dominated. (In fact there may be as many regions as there are purposes or functions.)
5. Because there must be a limit to the multiplicity of regions a fifth attribute must be found in the relative, composite homogeneity of the largest number of factors for the largest number of purposes in view, to the end that the region may be a practical, workable unit susceptible of both definition and utilization.
6. One of the key attributes of the region is that it must be a constituent unit in an aggregate whole or totality.
7. Another key attribute of the region is found in its organic nature. A region has organic unity not only in its natural landscape, but in that cultural evolution in which the age-long quartet of elements are at work—namely the land and the people, culturally conditioned through time and spatial relationships.

BASIC REGION-MAKING FORCES

The question arises as to how regions come to be basic configurations of human life. The answer to this question is found in three major forces that serve to unify the people living in such a large area into a homogeneous group.

GEOGRAPHIC AND PHYSIOGRAPHIC CHARACTERISTICS: The natural environment is readily recognized as one of the forces that tends to condition men to certain patterns of behavior. This fact was brought out earlier in discussions relating to socialization. Such differences, as those in occupation, dress, architecture, recreation, and food habits are readily linked to topography, soils, and climate. The mistake should not be made, however, of assigning overwhelming determinism to natural phenomena. It can readily be demonstrated that similar geographic features do not always mean similar socio-cultural characteristics. However, the physical environment is always a greater or lesser factor in regional differences.

[17] Howard W. Odum and Harry E. Moore, *American Regionalism* (New York, Holt, Rinehart and Winston, 1938), pp. 14-16.

HISTORICAL DEVELOPMENTS: Someone has remarked that accidents of history can become one of the most powerful forces operating to make a people stand apart. Wars, religious beliefs and practices, and disasters serve to bring people together through shared experiences. These experiences, in turn, lead to a strong consciousness of identity. To illustrate, in the United States, the historical facts of the race problem and the Civil War played a major role in molding the people of the South into a regional group. A recent volume edited by John McKinney and Edgar Thompson dramatically portrays developments that continue to give the South an unusual history.[18]

CULTURAL EXPERIENCES: It is well known that certain areas tend to develop cultural expressions that vary to some degree from the rest of the national society. It may be that it will be the way food is prepared, or a type of song or music or even a way of speech. These deviations are related to invention and cultural diffusion and are sometimes difficult to trace. The important fact for our discussion is that these differences serve to set the people in given areas off from the inhabitants of neighboring areas. To this extent cultural experiences serve as a region-making force.

In summary, it can be said that areal entities larger than communities gradually attain their individuality as regions because of the interplay of the three major forces discussed above. The related weight of a given set of forces can be assessed in a general way after thorough study and analysis.

CLASSIFICATION AND DELINEATION OF REGIONS

There are many ways one might divide a relatively large nation into subareas of relative homogeneity. Essentially, however, three major criterion are used to delineate regions. (1) The first criterion is the number of variables used in the delineational procedure. Regions that are determined on the basis of a single factor, such as a geographical or cultural characteristic, are differentiated from composite regions delineated on the basis of many factors. (2) The second criterion for determining types of regions is their subordinate or superordinate relationship to one another. In this regard, subregions are set apart from the major regions that they make up. (3) The third basis for classifying regional entities is whether or not political boundaries are made to coincide with the dividing lines between the various regions. Group-of-states regions or group-of-counties regions are classed as one type, whereas regions separated by broad zones of transition are considered a separate type.

Keeping the criterion named above in mind, delineational procedures for regions may be reviewed. One of two distinct procedures is generally utilized,

18 John C. McKinney and Edgar T. Thompson, Eds., *The South in Continuity and Change* (Durham, North Carolina, Duke University Press, 1965).

depending on the factors involved and the school of thought of the researcher. The first procedure, known as the cultural-diffusion method, attempts to delineate regions by tracing the diffusion of a culture trait or traits from its source of first use, that is, its origin. The core area of the region is identified as the area of highest use of the trait or traits selected and the boundaries of the region are marked where the trait or traits tend to be found only infrequently.

The second regional delineational procedure, and by far the most common, is the use of statistical indices to determine where one or a group of socio-cultural characteristics prevail. Sociologists have been more prone to use this approach and have developed several methods for refining data for the purpose of delimiting regions. The important tasks are the selection of and the weighing of the variables, which are the important indicators of regional homogeneity.

MAJOR APPROACHES TO REGIONAL STUDY

Regional sociologists have followed three major approaches in their studies of regions. First, they have attempted studies of composite regions, those which are based on many indexes and include all segments of the population in a given area. Second, they have focused attention primarily on what have been called the urban or metropolitan regions, those set aside primarily on the basis of urban characteristics. Third, they have concerned themselves with rural regions, or those that are delineated on the basis of agriculture as an occupation and type of farming or other cultural characteristics of rural populations. The work done in the United States will be used as an example of the various approaches to regional study, although similar studies might be found elsewhere.

Before describing and illustrating the various approaches to regional study, it is important to note that the content of regional sociology derives from the study of all types of regions. Regional sociology includes three types of information: (1) data useful in delineating regions; (2) analyses of all forms of human association within given regional environments; and (3) comparisons of regional social systems.[19]

COMPOSITE REGIONS: Three regional delineations of the United States based on composite characteristics stand out. Two of the studies are somewhat out-of-date, but they serve to illustrate this approach. The third study is relatively current and is used widely.

Under the title *American Regionalism*, Howard W. Odum and Harry E. Moore assembled, in 1938, what is still perhaps the greatest collection of re-

[19] See Alvin L. Bertrand, "Regional Sociology as a Special Discipline," *Social Forces,* Vol. 31 (December, 1952), p. 133.

gional materials with a sociological frame of reference in the nation. In general, they used criteria of three sorts to determine their regions: (1) the size of the region should not be too large for practical planning purposes, nor too small to include realistic subregions; (2) measures of physiographic homogeneities, historical development, folk culture, and population; and (3) statistical indices of technical, economic, and social facts. After a monumental collection of information, they divided the nation into seven groups-of-states regions. The specific characteristics of the six regions were carefully outlined by them and have provided the basis for much national planning to date. The names given the regions are Northeast region, Southeast region, Middle States Region, Southwest Region, Northwest Region, and Far West Region.

The second regional study classifiable as utilizing the composite approach is that of Carle C. Zimmerman. He followed the zone-of-transition method. His aim was to ". . . take the region-making factors which are general in nature and show their specific experience in creating the great regions of the United States." A composite of information from history, economics, culture, and geography was used to delineate his seven basic regions, which are named, respectively: the South, the Appalachian Ozarks region, the Northeastern Urban industrial region, the Cornbelt, the Wheatbelt, the Arid West, and the Pacific region.[20]

The third and most recent delineation of composite regions done in the United States is a phenomenal work in many ways. Donald J. Bogue and Calvin L. Beale collected and processed a veritable mountain of information in delimiting what they called *Economic Areas of the United States*.[21] Their sources included (1) the large body of data available from censuses and government reports on the economy and population of each county of the nation; (2) previous studies done by social scientists, which included descriptions and delineations of areas and regions, whether for a generalized or special purpose; (3) the opinions and suggestions of specialists having administrative responsibilities over particular areas or regions. On the basis of the data they collected, Bogue and Beale subdivided the entire land area of the United States into areas (regions) characterized by homogeneity in the way inhabitants obtained their livelihood and in socio-economic characteristics. Their procedure involved the grouping of counties with similar traits together to form *state economic areas*, which were then combined to form *economic subregions*. The latter were in turn combined to form *economic regions*, and finally, similar economic regions were formed into *economic provinces* or major composite regions. The economic regions and economic provinces delineated are shown in Figure 22-2. There are five provinces and 13 regions as follows:

[20] See the two works: Carle C. Zimmerman, *Outline of American Regional Sociology* (Cambridge, Massachusetts, The Phillips Book Store, 1947), and Carle C. Zimmerman and Richard E. Du Wors, *Graphic Regional Sociology* (Cambridge, Massachusetts, The Phillips Book Store, 1952).

[21] Donald J. Bogue and Calvin L. Beale, *Economic Areas of the United States* (New York, The Free Press, 1961).

FIGURE 22-2. *Economic Provinces and Economic Regions of the United States.*

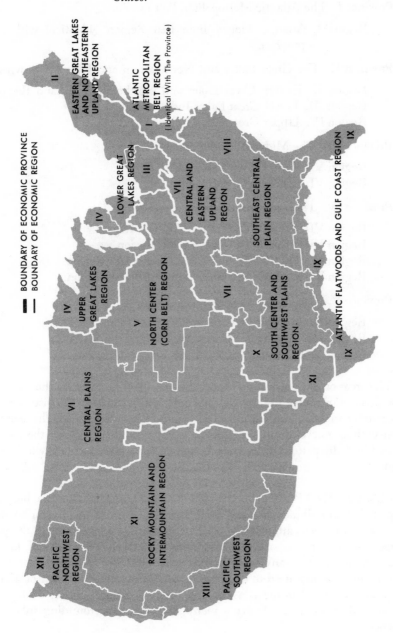

Province I. The Atlantic Metropolitan Belt Province

    Region I. Atlantic Metropolitan Belt Region (identical with the province)

Province II. The Great Lakes and Northeastern and Uplands Province.

    Region II. Eastern Great Lakes and Northeastern Upland Region.
    Region III. Lower Great Lakes Industrial Region.
    Region IV. Upper Great Lakes Region.

Province III. The Midwest Province.

    Region V. North Center (Corn Belt) Region.
    Region VI. Central Plains Region.

Province IV. The Southern Province.

    Region VII. Central and Eastern Upland Region.
    Region VIII. Southeast Coastal Plain Region.
    Region IX. Gulf Coast and Atlantic Flatwoods Region.
    Region X. South Center and Southwest Plains Region.

Province V. The Western Province.

    Region XI. Rocky Mountain and Intermountain Region.
    Region XII. Pacific Northwest Region.
    Region XIII. Pacific Southwest Region.

The areas or regions outlined above are described in detail by the authors. These descriptions serve to improve the analytic abilities of sociologists, economists, market analysts, and business statisticians. They also provide the average citizen with an encyclopedic type source telling how the people of the nation live, and how the pattern of livelihood changes from place to place within the nation.

URBAN OR METROPOLITAN REGIONS: The fact that the big city is one of the most all-inclusive and complex types of social agglomerations has always served to focus attention on it. This, perhaps, explains why in the past the regional idea has been more frequently associated with areas of metropolitan influence than any other spatial generalization. Although the term urban region was first used to designate a portion or ecological unit of a city, it was later modified to mean a city and its immediate environs. Today the term is used generally to signify a metropolis and its surrounding sphere of influence.[22]

The supporters of an "urban regionalism" point out that the lives of the farmer and villager as well as the suburbanite are conditioned to a great extent by the city. However, the question arises as to how much the reverse process

[22] Alvin Boskoff, op. cit., Chapter 7.

is true, that is, how much influence do local communities exert on the central metropolitan area. Leaving this question aside, one can readily see that, with some notable exceptions, most urban centers are inextricably bound by economic, cultural, and other ties to their surrounding hinterland. This is the rationale for the urban region.

Boskoff has worked out a schematic diagram of a typical urban region, Figure 22-3, which shows its various parts or specialized areas. The **central city** is, of course, the first and most important area of the urban region. This is where the vital economic, protective (fire and police), and educational functions center, and where the seat of government is located. Figure 22-3 shows how the central city may grow in size by annexing territory.

FIGURE 22-3. *A Simplified Ecological Diagram of the Urban Region.*

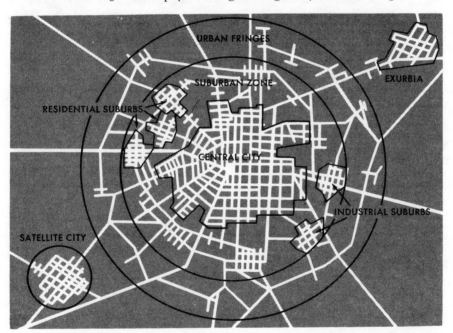

Source: Alvin Boskoff, *The Sociology of Urban Regions* (New York, Appleton-Century-Crofts, 1962), p. 132. Reprinted by permission of Appleton-Century-Crofts, Division of Meredith Publishing Company.

The second easily identifiable part of the urban region is the **suburban zone.** Suburbs are not a new phenomenon, but have developed to important proportions within recent years, as means of transportation and communication have improved. As Boskoff points out, suburbs are, ". . . those urbanized nuclei located outside (but within accessible range) of central cities that are

politically independent but economically and psychologically linked with services and facilities provided by the metropolis."[23]

Two major types of suburbs can be identified, residential and industrial,
although other types such as recreational and resort suburbs, appear less frequently. Residential suburbs are subdivided by Boskoff into three classes: (1)
The traditional upper-class suburb, which includes a preponderance of long-
established, high status families and has little property turnover. (2) The
stable middle-class suburb, which attracts families from the middle income and
middle status groups. (3) The "packaged" suburb, which is characterized as
mass produced, with only one or two house designs, and as springing up overnight. Most of the residents of these latter suburbs are highly mobile, comparatively young, and hold junior executives type jobs.

Industrial suburbs include for the most part persons who are employed
as skilled or semiskilled workers and who fall in the lower middle class or
lower class strata of society. Within recent years industrial suburbs in the
United States have grown at a slower rate than residential suburbs, probably
reflecting the fact that occupational structures have changed to include more
professional and specialized positions.

The **urban fringe** is the third specific area found in urban regions. This
area is not easily described, although it can be readily identified. It includes
the territory beyond the suburban zone where land-use patterns tend to be
rather mixed, with residences, industrial installations, commercial establishments, hospitals, and cemeteries being interspersed with considerable amounts
of agricultural and vacant land. The employed populations living in the fringe
tend to be from the lower classes, and to be willing to do without certain urban
services, such as sewerage lines, paved streets, and fire protection.

Satellite cities represent a fourth specific ecological unit or area within
urban regions. These cities are located at the outer edge of the urban fringe.
Not infrequently they were founded at the same time or before the central city,
but for some historical or economic reason did not match its growth. Satellite
cities supply their residents with all the services they need, but cannot match
the quality of service to be found in the central city. That is, they do not have
the range of goods and services of the larger cities. To this extent, they are
quasi-dependent on the latter. This dependency is what identifies them as
part of the given urban region.

Exurbia is said to be ". . . the farthest thrust of the urban region. . . ."
Only the largest cities develop this type of area, which is located beyond the
urban fringe in what was formerly rural areas.[24]

Exurbia is linked with the central city in a real way, since its residents
maintain occupational positions in the city. The residents of exurbia are
typically in what has been called the "creative" branches of the communications industry—advertising, commercial art, television, radio, popular maga-

[23] *Ibid.*, p. 133.
[24] *Ibid.*, p. 434.

zines—and are characterized by a desire to escape the conventionality of the suburbs as well as the cramped quarters of the central city. They may commute as much as 50 or more miles to accomplish this escape. Many exurbanites do much of their work at home, and show up only occasionally at their "downtown" office. They are usually in the salary brackets which permit them to be pacesetters in urban fashions. Rigid control is maintained over their residential areas in attempts to retain a low density of population and a high social status. This control has been referred to as "snob zoning."

RURAL REGIONS: Sociologists began making systematic studies of rural regions in the United States in the 1930's and 1940's. Several regional studies have appeared for the nation as a whole, and every state has been divided into rural areas or subregions. The approaches taken to the study of rural regions necessarily have been different from the approaches made to the study of urban regions. One or the other of the two approaches described below has generally been followed in delineational procedures.

The first approach is the statistical index approach described earlier. It is typified by A. R. Mangus' study done in 1940.[25] Mangus' specific reason for attempting a delineation of rural regions was to contribute to the rural relief problem of the 1930's by giving it a geographical setting. His delineation was based primarily on nationally distributed variables such as rural plane-of-living indexes, rural fertility indexes, farm income, tenancy rates, land value, and farm residence. Each of the factors selected by him was carefully weighted in an attempt to objectively measure differences between geographic areas. In addition, physiographic and residence features were taken into account in the final delineation of his 34 rural cultural regions.

The study of Carl Taylor and his associates done in 1949 exemplifies the second approach to the delineation of rural regions.[26] Their procedure differed from that of Mangus in that they used one primary factor—type-of-farming. They made a case for major type-farming areas as rural cultural universes by pointing out that the production of the same crop or combination of crops results in many common activities among people and therefore in broadly similar interests, attitudes and values. They further defended their approach by noting that in type-of-farming areas, marked differences arise in response to a combination of physical, economic, and historical factors. The names of the seven regions delineated by this group are indicative of their distinctiveness: (1) the Cotton Belt, (2) the Corn Belt, (3) the Range-Livestock Region, (4) the Wheat Region, (5) the Dairy Region, (6) the Western Specialty-crop Region, (7) the General and Self-Sufficing Region.

---

[25] A. R. Mangus, *Rural Regions of the United States* (Washington, D. C., Government Printing Office, 1940).

[26] Carl C. Taylor, *et al.*, *Rural Life in the United States* (New York, Knopf, 1949), Part IV.

SUMMARY

The study of the relationship between man and his environment, human ecology, is an important part of sociology. This study encompasses the nature and types of ecological entities as well as the characteristics of these entities and the processes that are important to their existence.

The community is looked upon as a major ecological unit. It is considered to be a particular type of social system—one which is made up of individuals, groups, and organizations, and includes a sufficient number of institutionalized structures to satisfy the basic needs of its members. The people in the community are linked through a system of symbiotic role relationships. A community is larger than a family or neighborhood and includes a wider variety of role relationships. The two methods most commonly used to delineate communities are the individual identification and neighborhood cluster methods.

Two major types of communities are recognized—rural and urban. They are distinguished on the basis of size and the interactional patterns which characterize their members. Urban communities are generally more complex in organization than rural communities and tend to be larger in size. Several ecological processes account for crucial change in both urban and rural communities, including aggregation, concentration, centralization, segregation, invasion, succession, and decentralization. Several approaches have been used in the delineation of ecological units within urban communities: natural areas, concentric zones, sectors, nuclei, census tracts, and social areas.

Regions represent ecological units which are larger than the community, but smaller than the society. They come into existence because of geographic, historical and cultural characteristics which make them unique. Three basic types of regions are recognized by sociologists. The major composite regions are set aside on the basis of a large number of variables which give them an aspect of homogeneity. Urban or metropolitan regions are delineated with large cities at their center and the surrounding hinterland as their sphere of influence. These regions encompass suburban zones, urban fringe areas, satellite cities, and exurbia areas. Rural regions are delineated on the basis of type-of-farming characteristics and the way of life of rural people.

Supplementary Readings

Anderson, Nels, *The Urban Community: A World Perspective* (New York, Holt, Rinehart and Winston, 1959).

Bertrand, Alvin L. "Regional Sociology as a Special Discipline," *Social Forces*, Vol. 31 (December, 1952), pp. 132-136.

Boskoff, Alvin, *The Sociology of Urban Regions* (New York, Appleton-Century-Crofts, 1962).

Firey, Walter, "Sentiment and Symbolism as Ecological Variables," *American Sociological Review*, Vol. 10 (April, 1945), pp. 140-146, and also in O'BRIEN ET AL. and BM.

Hawley, Amos., "Ecology and Human Ecology," *Social Forces*, Vol. 22 (May, 1944), pp. 398-405, and also in LASSWELL ET AL. and BM.

Odum, Howard W., and Harry E. Moore, *American Regionalism* (New York, Holt, Rinehart and Winston, 1938).

Sanders, Irwin T., *The Community: An Introduction to a Social System*, 2nd ed. (New York, The Ronald Press, 1966).

Taylor, Carl C., *et al.*, *Rural Life in the United States* (New York, Knopf, 1949), Part IV.

Warren, Roland L., *Perspectives on the American Community* (Chicago, Rand McNally, 1966).

Zimmerman, Carle C. and Richard E. Du Wors, *Graphic Regional Sociology* (Cambridge, Massachusetts, The Phillips Book Store, 1952).

NAME INDEX

SUBJECT INDEX